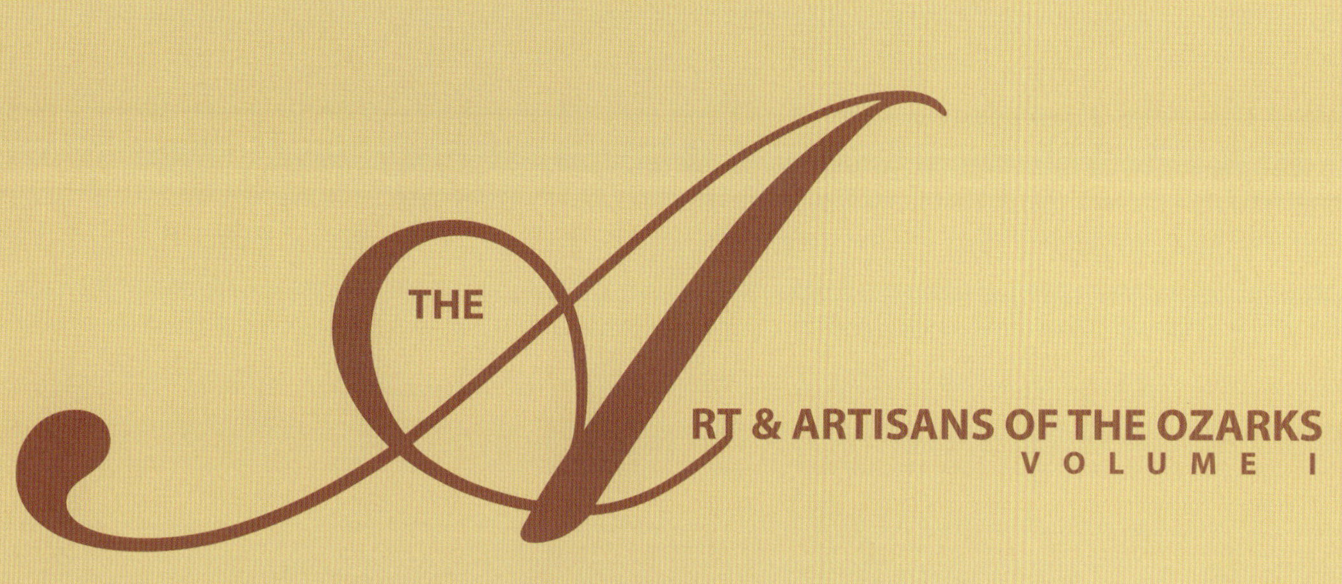

PRESENTED BY THE PALETTE ART LEAGUE

http://paletteartleague.org

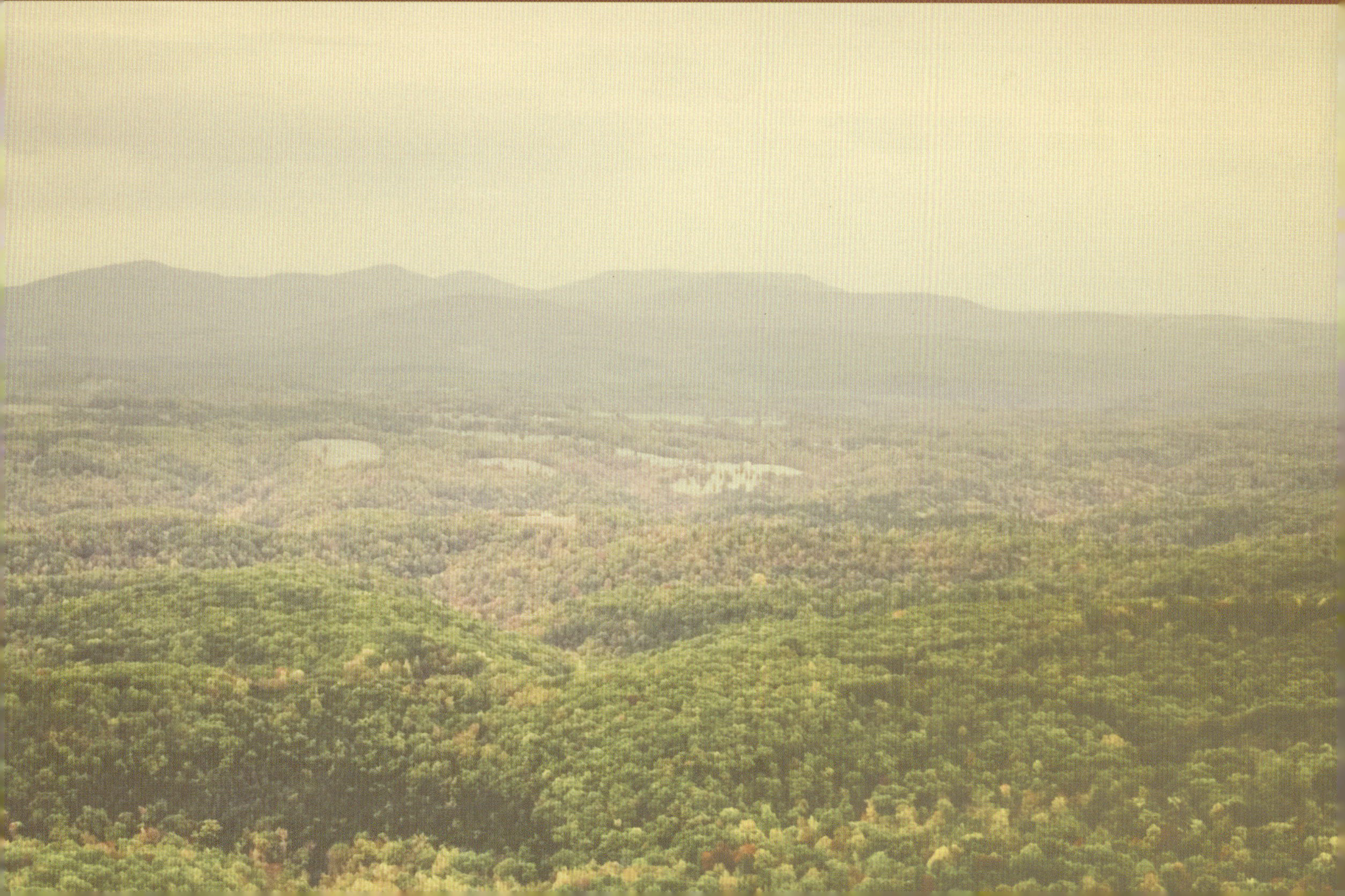

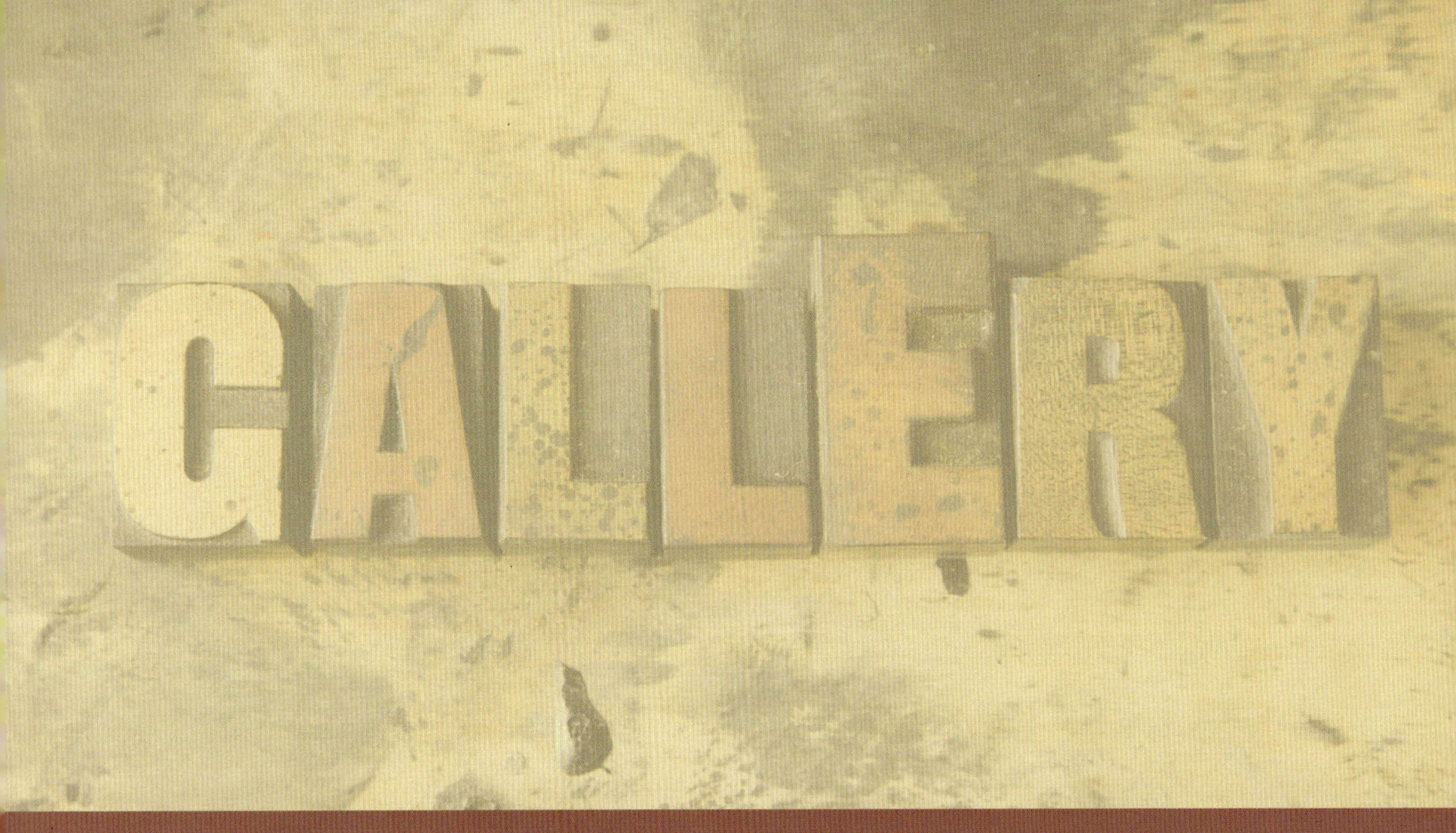

PALETTEARTLEAGUE.ORG

The Art & Artisans of the Ozarks, Volume One

The Palette Art League
300 Hwy 62 West
Yellville, Arkansas 72687
Website: http://paletteartleague.org
E-mail: info@paletteartleague.org

Published by:
Whitehall Publishing
PO Box 548
Yellville, Arkansas 72687
http://whitehallpublishing.com
info@whitehallpublishing.com

Cover and interior design crafted by:
Ascender Graphix, Norfolk, NE.
http://ascendergraphix.com/

Photography by:
K.R.P. Photography
Keith R. Probert
PO Box 548
Yellville, Arkansas 72687
Krpphoto1@aol.com

The Art & Artisans of the Ozarks: ISBN# 978-1-935122-23-4
Retail Price: $24.95

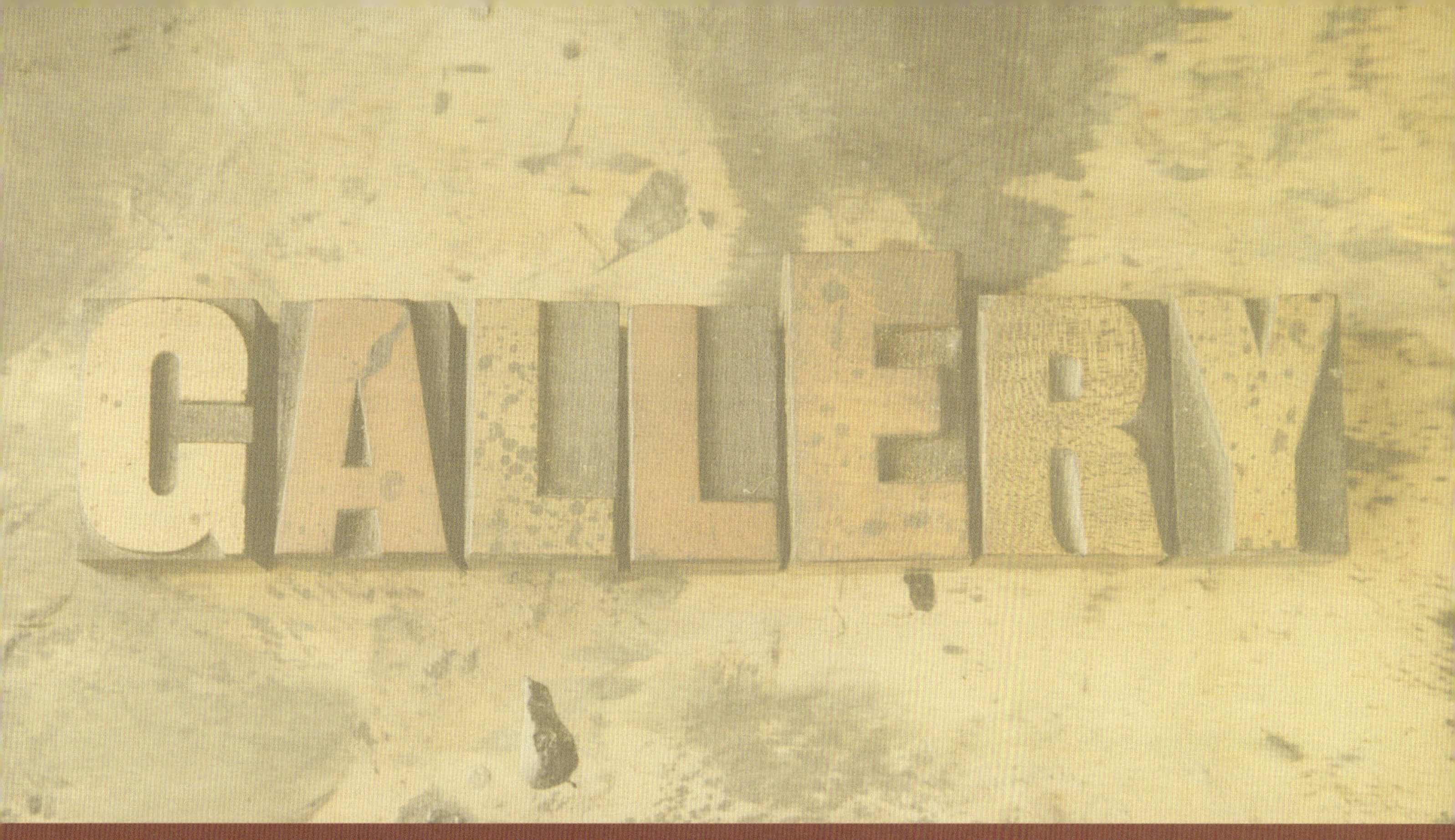

DEDICATION

A pioneer of fine art in the Ozark Mountains, artist, teacher and mentor Jo Rowell, with a small group of dedicated fellow artists, believed enough in the artistic talent here in the Ozarks that they formed the Palette Art League more than a decade ago. Mrs. Rowell with other dedicated artists went on to locate and purchase the building that would become today's Palette Art League Gallery in Yellville, Arkansas.

Jo Rowell has taught and inspired young artists for half a century, teaching her students all the skills required to achieve success as an artist and success in life. She is tenacious in her quest to nurture and showcase the talent here in the Ozarks and without that tenacity; the Palette Art League would not exist.

The members of the Palette Art League, and the hundreds of artists she has inspired and taught over the years are proud to dedicate this book to Mrs. Jo Rowell.

GALLERY

ABOUT US

The Palette Art League was formed by a group of dedicated Ozark Artists and Art lovers in the early 1980's. Spurred by their desire to promote the Arts and to encourage people to explore their artistic talents, this small band embarked on a journey that continues to grow today.

The group purchased the Palette Art League Gallery in Yellville, Arkansas in 2002 and filed for, and received their 501(c) 3 (non-profit recognition) in 2009 and launched their large website and shopping cart (http://paletteartleague.org) shortly thereafter. All of this was done with a clear mission statement focused on education and Art appreciation.

The founding members of the Palette Art League understood then and feel even more strongly now that Art is important to the development and well being of children and adults alike. Art provides a mirror for our society and reflects who we are as individuals and as a society. A world without the Arts would be a very poor one, intellectually and spiritually, because art connects us to the human imagination and once we tap into that, anything is possible.

Whether your interests include painting or wood work, quilting or pottery, creating jewelry or glass blowing, what is most important is that you are exercising your creativity, expanding your thought processes, discovering an enjoyable hobby (or in many cases) a new career that is fun, relaxing and creative. That is the power of the Arts and the mission of the Palette Art League is two-fold:

* To share the art that is already happening right now in the Ozarks, with the hope that it will inspire you to pick up a brush or a wood working tool or whatever art medium you fancy and start making your own art.
* To provide education in all mediums of art so aspiring artists can enhance their skills and achieve their artistic dreams.

DIANA HARVEY

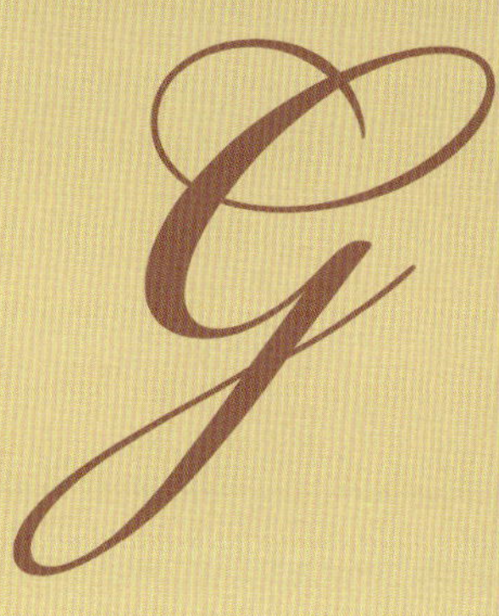

rowing up in a military family was the formative beginning to Diana's experience of the world and its cultures. She delighted in being tutored at the Prado Museum in Madrid, then returned to the States for a B.A. in archaeology. Love of art drew her to a successful career in etching, but when the physical stresses of years of printmaking appeared, she turned full attention to her "hobby" of painting. She feels she is doing her finest work now, with serene, evocative images reflective of the early European training, and her contemplative nature. Recently these works of quiet beauty have appeared in prestigious national shows including American Art in Miniature, Gilcrease Museum; Masterworks 2009, Gallery One; 35th International Miniature Art Exhibition, Leepa-Rattner Museum. **For more information on Diana's work, visit http://paletteartleague.org/DianaHarvey.html.**

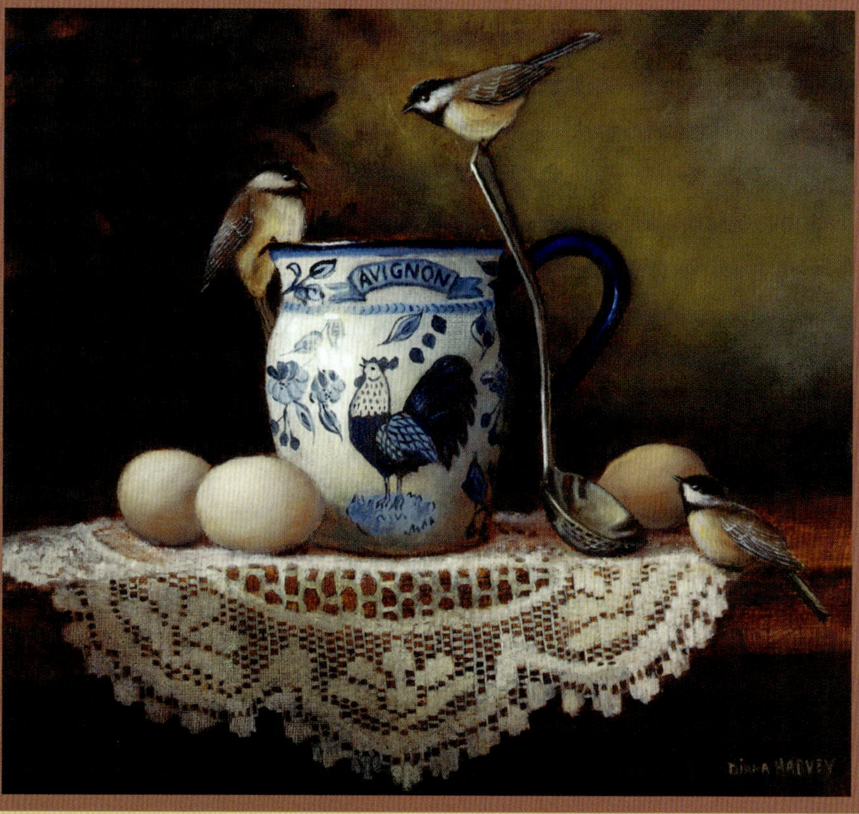

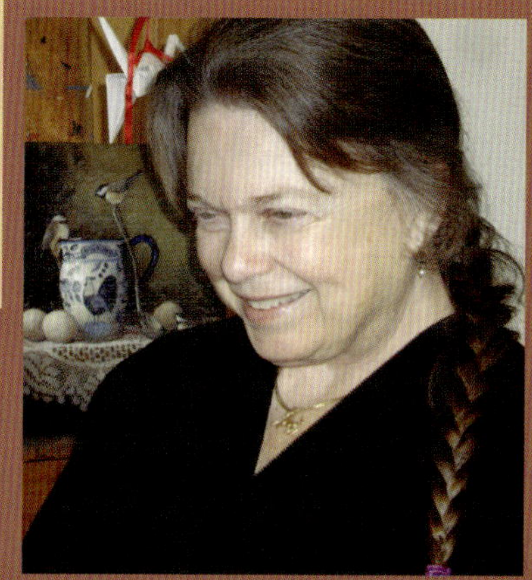

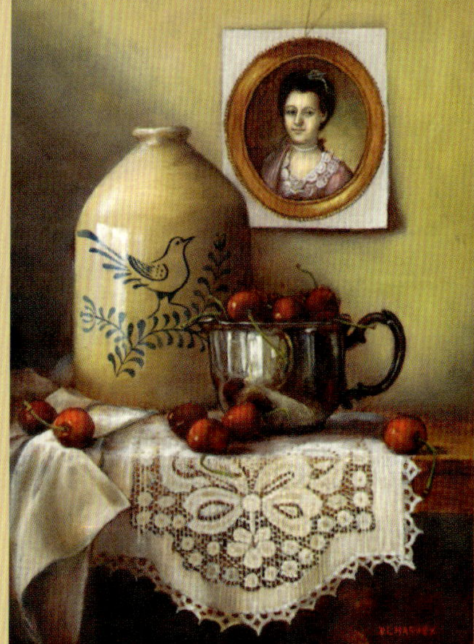

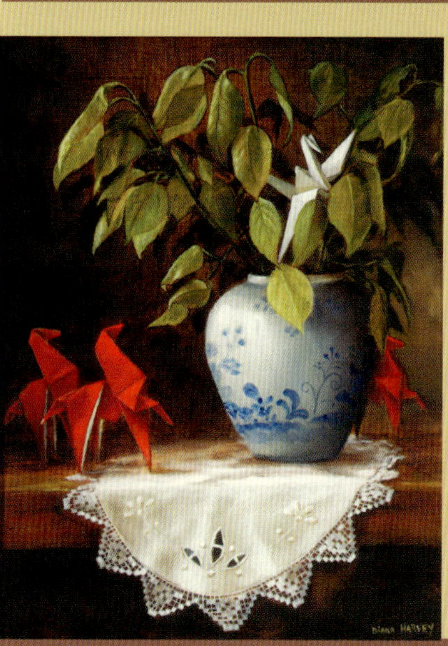

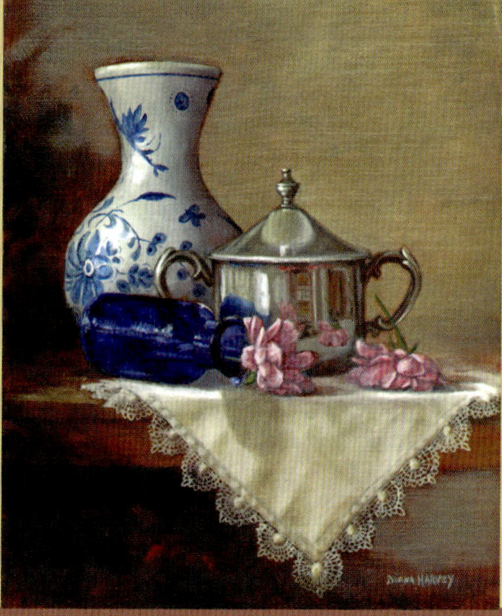

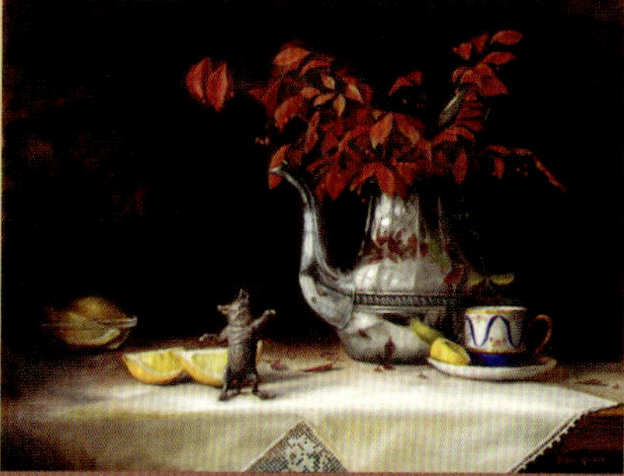

Jim Young MASTER POTTER, ROGERS, ARKANSAS

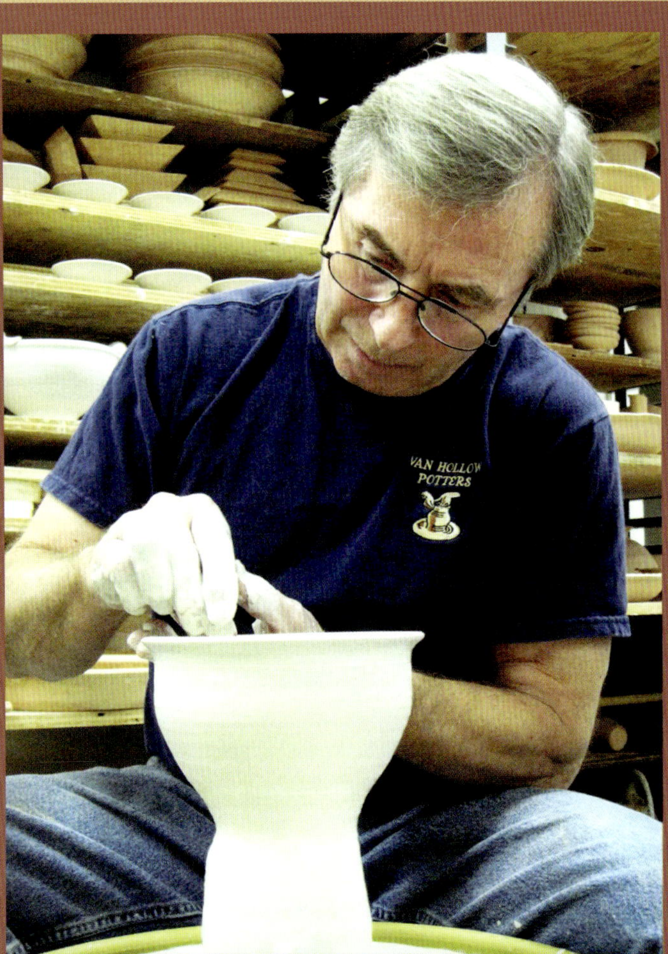

Jim Young has been a potter for 38 years. He is a member of the Arkansas Craft Guild and teaches pottery at his studio in Rogers.

Jim's functional high-fire stoneware pottery is brilliantly decorated with multiple layering of handcrafted glazes that melt and blend together in temperatures that will melt steel (2400°F).

"It's all in the details," says Jim. "I airbrush the glazes to produce subtle variations resembling the work of Nature. In fact I believe that Creation and creating are closely intertwined. My purpose in life, I feel, is to take in my surroundings and to express them through my work. The Ozarks offer a wonder palette of intricate details for my pottery."

www.vanhollowpottery.com

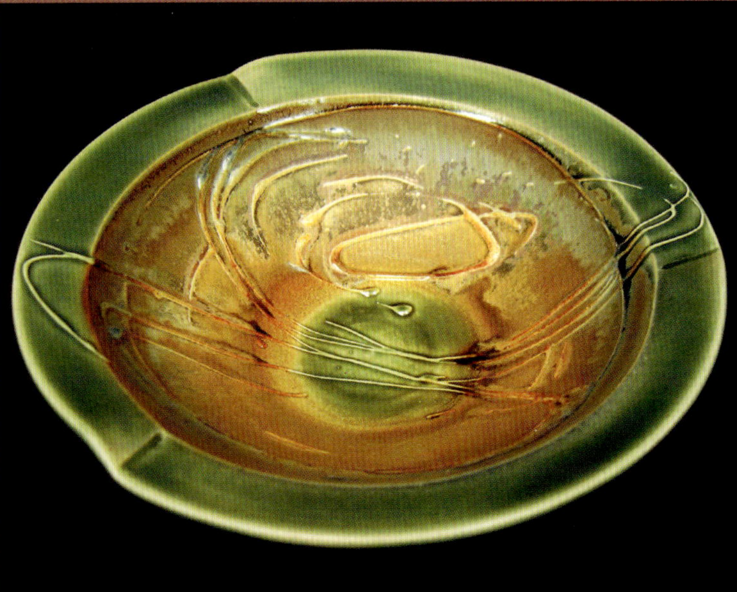

Stoneware bowl 8" diameter X 2 ½" high with a fluted border, multiple glazes and raised slip designs.

Close-up of bowl showing complex variation in surface texture and glaze effects.

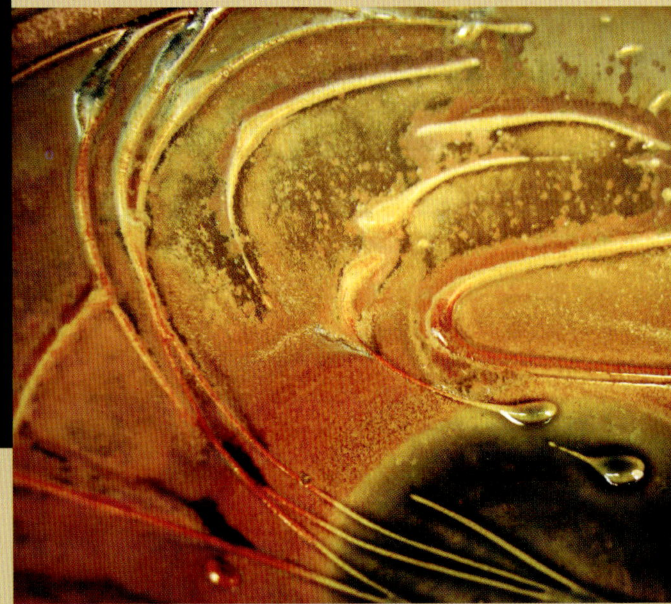

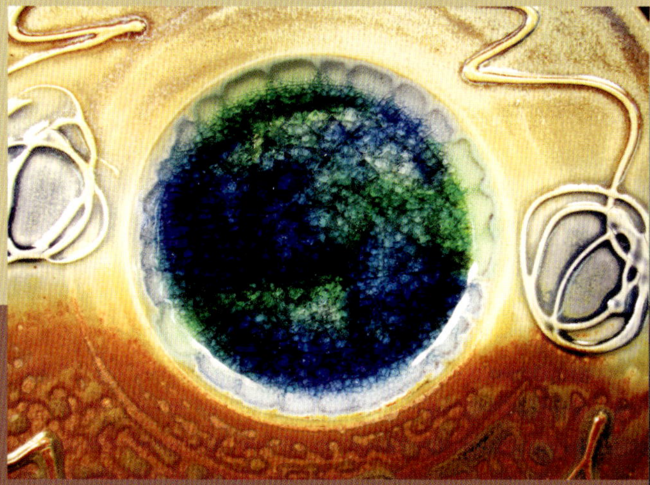

Above: Shards of stained glass are arranged in the center and fired to produce a pool resembling Earth as seen from space.

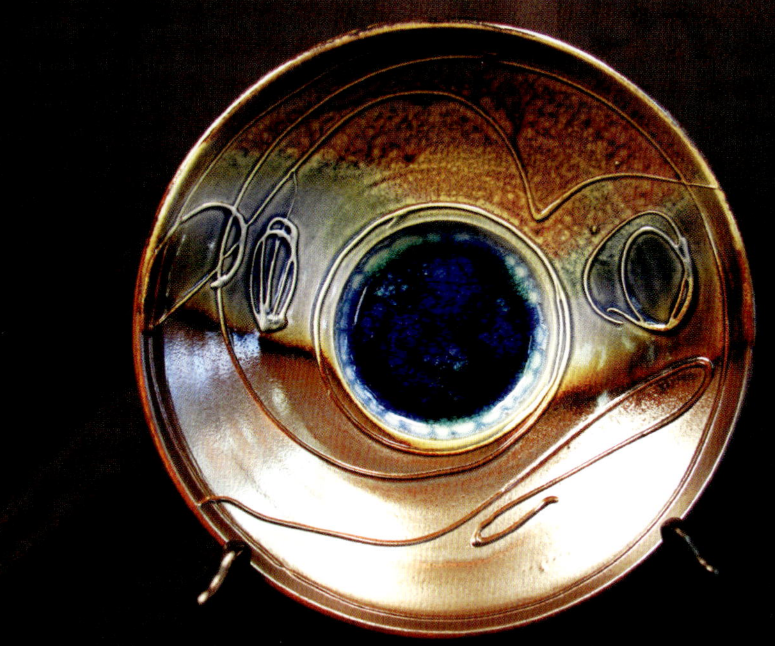

Above: "Pool of Wonder" stoneware bowl 10 ½" wide X 2 1/2" deep with stained glass center, sprayed hardwood ash glazes and raised slip.

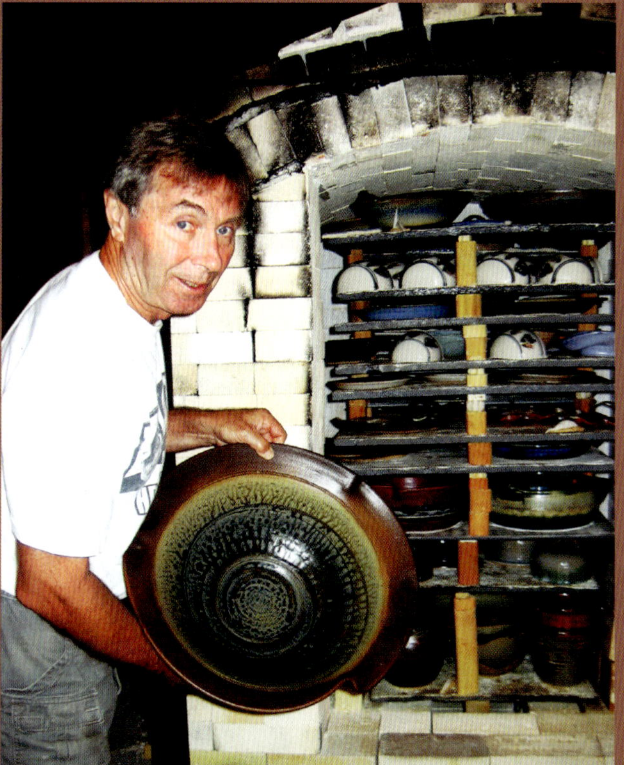

Below: Detail of bowl showing the watery melt of the hardwood ash glazes.

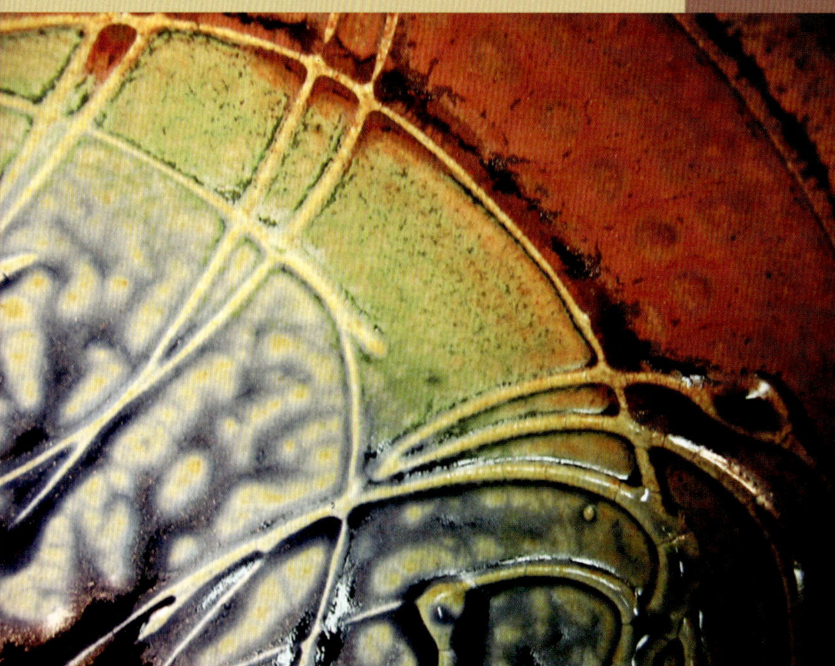

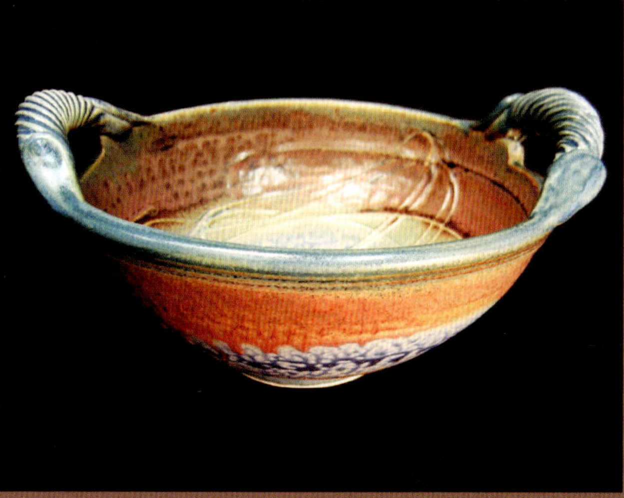

Left: Stoneware bowl with spiral handles 7 " wide X 3" high with multiple glazes and raised slip designs.

Stoneware hanging platter 22″ wide X 5″ high with multiple glazes and raised slip designs. This bowl features the containment of the circle (the bowl itself) and the excitement of the decorations. All glazes are made of natural, non-toxic materials.

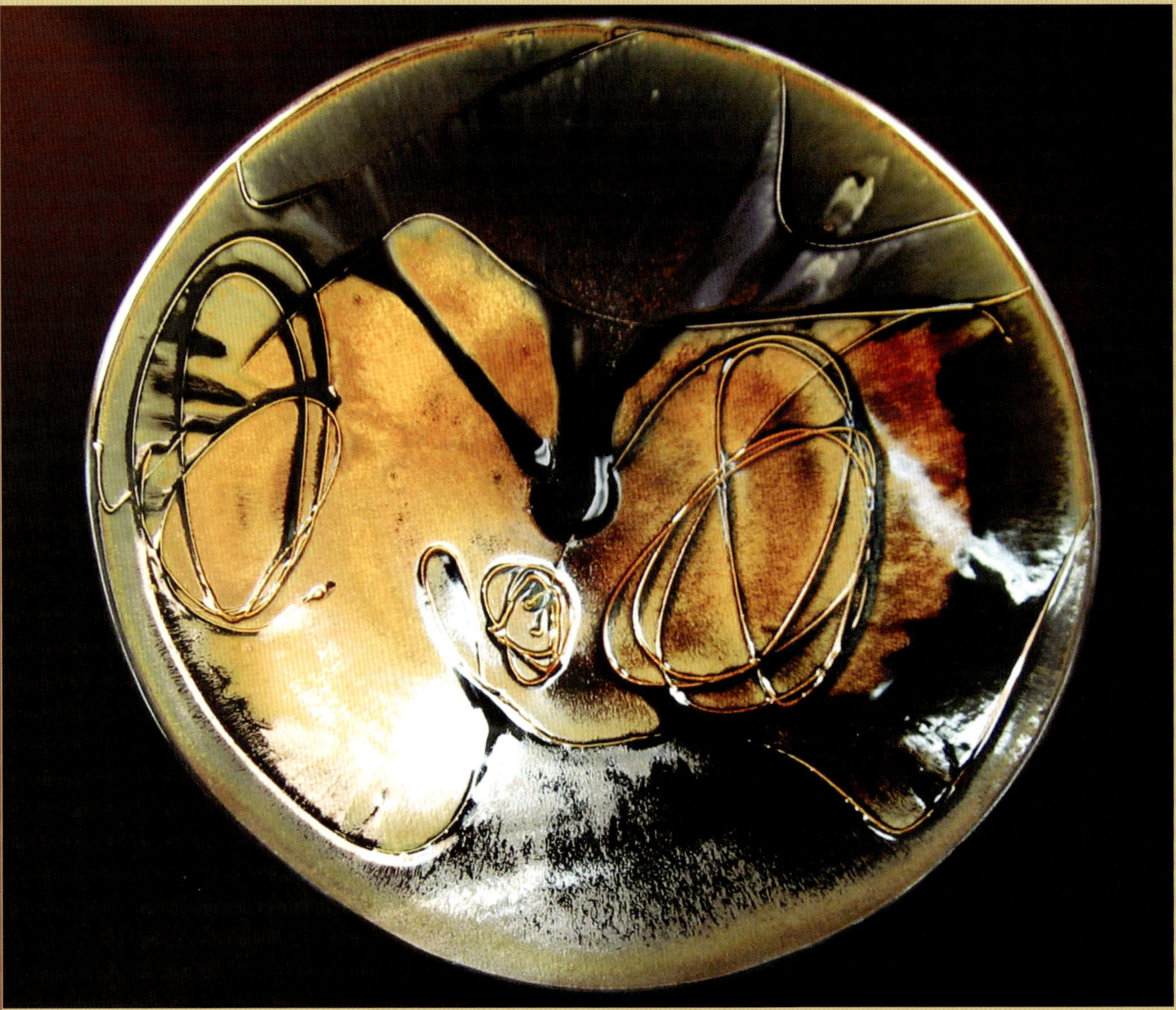

Below: Close-up of platter details.

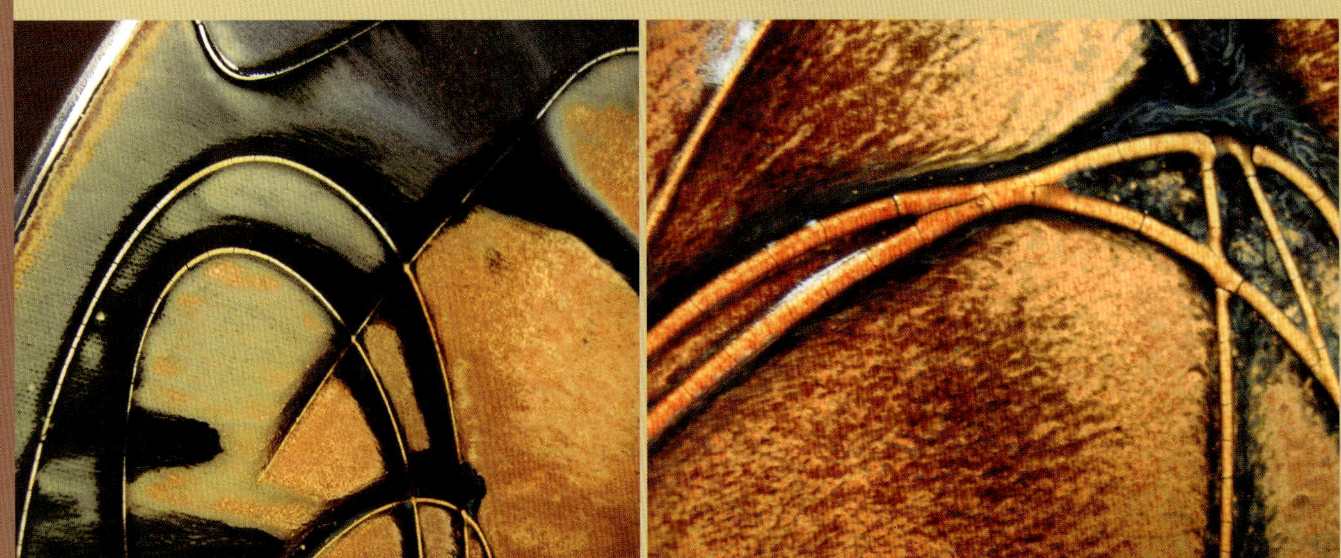

Stoneware hanging platter 21″ wide x 4 ½″ high with raised slip designs and all natural glazes. Van Hollow Pottery uses over 100 glazes in multiple combinations to produce sensuous earth tone tapestries.

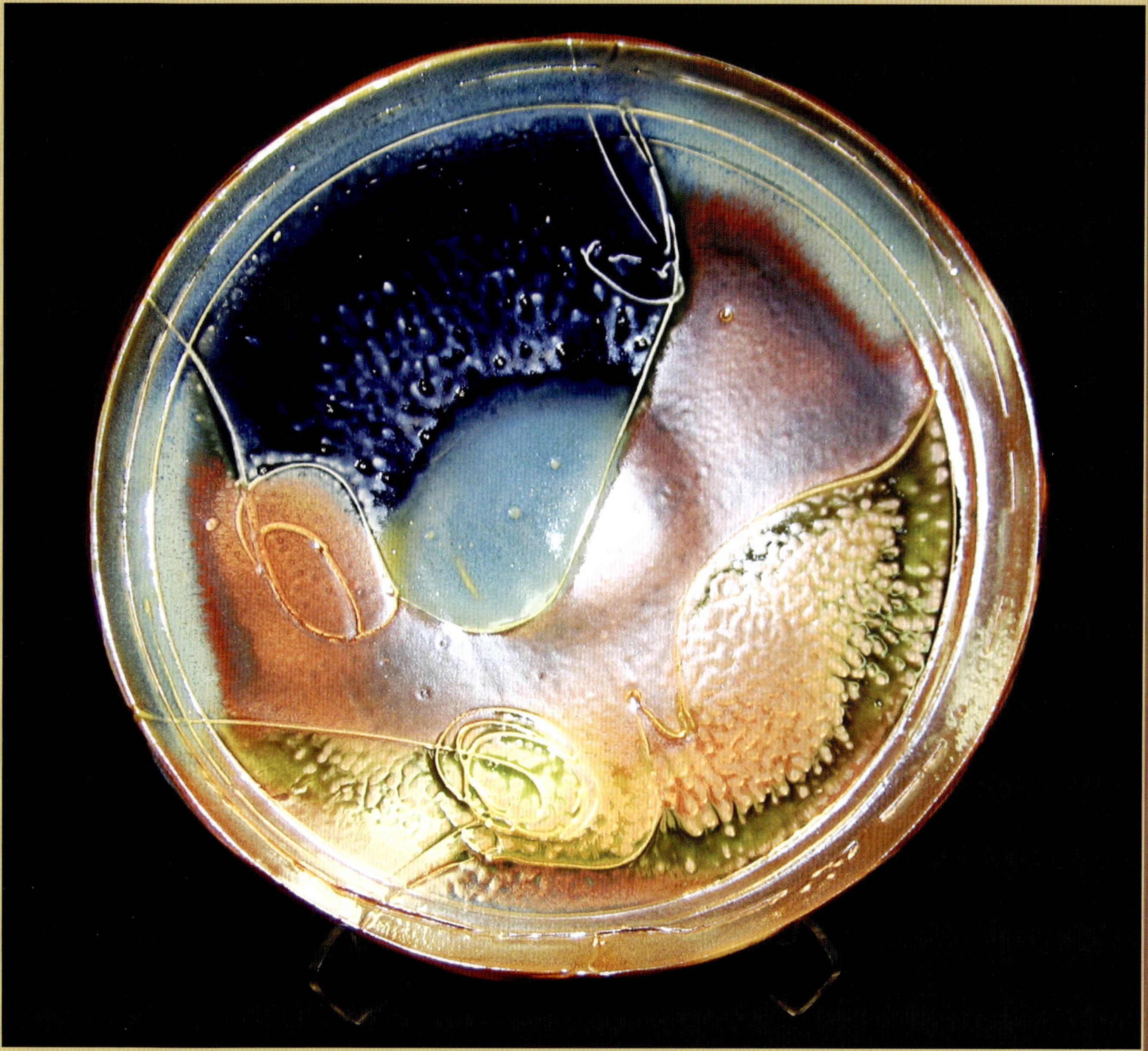

Below: Details of hanging platter showing the intricate variation made possible through intense heat and layered glazes. There is no more durable pottery, and it is all oven, microwave and dishwasher safe.

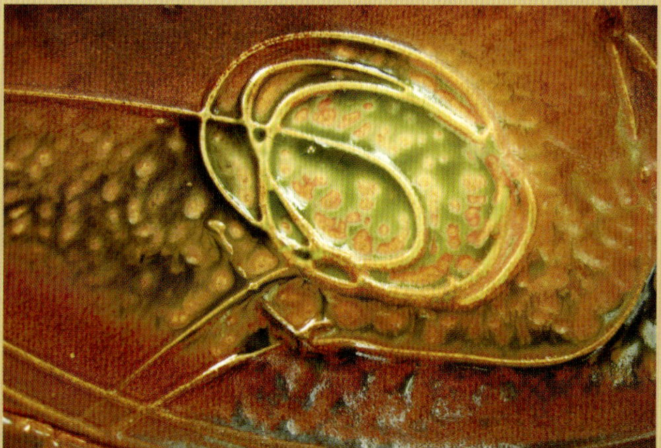

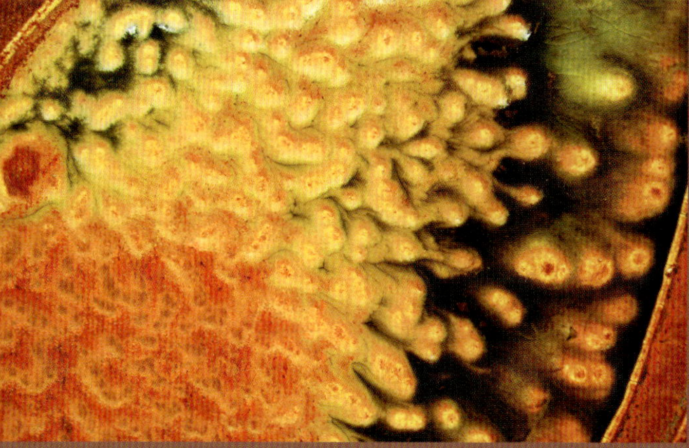

MARGIE PAYTON

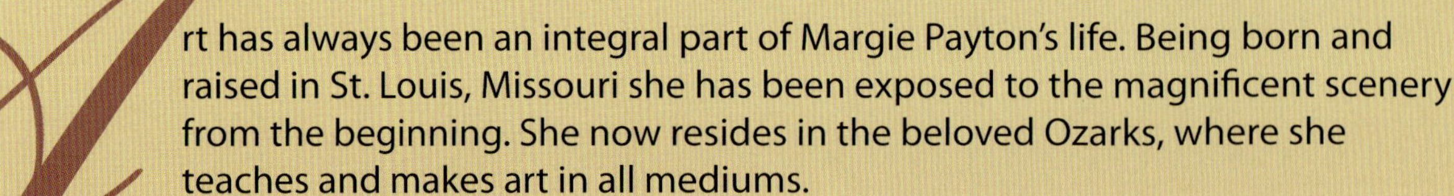

Art has always been an integral part of Margie Payton's life. Being born and raised in St. Louis, Missouri she has been exposed to the magnificent scenery from the beginning. She now resides in the beloved Ozarks, where she teaches and makes art in all mediums.

Margie's paintings are created to bring comfort and happiness to all who view or own them. Many of them reflect the panoramic lake view of her hilltop home. More can be viewed at **http://paletteartleague.org/MargiePayton.html.**

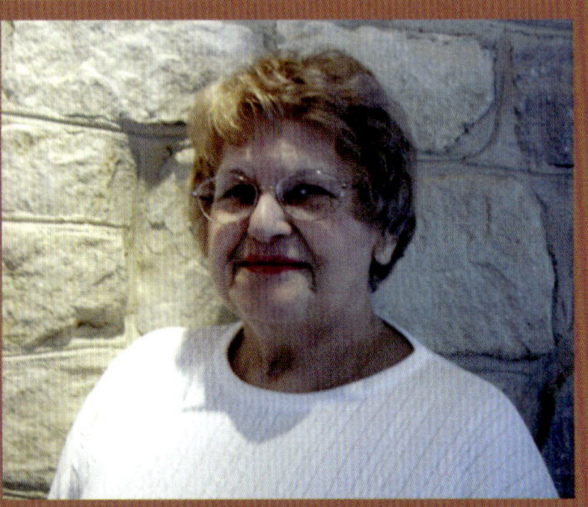

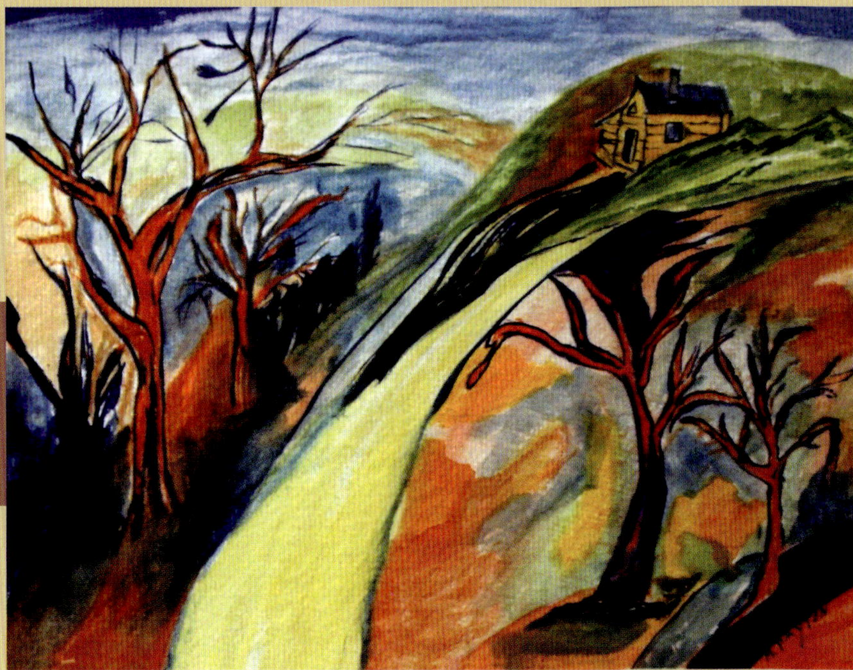

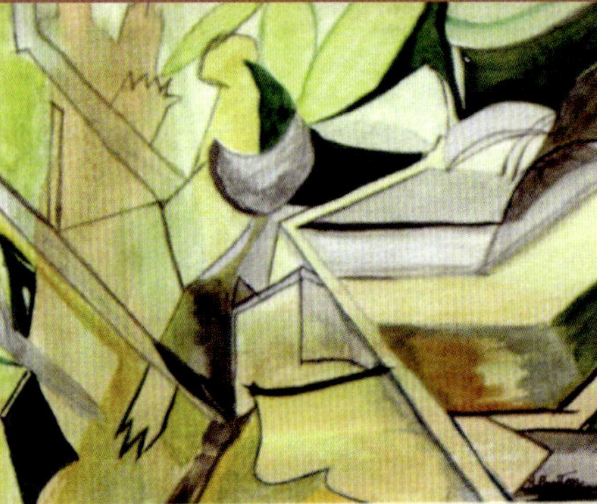

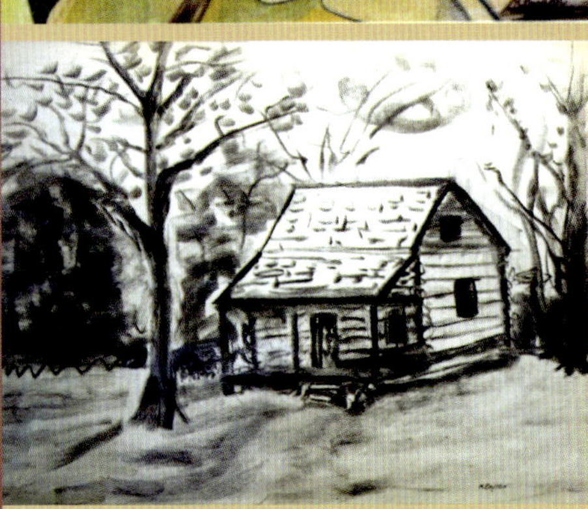

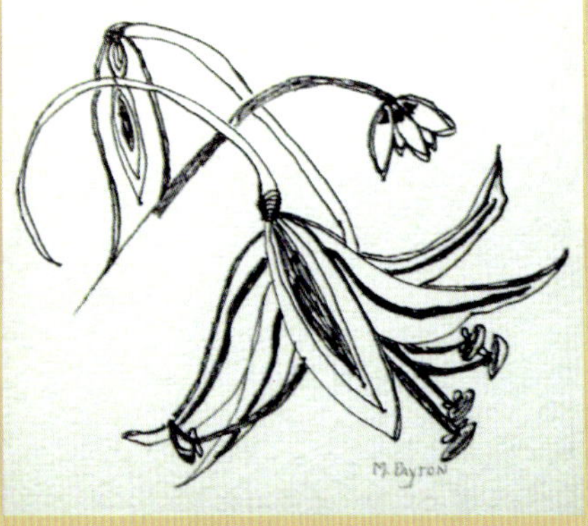

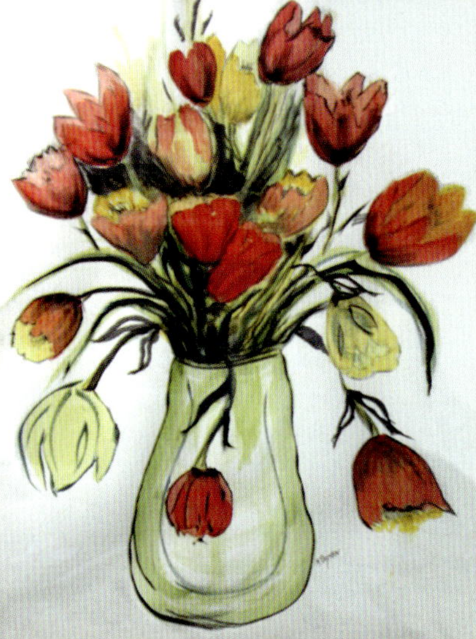

JEANNE ROTH

I have been interested in art as long as I can remember. In St. Louis, I taught elementary and high school art for a total of 20 years, and also in an after school gifted art program for 9 years.

Since retiring, I have been active in local art clubs and in 2010, served for a second time as President of Area Art Club. I am also currently President of Artists of the Ozark, a member of Bull Shoals Art Club and Hill Country Art Gallery, and I was an Advisory Board Member for the Cultural Arts Society.

My life is "artful" as I participate in shows, exhibitions, teach workshops in painting and collage and create in my studio in Gamaliel, Arkansas. For more information on Jeanne's work, visit **http://paletteartleague.org/JeanneRoth.html.**

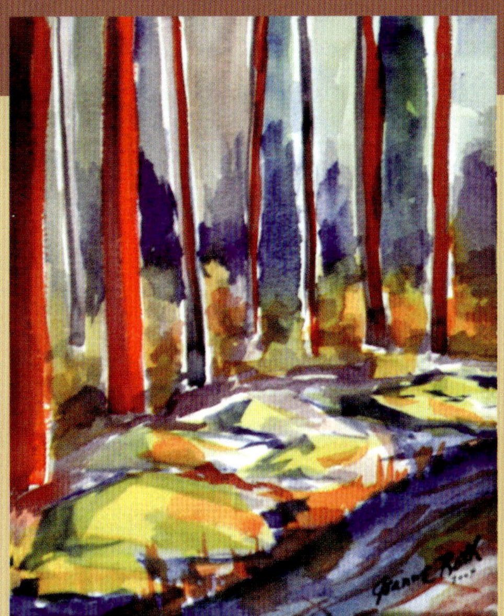

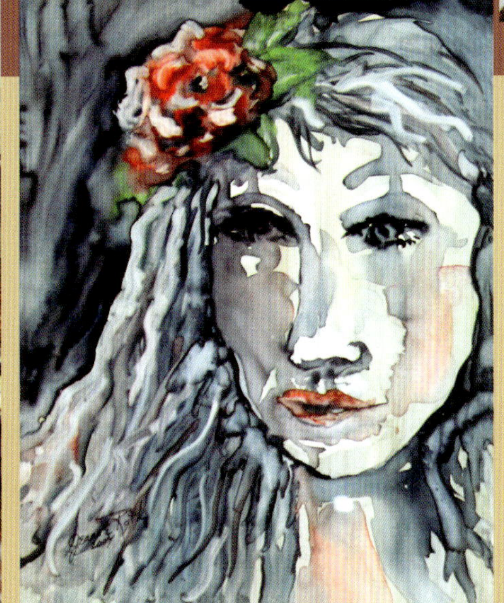

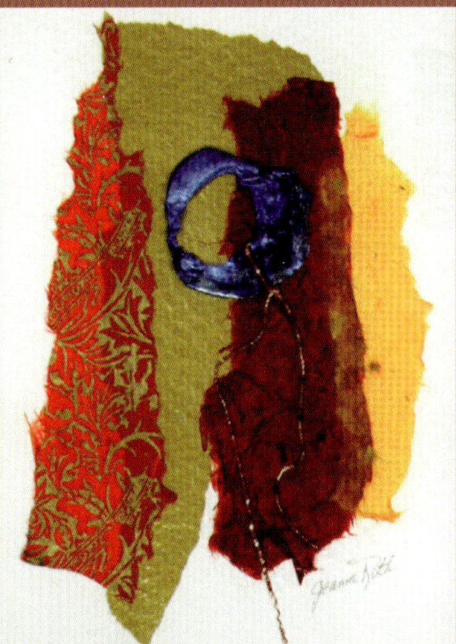

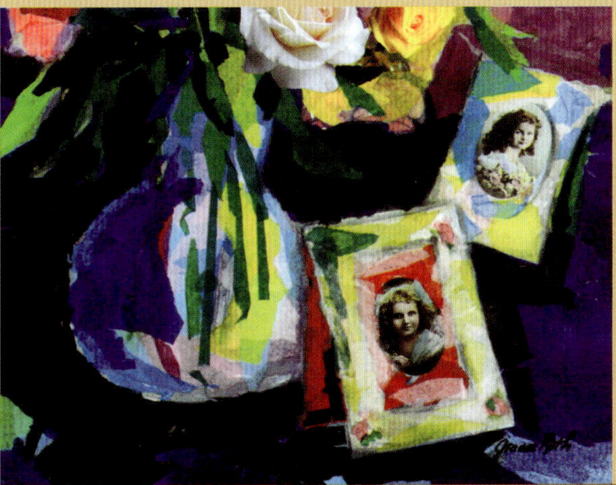

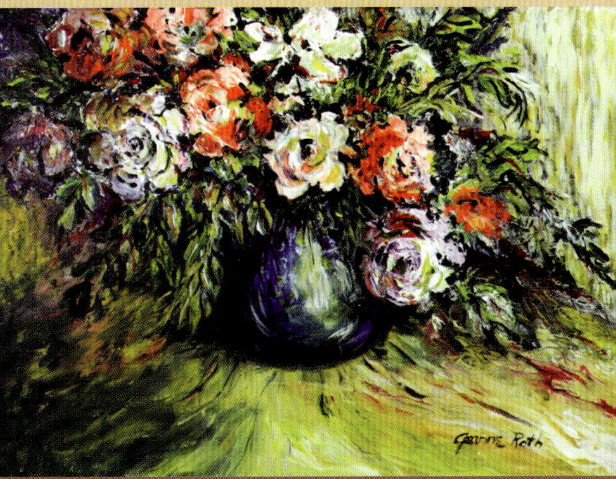

CRAIG & LORNA TRIGG HIRSCH

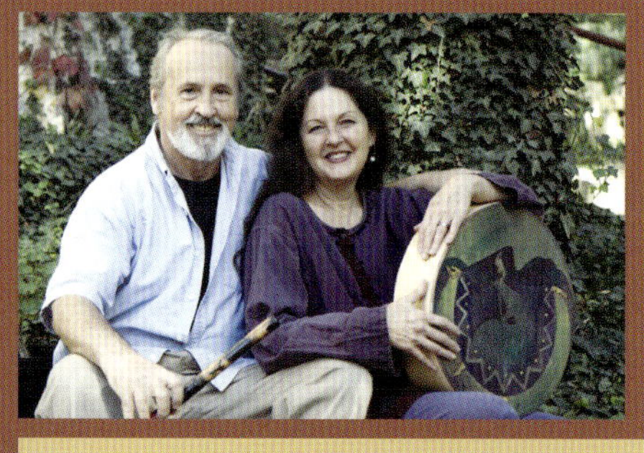

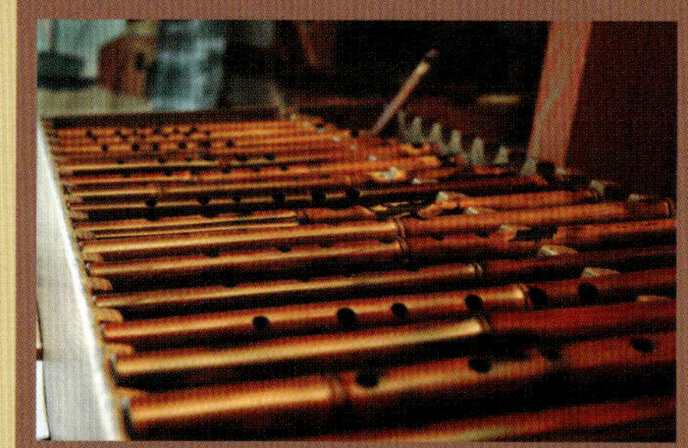

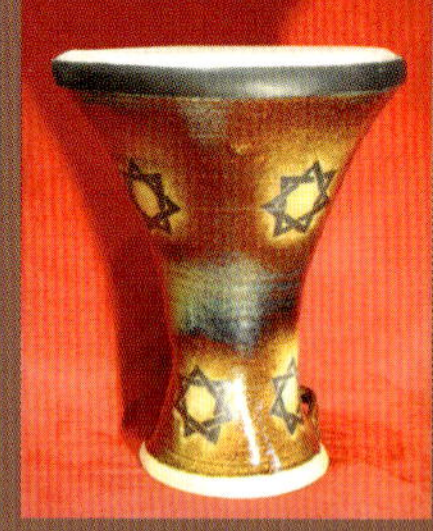

Fire Om Earth is the collaborative creativity studio of Lorna and Craig Trigg Hirsch. Emphasizing the hand crafting of musical wind and percussion instruments representing the Renaissance period, and the influence of a world traveled by troubadours, merchants and crafts people.

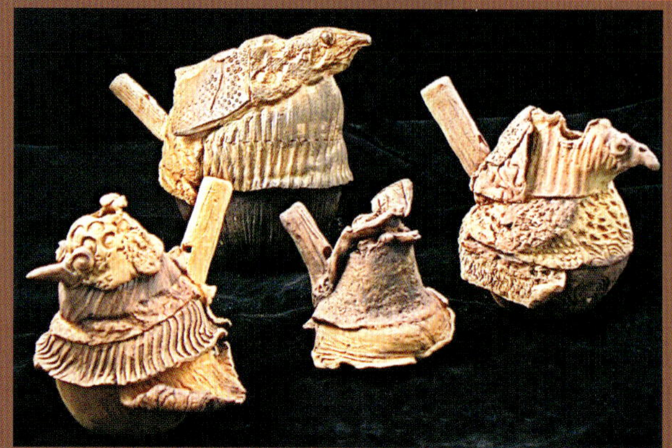

Craig is a Master wind instrument builder specializing in breath work instruction and Lorna is a Creativity and Movement Facilitator. Her lifelong study has focused on the use of rhythm instruments and dance of indigenous people. For more information on workshops, retreats and instruments created by this creative team visit their website at **http://www.fireomearth.com/ or E-mail them at info@fireomearth.com.**

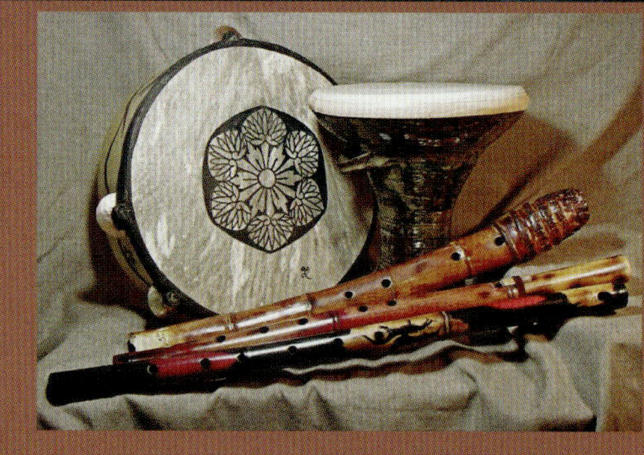

GINNY LUTTRELL

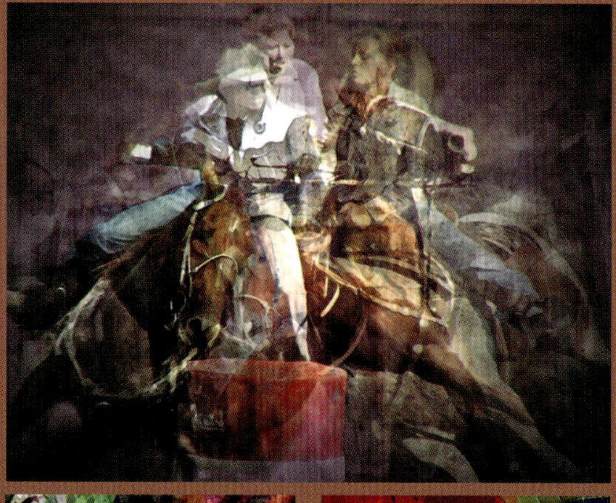

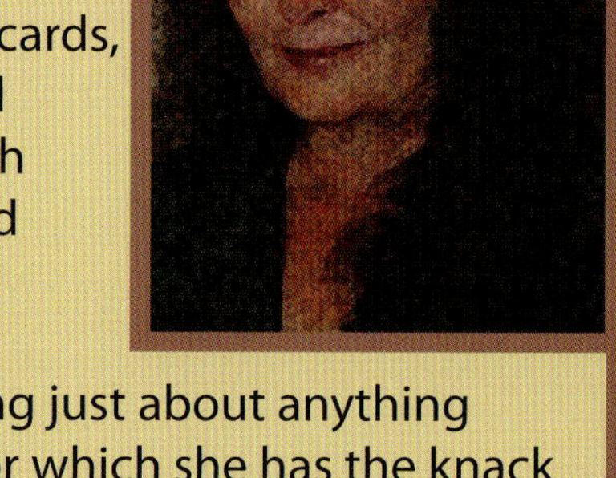

Ginny has enjoyed photography all of her life. Upon retirement she started her own photography business, Memories by Gin, which features her artist cards, fine art photography and commissioned works with a Photo Shop twist added for your enjoyment.

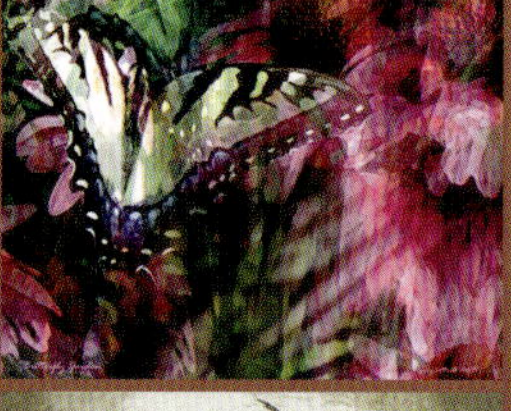

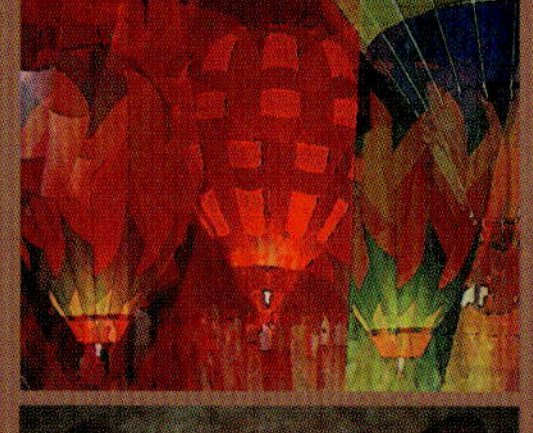

She enjoys photographing just about anything but especially animals, for which she has the knack of capturing their inner essence, beauty and character.

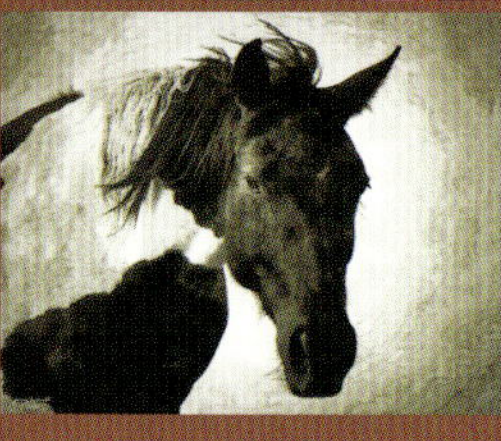

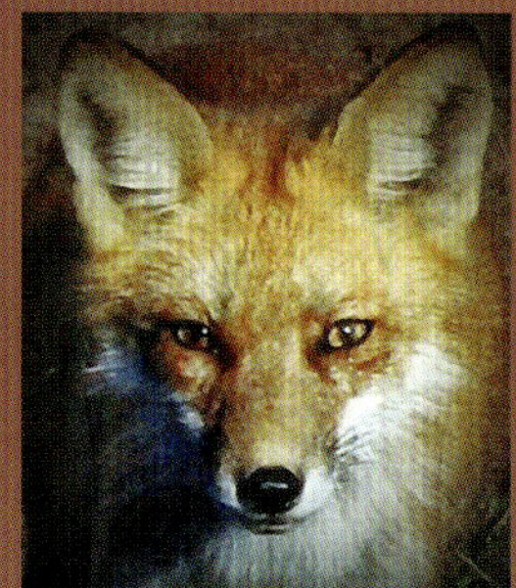

Her works can be seen at Poor Richard's Art Gallery in Rogers, Arkansas, various shops in Topeka, Kansas and have been sold worldwide through her shop on Zazzle.com. She is also a member of the Eureka Springs Artist Registry in Eureka Springs, Arkansas. **For more information on Ginny's work, visit http://www.memoriesbygin.net or http://www.zazzle.com/ginnyl52.**

Terry has been painting since childhood. Her major work is in oil. One style she uses is flowing and dynamic to express her spiritual nature. She allows her brush to flow freely over her canvas and floods the canvas with the essence and richness of her visions and dreams.

Terry has been in many juried art shows, competitions, and galleries. Her paintings are included in private and corporate collections worldwide. She currently shows and sells from her home and studio and often works on commission. Terry is always happy to discuss ideas with the client. She may be contacted by phone at 870-453-6123 or by email tlzarate@flippinweb.com. **More of her work may be seen on her website www.dreamworldsart.com.**

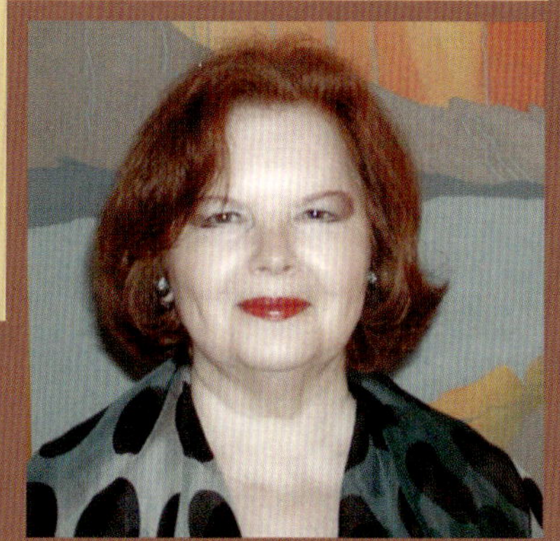

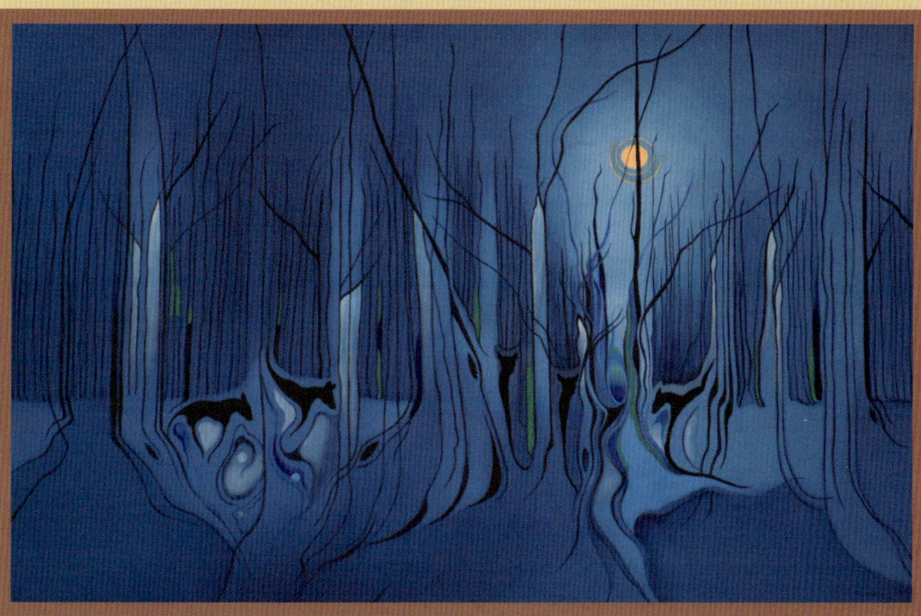

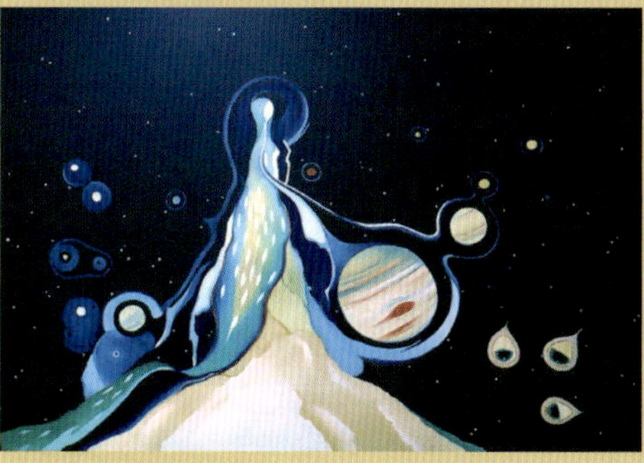

Top: Enchanted Forest,
Above: Juno Ordering The Universe,
Right: Autumn

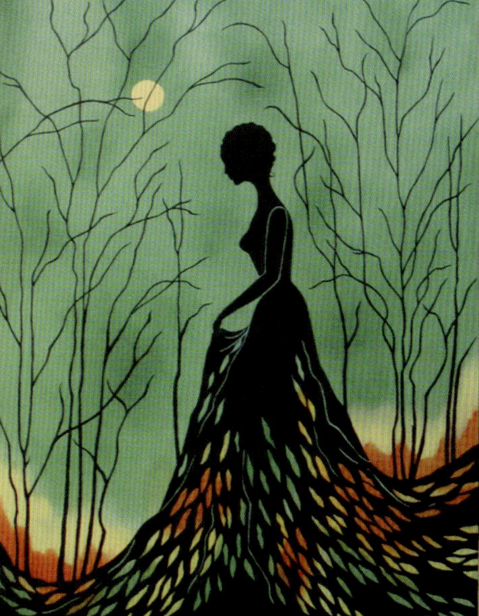

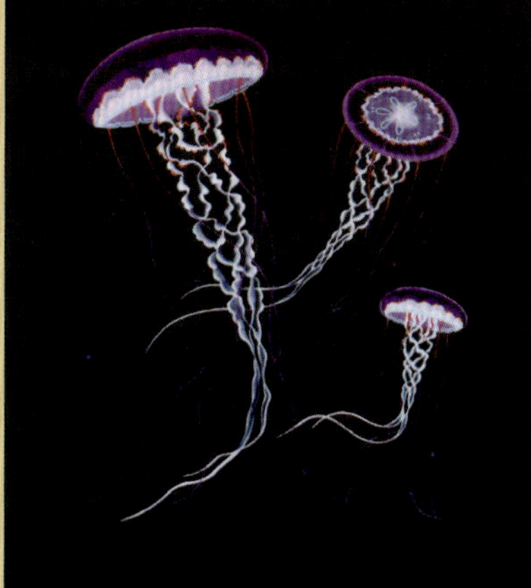

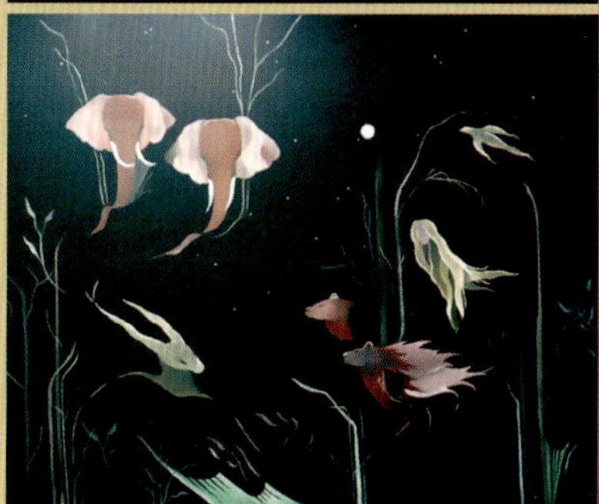

Top: Jellies,
Above: African Queen

CAROLE TORMEY JONES

Carole grew up in the horse country of Oyster Bay, Long Island, New York.

Her love for all animals and an ability to draw, inspired her to attend "The Art Students League" in New York City. Here, she was able to study illustration with Earl Mayan of the Saturday Evening Post and Steven Kidd of the New York Daily News. She also studied anatomy with Robert Hale. Later, she furthered her education in England at Sir John Cass College, studying drawing, painting and illustration. She continued her study of anatomy at the Royal Academy.

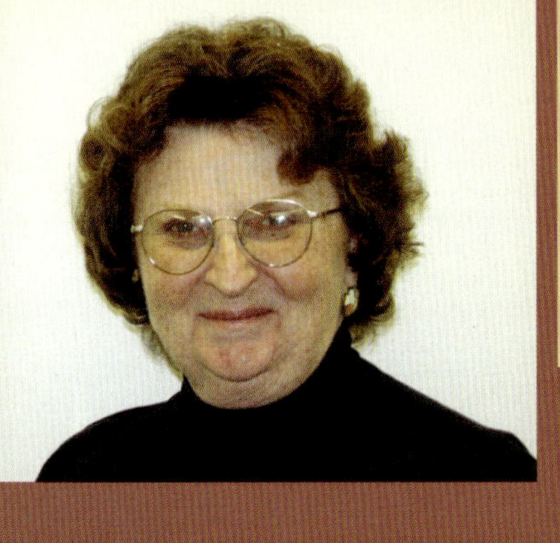

Carole is available for commission portrait work, book illustrations and you can learn more about her work by visiting her website at: http://paletteartleague.org/CaroleJones.html.

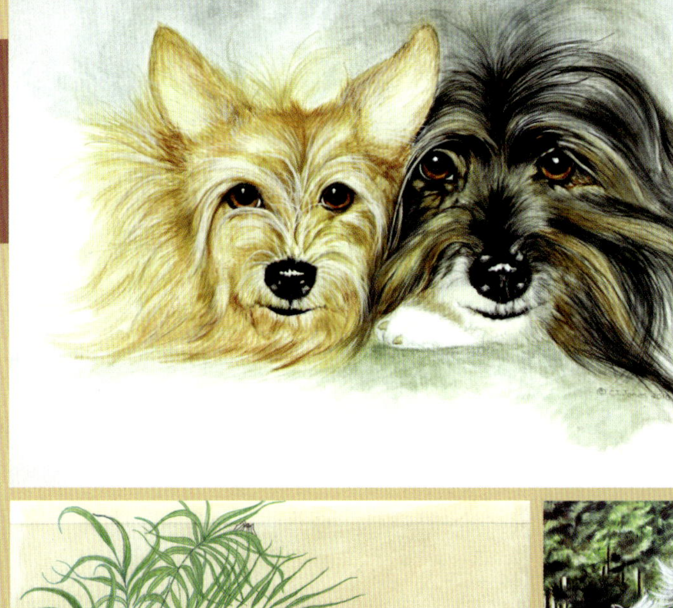

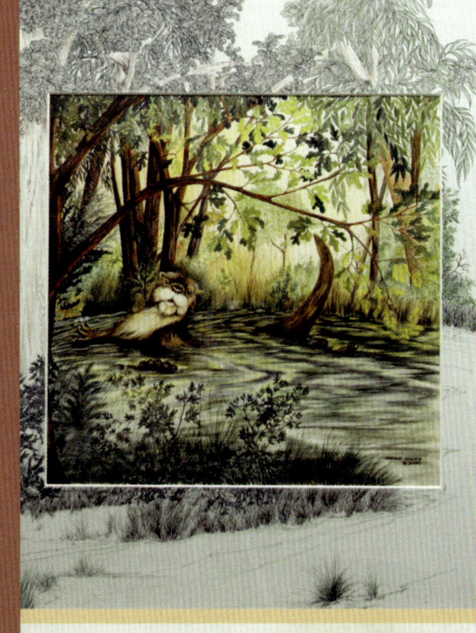

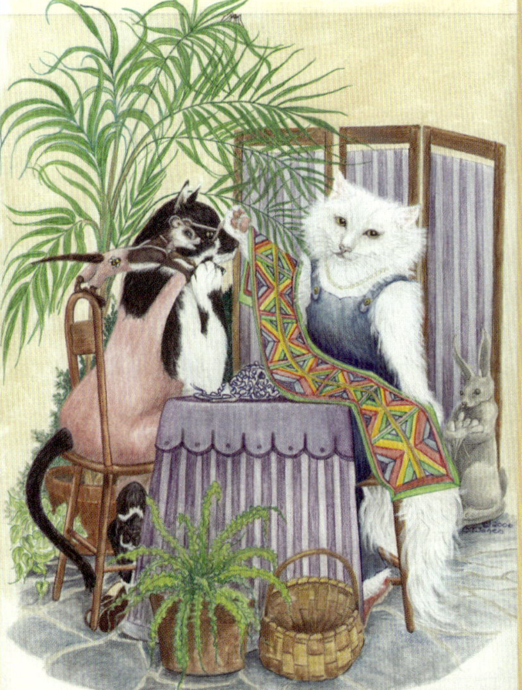

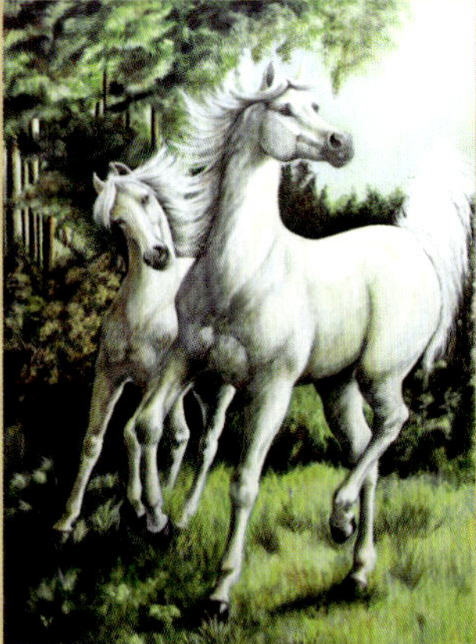

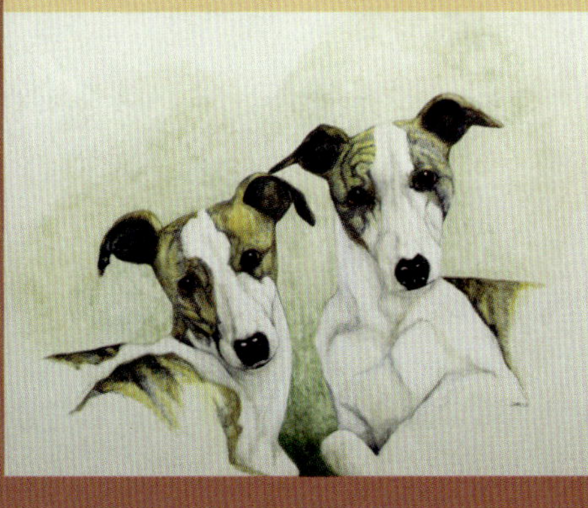

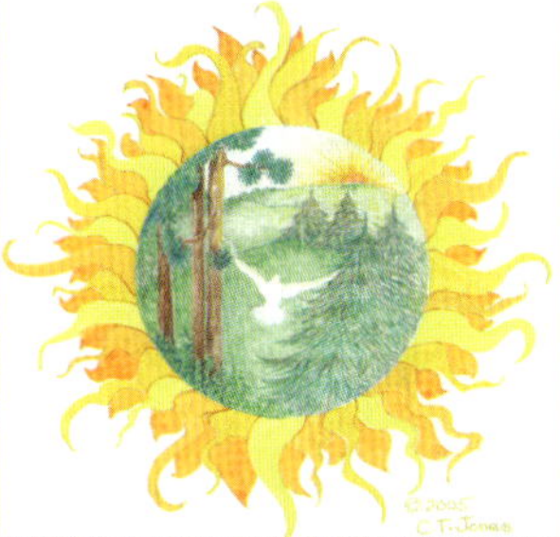

Les Casteel is an Arkansas based woodworker, furniture designer, writer, and instructor who specializes in designing and building sculptured rocking chairs, as well as other classic types of seating. Both the influence and association with the legendary chair maker Sam Maloof, continues to inspire Les to design and build complex sculptured pieces of furniture from various types of fine wood.

Les is also an accomplished woodturner and is fond of creating segmented objects of art from waste wood that is destined for the land fill. Les is currently working on a series of new woodturnings employing classical shapes and color patterns which are often found in old pottery.

You may contact Les at his mountain-top studio near Harrison, Arkansas at:
http://www.woodthatrocks.com
or les@woodthatrocks.com.

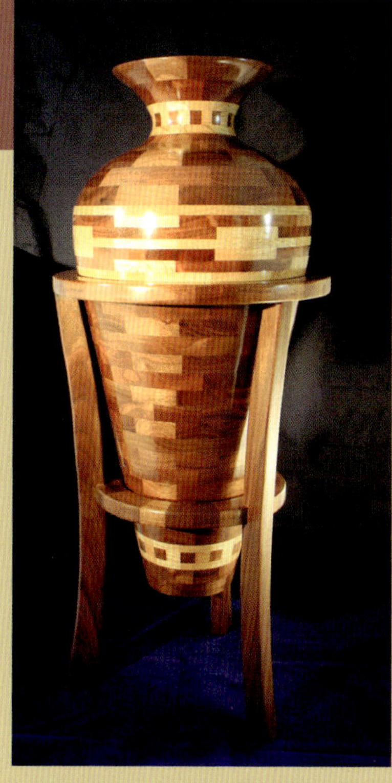

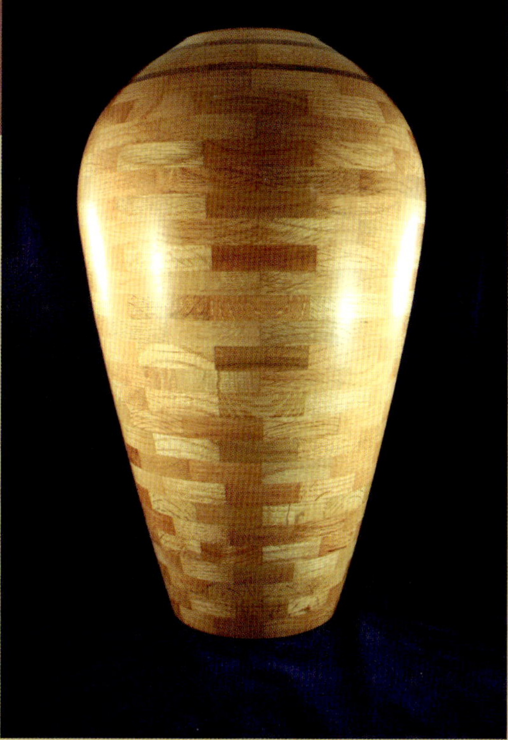

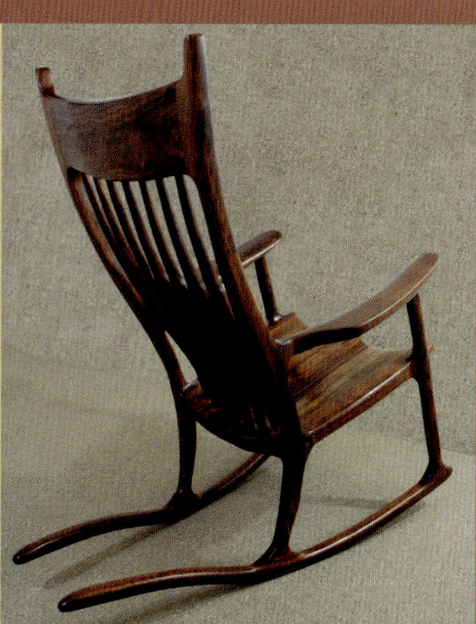

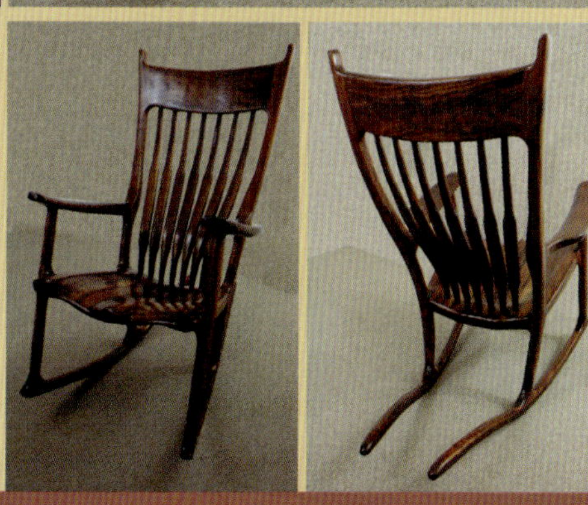

MICHAEL AND KAY ANDREWS HARRISON, ARKANSAS

Michael Andrews was practically born with a pencil and paper in his hands. He recalls pursuing his art as far back as his earliest childhood memories.

Michael attended Kansas City Art Institute before embarking on a series of art-related jobs in the years that followed which included designing a prayer chapel for the New York World's Fair, freelance work for newspapers, print shops, magazines and even a theme park!

In 1984, Michael and his wife Kay made a decision to focus on full time commission work, painting the working ranch cowboy, and the culture of the Ozarks. Michael has exhibited his work across the USA and was named winner of the first Will Rogers Award presented by the National Academy of Western Artists for the Cowboy Artist of the Year.

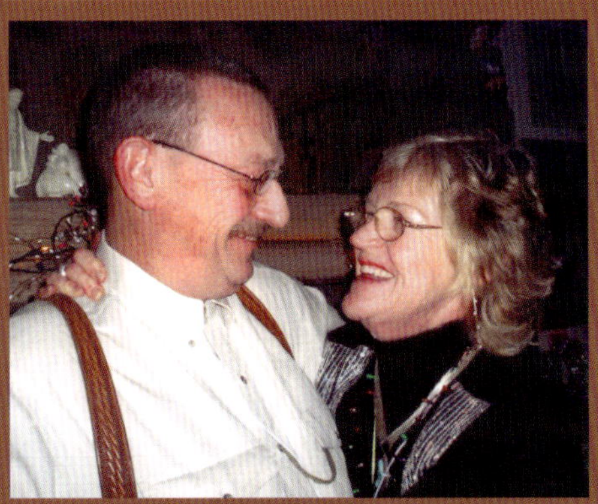

Michael specializes in commission portrait work from photographs. **For more information on Michael Andrew's work, call 870-743-5009 or visit: http://paletteartleague.org/MichaelAndrews.html.**

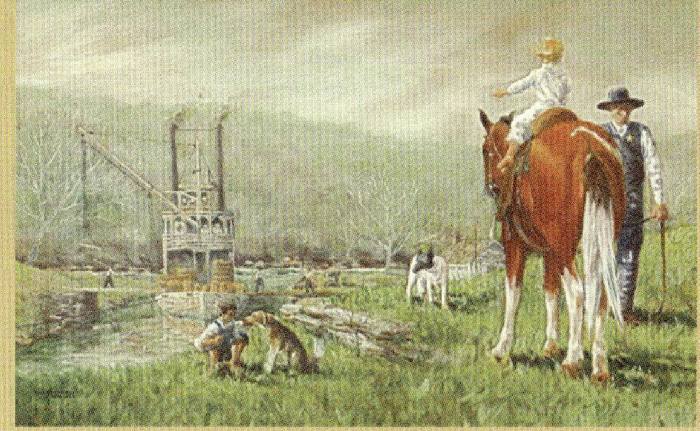

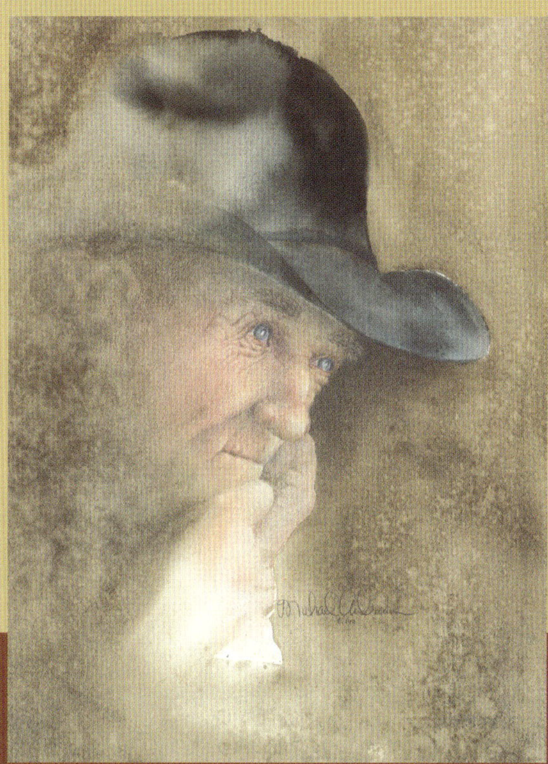

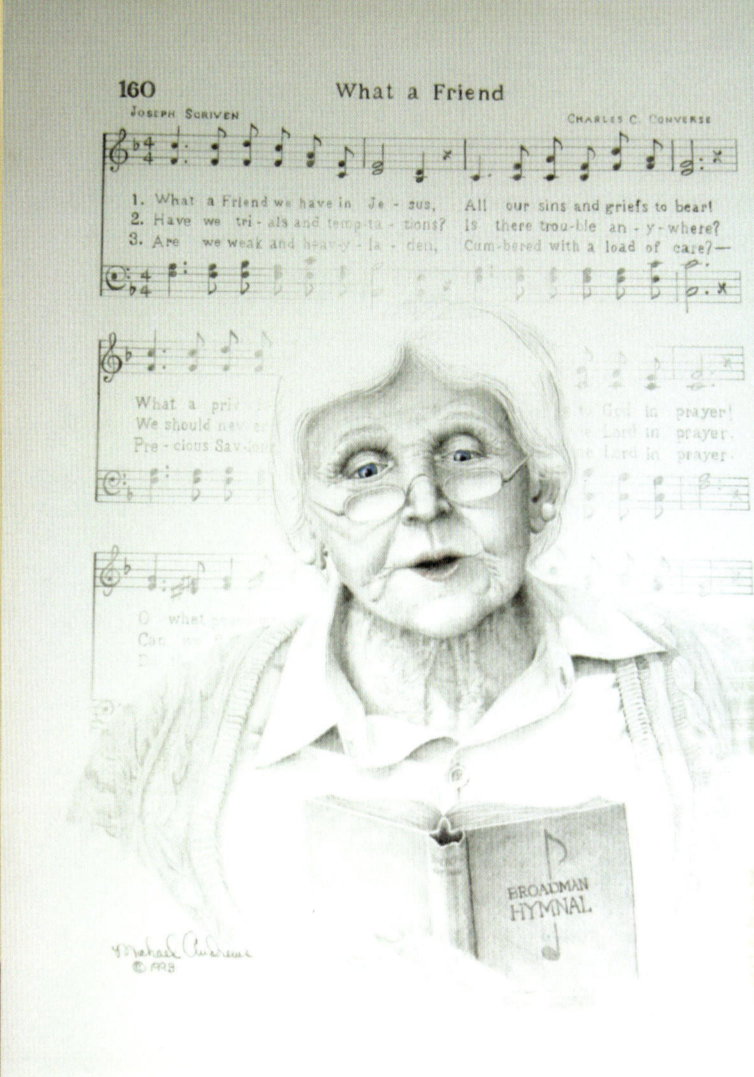

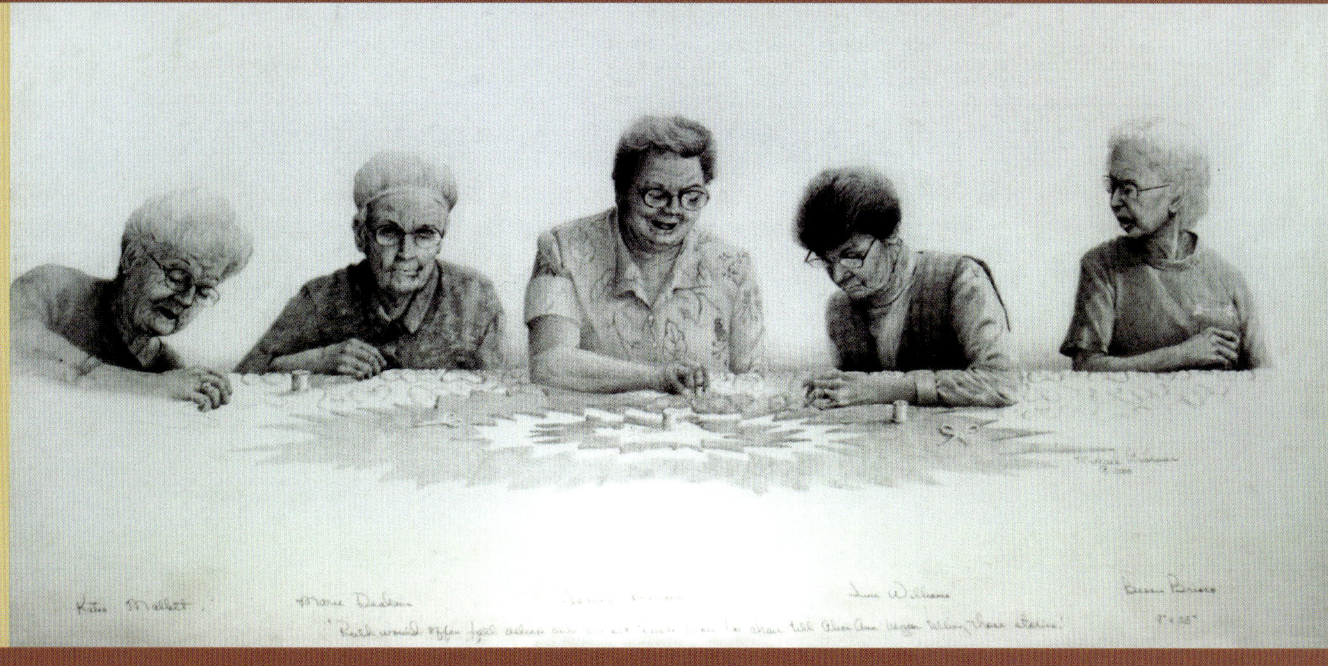

MICHAEL AND KAY ANDREWS HARRISON, ARKANSAS

DOROTHY ANDERSON

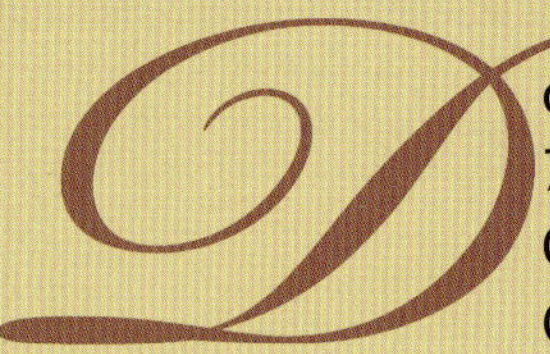orothy Anderson was born in Georgetown, Texas. She moved to Arkansas in the 70's when her husband Bobby retired from the Army after 20 years of service. Over the years, they traveled the United States and Europe and chose the Ozarks as their permanent home!

Always interested in art, after her children were grown, Dorothy studied with a well known artist in Arkansas and then attended courses at the local college where she studied art and creative writing.

Dorothy likes all mediums of art: oil, pastel, pen and ink, and pencil. Some more than others but still her favorite are pencil and colored pencils. She is always learning new art forms whether on canvas, paper, cloth, or wood. To learn more about Dorothy's work, **visit her at: http://paletteartleague.org/DorothyAnderson.html.**

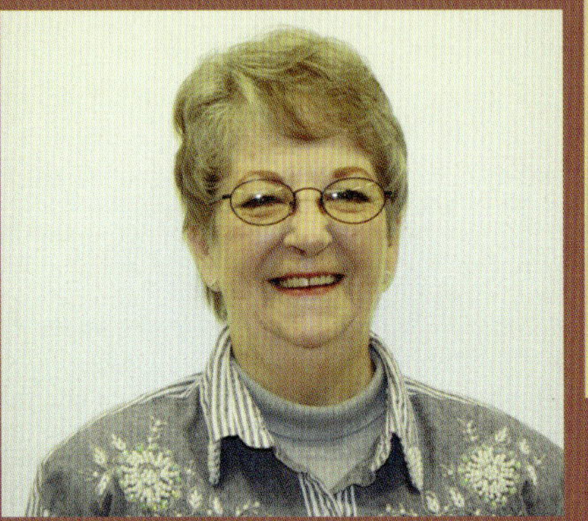

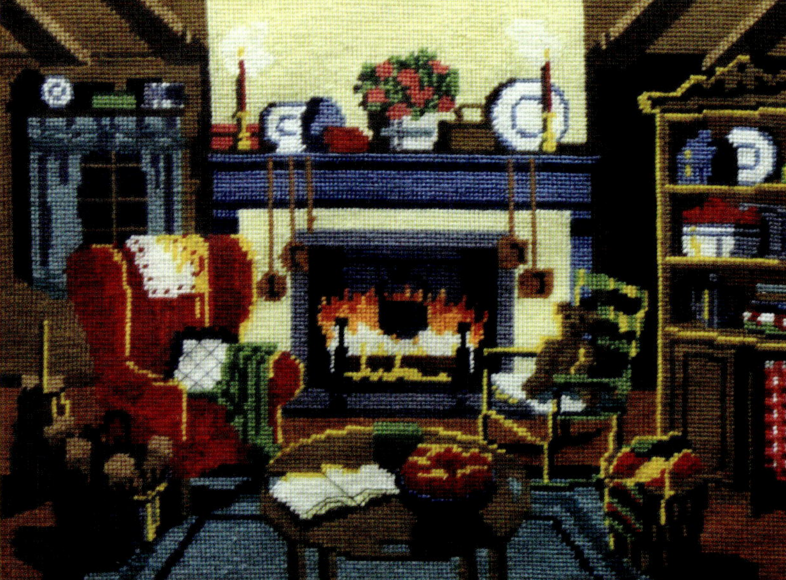

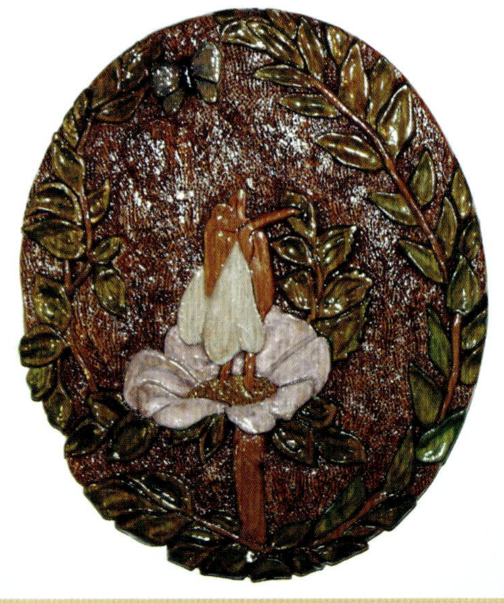

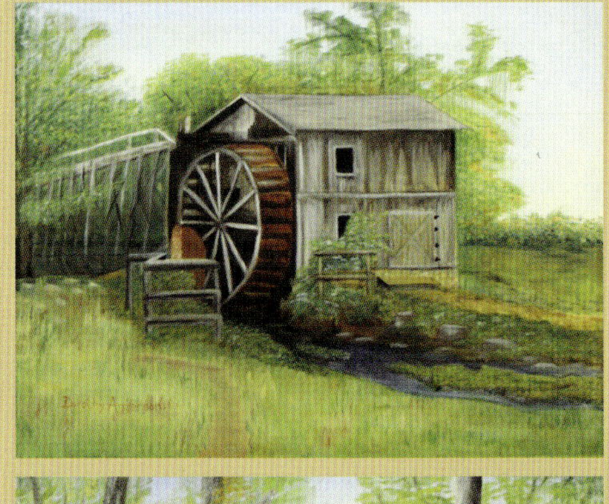

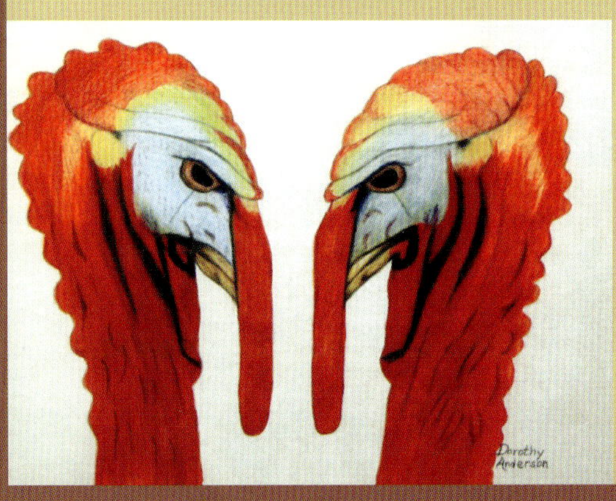

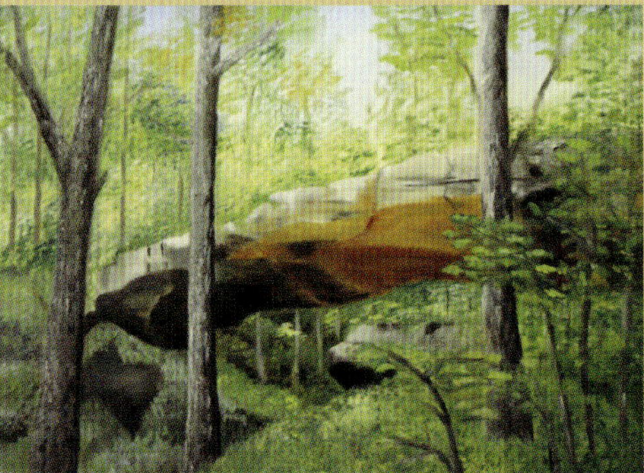

ELISSA GORDON

I studied art during high school and college. When I retired to Mountain Home, Arkansas after working in advertising for more than 25 years, I took classes in drawing, pastel and design. Pastel, acrylic, collage and photography are my mediums. While I have never met a medium that I didn't like, pastel is my favorite because I feel so connected to the work and the colors are magnificent.

As a member of Area Art Club, Artists of the Ozarks, Bull Shoals Art Club and Hill Country Art Gallery, I participate in numerous local art shows and exhibits. I have a studio in my home where I am currently focusing on watercolor.

For more information on Elissa's work, visit http://paletteartleague.org/ElissaGordon.html.

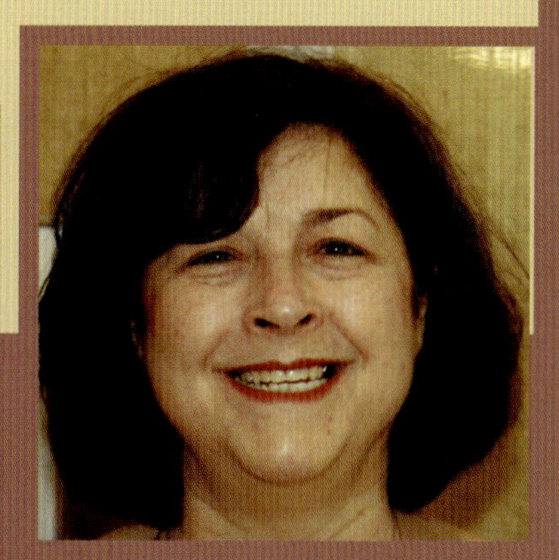

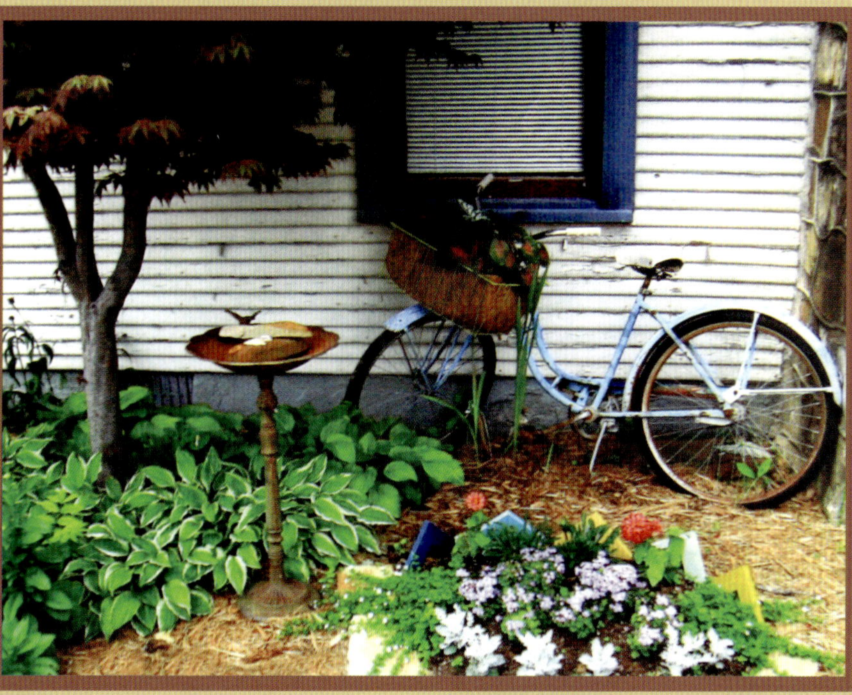

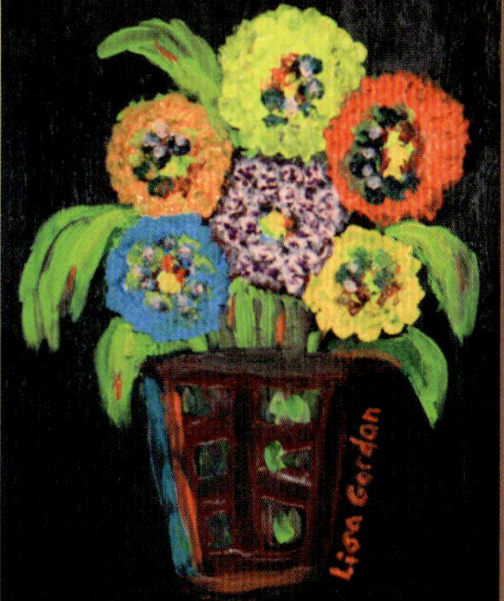

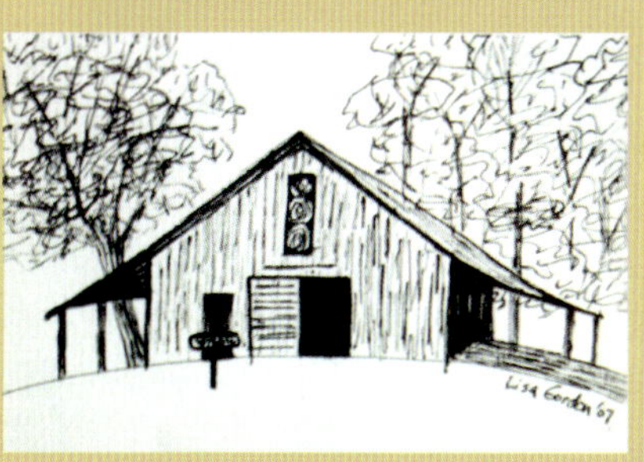

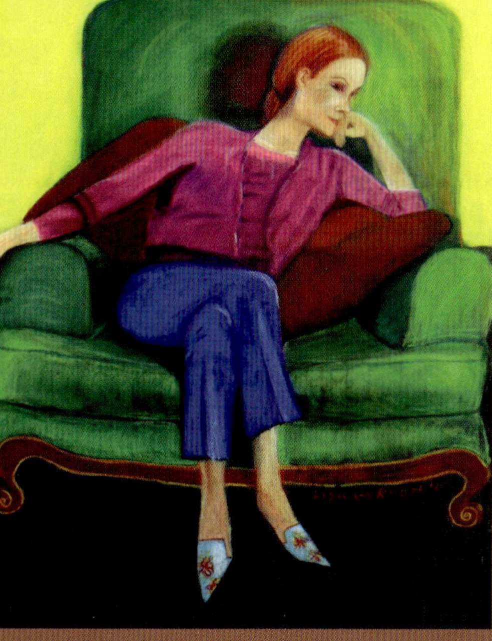

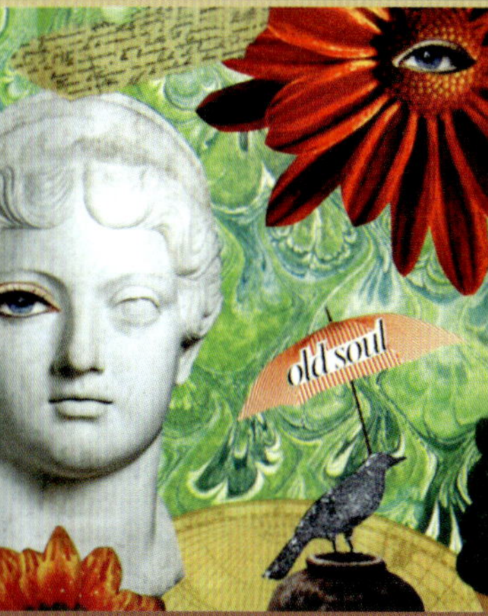

Martin is a native Missourian, born in 1960. It was there, growing up on his family's farm that he learned to appreciate the beauty of the land and the seasons. Martin now resides in Columbia, Missouri.

Martin is a self-taught photographer who took up the serious art of photography in 1999 at the urging of friends who admired his images from his cross-country travels. In 2004, Martin became a "juried artist member" of the Missouri Artisans Association, D.B.A "Best of Missouri Hands".
For more information about Martin's work, visit his website at http://www.MartinSpilker.com or e-mail Martin at martinspilker@me.com.

"Reading about nature is fine, but if a person walks in the woods and listens carefully, they can learn more than what is in books, for they speak with the voice of God." George Washington Carver.

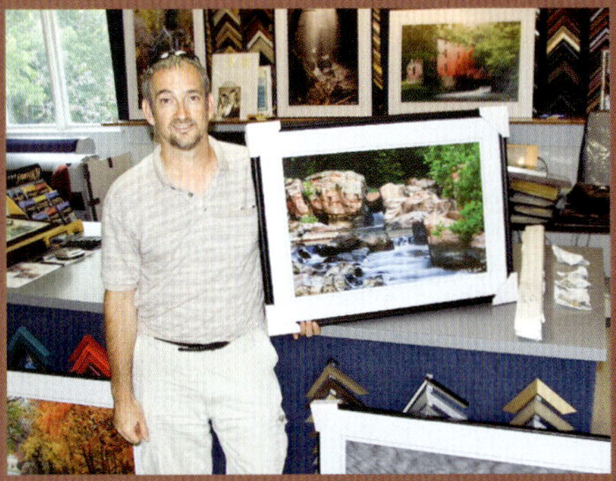

www.MartinSpilker.com

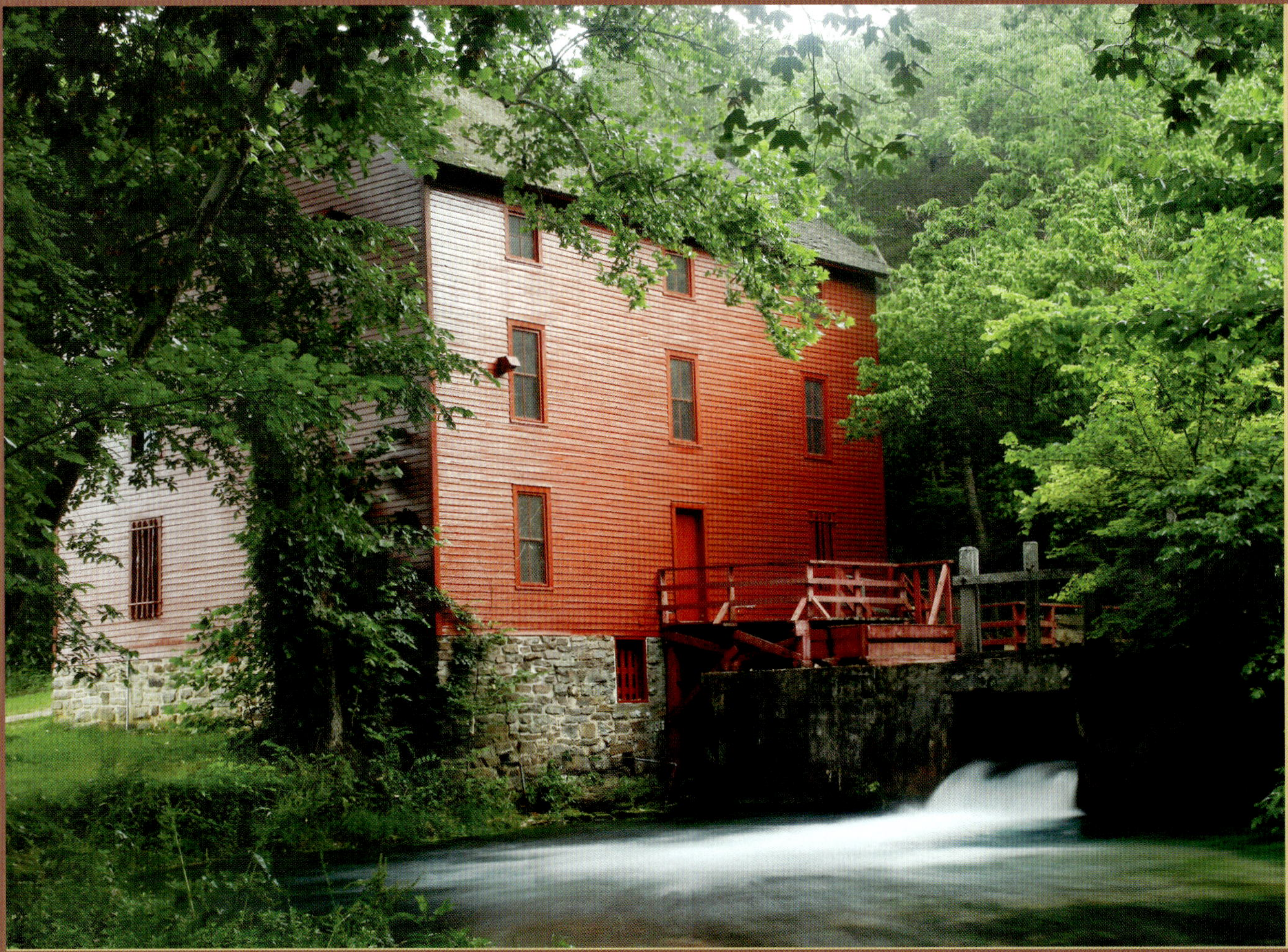

MARTIN SPILKER

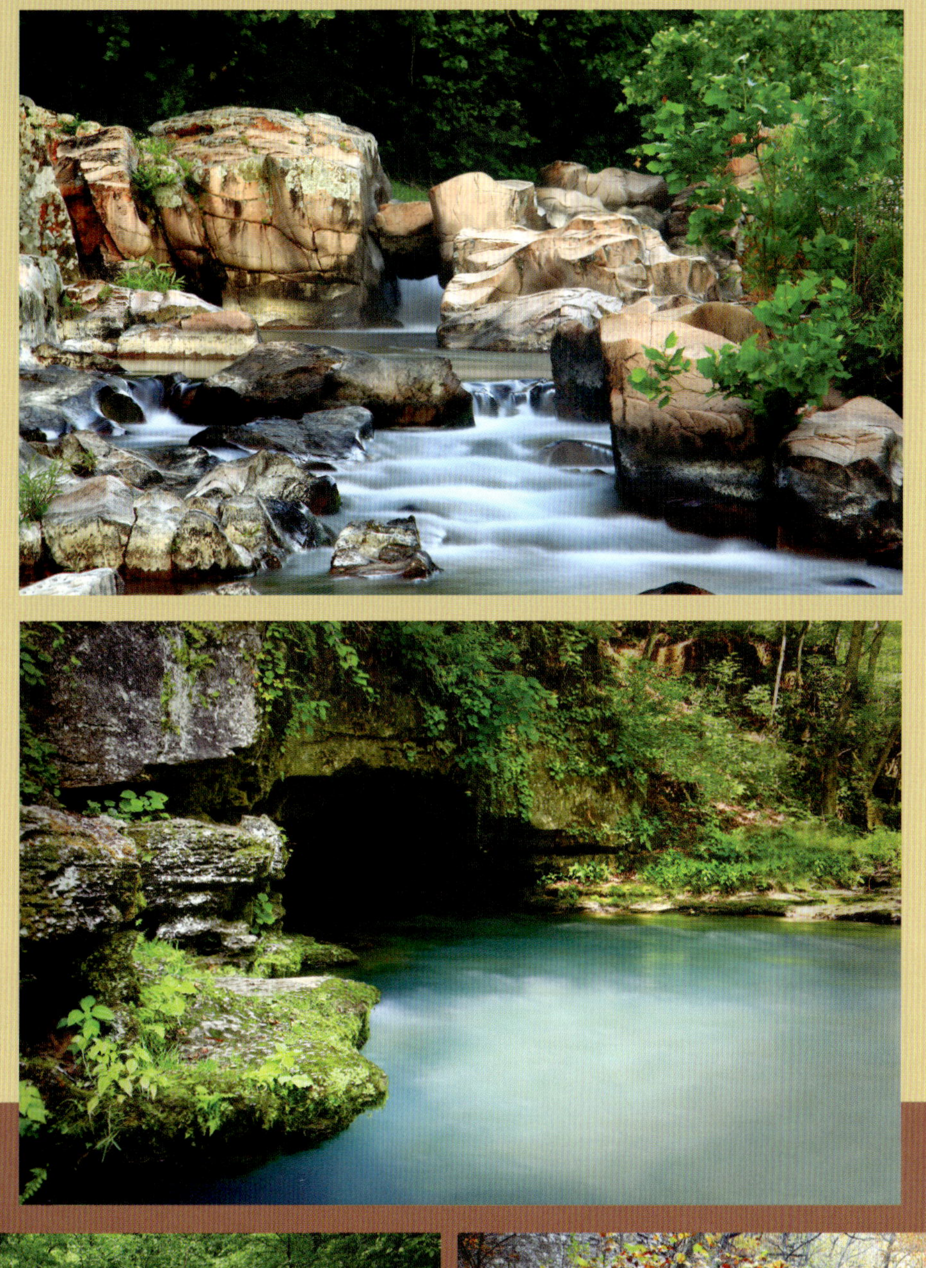

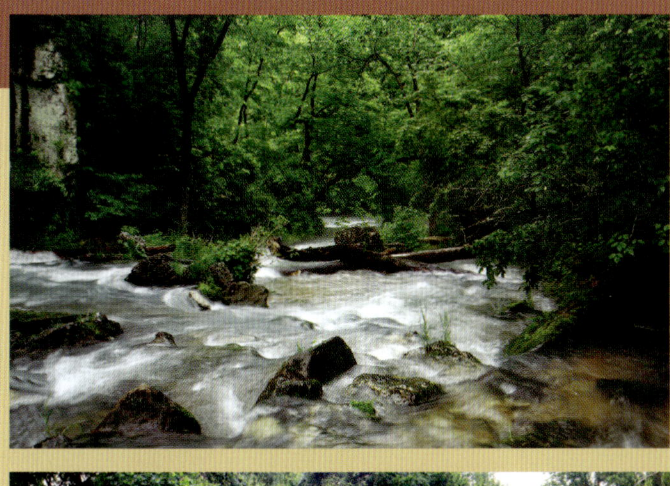

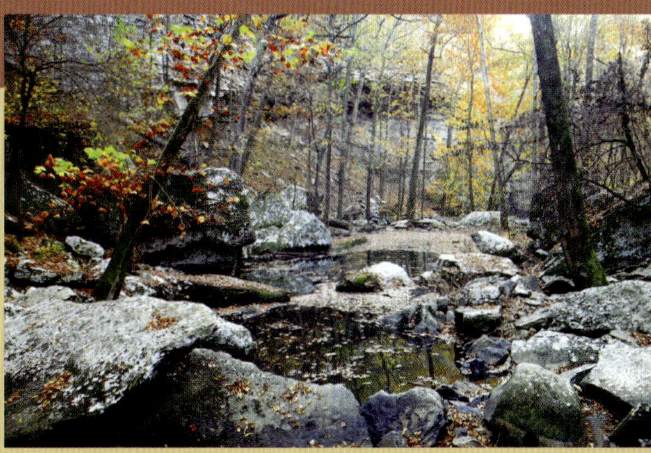

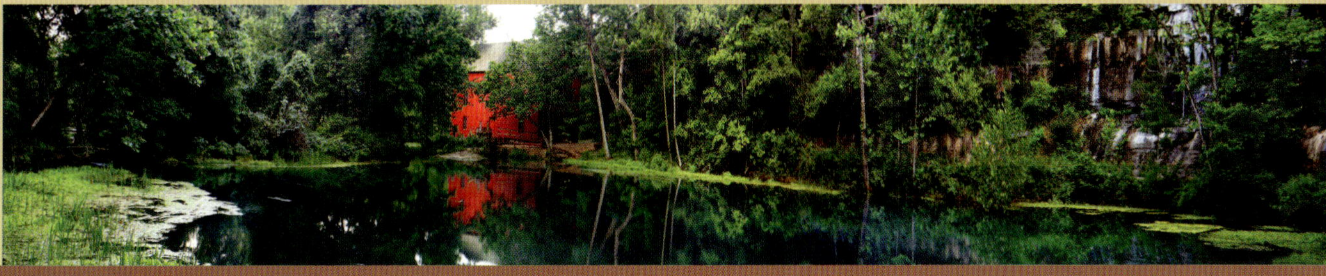

MARTIN SPILKER

ROGER KING

Roger King is a native of West Virginia who majored in Fine Arts at W.V. University before transferring to the Art Institute of Pittsburgh PA, where he studied Interior Design. After graduation, Roger moved to Phoenix Arizona where he lived until he retired to Arkansas in 1990. While living in Arizona he was a member of the National Society of Interior Designs, American Interior Designs, Arizona Watercolor Association and the Arizona Artist Guild (all juried organizations).

Roger taught painting techniques on TV in Huntington, West Virginia and Phoenix, Arizona. He has hosted seminars in Arizona and in Taos New Mexico and was a private teacher for many years in Scottsdale Arizona. His love of the woods, and the Arkansas seasons has provided him with some dramatic landscapes. **For more information on Roger's work, visit his website at http://paletteartleague.org/RogerKing.html.**

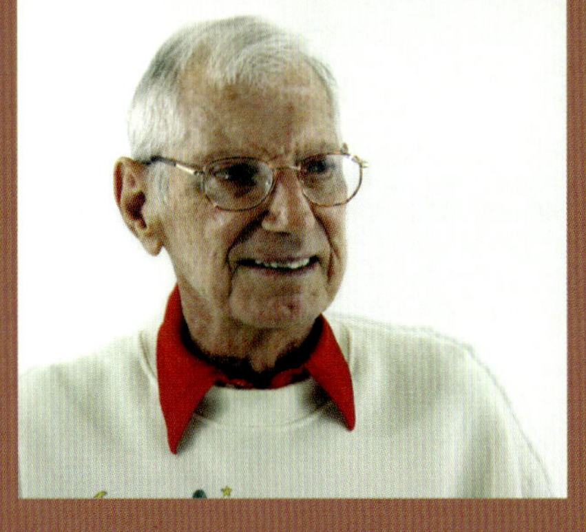

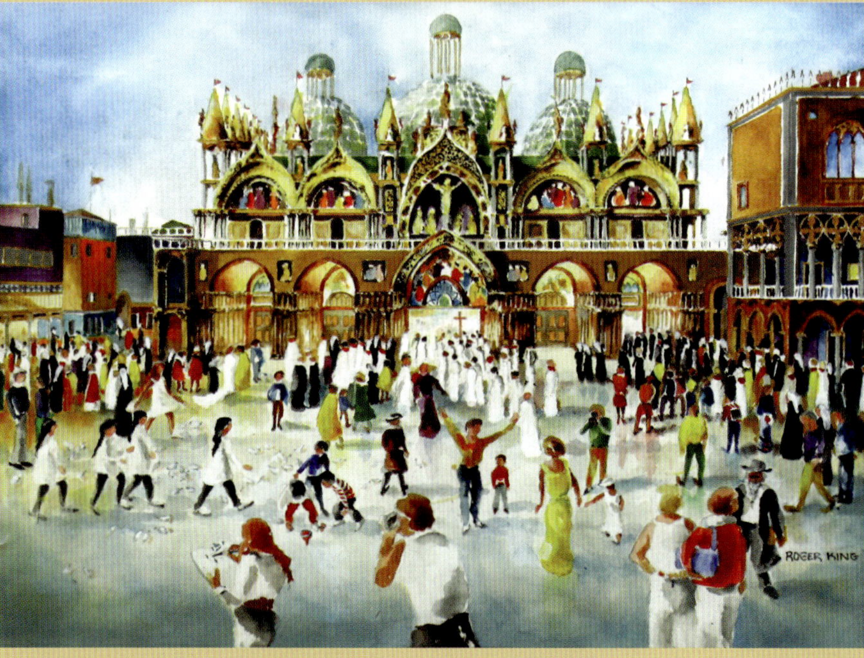

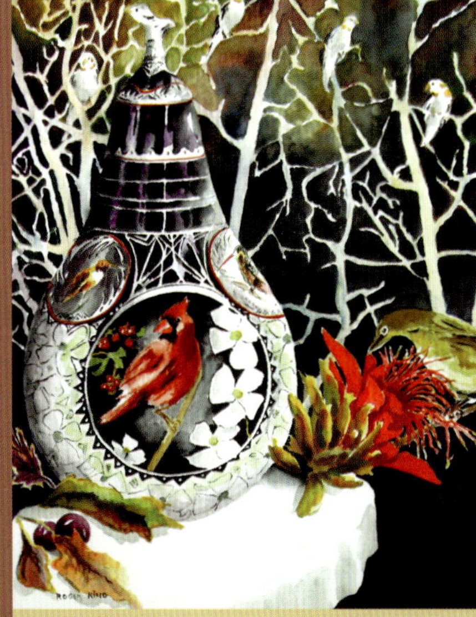

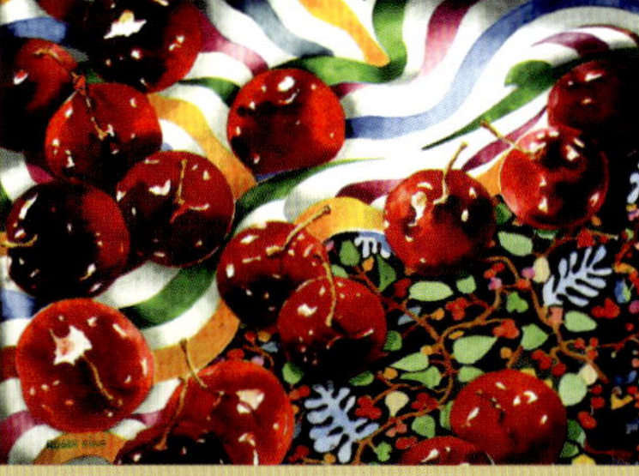

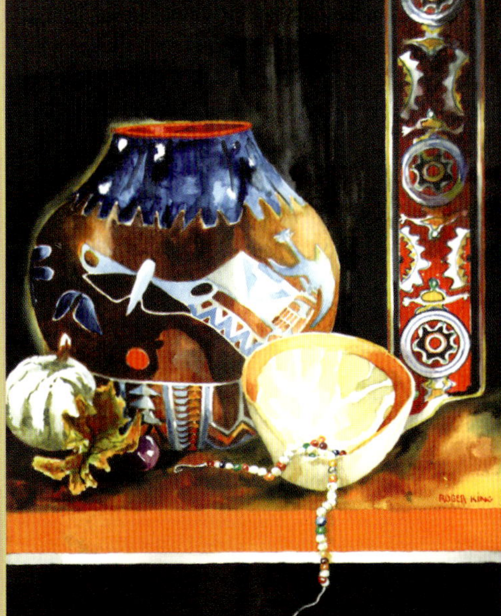

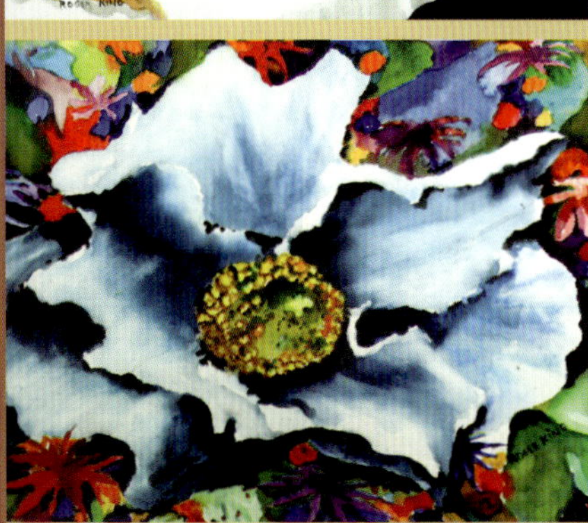

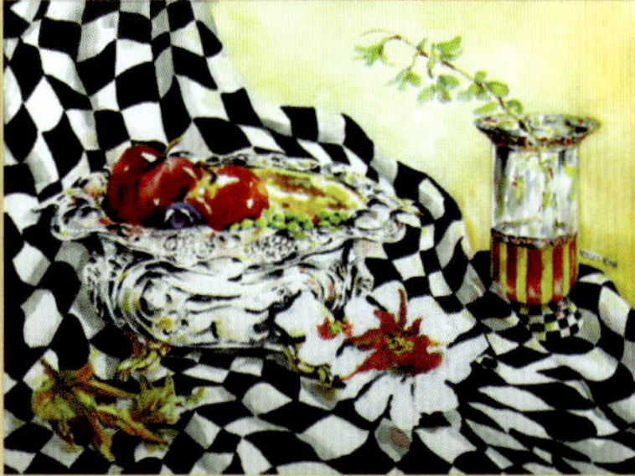

A lifelong Arkansas native and Conway resident since 1984, Mark Cothren became fascinated with woodturning after seeing a friend create a bowl in 2005. Since then, he has grown rapidly as a woodturning artist, and has pieces on display in the Arkansas State Capitol and at the Historic Arkansas Museum. His work is also in many private collections around the country, including a bowl purchased personally by woodworking legend Sam Maloof. Despite his early success, Mark still considers himself a student of the craft, and is continually trying to learn and expand his range. He is truly humbled by the unique beauty God creates in each piece of wood, and is honored to be allowed to reveal and share that beauty with others. **For more information on Mark's work, visit his website at: http://www.flyingcurls.com.**

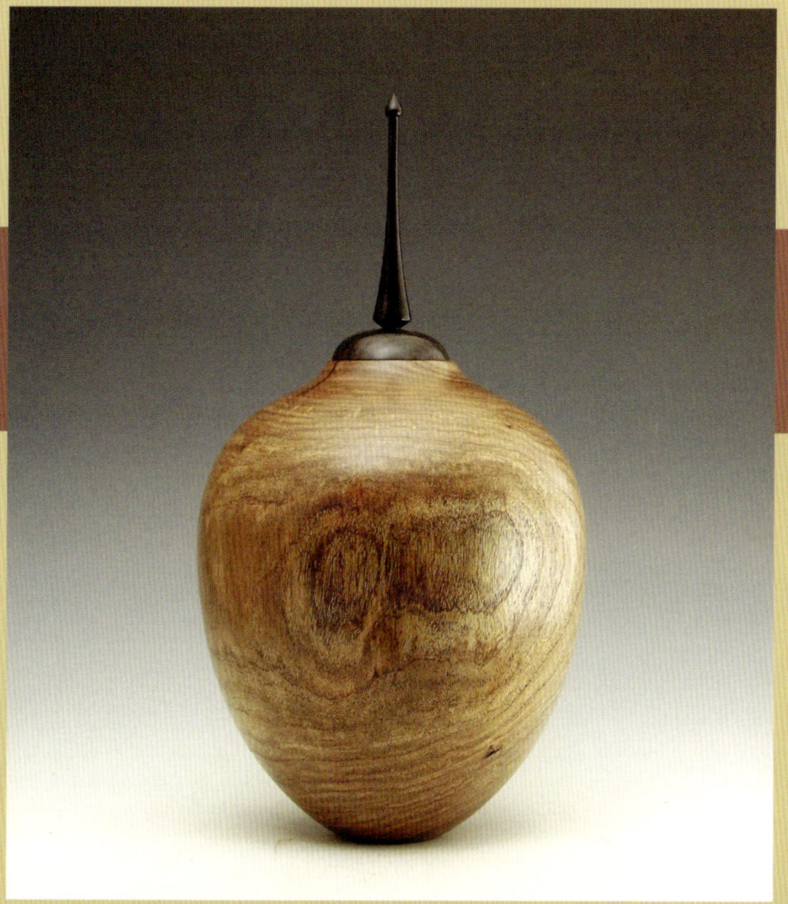

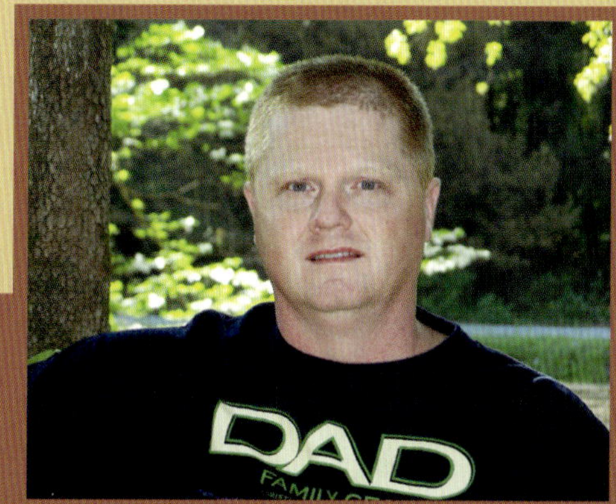

MARK COTHREN

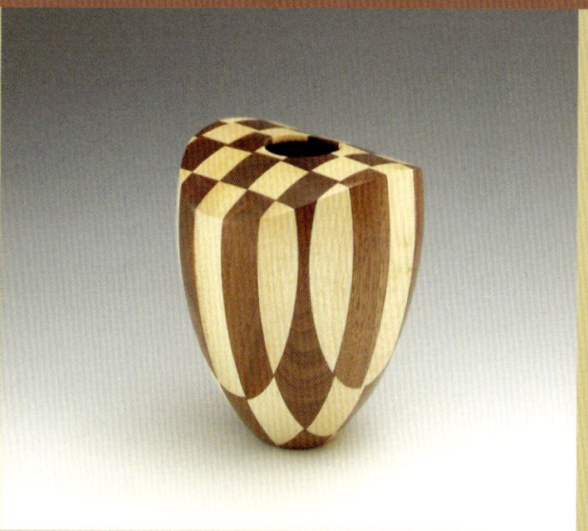

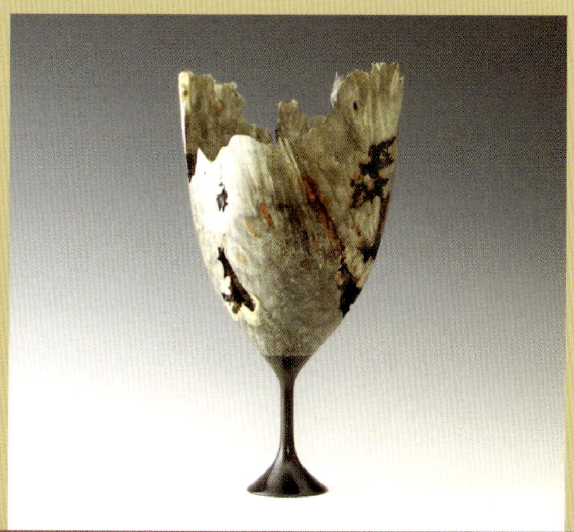

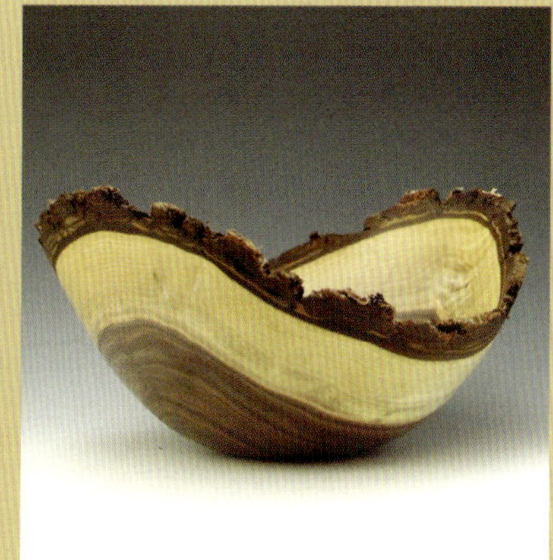

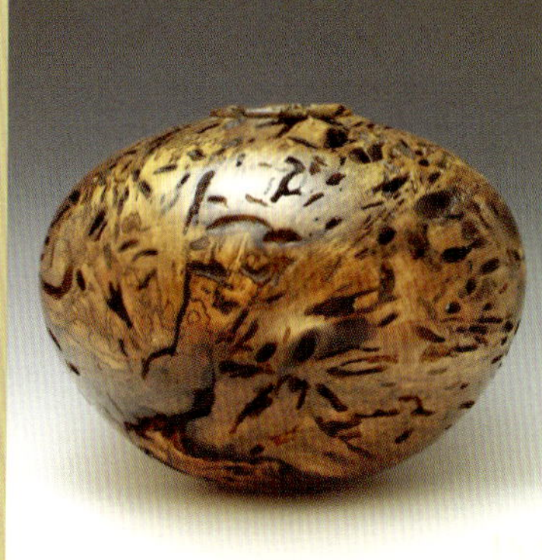

SARAH TOMLIN

Sarah Tomlin was born and raised in East Texas and recently moved to Northwest Arkansas with her husband. Being raised in a small town and having lived in the city, Sarah is able to capture the essence of both worlds in her art. She is completely self-taught and a bit of a newcomer to the photography world and has already garnered much praise. She has been showcased in websites, magazines, festivals and shows. Her point of interest is landscape and still life, but she has a knack for portraiture as well. Sarah embraces all types and genres of art and incorporates that into her artwork. For her, photography is not just a hobby, it is a passion. Sarah's favorite quote is:
"We look at the world and see what we have learned to believe is there. We have been conditioned to expect.... but, as photographers, we must learn to relax our beliefs." -Aaron Siskind"

You may contact Sarah through her website at http://Sarahtomlinphotography.com.

Sarahtomlinphotography.com

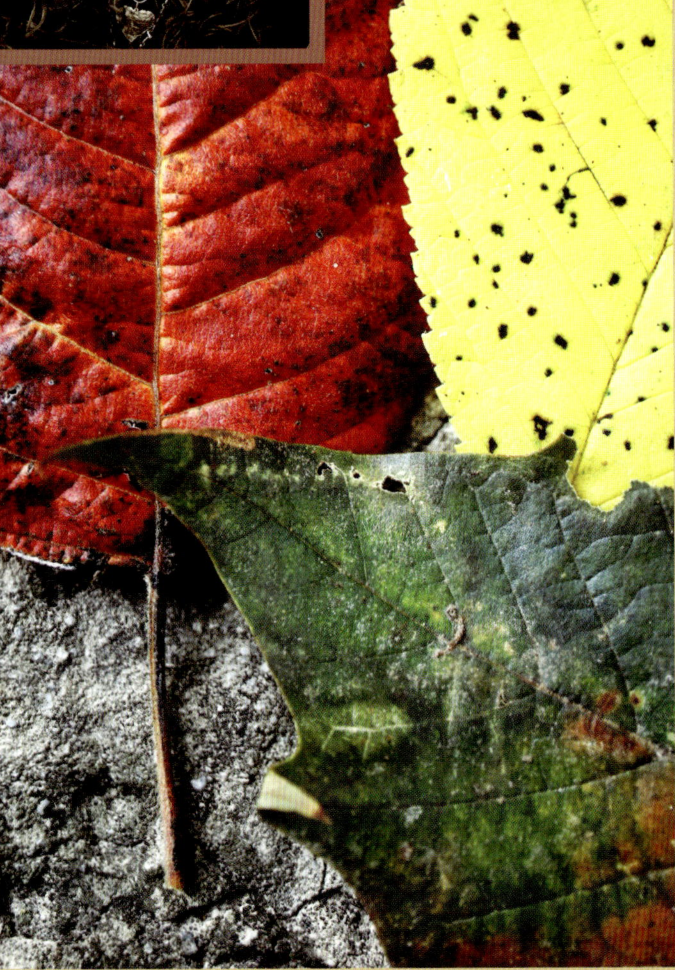

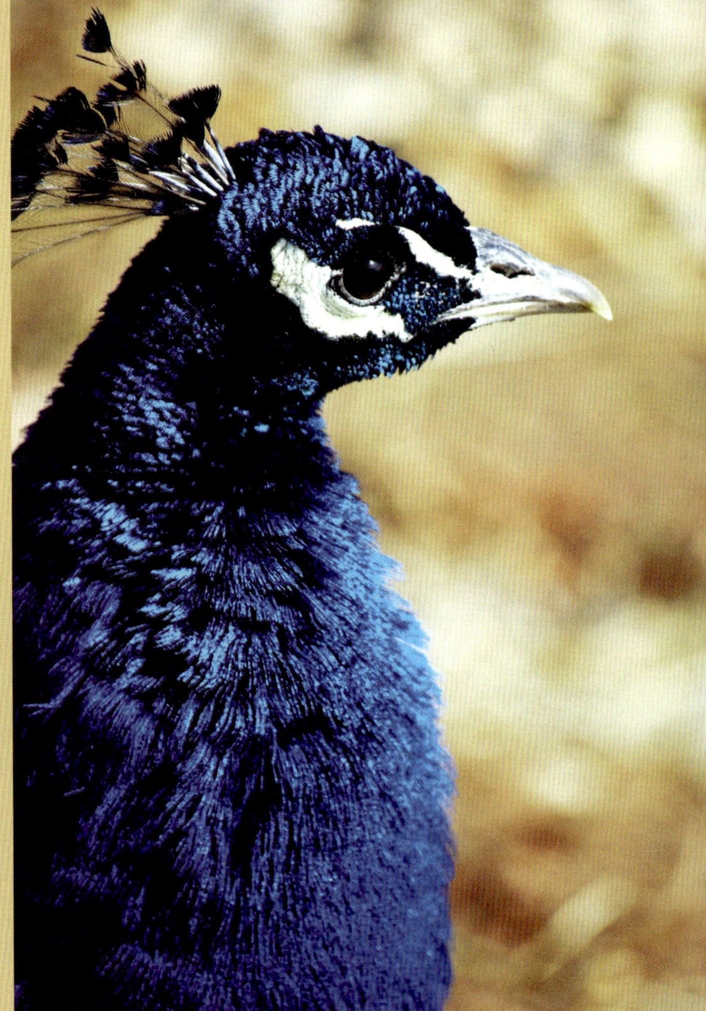

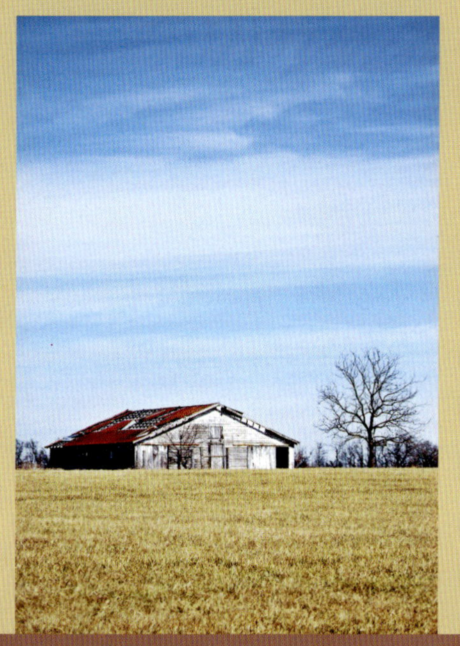

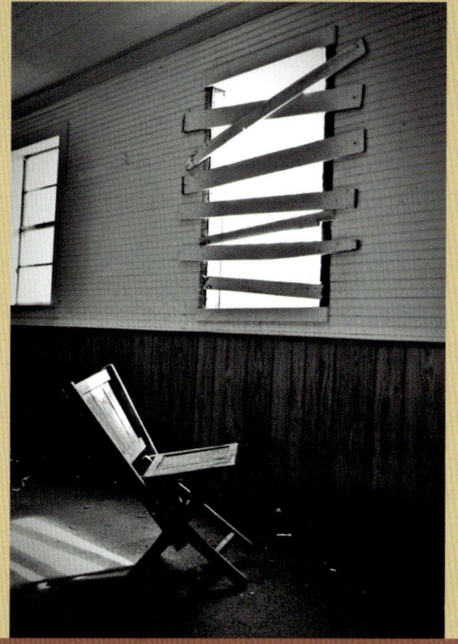

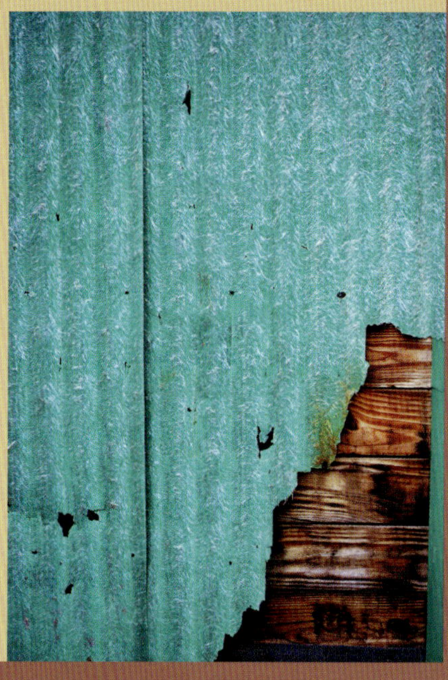

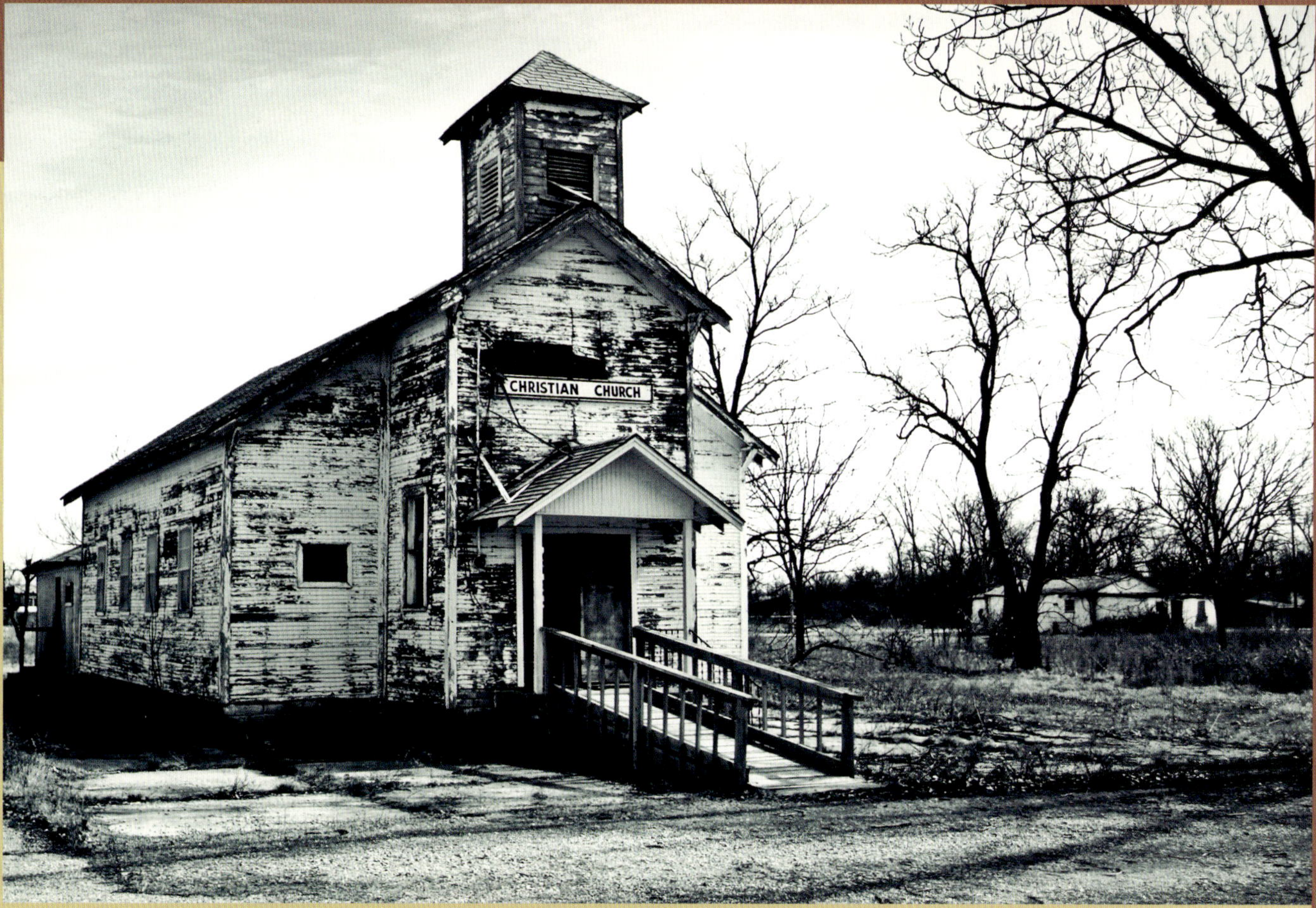

SARAH TOMLIN

CHRISTIAN CHURCH

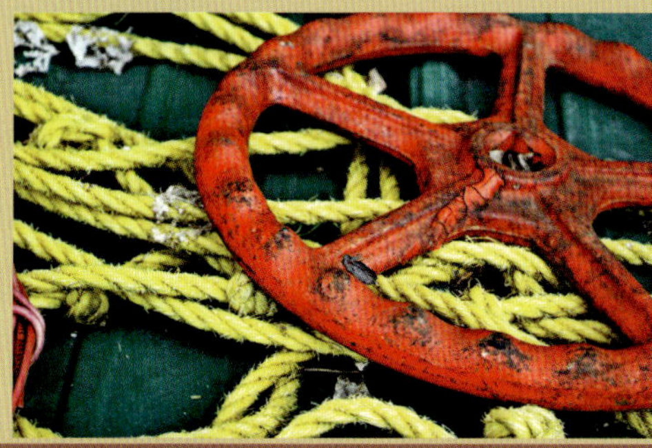

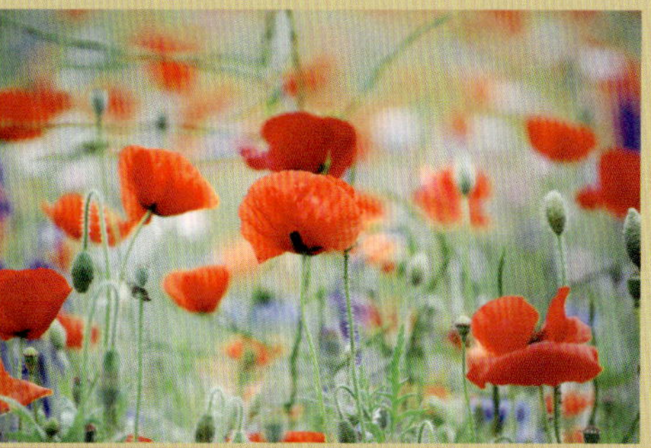

MICHAEL DON FESS

Michael Don Fess is not just a Master Gardener, he is also a Master at creating Garden Sculptures that will distinguish any garden. Born in Louisiana, Michael and his family relocated to Arkansas where he attended school, earning a degree in Engineering and Michael went on to earn a B.S. in Physics before marrying his high school sweetheart Martha Sue Wilson and raising their four children. **To learn more about Michael's work visit www.FessArt.info.**

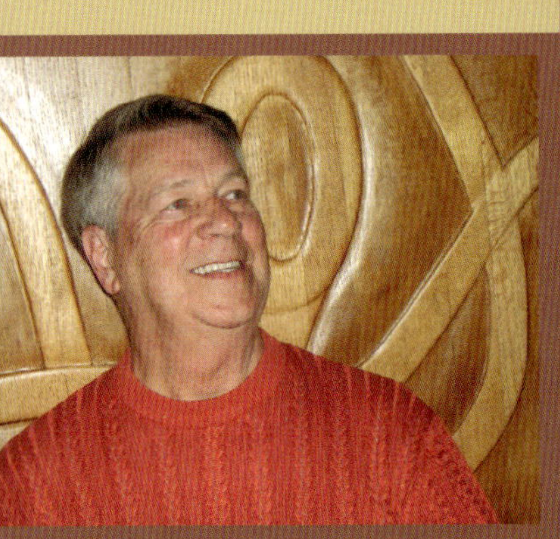

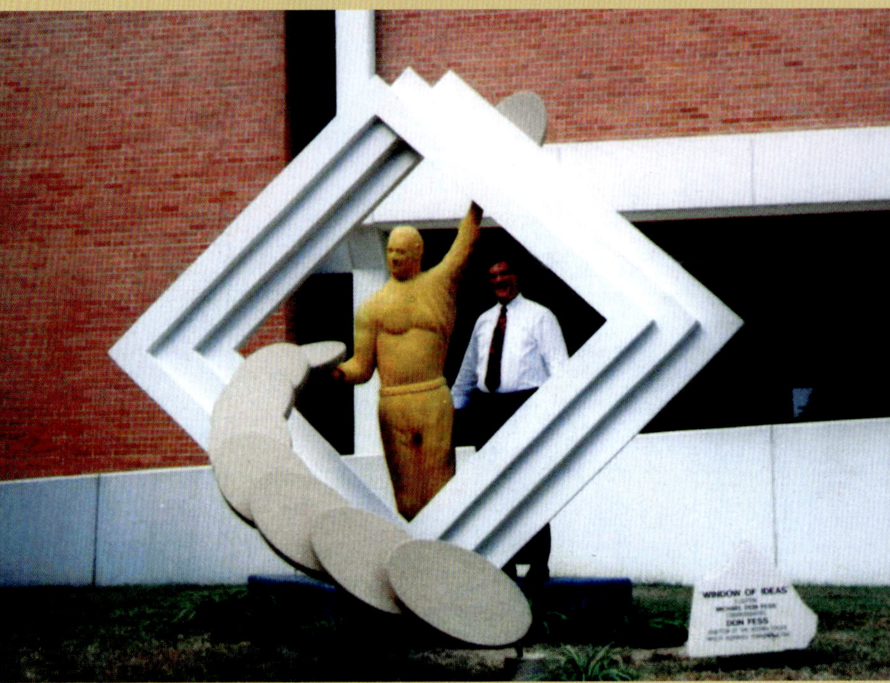

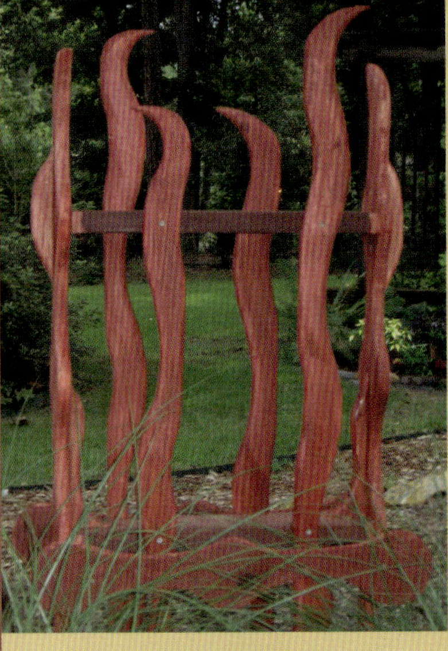

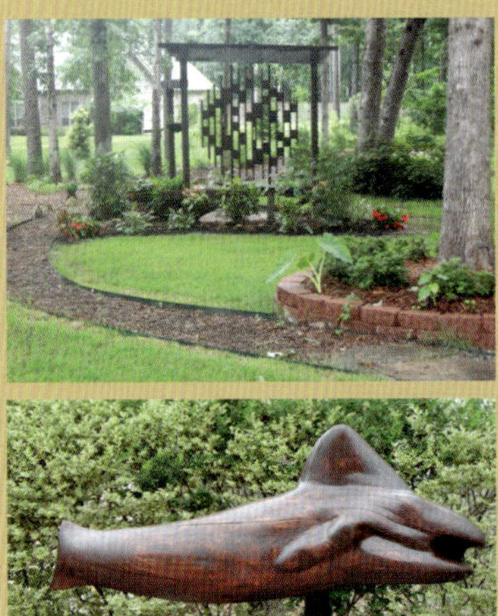

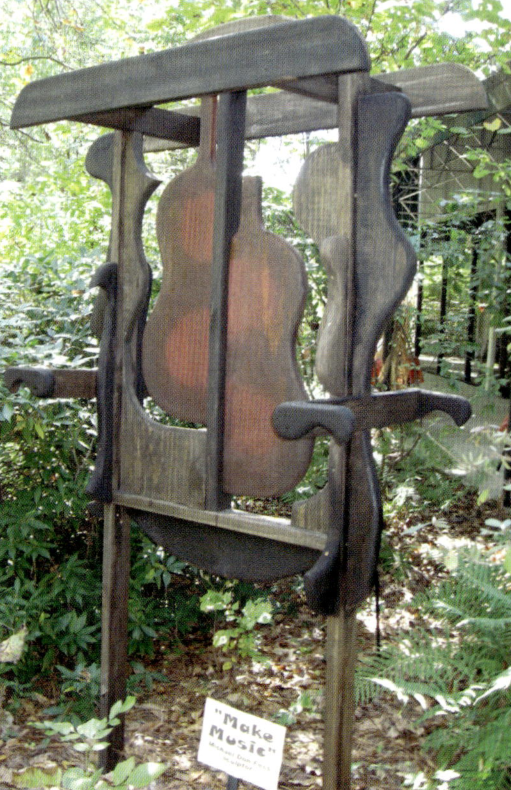

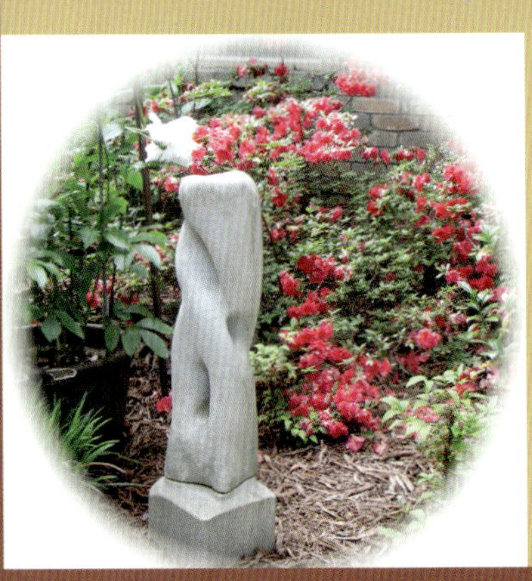

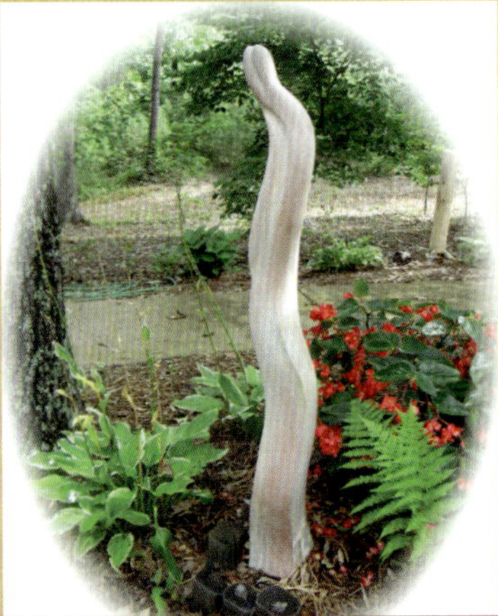

"Coup de Rouge" is French for "A Touch of Red." The touch of red refers not only to the color of the artist Janet Bujarski's hair but also refers to her trademark red seed bead at the end of her jewelry. When you see the red beads you can be assured of a quality product and original design work.

Coup de Rouge has grown from an artistic pursuit into a small business with sales from art shows, art galleries, studio visitors and the internet. Since becoming a full time designer, Janet's reputation has grown and she is well established in the Missouri Ozarks as an artisan of great talent. **You can learn more about Coup de Rouge and buy beautiful jewelry at http://coupderouge.com.**

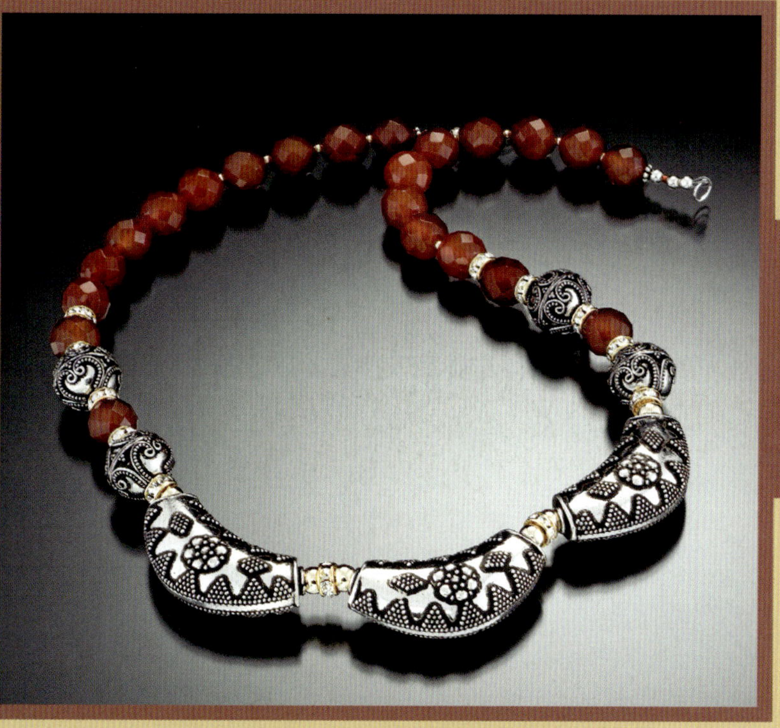

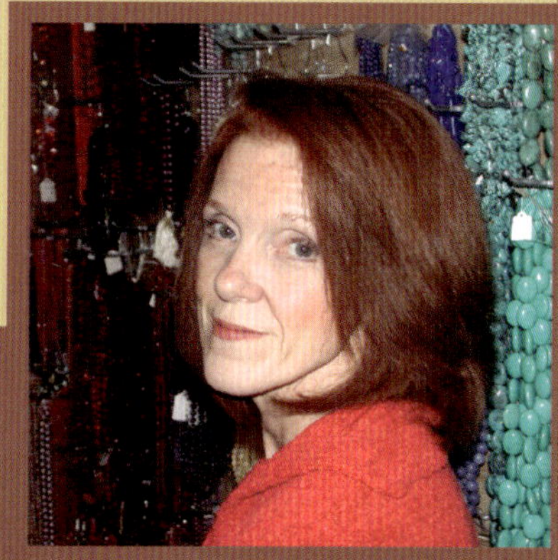

JANET BUJARSKI

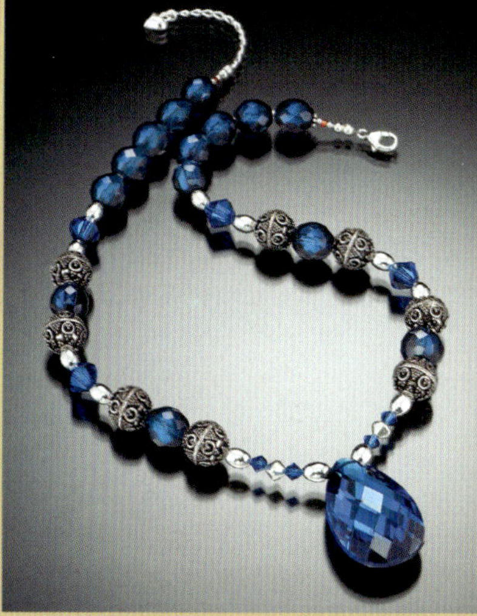

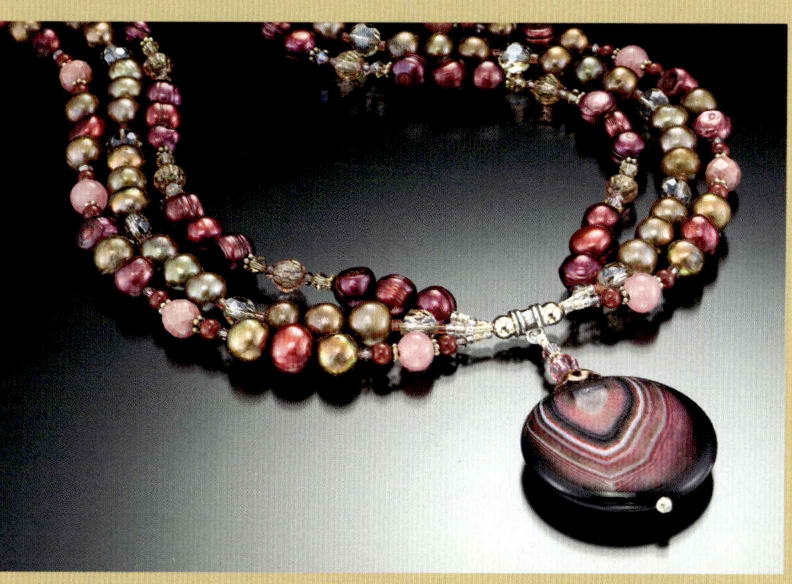

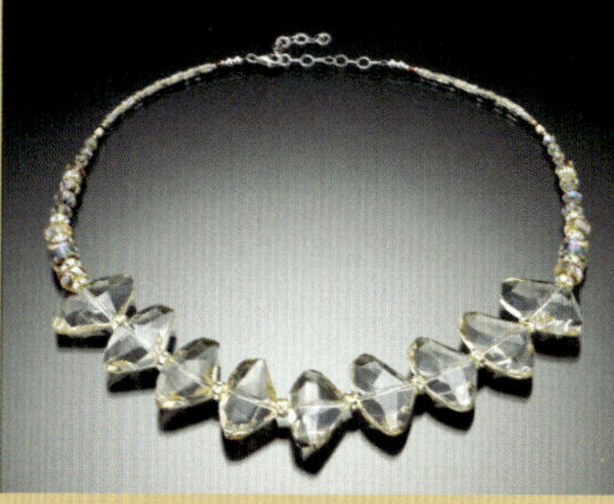

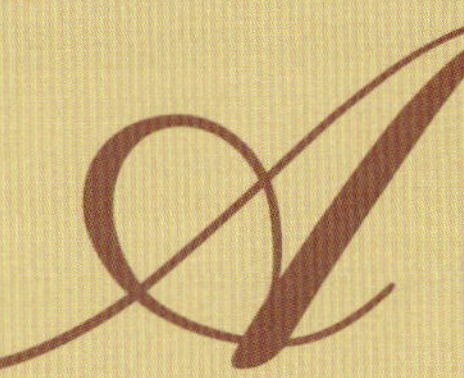

Although born in Denver, Colorado, Karen spent 48 years in Northern California before retiring and moving to Norfork, Arkansas with her husband Don in late 2007.

Karen embraced a love of drawing animals since childhood. She took high school and some college art courses, but is mostly a self taught artist. In fulfilling her mother's request for a horse portrait, Karen discovered an affinity for colored pencils. This led to Karen's first recognition for her artwork at the Area Art Club Art show in Mountain Home, awards from the Bull Shoals Art Club and Stone County Fair, and to her first commissioned pet portrait. Karen also works in pastels and watercolors. **For more information on Karen's work or to discuss a commissioned portrait of your favorite pet, e-mail: kajon@inreach.com.**

KAREN L. JONES

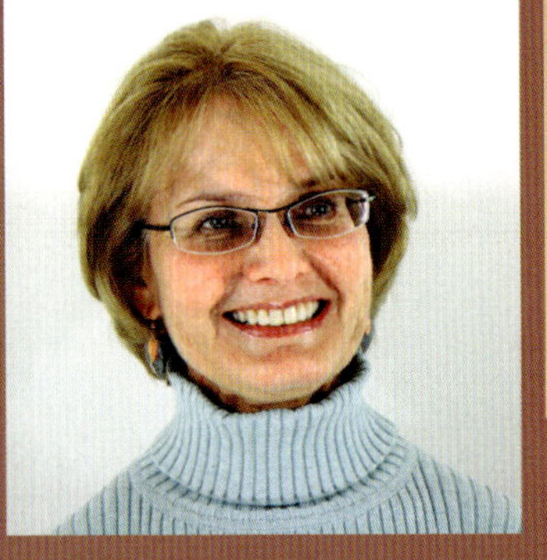

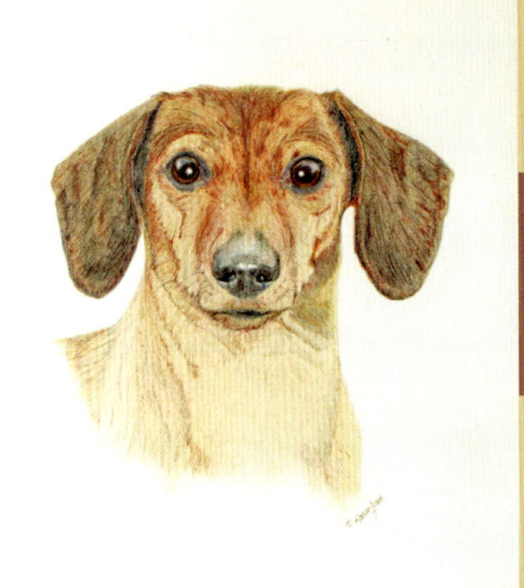

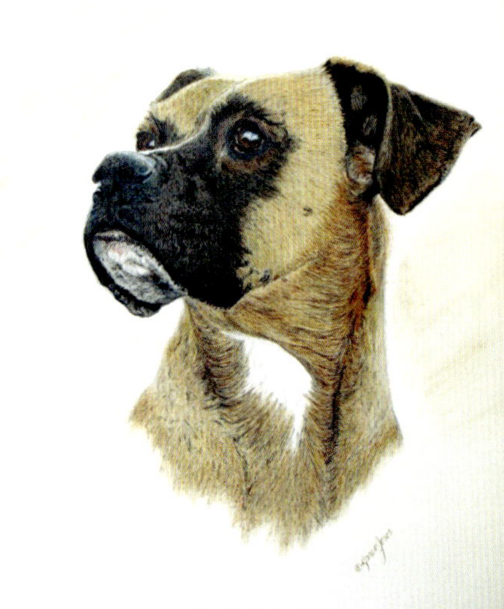

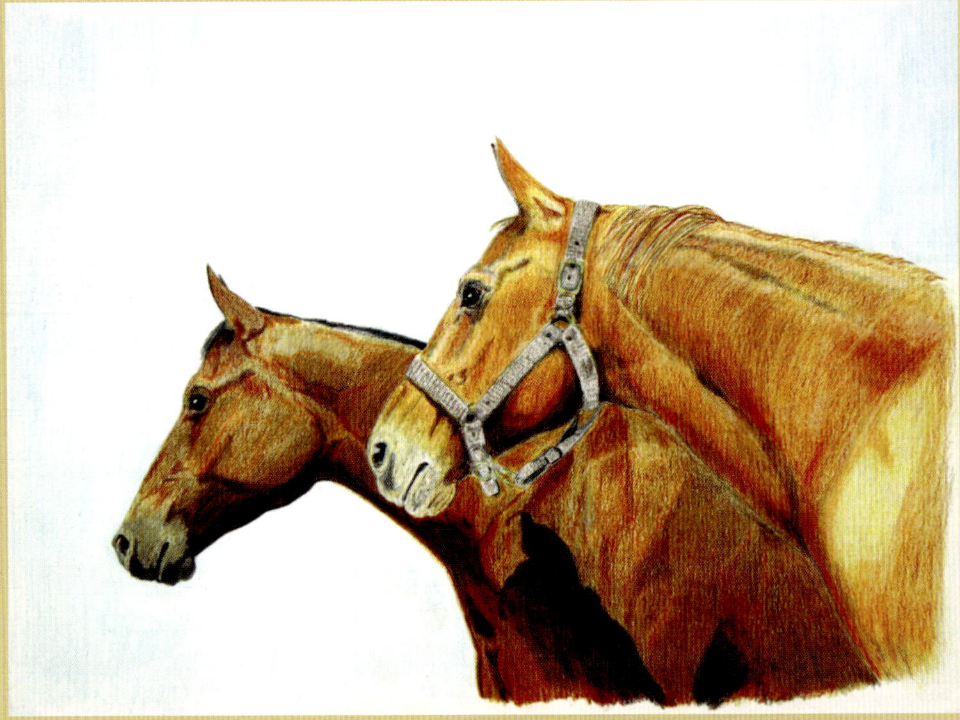

Jody Ratliff was born in Mt. Clemens, Michigan but moved to the Twin Lakes area of Northern Arkansas in 1967, where he grew up and lives today. His interest in art began at an early age but didn't become a passion until 1990 while living in Scottsdale, Arizona. Jody had the opportunity to work directly with many of the professional artists who resided in or displayed their works in local galleries. Since that time his work has been displayed in the Masterpiece Collection of Scottsdale, the Baxter County Library in Mountain Home, Arkansas and was recently featured along with other area artists in the Annual Art Show and Competition of West Plains, Missouri.

Although the majority of his work is done in acrylic, he also enjoys working with oils and pastels. Paintings are available framed or unframed. **For more information on Jody's work, you can contact him at 422 W. Old Main Street, Yellville, Arkansas 72687 or call 870-718-2487 or 870-449-2013.**

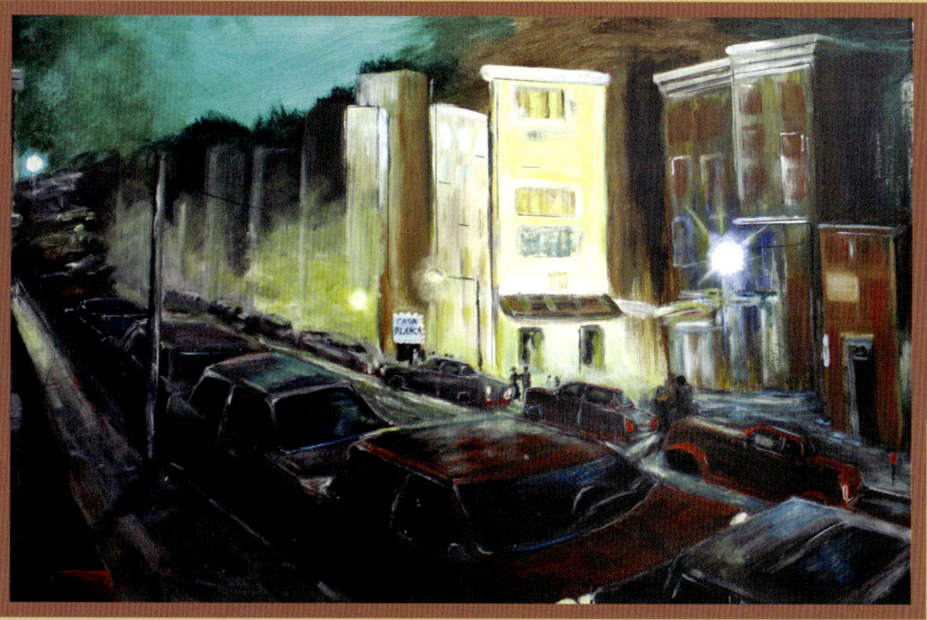

The Marquee | 24 X 36

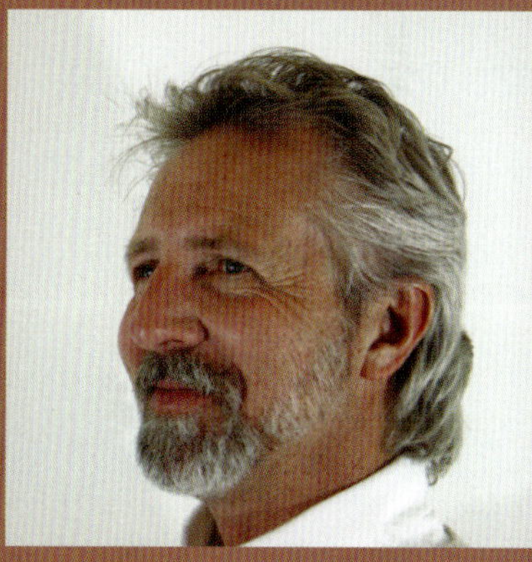

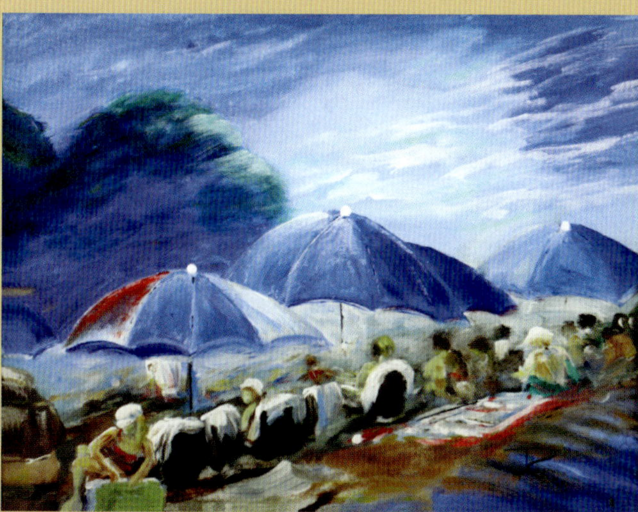

Blue Parasols | 16 X 20

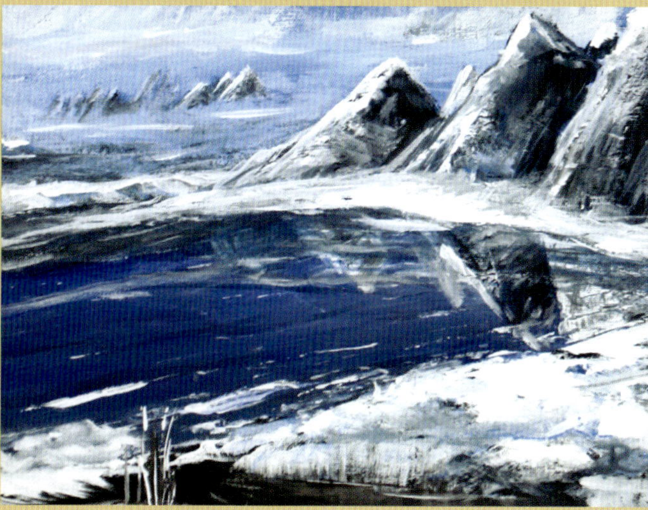

Artic Breeze | 12 X 14

PAT CHURCH

Brightly colored, whimsical, graphic describes the work of Pat Church, founder of LPOMA hand-painted dinnerware. Pat's self-taught art of ceramic painting, glazing and firing began 18 years ago in her home studio in Rogers, Arkansas, at 479-631-1596.

"My designs just come to me, and it can be something I dream, or a scrap of patterned fabric that catches my eye, or a trick of shadow and light in nature. They come to me as color combinations first, then I arrange them into patterns, adding dots or stripes, etc., for texture and a little whimsy."

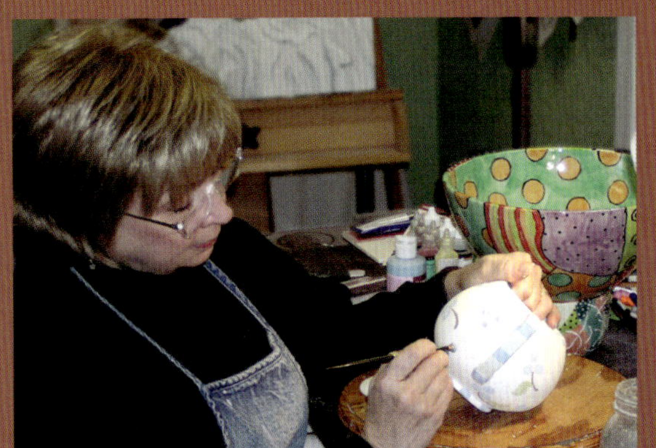

All of Pat's dinnerware is triple-glazed and kiln-fired to make them food and dishwasher safe. **Her work is sold at juried art shows and online at www.LPOMA.com. LPOMA stands for "Little Piece of MY Art."**

www.LPOMA.com.

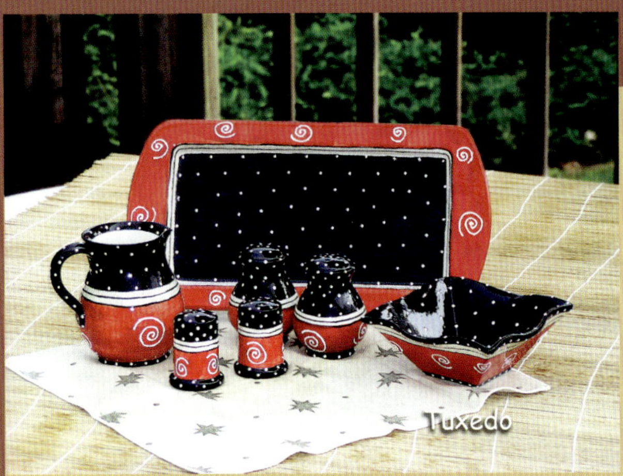

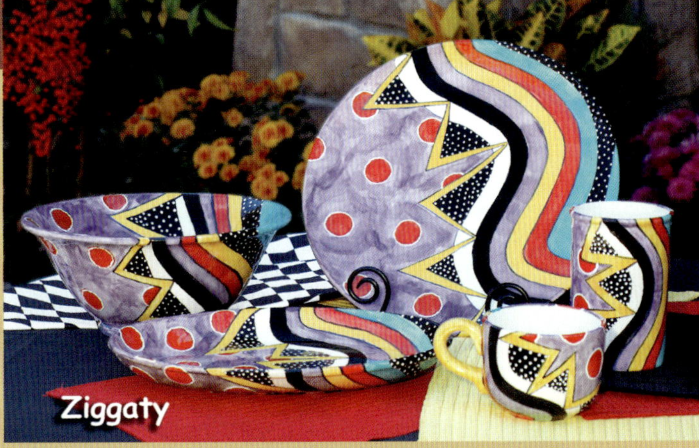

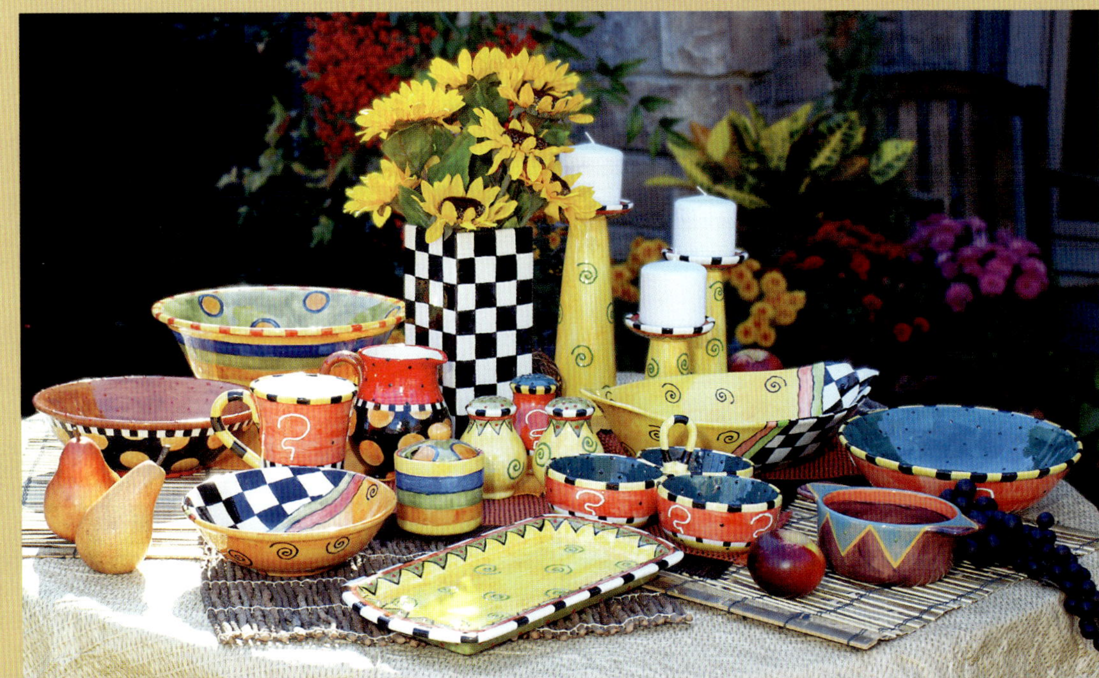

MARY JANE TURAN

Mary Jane Turan was born and raised in Yellville Arkansas and retired there after 30 years in the medical profession. She lives on the same family property she was raised on and treasures living in the Arkansas mountains near lakes and water. She raised two sons and did all the things families do.

Hobbies and interests include painting, sewing, quilts, photography, antiques (old houses, barns, and collectibles), music, opera, reading and would like to travel the world with lifelong classmates who are all still close friends.

In her retirement, Mary Jane has had the time to finally follow a lifelong ambition to play the piano. Self taught, MJ now enjoys playing every day, proving that it is never too late to follow your dreams!

Art instruction began in pastels and oils after assurance and encouragement from the instructor, family and art friends. My mentor, Henry Ratliff, shared his knowledge and vast art library further inspiring me. After her family, painting became the most enjoyable activity in her life and remains so. She has been a member of the Palette Art League for 20 + years and is passionate about the "Gallery". **For more information on Mary Jane's work, visit: http://paletteartleague.org/MJTuran.html**

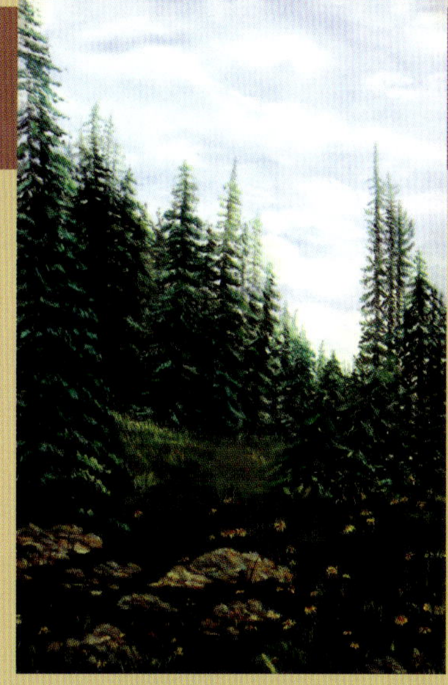

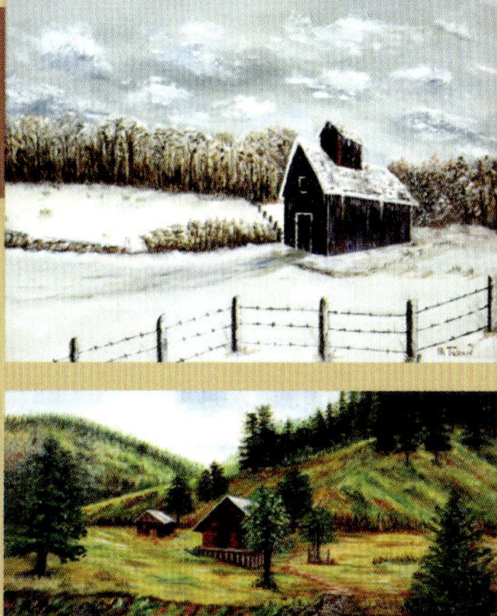

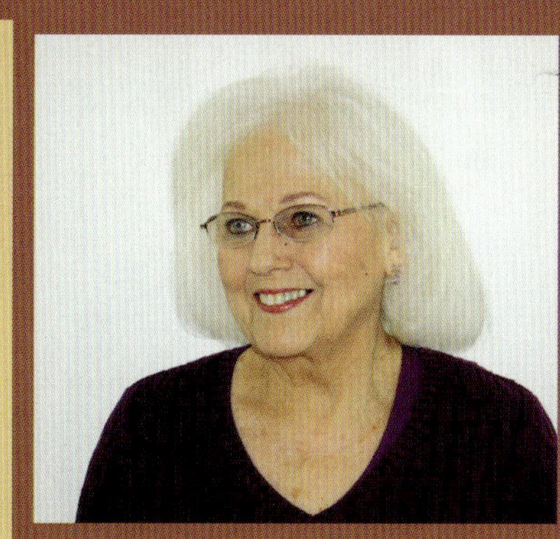

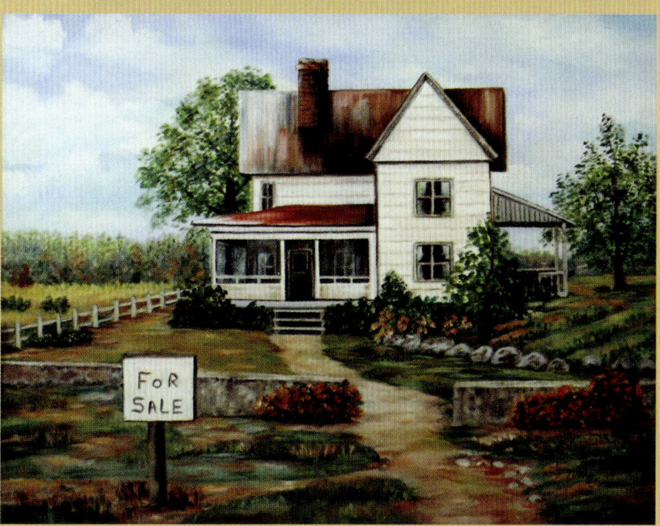

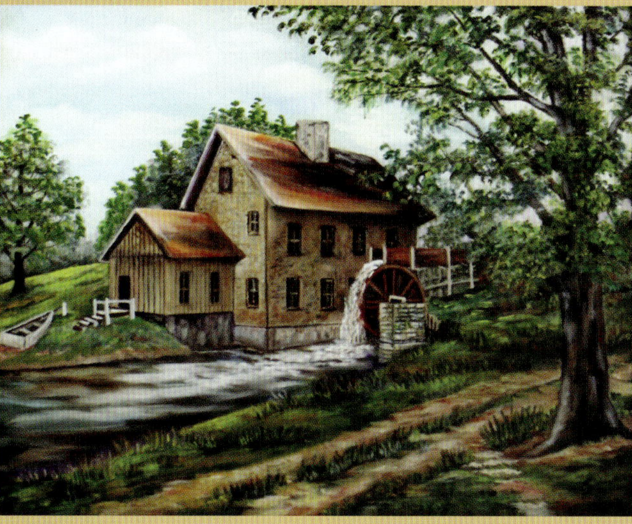

RICHARD NEUBAUER

Richard Neubauer is a portrait artist who loves the natural beauty of the Ozarks and the wonderful fishing there.

Previously, he made one-of-a-kind stain glass doors for churches and custom homes in his studio in Las Vegas, Nevada. Richard worked in "Dalle De Verre" glass. A unique one-inch thick glass. He has been a featured artist and blue ribbon winner with his beautiful doors.

Richard studied portrait painting and figure painting in Sedona Arizona for two years. His goal is to capture the living essence of his subject. "When I am done, I want the viewer to say, WOW! In that perfect moment, I know I have succeeded." **To see more of Richard's work or to contact him for commission portrait work from photographs, he can be reached by visiting his website at http://paletteartleague.org/RichardNeubauer.html.**

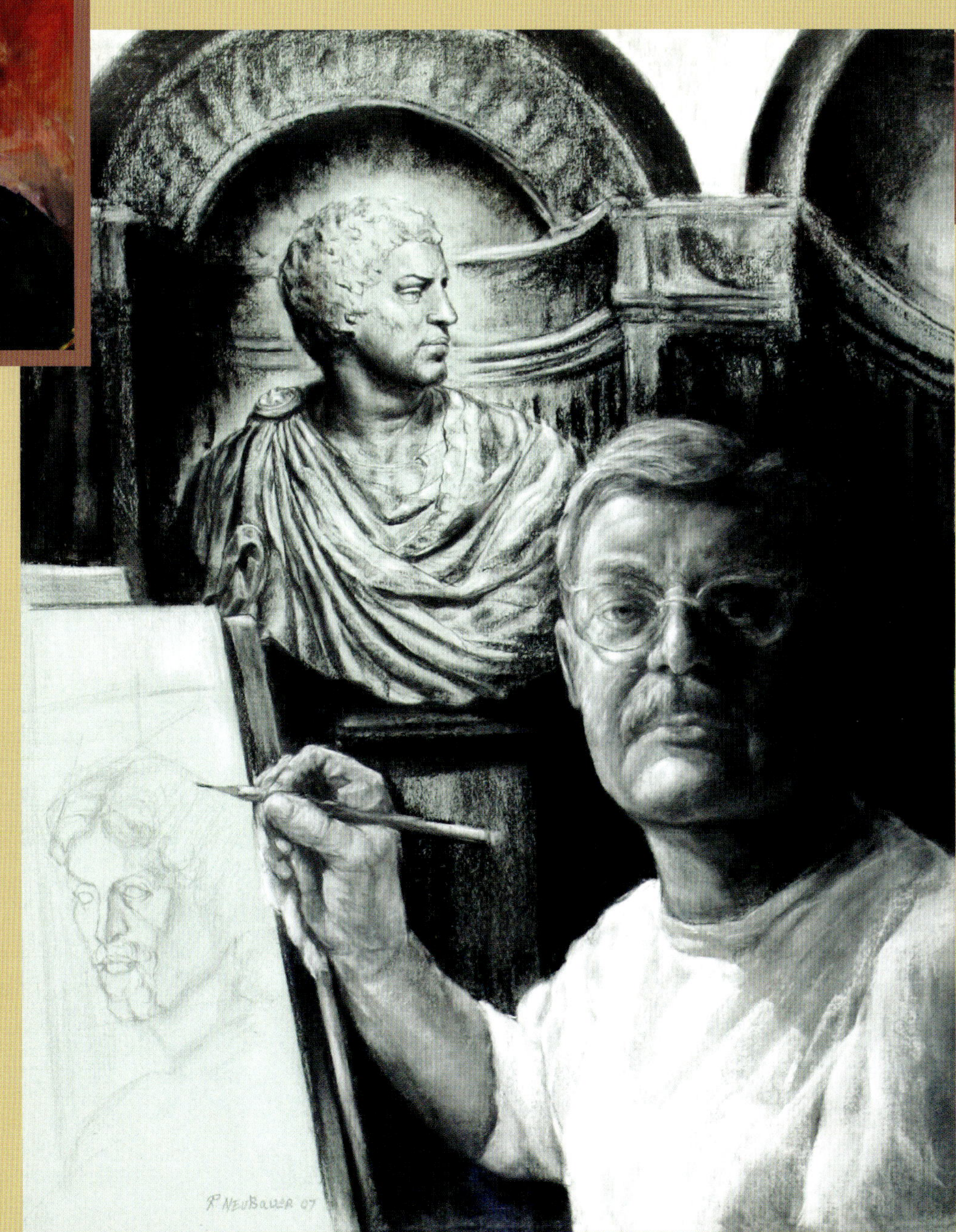

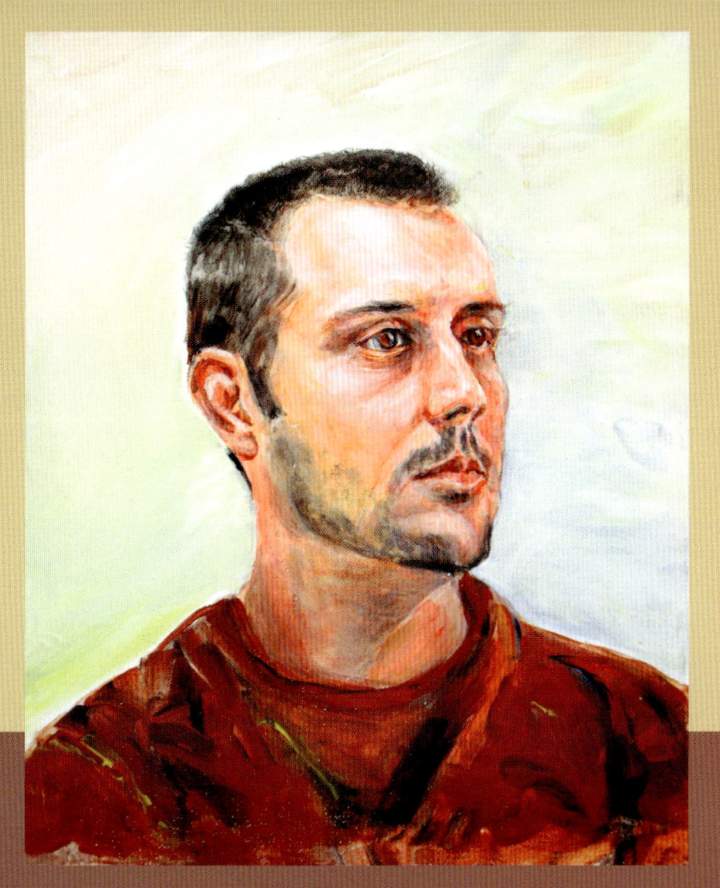

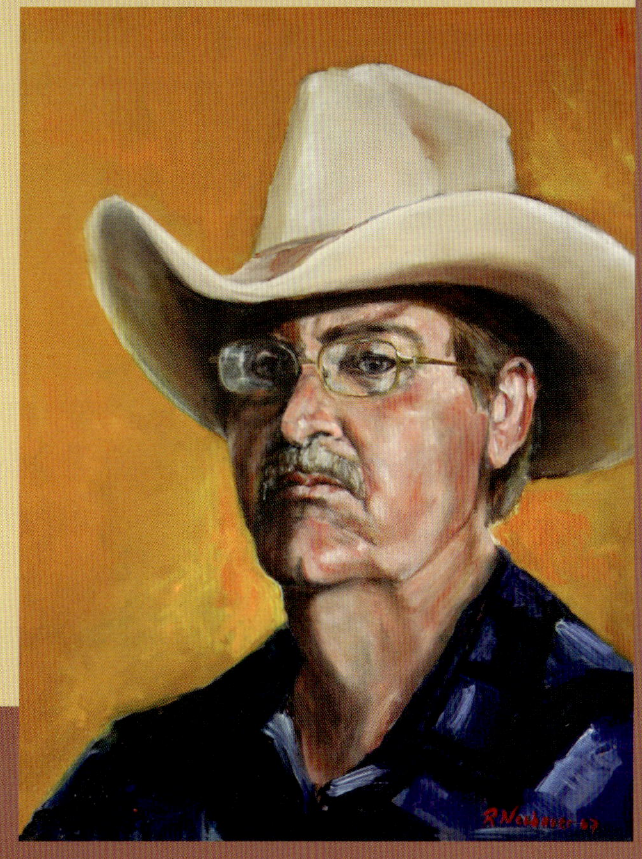

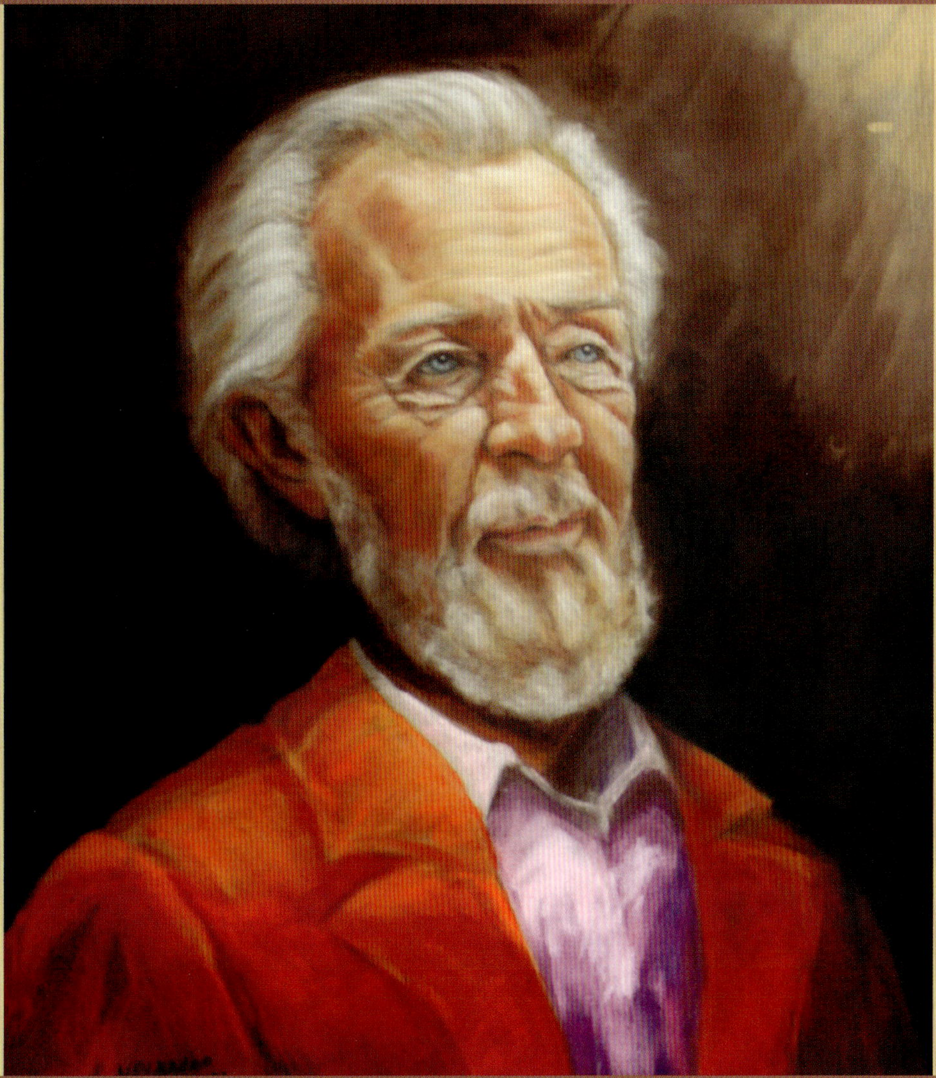

One of Susan McSherry's entrepreneurial projects led her to her current location in the Erbie neighborhood of the Buffalo River in NW Arkansas. Here she "transmogrifies" plain old cast off items into art and just plain old fun stuff. This isn't a new activity, but it has taken on a more organized tone. This organized sortie into the art world has yielded some notable results.

Acceptance into juried art shows, winning awards in juried art shows, teaching opportunities at art galleries, and publication of the Ozark Vernacular Bird House #1 in the Arkansas Governor's Mansion Day Planner 2009, Pink Foo Foo Clock in Arkansas at Home, June 2009, and Flower Hat Lady in the 2010 Mosaic Yearbook.

For further information: e-mail Susan through her web site: info@art-and-artifacts.com.

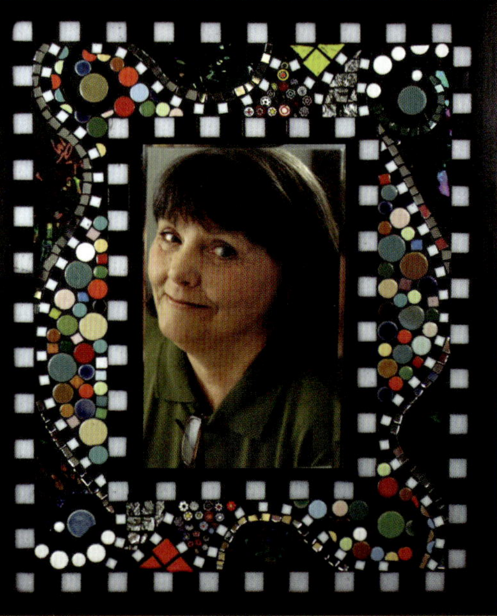

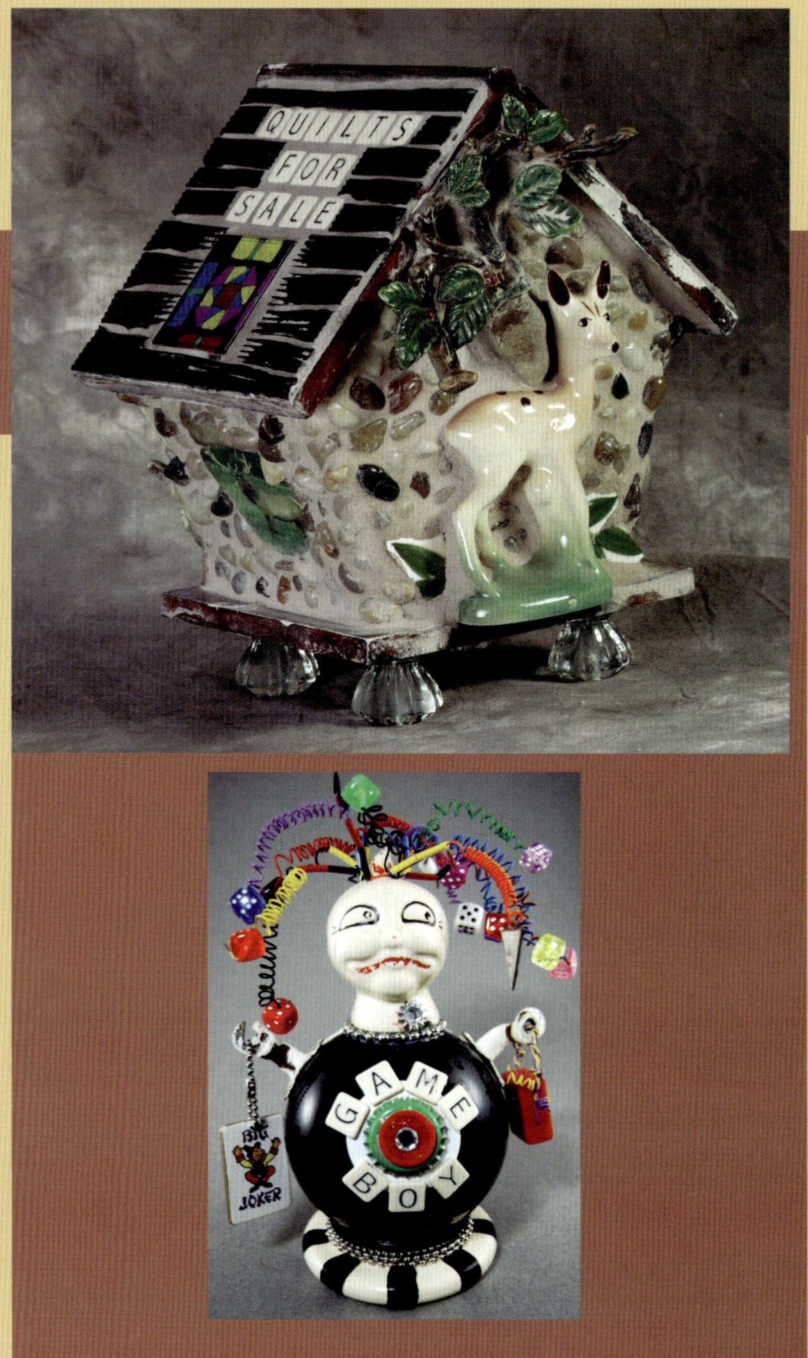

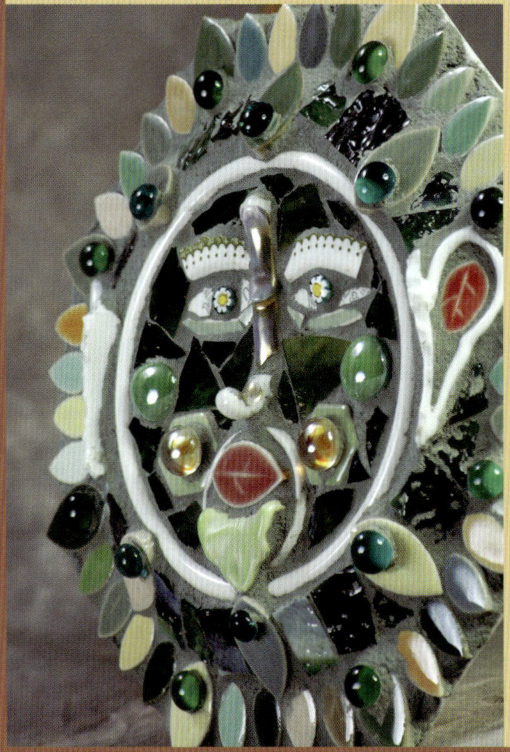

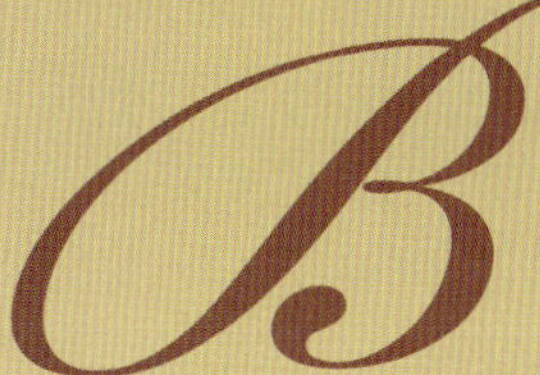

ill Wright has been capturing peace and harmony on film for many years. "My favorite time of the day is early morning. My favorite place to be is in the woods or along a stream. A place that is quiet and tranquil is where I create.

My goal is to bring you there, through my images. I want to capture on film the peace and tranquility I experienced while taking the image so you can go there every time you see the image on your wall. Not everyone can experience these wondrous places in person but my desire is to share them with you through my work."

For more information on Bill Wright's work, visit: http://mariahphoto.com/ or http://eurekaspringsartists.com/artistdetail.php?id=222 or e-mail Bill at billmariah@aol.com. You can also visit Bill at: http://paletteartleague.org/BillWright.html.

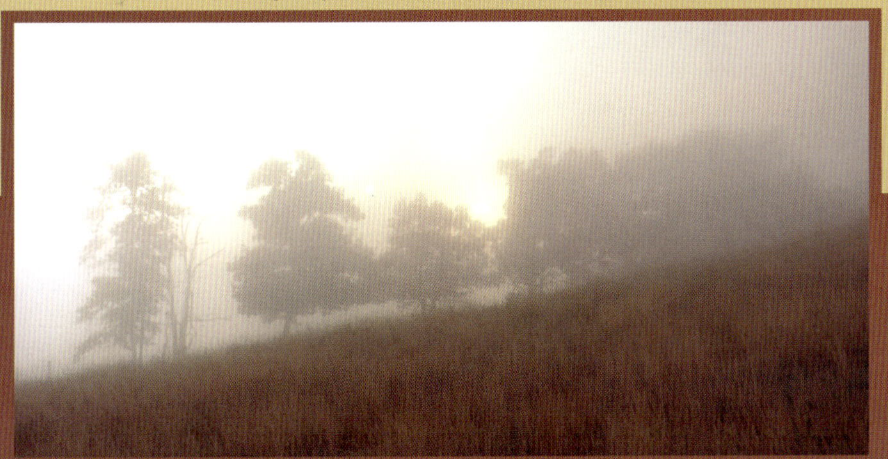

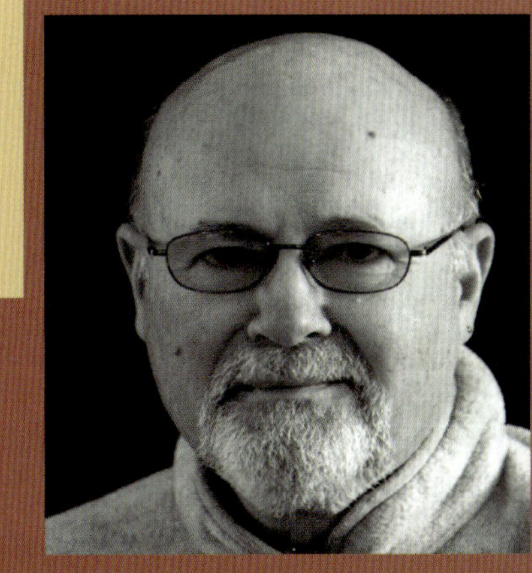

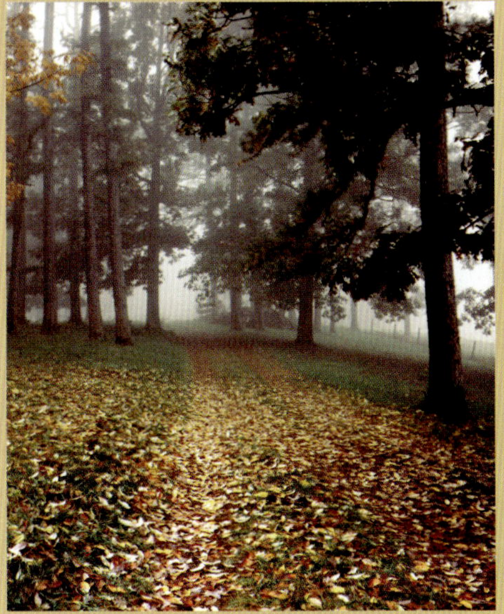

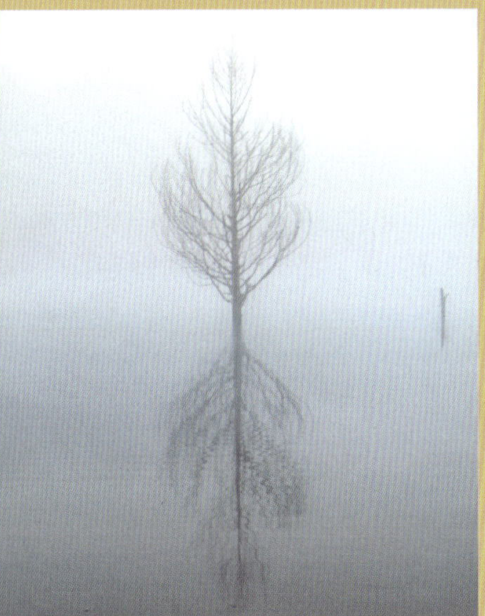

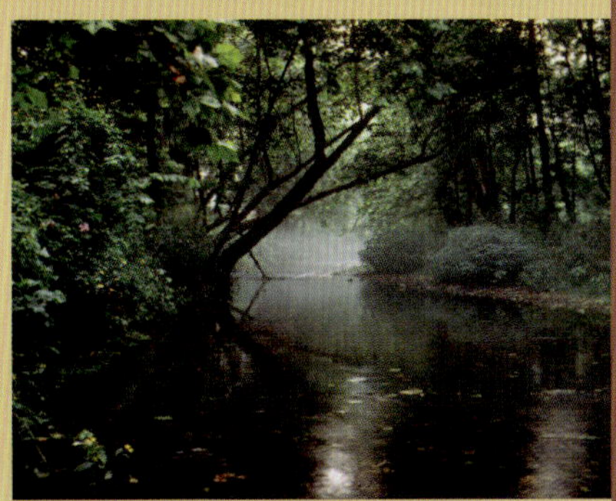

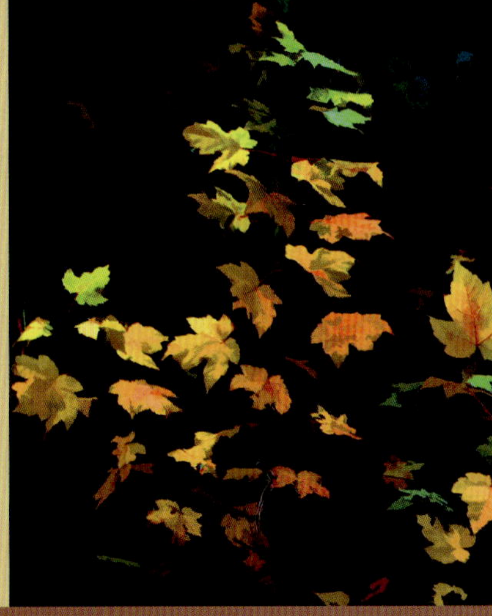

"I want to slow down and become a part of the flow of the surroundings. I want to see these surroundings thru the lens of my camera. I want to study this scene until it becomes a picture in my mind. I want to study it until it is a shock if anything moves in this picture. When this happens it is time to expose the film." Bill Wright.

VAL WRIGHT

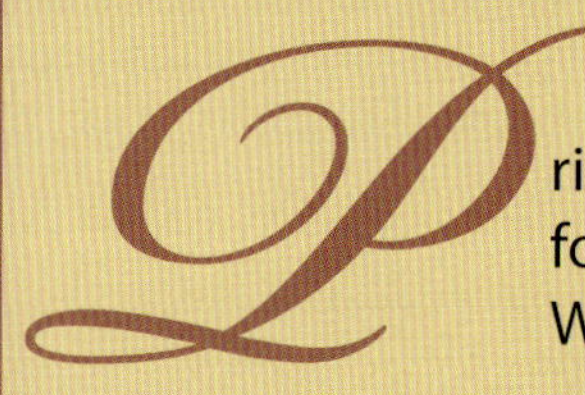

Primarily a plein air painter, Wright is captivated by the movement and repetition found in nature. To best capture the transient atmosphere of the natural world, Wright most often paints on location or from sketches she makes while outside.

Movement is the theme of her current work-movement of figures, trees, water, and even patterns of birds and fish in the water. Transparent watercolors are most effective at implying there is an underlying force controlling the painting, whether it is the dark shadows of a lily pond or a hot blast from the sun.

Wright is a member of Watercolor USA Honor Society and a signature member of the Florida Water-color Society, Mid-Southern Watercolorists, Georgia Water Color Society and the Texas Watercolor Society. She is also a juried member of the Southern Watercolor Society and the Southwest Watercolor Society.

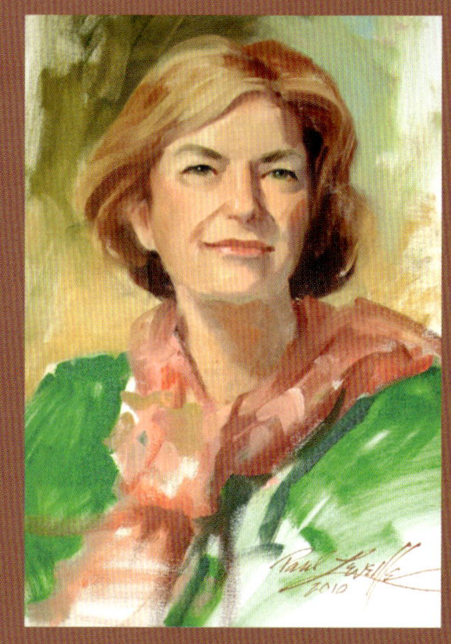

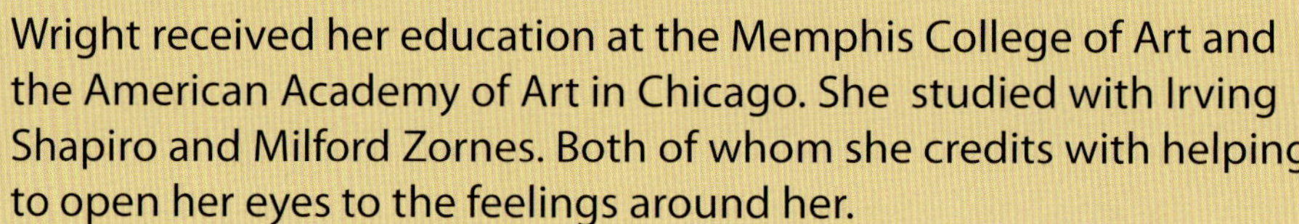

Wright received her education at the Memphis College of Art and the American Academy of Art in Chicago. She studied with Irving Shapiro and Milford Zornes. Both of whom she credits with helping to open her eyes to the feelings around her.

"My work is included in many corporate and private collections. I participate in national juried competitive shows from Maine to California and have won awards over the years." **For more information on Val's work, visit http://paletteartleague.org/ValWright.html.**

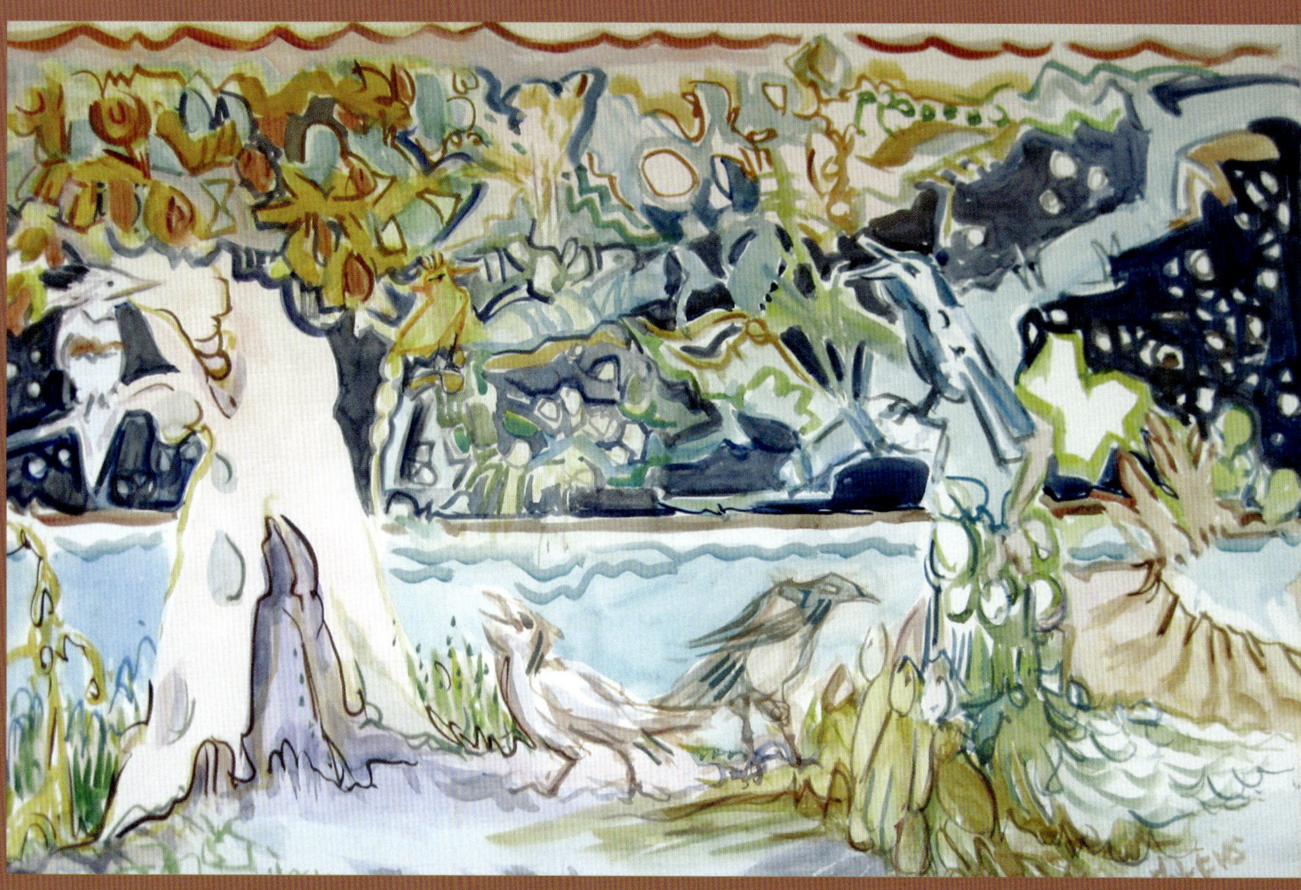

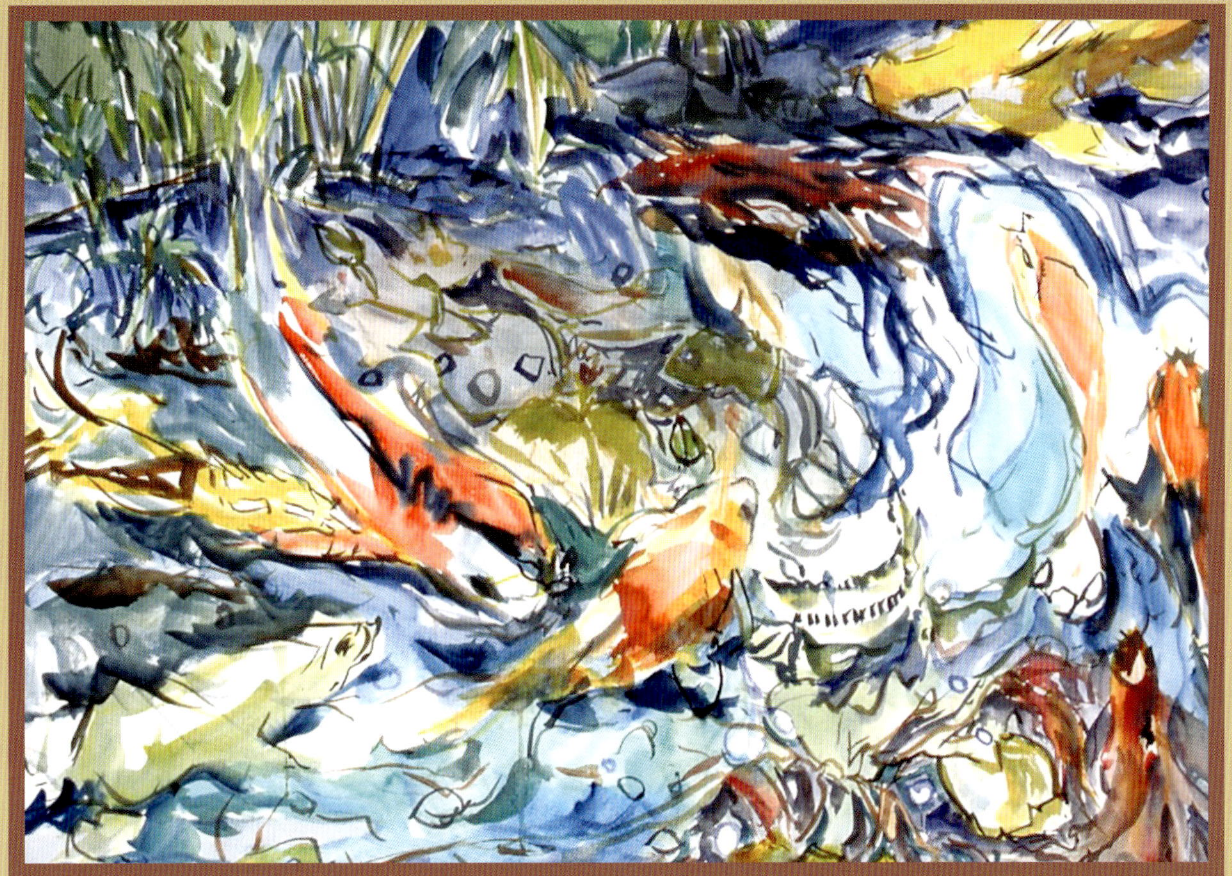

VAL WRIGHT

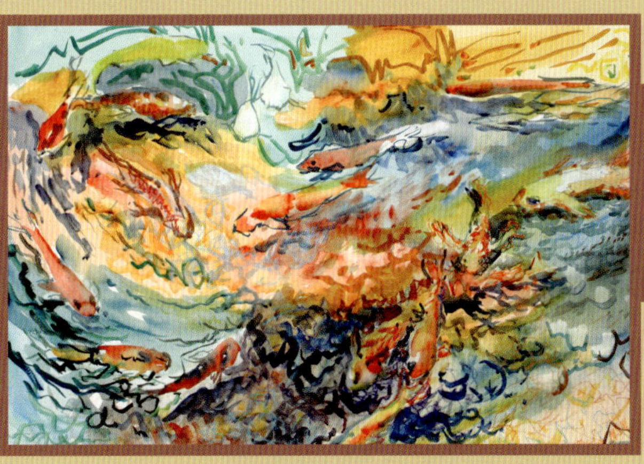

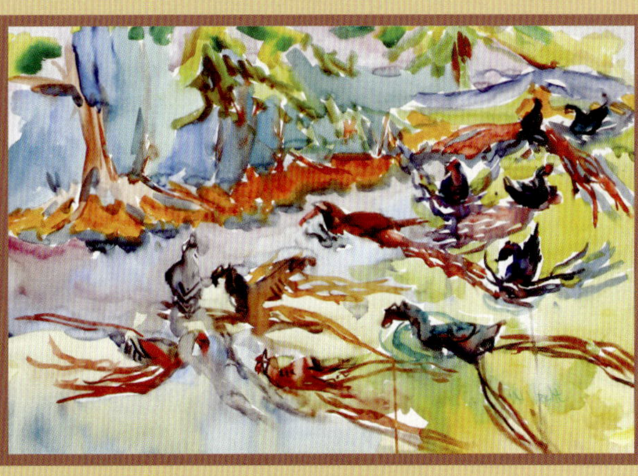

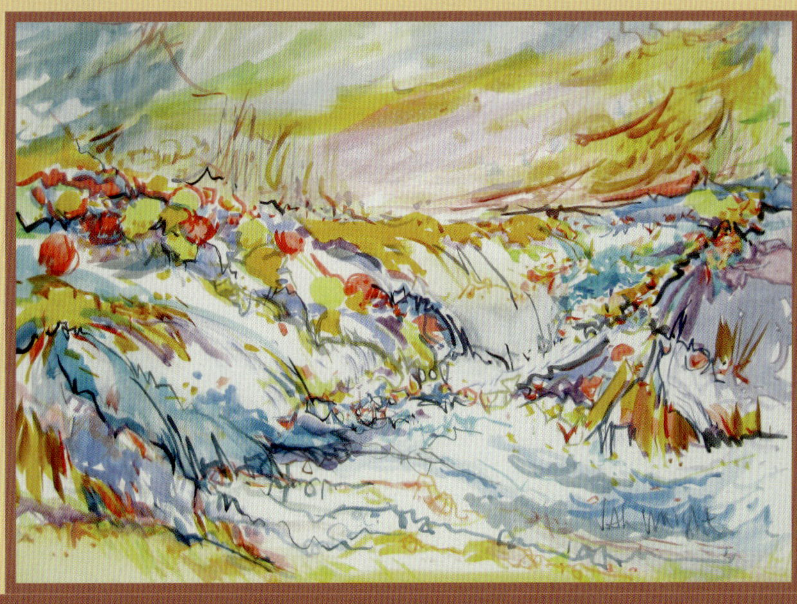

EDITH THORNBURG

The first 57 years of my life were spent in Western Illinois. My husband and I moved to Arkansas in 1998 when we retired. It was then that I realized a lifelong dream of taking art lessons. I took lessons for approximately 7 years; the rest was self-taught. I work in pastels, oils and colored pencil. My favorite subjects are portraits, pet portraits and still life. I have won numerous awards at local art shows and was featured in the Harrison Arkansas newspaper.

I can be reached at edierachel@yahoo.com or at my website at: http://paletteartleague.org/EdithThornburg.html.

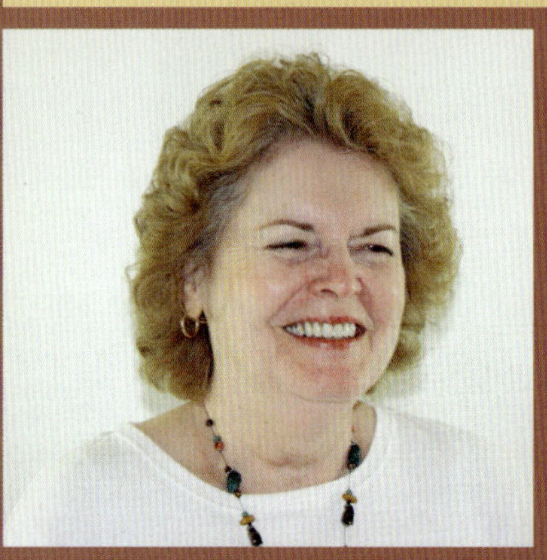

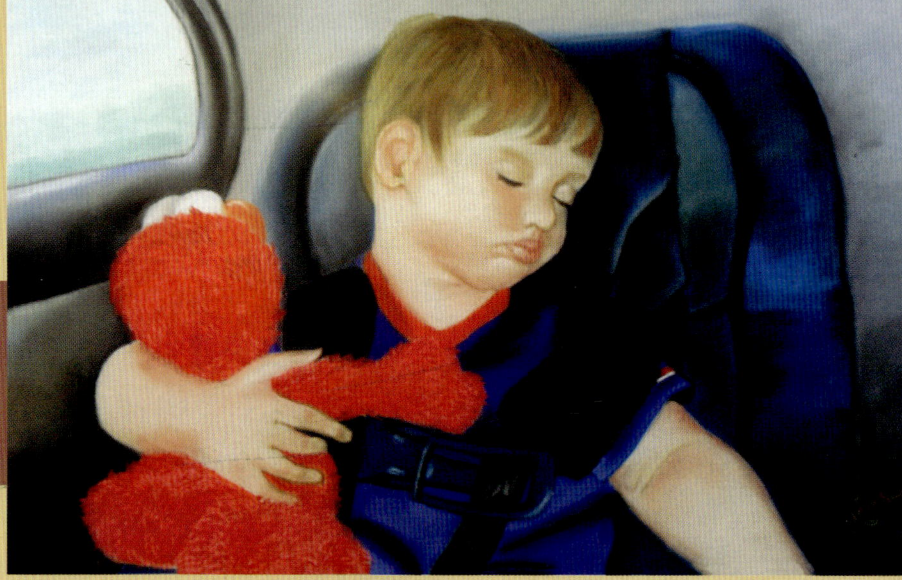

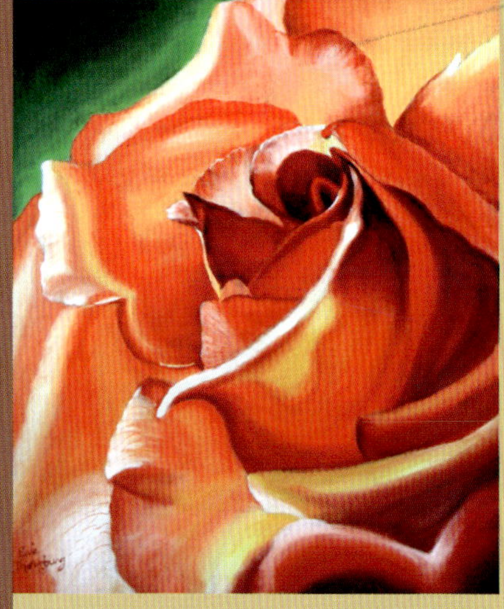

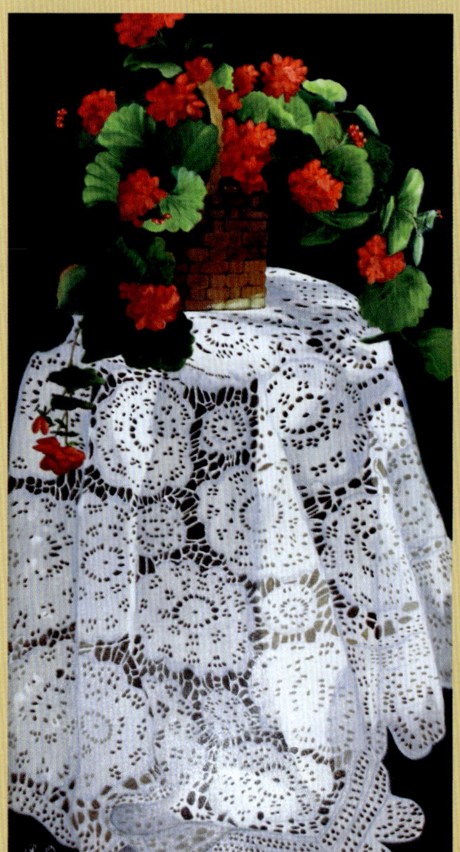

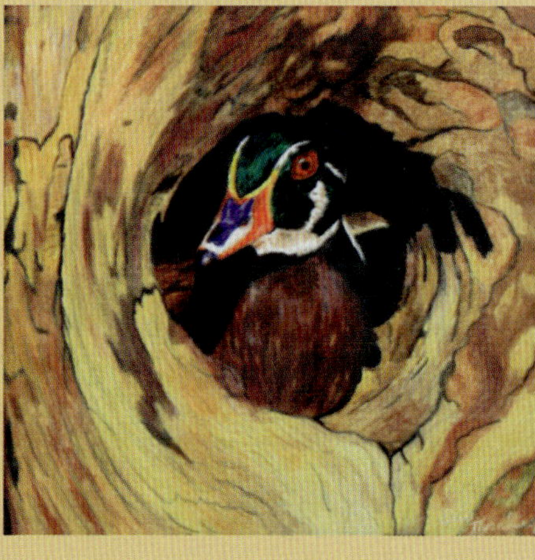

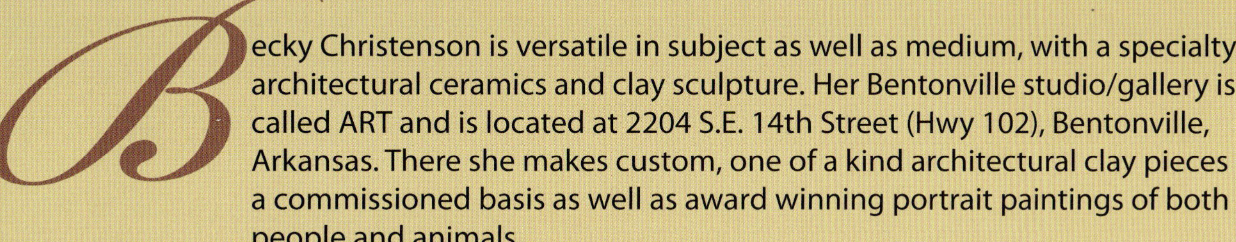

Becky Christenson is versatile in subject as well as medium, with a specialty in architectural ceramics and clay sculpture. Her Bentonville studio/gallery is called ART and is located at 2204 S.E. 14th Street (Hwy 102), Bentonville, Arkansas. There she makes custom, one of a kind architectural clay pieces on a commissioned basis as well as award winning portrait paintings of both people and animals.

Becky is Past President of the Associated Artist's of Phillbrook Art Museum in Tulsa, Oklahoma. She has studied under several national and internationally known artists and has a degree in graphic design. Becky has completed many commissioned works and was chosen to do a public installation of painted clay tile at Creation Park in Rogers as well as a large mosaic and tile installation at Benton County School of the Arts in Rogers, Arkansas.

For more information on Becky Christenson's work, visit http://www.ARTon102.com or e-mail Becky at bcstudio@sbcglobal.net.

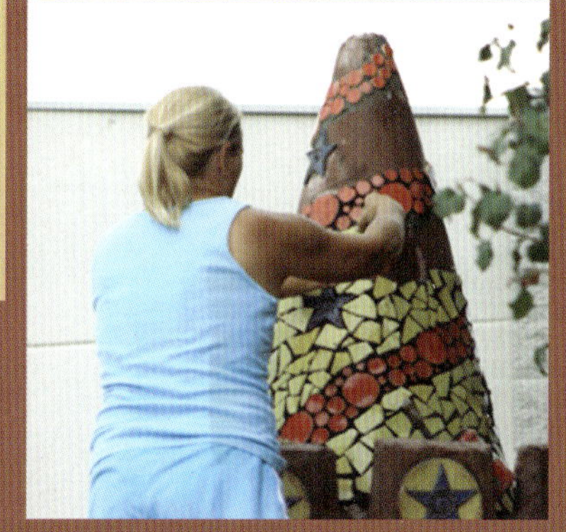

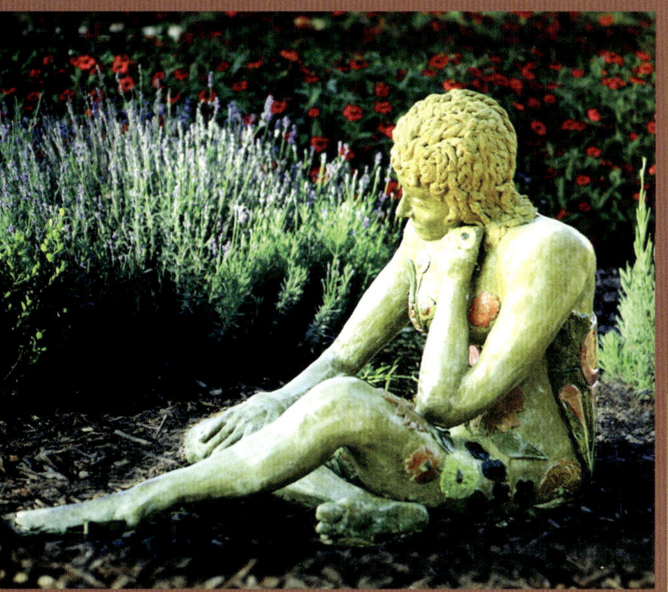

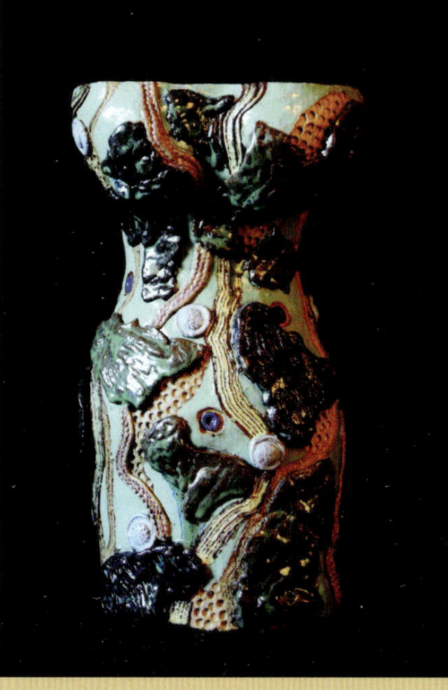

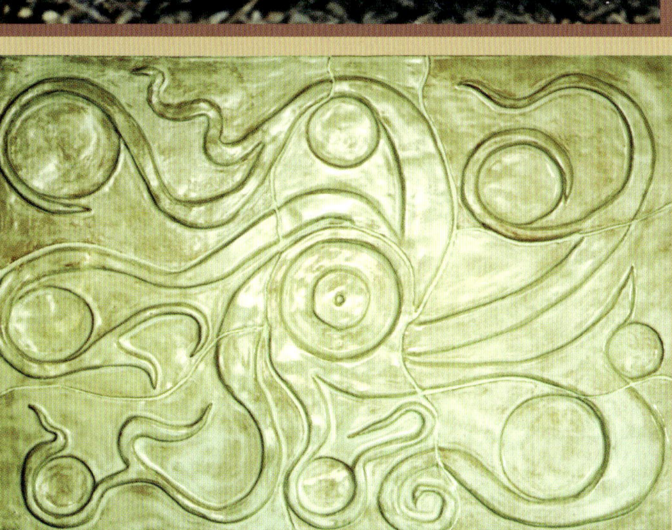

Becky Christenson ART | 2204 SE 14th Street | Bentonville, AR 72712 | 479-273-0668
www.ARTon102.com | bcstudio@sbcglobal.net

JANIS GILL WARD

Janis Gill Ward is a signature member of Mid-Southern Watercolorists, winner of 3 "Best of Shows" and other awards. She has Participated in more than 50 watercolor workshops. Janis is a private teacher in Fayetteville, Arkansas.

"As a teen my friends and I walked along the Arkansas River hunting sparkling crystals and wading in the shimmering waters. Allsopp Park Bird Sanctuary was my backyard, and I loved hearing the chirps of the birds as I hiked through the rustling leaves."

Painting some of the Arkansas Nature Conservancy lands became important to me as I began to hear of "extinction" of our wildlife creatures.

To my adventuring grandchildren, Del Ray, Gilly, Hollis, John, Josh, Aubrey, Susan, Blaise, Maggie, Marty, Kyle and Kaylee...LISTEN... GO EXPLORE and help preserve disappearing habitats..."

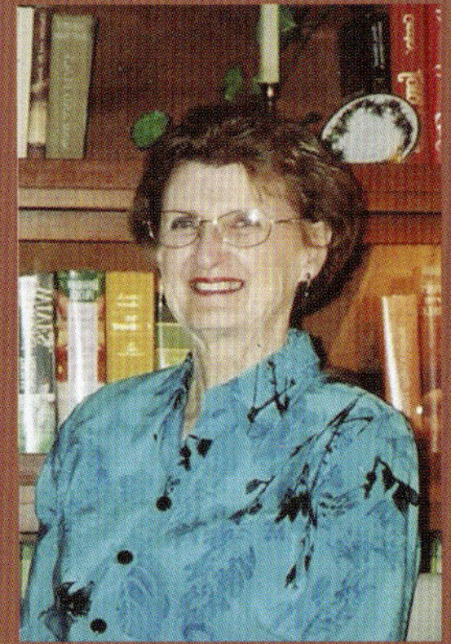

To learn more about Janis's work, e-mail her at: wrdjh@yahoo.com.

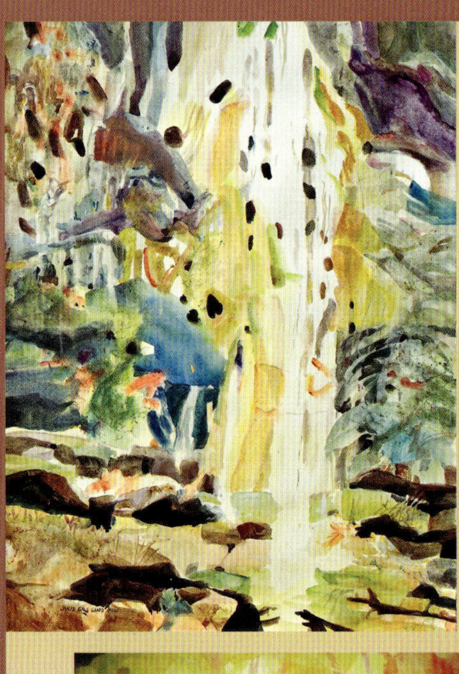

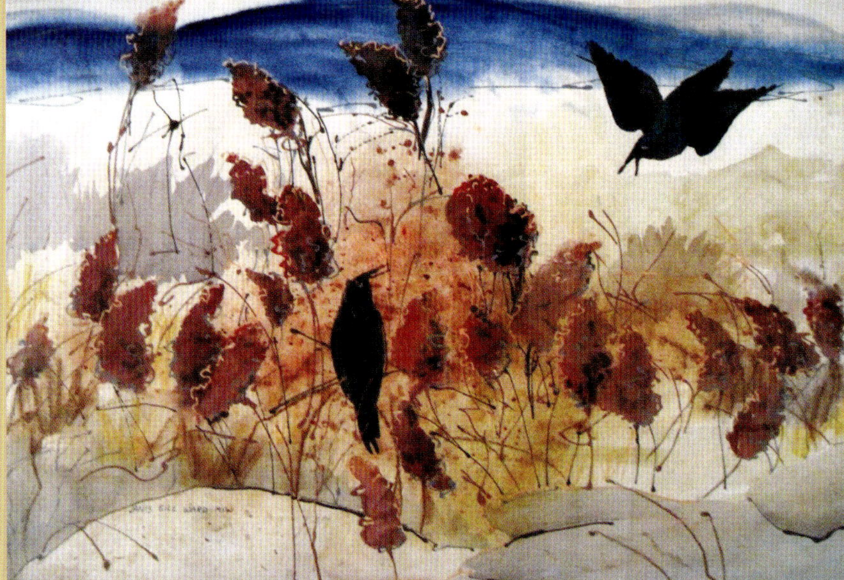

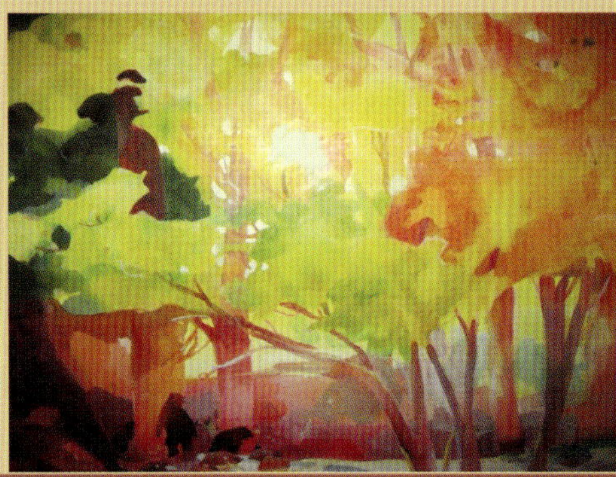

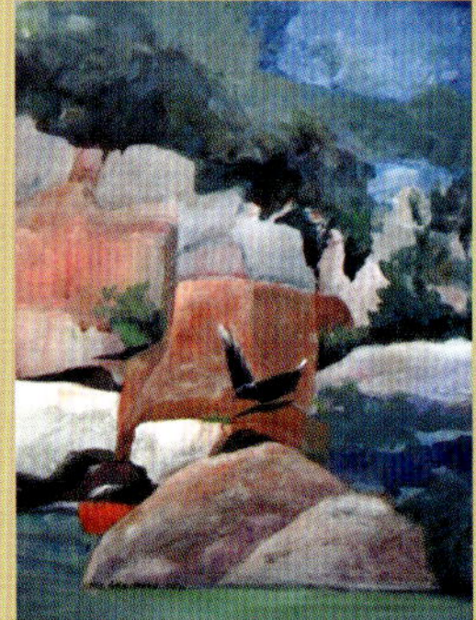

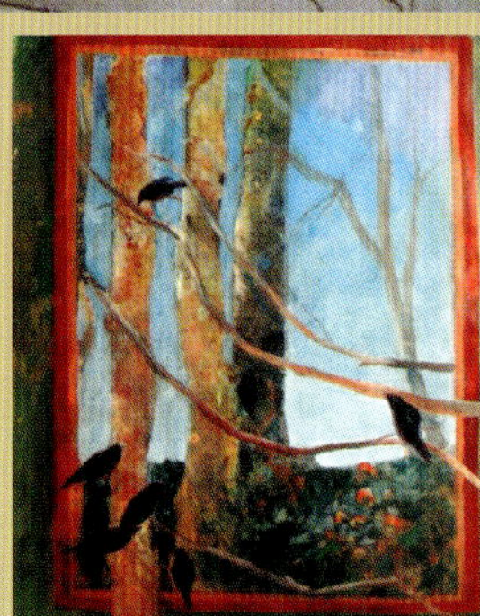

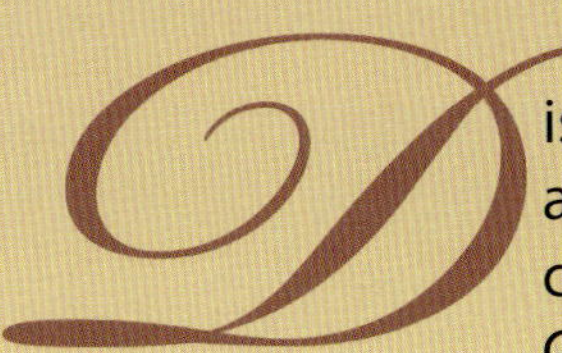

Displaced by Hurricane Katrina four years ago, my husband Jim and I looked for a new home. Taking into consideration fishing and the proximity to our seven children – Mountain View Arkansas was a natural fit with great fishing and GREAT people.

My interest in glass started 14 years ago when I wanted to make a stained glass totem pole. After lessons and much practice, the totem pole became a reality and I was hooked on glass. The four foot high totem pole is on display in my studio.

Photography, my other passion, is a 40 year obsession. I use it in conjunction with glass pattern making and Photo Art. With nature's never ending wonders here in the Ozarks, subject matter is just a click away.

For more information on Gwen's work, visit her website at: http://offthebeatenpath.com or you can e-mail her at jgfurey@gmail.com.

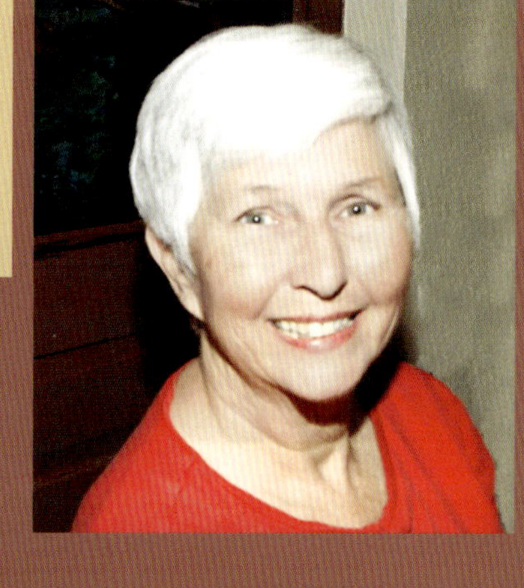

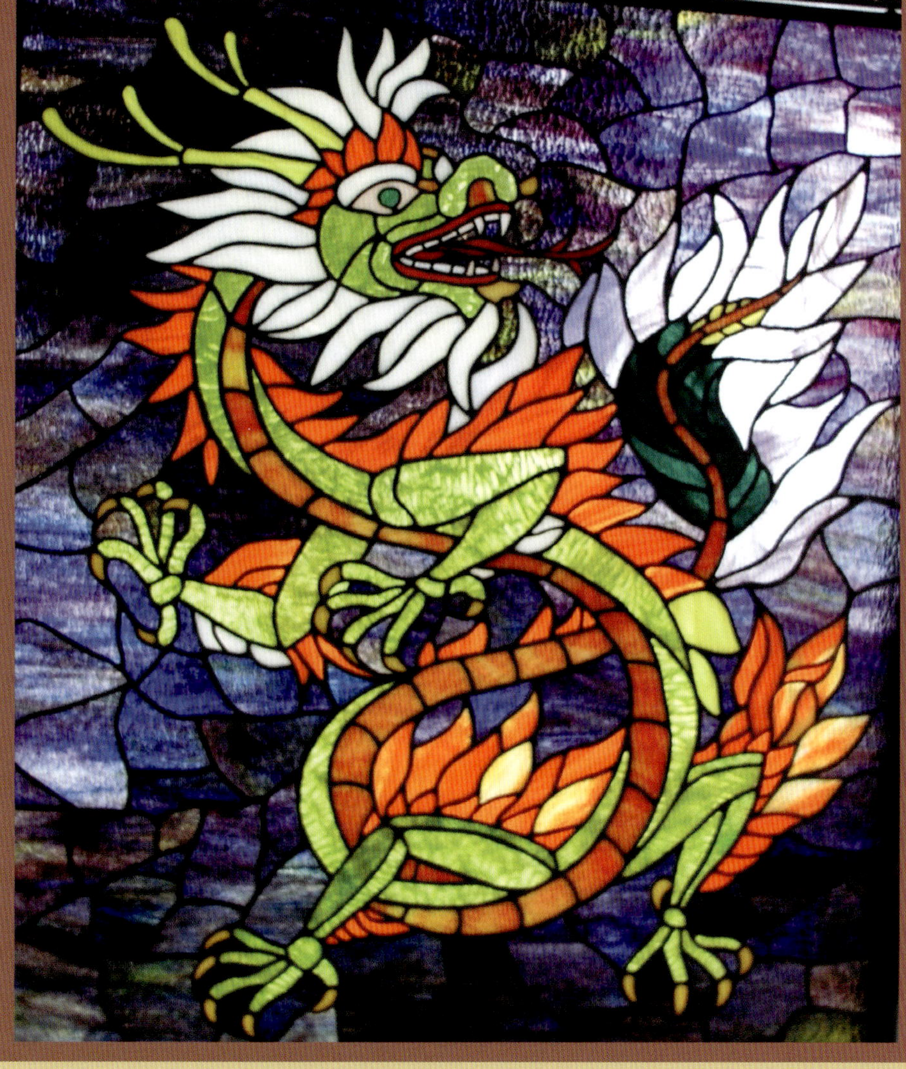

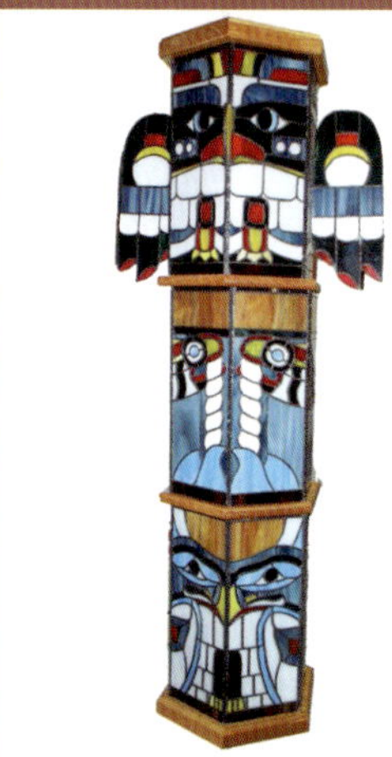

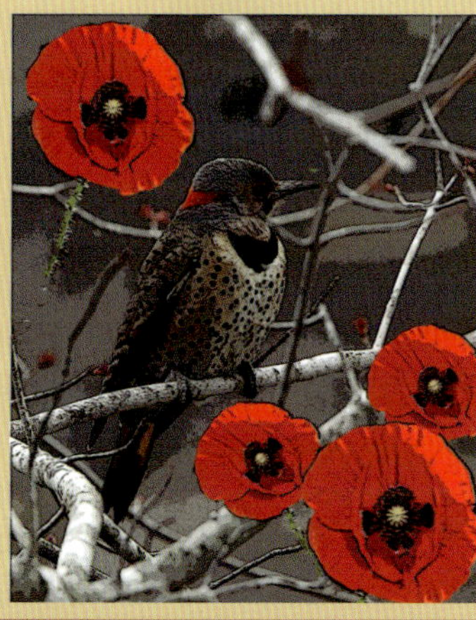

COURTNEY TRIMBLE

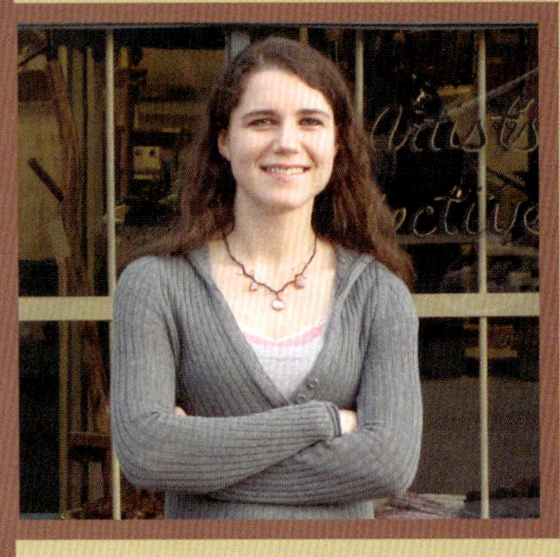

Nature illustration has always been the main focus of my work. I have illustrated interpretive panels for the Arkansas Forest Service, Arkansas State Parks and the Pineywoods NativePlant Center in Nacogdoches, Texas.

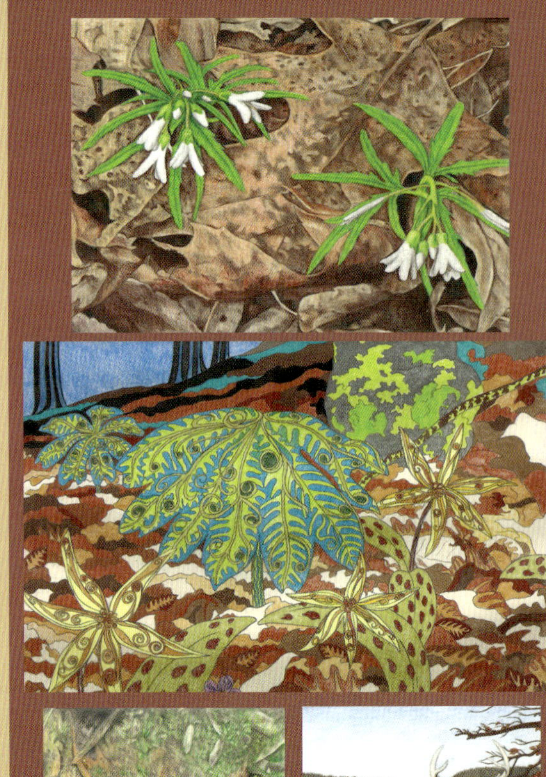

My preferred medium is colored pencil, but I also work with pen and ink, watercolor, and graphite. I make both realistic and more abstract work, which was inspired from Celtic knotwork and the paint-by-numbers of my childhood.

In 2007 I graduated with a Bachelor of Science in Biology and moved to Fayetteville the following year. I am currently working on a book about Ozark plants and wildlife that will be a collection of my nature art. My goal is to promote the incredible beauty and diversity of Ozark nature.
For more information on Courtney's work, visit http://paletteartleague.org/CourtneyTrimble.html.

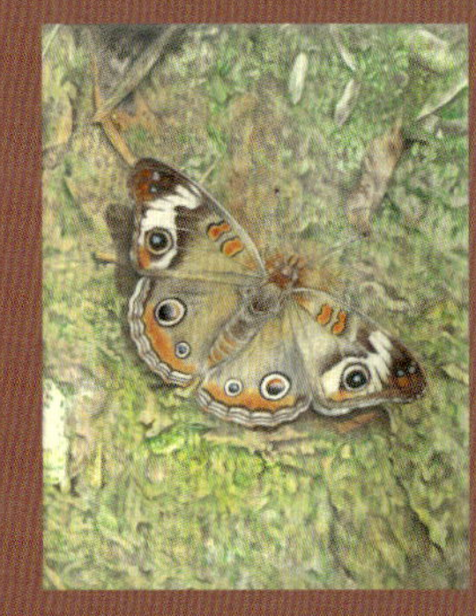

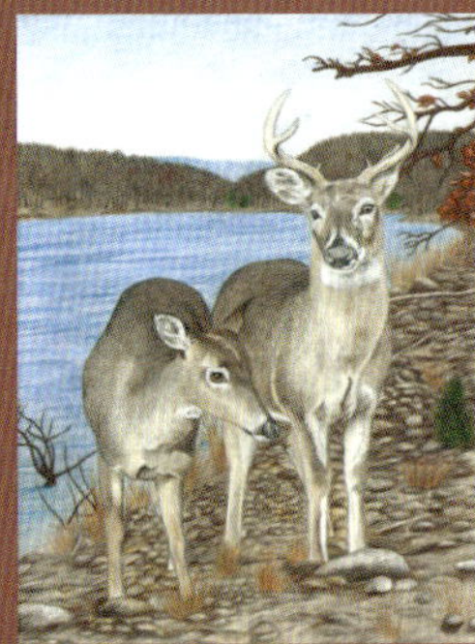

J.P. ROSENQUIST - SILVERSMITH

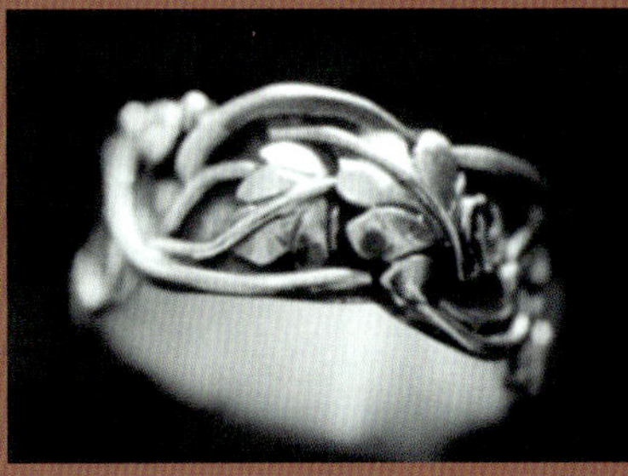

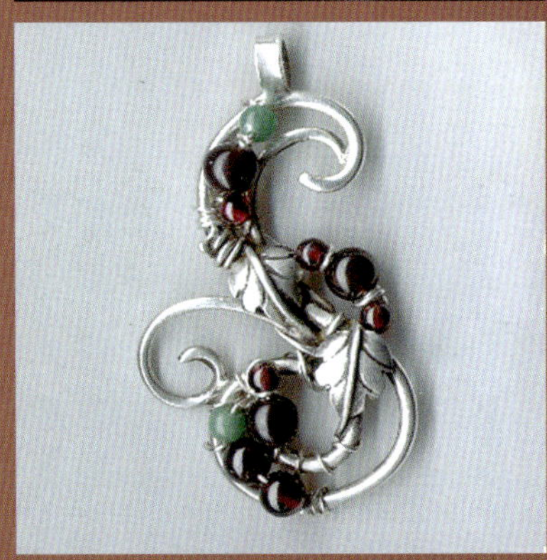

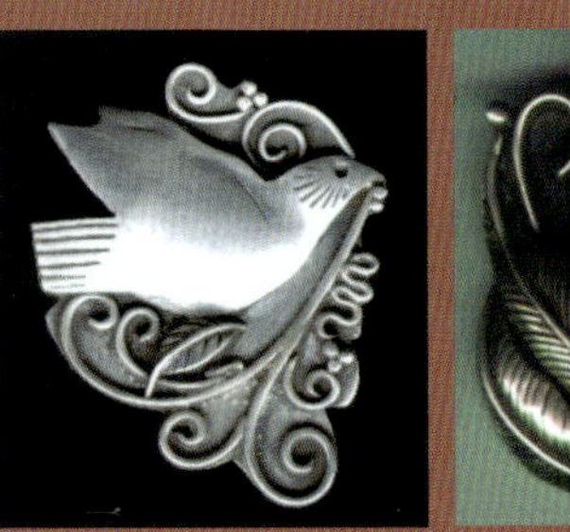

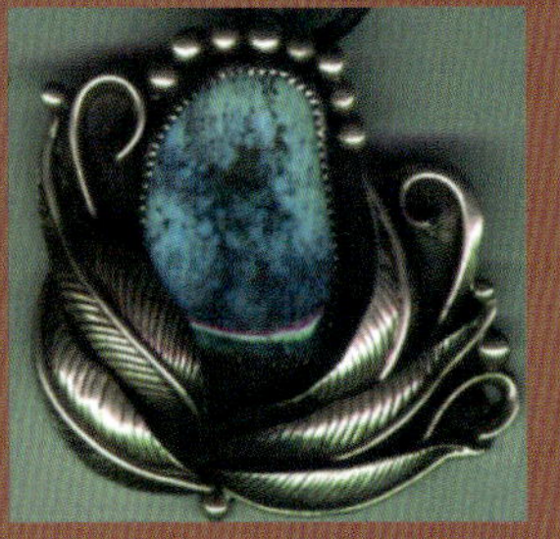

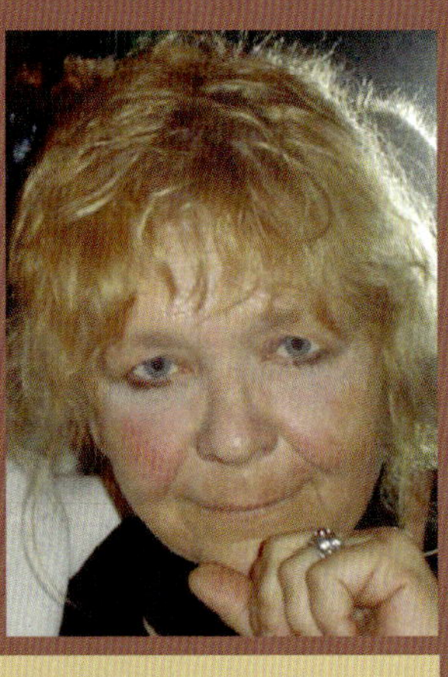

J.P. has pursued the life of an artist for over 30 years. Silversmithing has been her major media and focus, sculpturing intricate designs in silver since the mid 70's.

Considering design, structure and comfort, she creates one of a kind jewelry that is literally wearable art. Leaves, birds, suns, and moons are a few of her representational pieces. Nature's flowing lines, twisted vines and intriguing shapes all contribute to her inspiration.

Amethyst, garnets and topaz often are incorporated into her work. The colors are brilliant along with the moonlight color of silver.

You can find her work at the "Arkansas Craft Gallery" in Mountain View, Arkansas. **For more information visit her website at www.jprosenquist.com**

Janet Goodyear has been a painter and printmaker for 25 years. Born in Pensacola, Florida to a Navy Surgeon, she was one of eight children. Always fascinated by arts and humanities, she has traveled extensively throughout Europe, Mexico, Canada and the United States visiting museums and art collection. After receiving a BFA from Indiana University, she continued her studies at the San Francisco Art Institute and the University of New Orleans. She has won numerous awards for printmaking and painting throughout the years.

In the aftermath of Hurricane Katrina, Janet relocated to Eureka Springs from New Orleans where she has become fascinated with the shapes and patterns of nature. **For more information on Janet, visit her website at: http://janetgoodyear.net or check out her work at: http://paletteartleague.org/JanetGoodyear.html.**

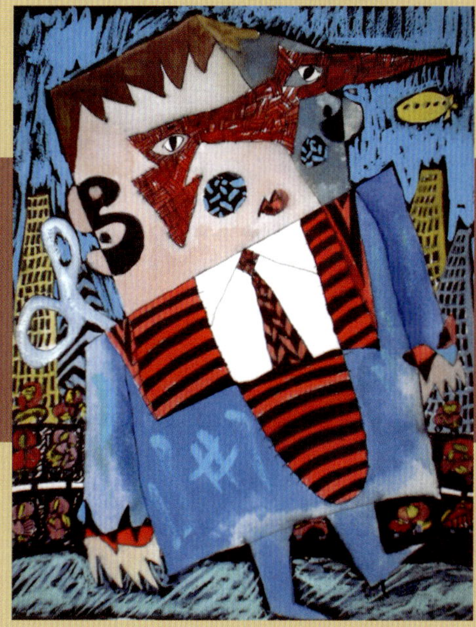

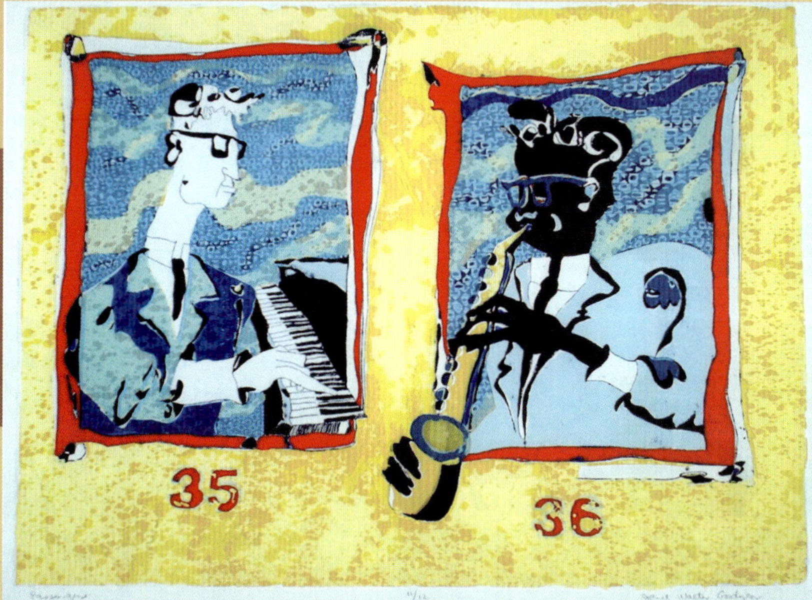

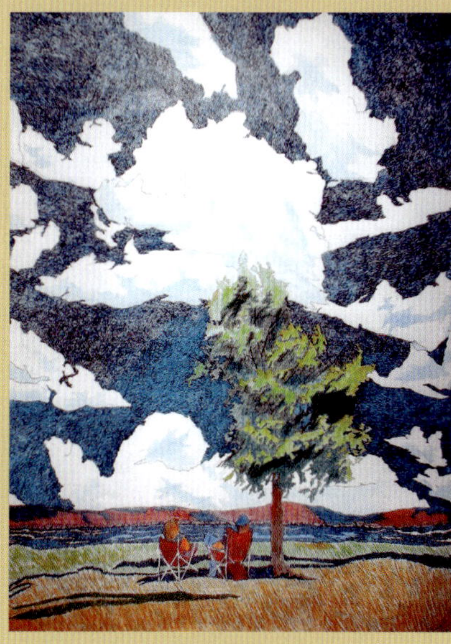

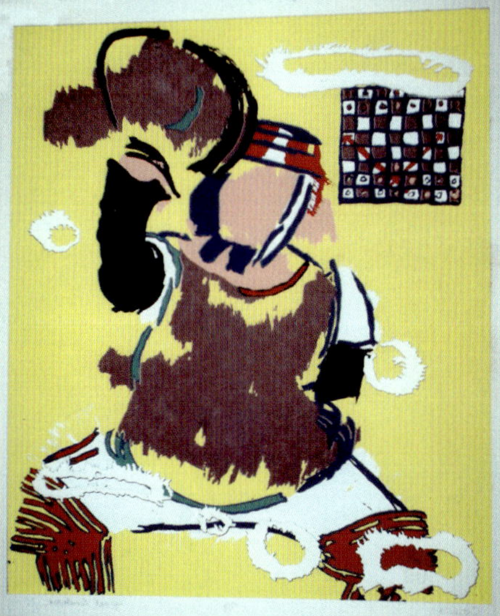

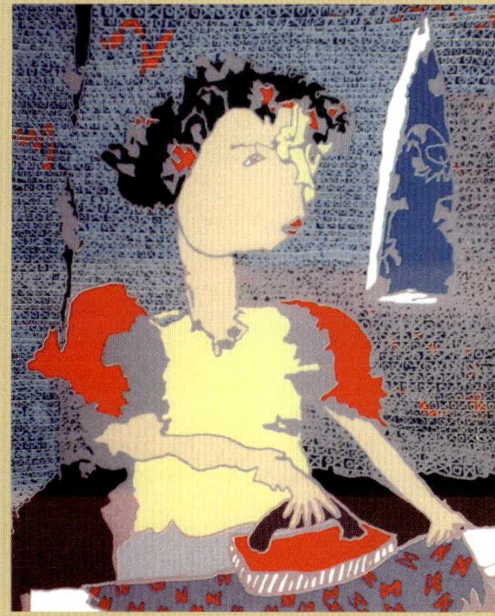

BETH IVENS

I was born in Kankakee, Illinois in 1962 and moved to Mountain Home, Arkansas in 1970. I graduated from Mountain Home High School in '80 where I later returned and currently teach art. I received my BSE at the University of Central Arkansas in '84 and I have taught elementary, middle, and high school art for 23 years. In 1985 I married my high school sweetheart, Larry, and we have two children, Mike, and Heather.
We live in Henderson, Arkansas.

Throughout my teaching career I have spent years creating art samples for my students but I felt compelled to "practice what I preached". So as our nest has emptied I have begun to carve out even more time to develop my own artistic voice. Some of my favorite subjects include my children, landscape, and preserving memories through still-life.
I especially love working with pastel, batik, oils and mixed media jewelry. **For more information on Beth's work, visit http://paletteartleague.org/BethIvens.html.**

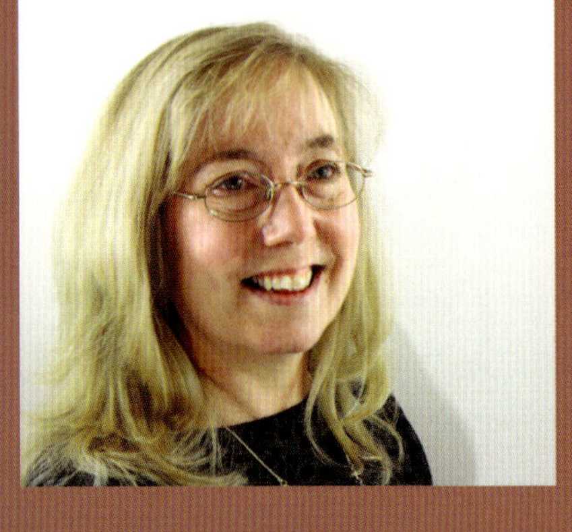

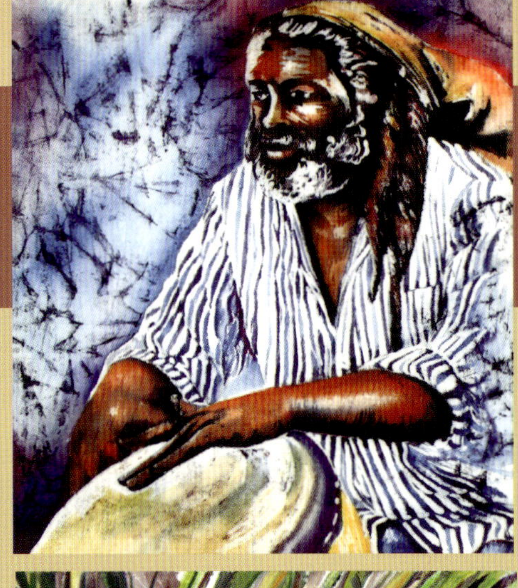

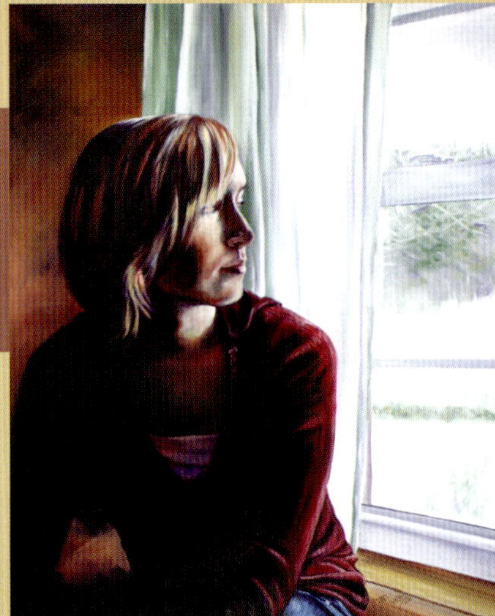

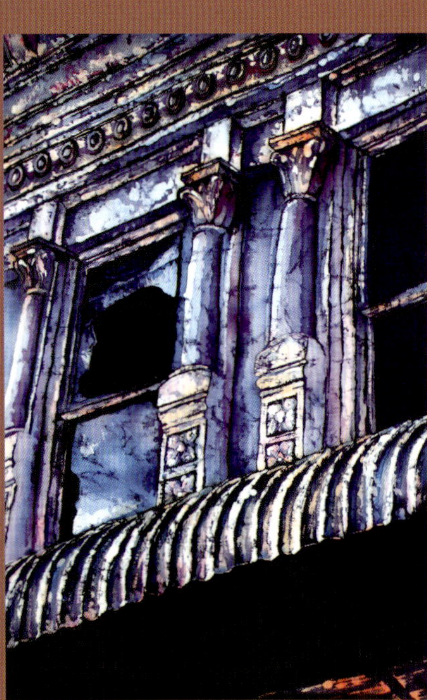

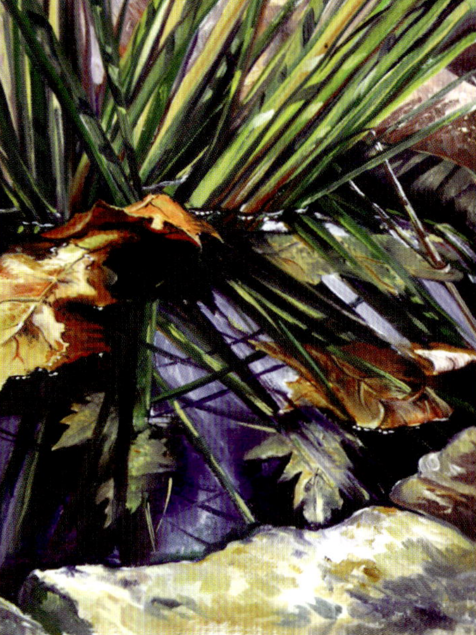

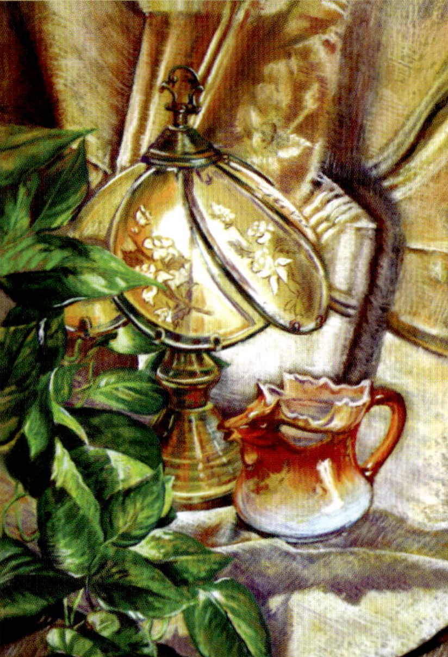

I was born in Mountain Home, Arkansas in 1990 to a very talented family. With a musician for a father and an artist as a mother, it's only natural that my brother and I would seek paths in life that would keep our creativity flowing. My parents encouraged me throughout my younger years to express myself with art and music and I have continued to do so since.

In 2008 I graduated from Mountain Home High School and am currently attending Arkansas Tech University in Russellville, Arkansas where I major in fine art. I have spent my time here developing my own style in oil paints, watercolor, chalk pastels, and charcoal.

For more information on Heather's work, visit her website at: http://paletteartleague.org/HeatherIvens.html

HEATHER IVENS

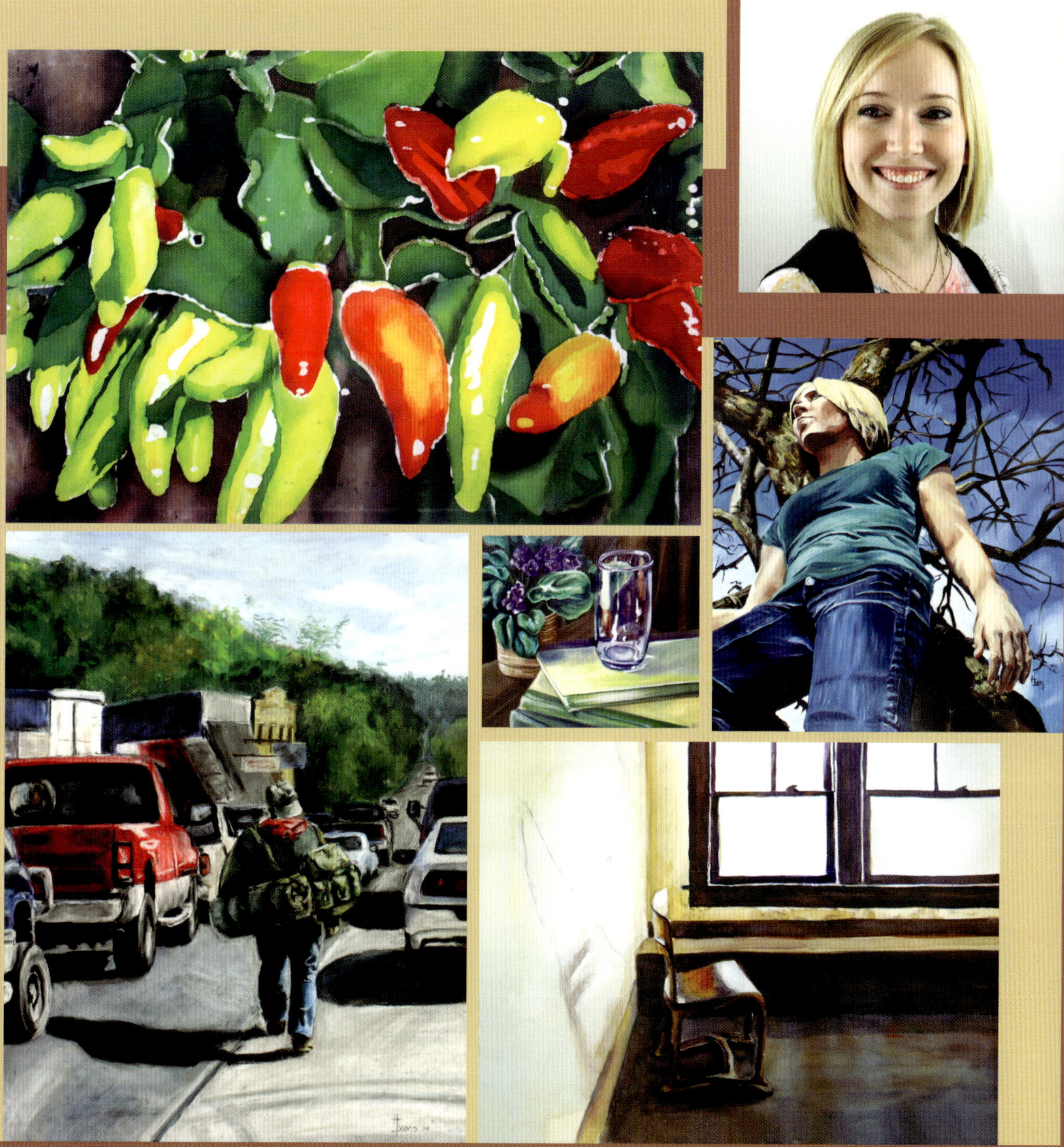

VERLE LAFARRA

I am Verle LaFarra from McGehee, Arkansas. I am a retired registered nurse and probably an octogenarian, whatever that means. My second calling is a quilter.

I first learned to quilt at my Mother's knees. She Made me learn. I rebelled and hated it. While watching the ladies who lived in the nursing home hand quilting, I thought, 'You ought to help them. Their hands aren't working too good any more."

I tried it. Much to my surprise, the stress just melted away. I thought, "This is wonderful! I can do this." Geneva Gates Quilt is named for one of those ladies who lived in that nursing home.

I found quilting with a hoop much easier than the traditional frame. You only have to quilt in one direction. I prefer doing patchwork quilting like my Mother did; using old fashioned patterns in brighter colored combinations. You never know how a quilt will turn out. It just takes on a life of its own as you add, subtract and combine the fabrics. You don't want to stop to cook and eat and never mind the threads and scraps on the floor. All that can wait.

For more information on Verle's work, e-mail: bandvgen@att.net

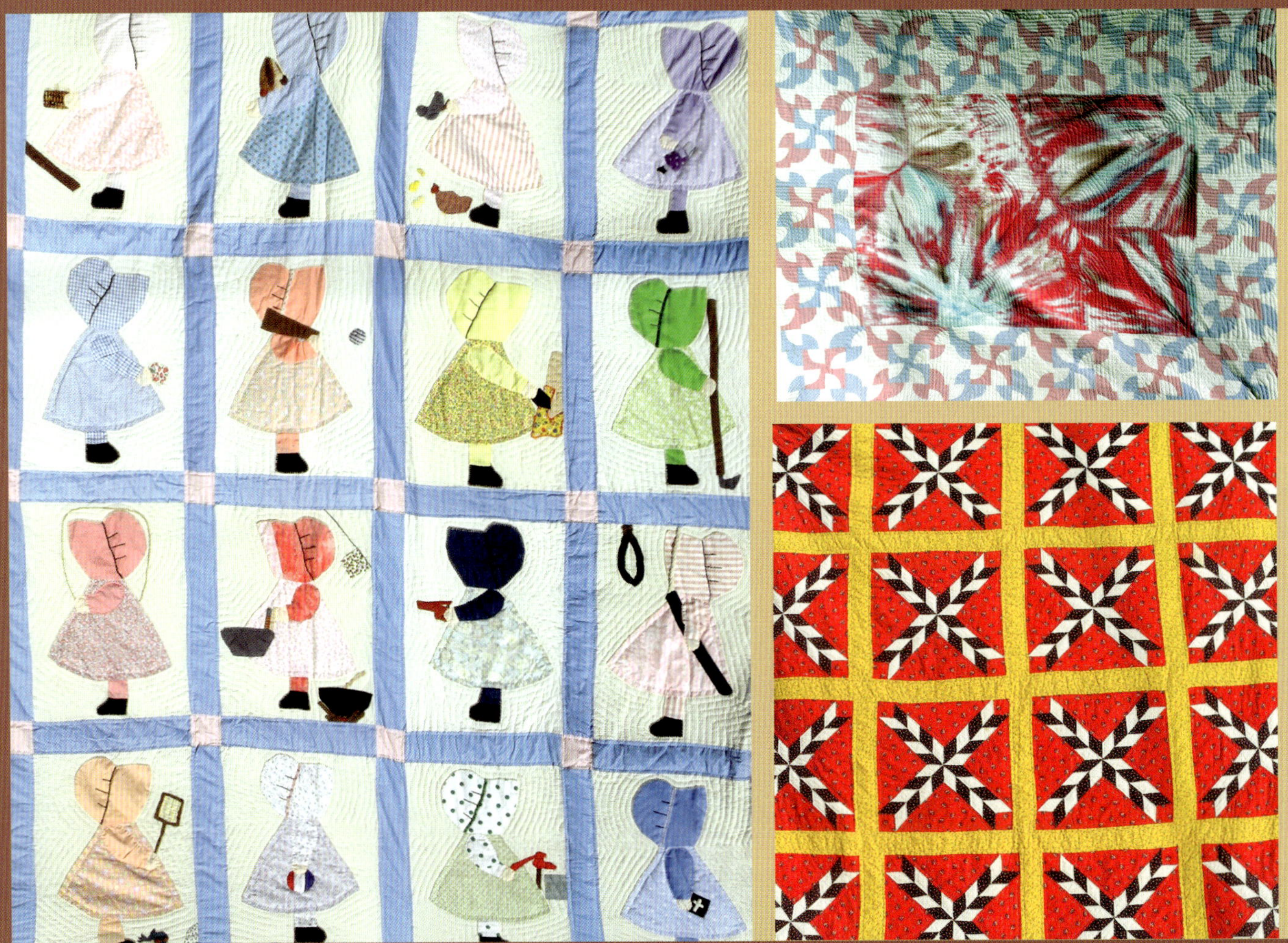

NANCY LAFARRA WILSON

Nancy LaFarra Wilson has a bachelor's degree in art education from the University of Arkansas at Monticello. She teaches art to kindergarten through sixth grade students at McGehee Elementary School in McGehee, Arkansas. She enjoys painting in oils and watercolors. Nancy's subjects include portraits, landscapes and animals. Her artwork consists of things she has seen, places she has been and things familiar to her.

Nancy grew up in the delta region of Arkansas and loves to paint the beauty of the land surrounding her. She especially loves the cotton fields and the agriculture of the area and is always looking for unique ways to portray these things.

Nancy's artwork has been in numerous solo \and group exhibits across the United States. **Her artwork can be viewed at the following websites: www.arkansasdeltamade.com www.arkansasartists.com www.arkansasarts.org/programs/registry**

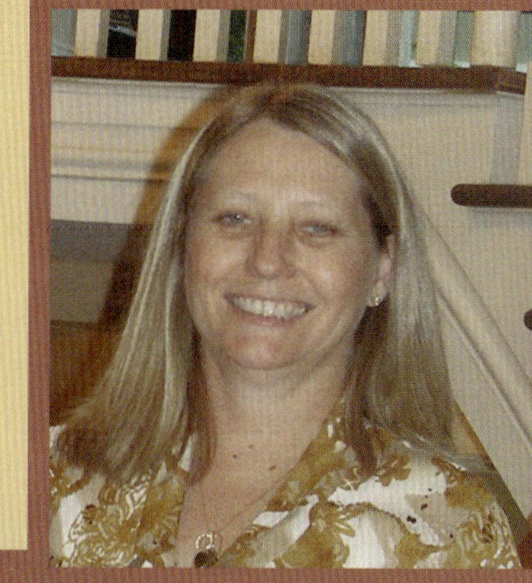

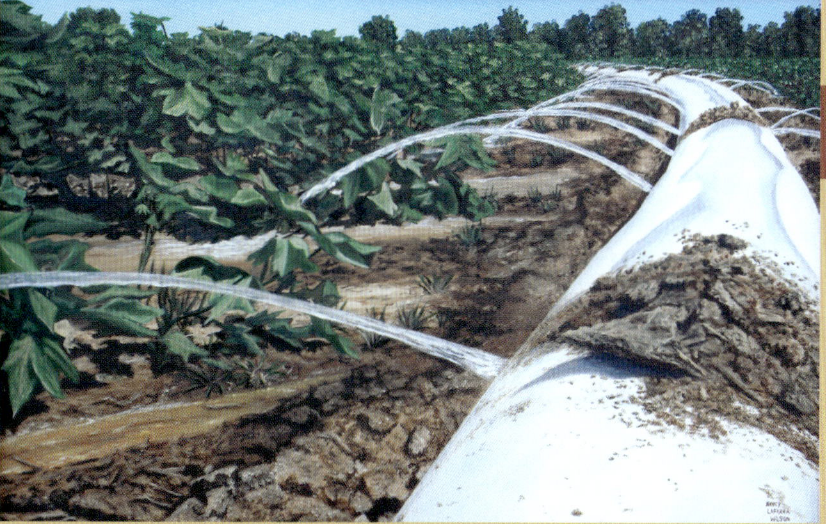

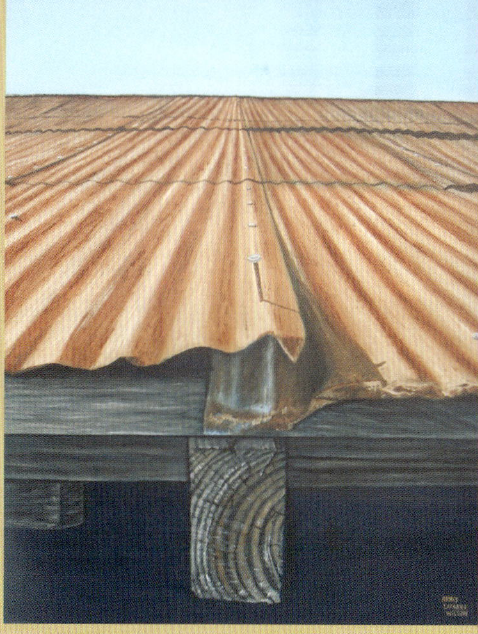

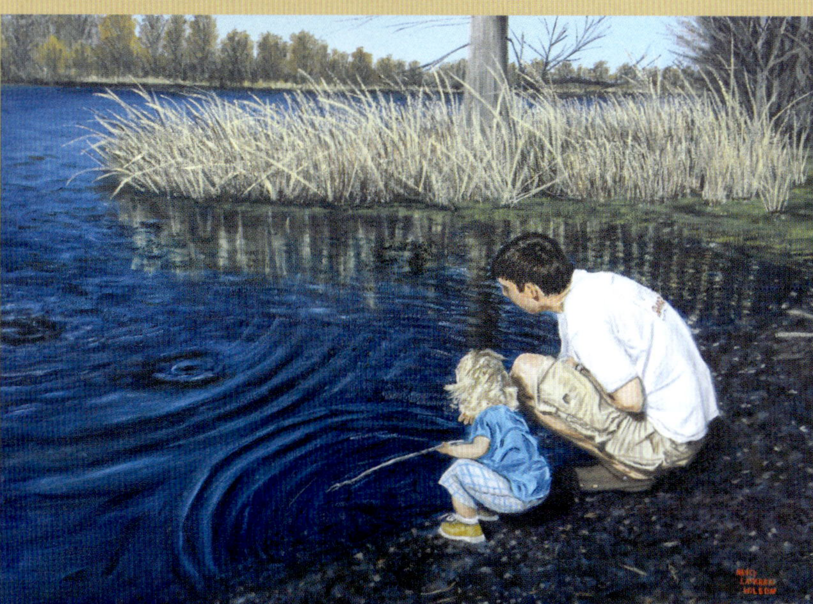

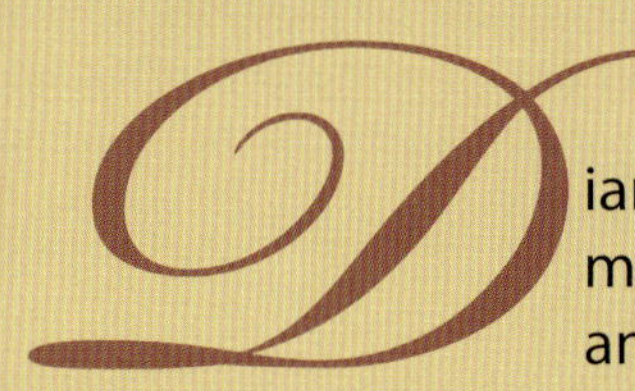

Diane's long career has been as eclectic as her art. She was an eighth-grade math and science teacher, electronic draftsperson, reporter, technical editor and corporate trainer. But, always, art was present in one form or another.

Her latest artistic endeavor involves transforming discarded, reclaimed and collectable objects into something entirely new and beautiful. The inspiration for her kaleidoscopes, reminiscent of old Victorian Parlor Scopes, started with a discarded brass lamp she found in a salvage yard in Fayetteville, Arkansas.

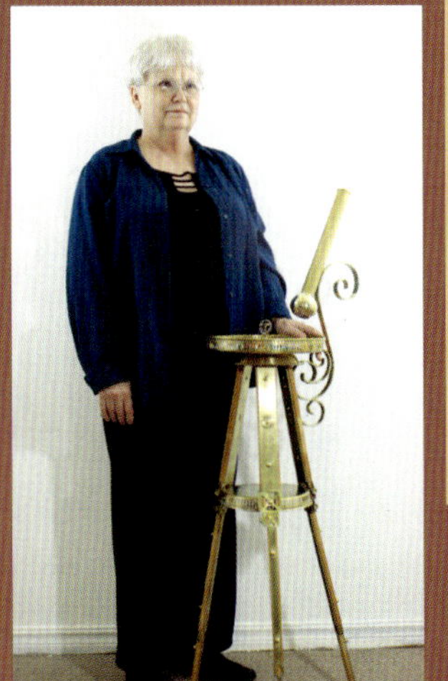

Much of the metal and glass in her recycled creations comes from flea markets, garage sales, thrift shops and E-bay finds. She uses everything from curtain rods and broken jewelry to vintage glassware in her scopes.
For more information on Diane's work, visit:
http://paletteartleague.org/DianeHill.html
or e-mail her at theartist@uncommonscopes.com

DIANE HILL

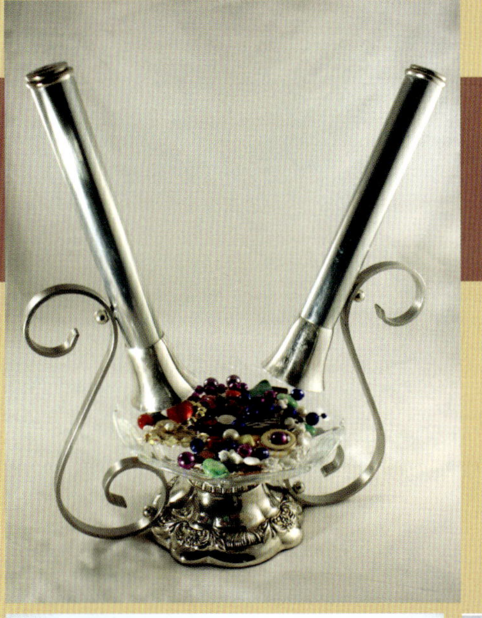

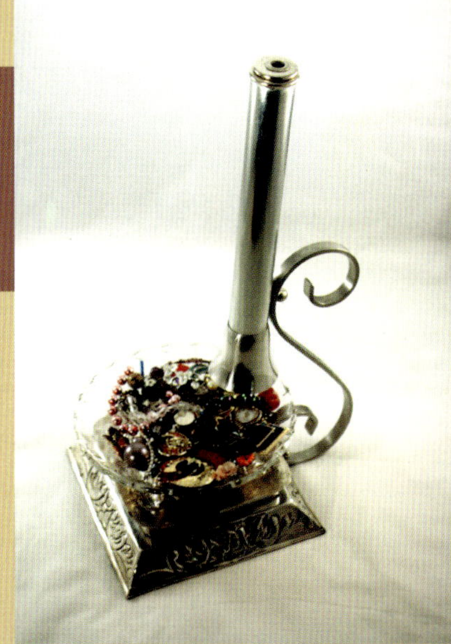

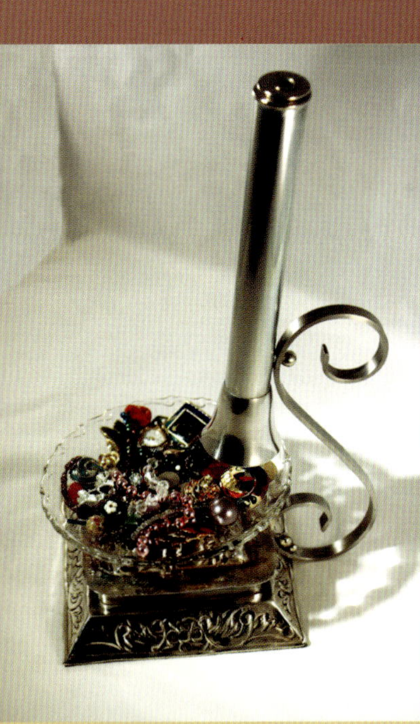

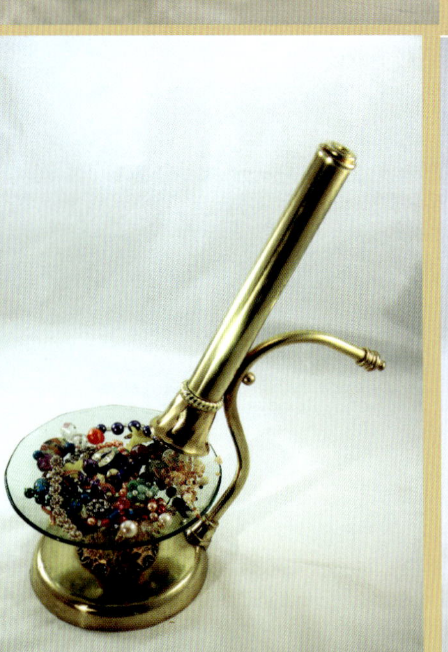

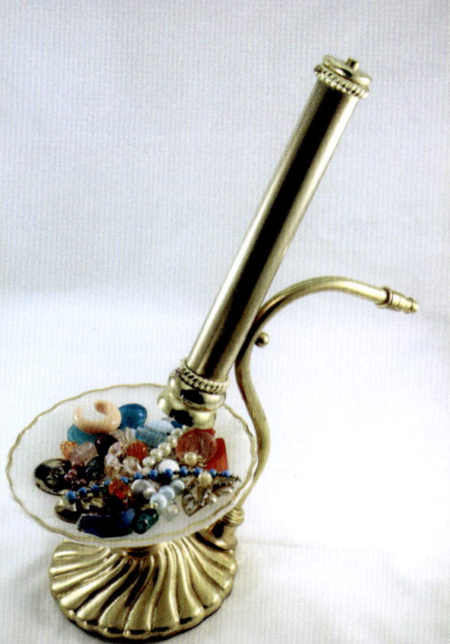

Miriam Krone grew up in Toronto, Ontario. She spent her formative years playing outdoors. Although she showed a talent for art early on, Miriam's thirst for knowledge about the living world led her to pursue a career in environmental education. In 1987, she moved to Missouri where she lives on a small farm in the northern Ozarks.

After 20 years in outdoor education, she returned to school to follow her dream of studying art. Watercolor became her passion. Miriam's attention to detail and focus on the individuality and beauty of living things is evident in her paintings. Currently she exhibits her award winning art in many art fairs and shows around the Midwest.

For more information, to see more examples of her work and contact Miriam, go to www.miriamkrone.com.

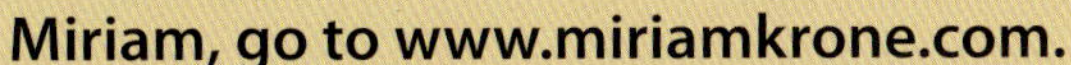

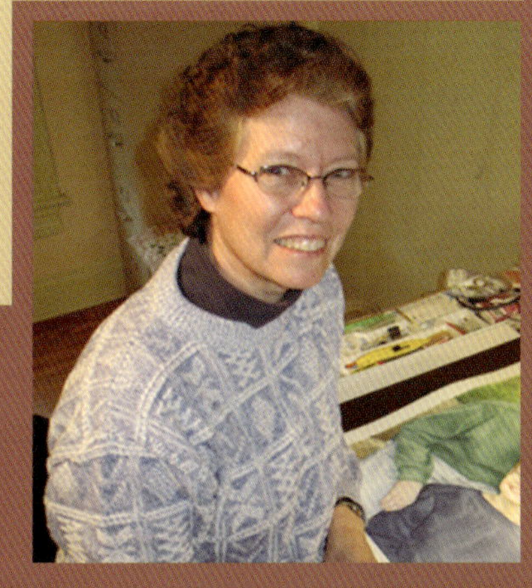

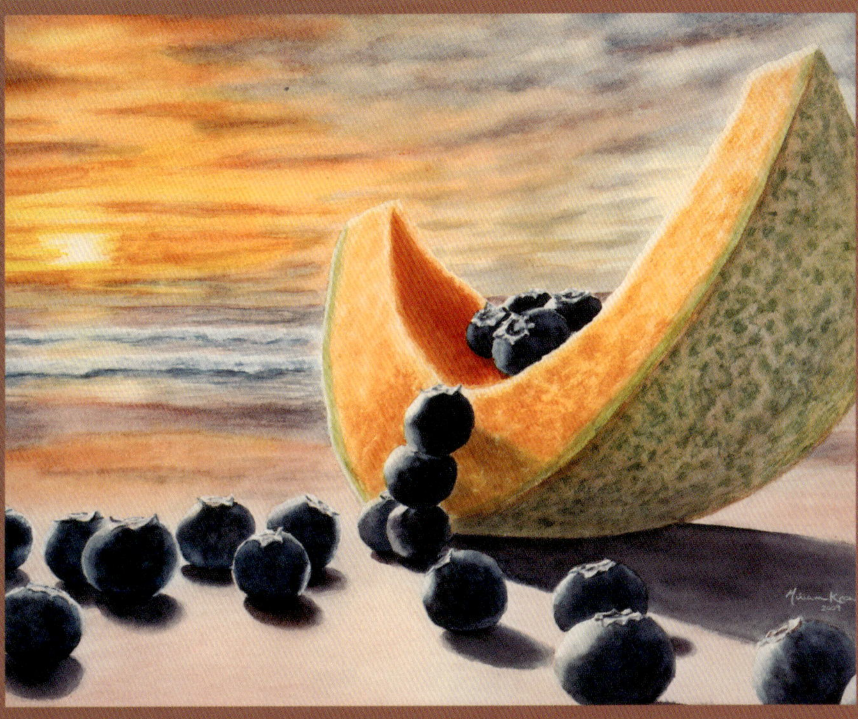

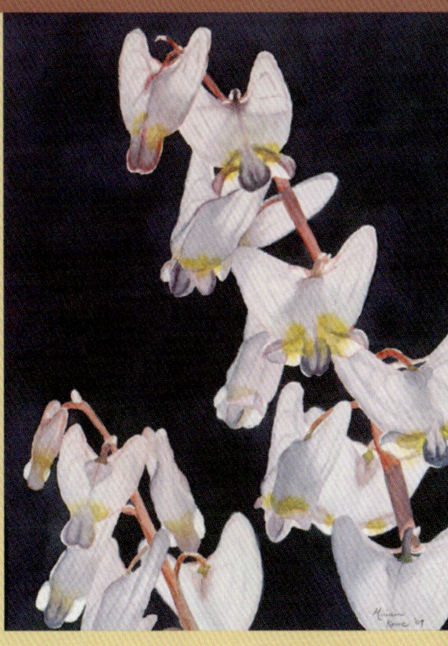

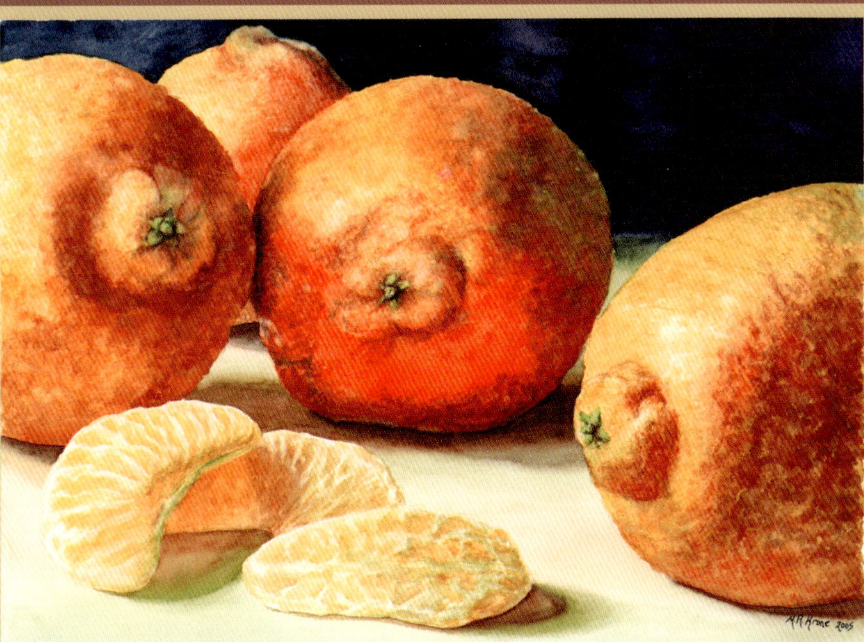

PATRICIA SINGH

Patricia Singh was born in Southeast Arkansas and resides in McGehee, Arkansas. Ms. Singh earned her BA at The University of Arkansas at Monticello and her Masters of Studio Art at The University of Arkansas at Little Rock. She teaches art at McGehee High School and Art History Classes for Phoenix University.

Patricia has been included in many juried shows, including The Delta, Helena Watercolor Exhibit, South Arkansas Art Center, Small Works on Paper, and a solo exhibit at the Arkansas Museum of Natural Resources to name a few. She is a member of the Arkansas Artist's Registry. Patricia enjoys working in Pastels, watercolor, and Acrylic.

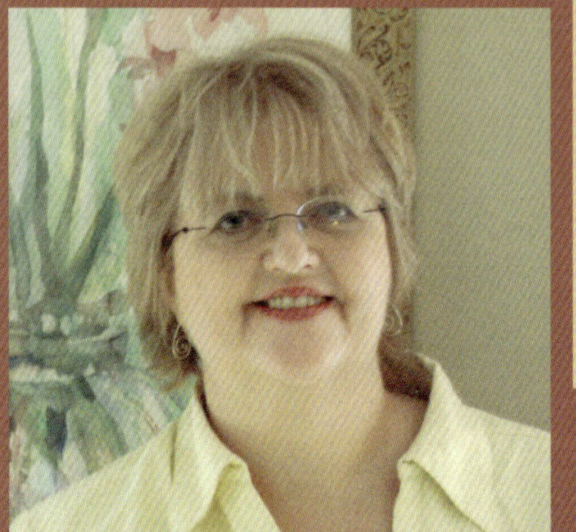

"I try to capture a feeling or mood reflected in the landscape. The work ultimately came to be about meditation, reflectiveness, movement, and sound. I am drawn to that play of light and shadow in the work. Each is a reflection of life's journey."

For more information on Patricia's work, e-mail her at: psingh57@yahoo.com.

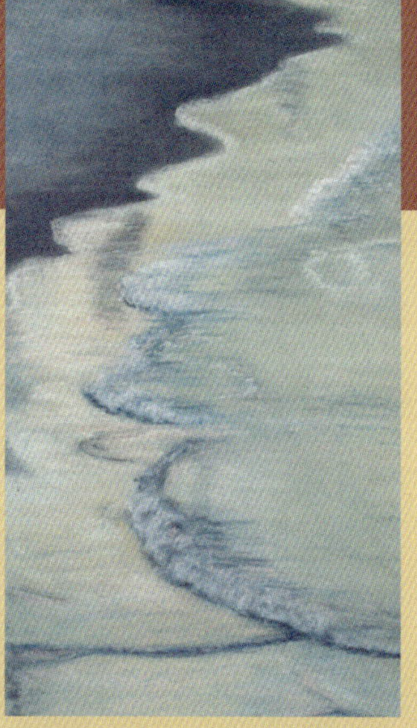

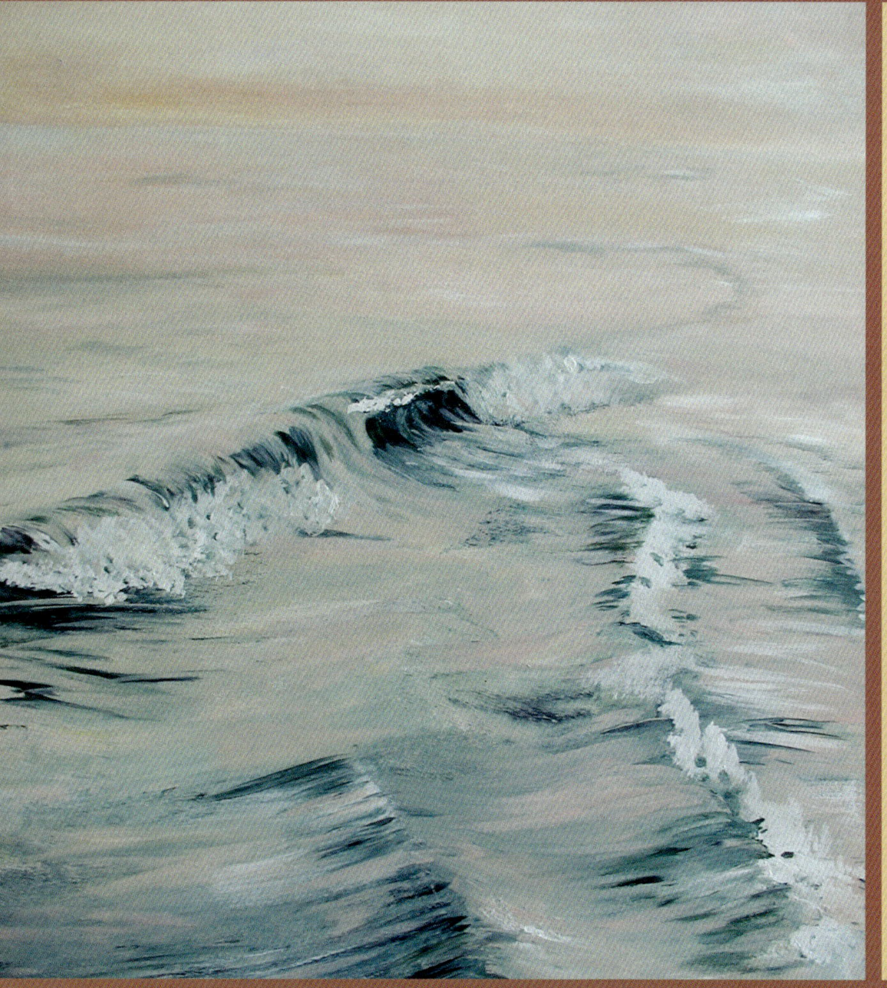

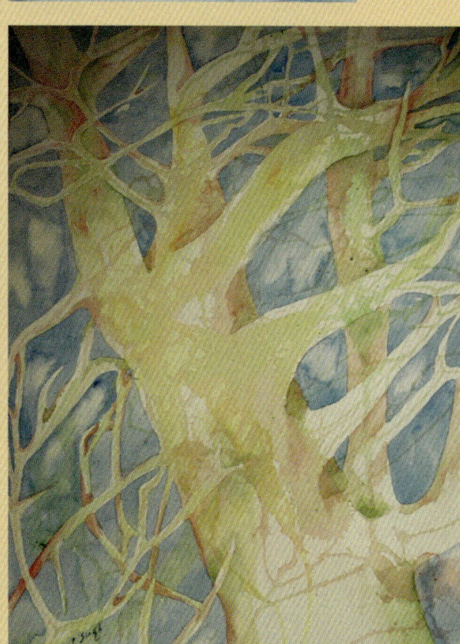

manda Singh, born in south Arkansas, now resides in Springdale Arkansas. Amanda earned a degree in art with a drawing and painting emphasis from the University of Arkansas at Little Rock. Many would consider her an abstract artist, however; in the words of Frieda Kahlo, "I never paint dreams or nightmares. I paint my own reality."

Due to a condition called Juvenile Rheumatoid Arthritis, Amanda's vision fluctuates between blurry and manageable. She draws as she sees the world; distorting and blurring out part of her drawings.

When drawing, Amanda begins with a color field - it is somewhat like the Abstract Expressionists except with pastels. Space and actual texture is an important aspect of her drawings as well as her paintings.
To see more of Amanda's work, visit: www.arkansasarts.org/programs/registry/ or e-mail her at: amanda.tyree@yahoo.com

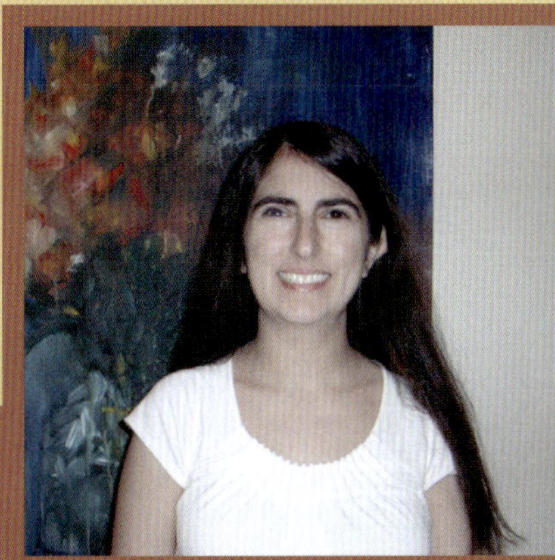

AMANDA SINGH

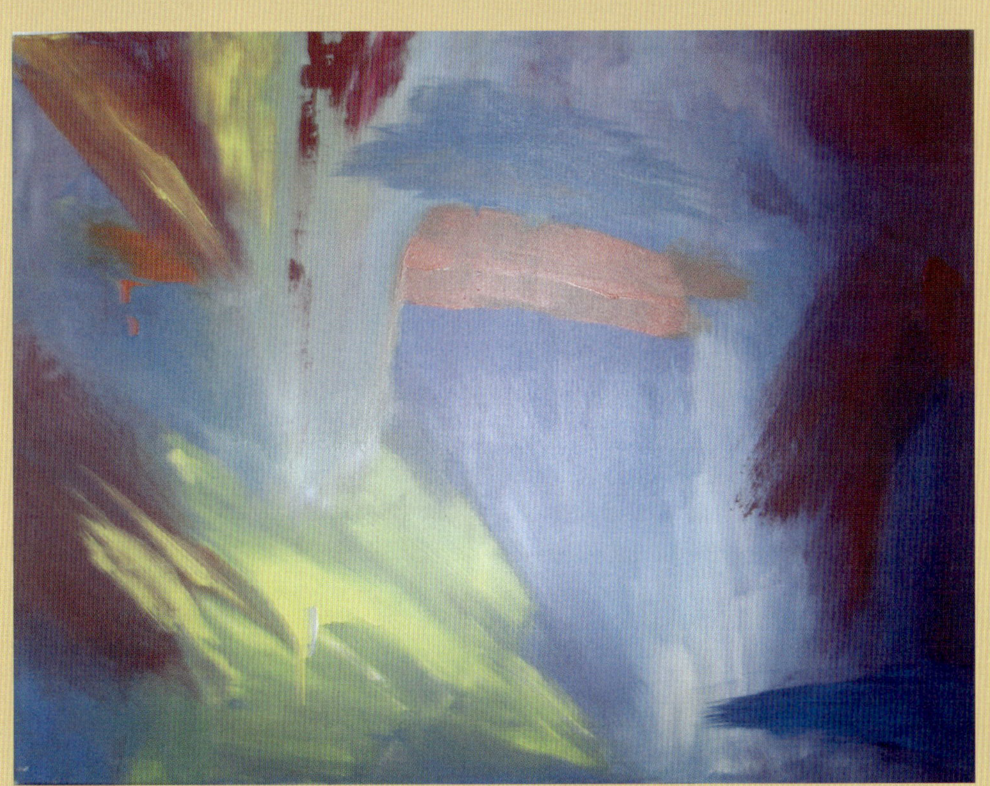

September 10th 37" x 48"

The Red Door Leads Nowhere 5" x 7"

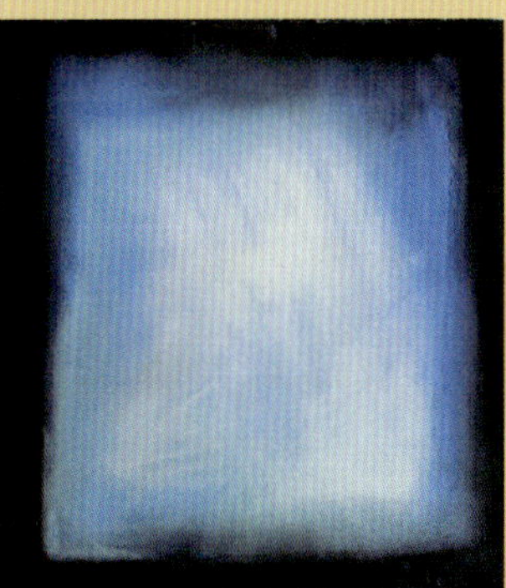

The Blue Room 8.5" x 9.5"

DAN COHEE

Dan Cohee was born in California but was raised in the heart of the Ozarks where he studied and honed his painting skills. Dan returned to California where he studied the works of L. Ron Hubbard, including film and art, until he was diagnosed with a serious, life-threatening illness. That is when he discovered just how much he missed the peace and tranquility that he knew in the Ozarks.

Dan returned to his beloved Ozarks in 2003 where he has been celebrating the peace and solitude that only the Ozarks can bring. Dan paints landscapes that bring him peace of mind and his goal is to share that peaceful feeling with all who enjoy his work. In the fast paced world that we all live in, Dan's work will center you and give you a sense of peace.

Dan does custom paintings and **for more information about Dan's work, visit: http://paletteartleague.org/DanCohee.html**

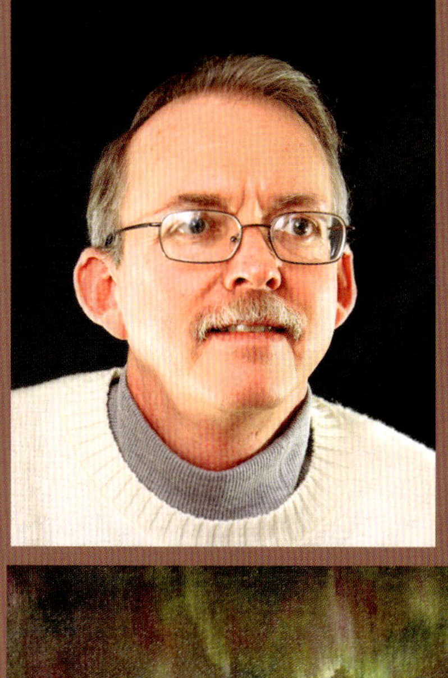

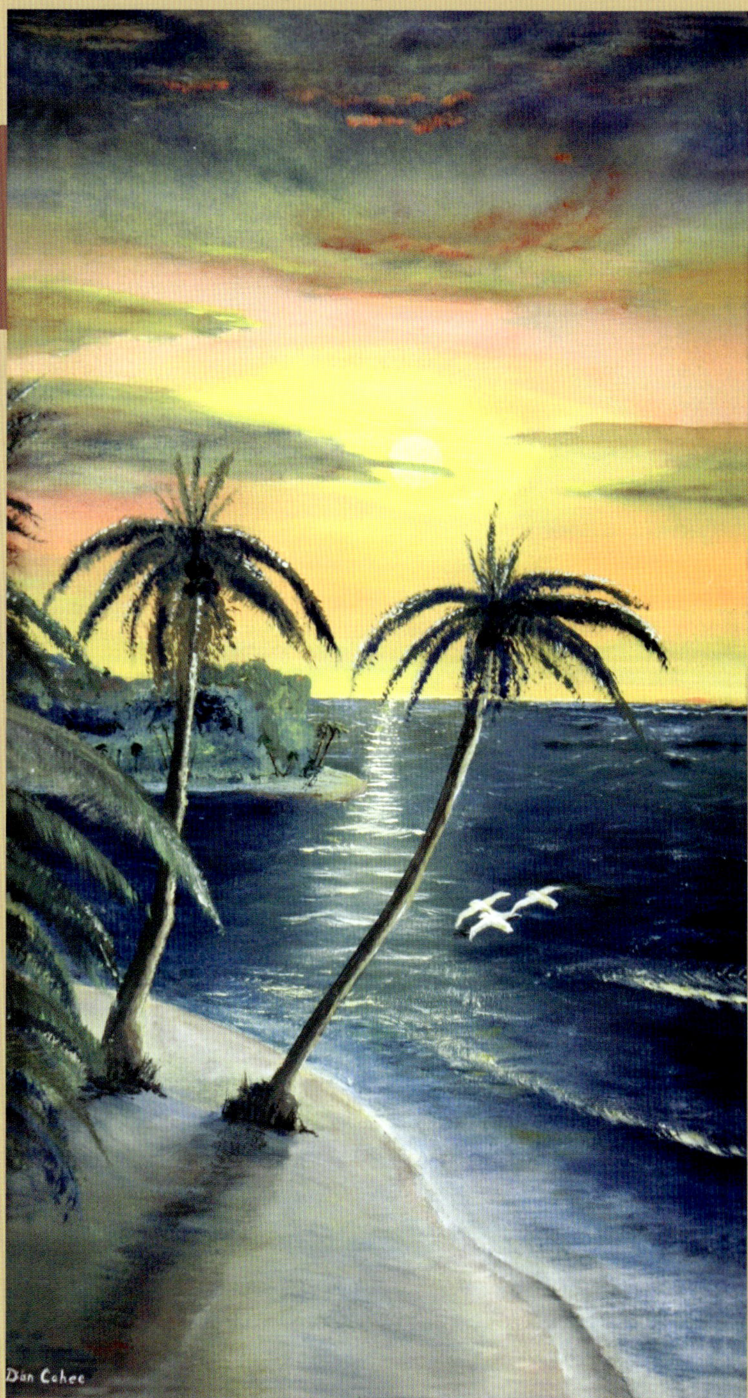

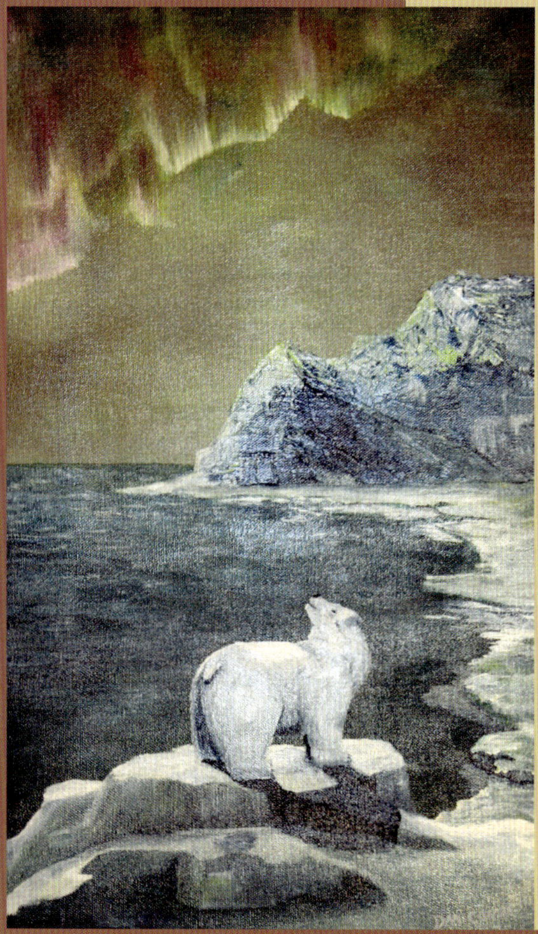

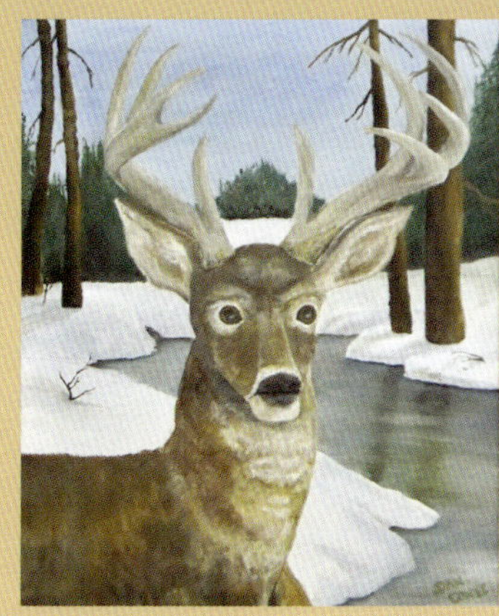
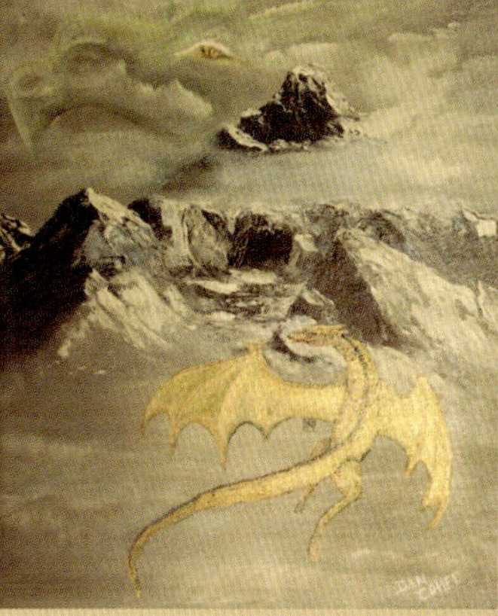
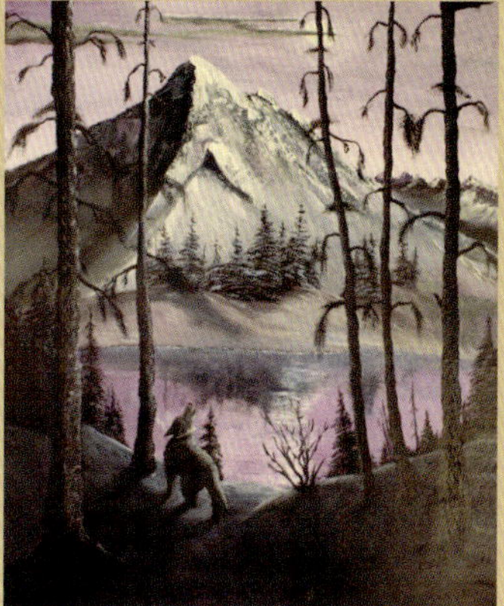
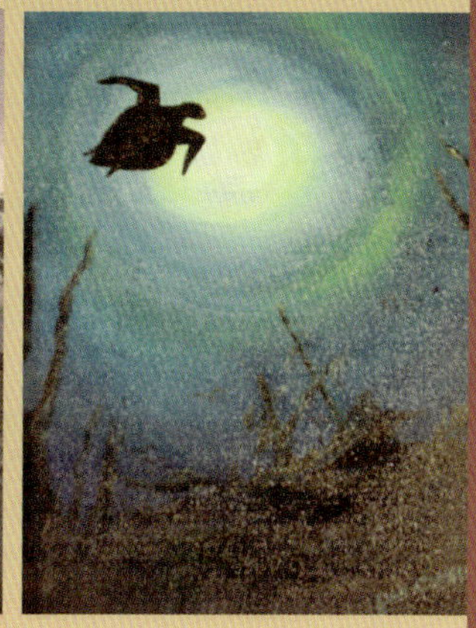
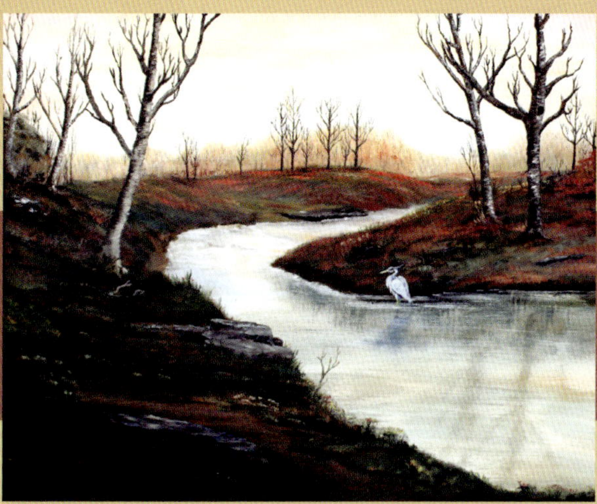
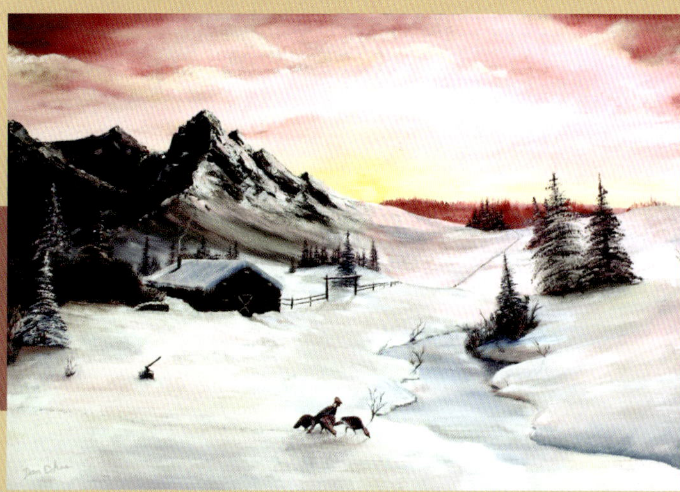

DAN COHEE

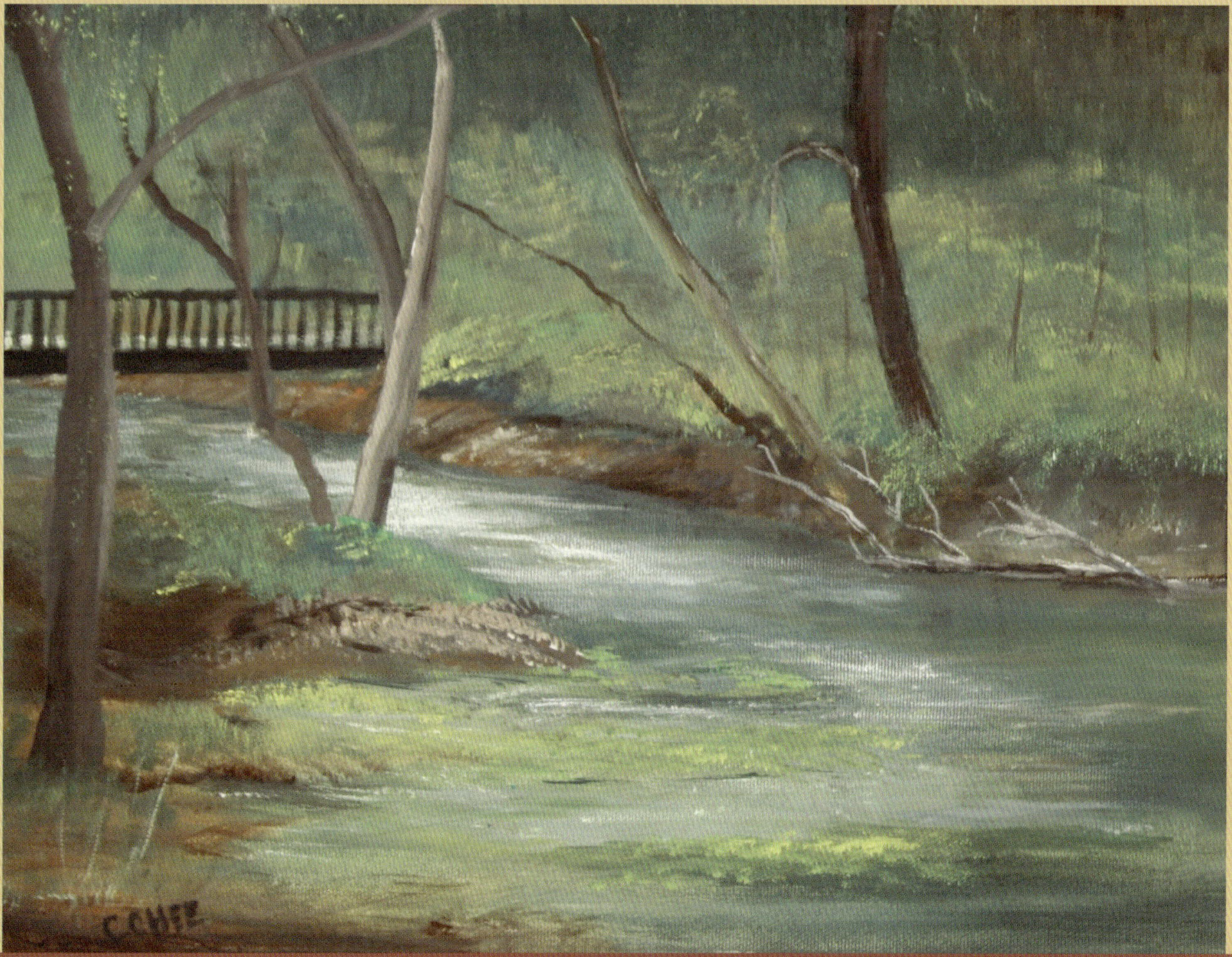

Wood Fired Ceramics

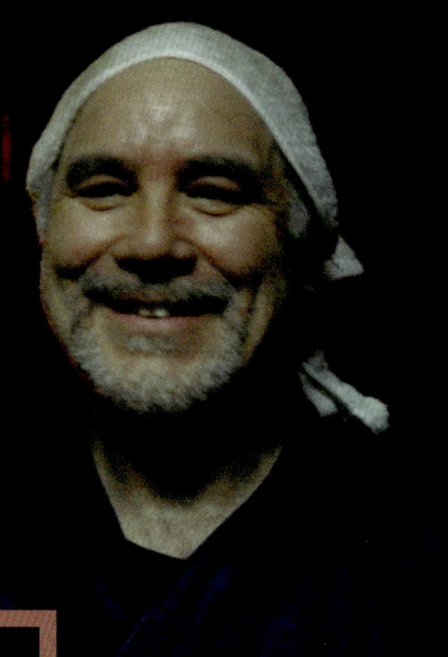

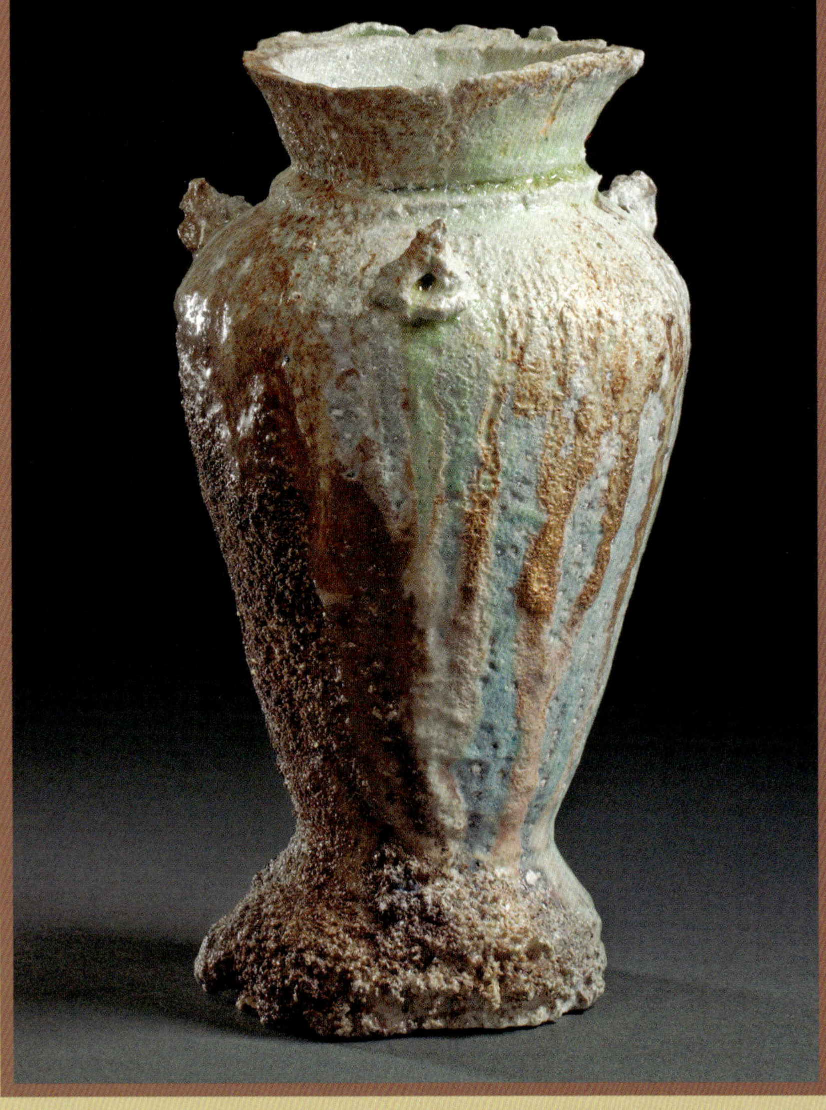

www.joebruhin.com

"By being in harmony with the elements and forces of nature the work becomes a sacrificial offering surrendered to the flames and reborn, it aspires towards the ideal of timeless beauty. Complacency is not an option. Each firing gives information to grow from and inspires me to dive deeper, which keeps the work fresh and enables me to express with heart and spirit. My goal and ideal is to make objects of beauty that have a transcending quality which can inspire another human being, bring a little joy or add a positive presence to one's living environment. For me, working with clay and being a fire artist is a vehicle for spiritual growth. One can say that my pots are offerings or prayers and my kiln the temple to manifest them."

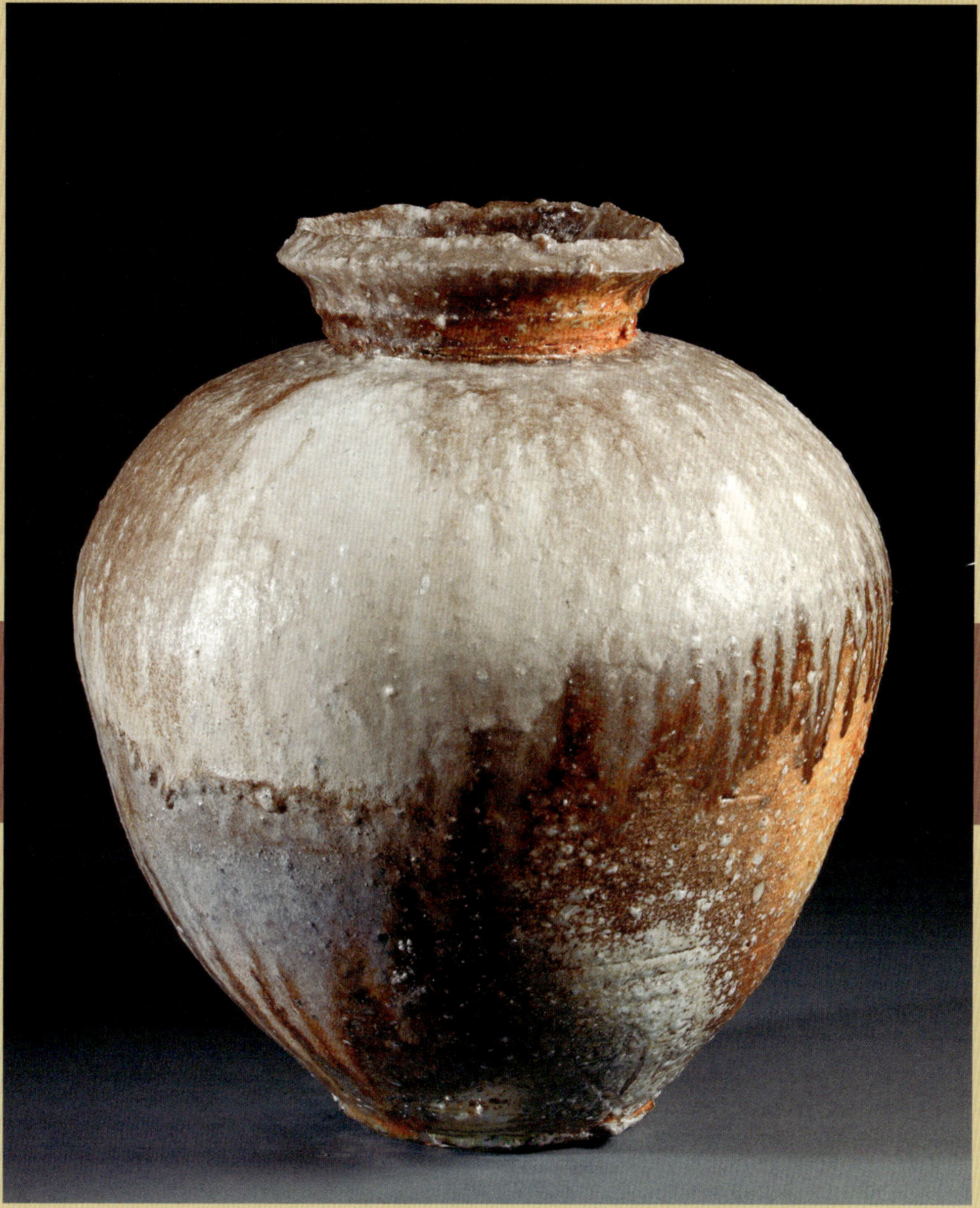

"Iga Jar . . . Duality" in memory of my mother and father

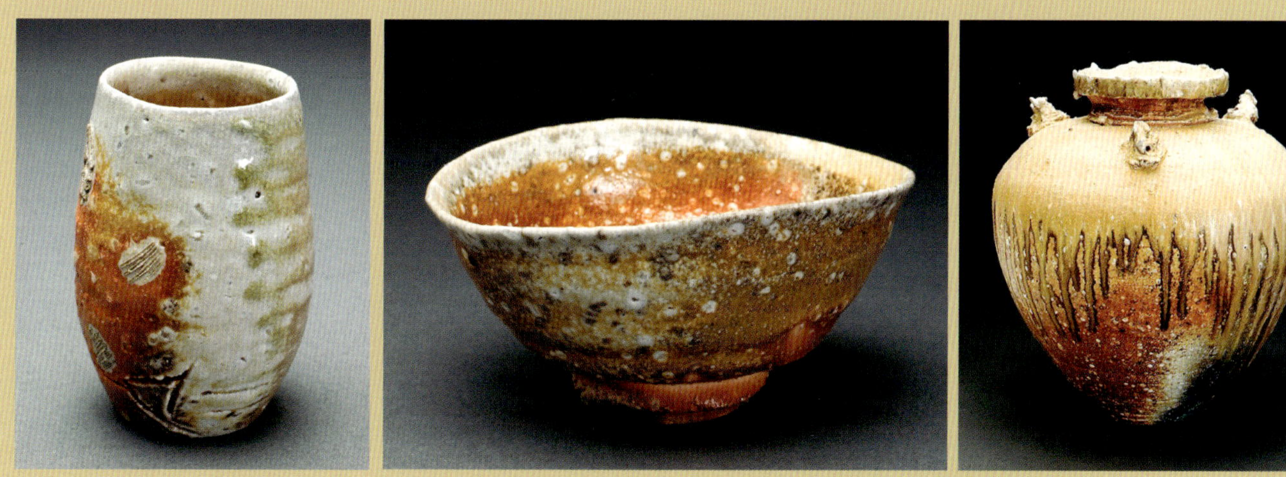

JOE BRUHIN

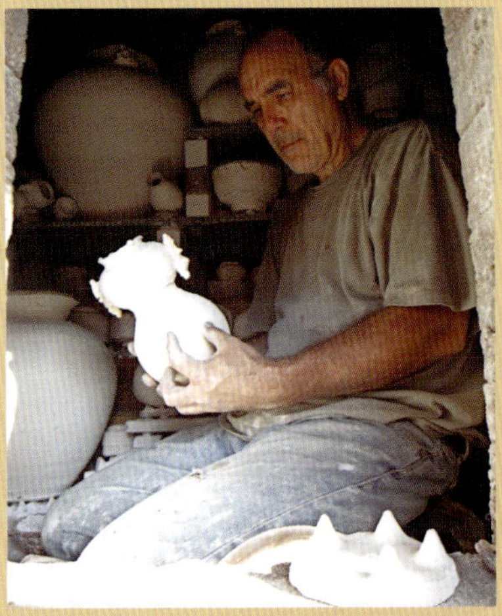

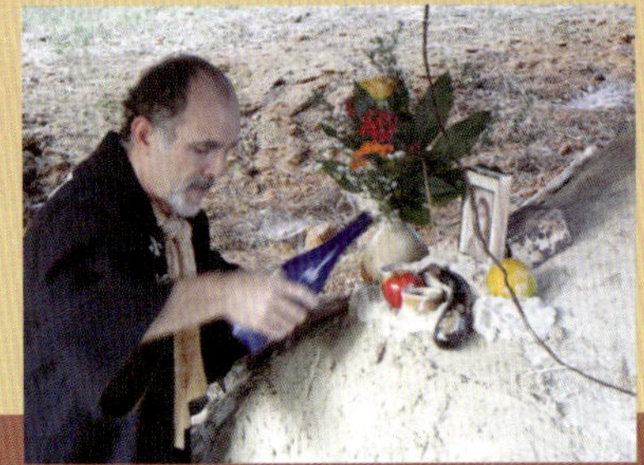

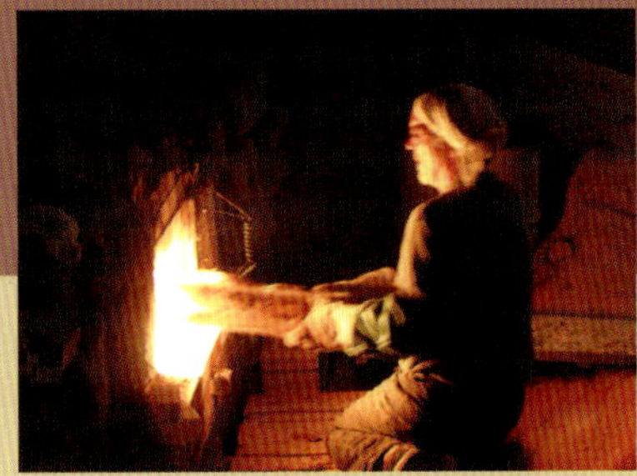

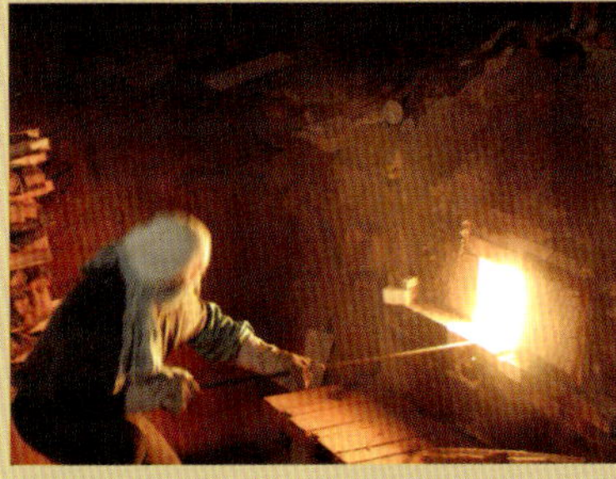

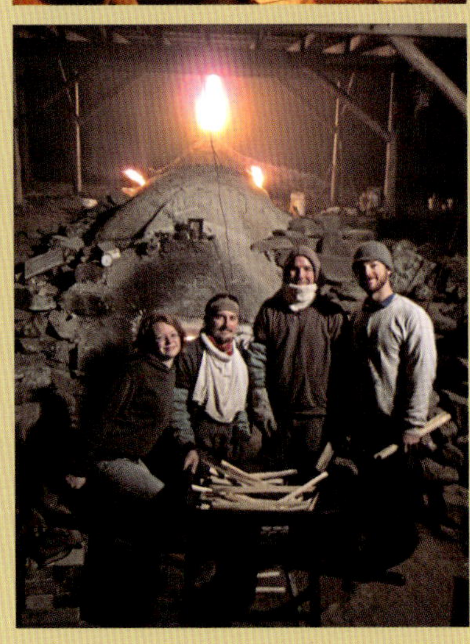

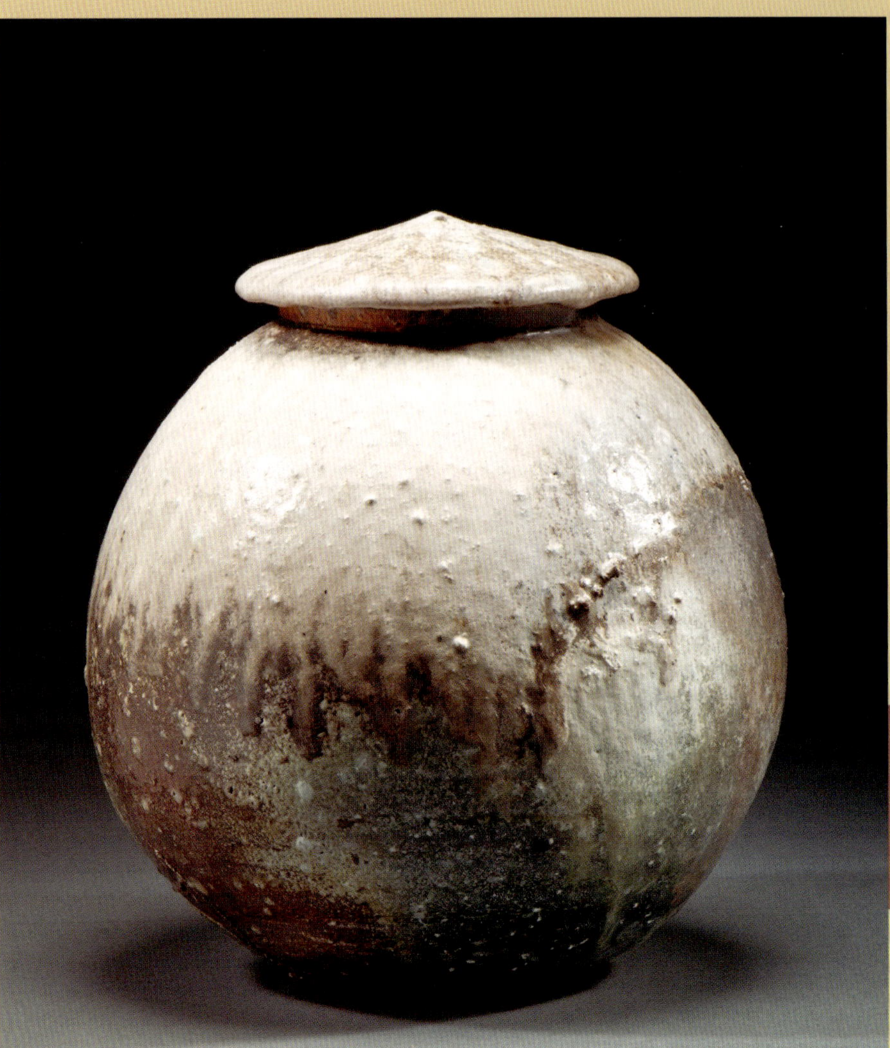

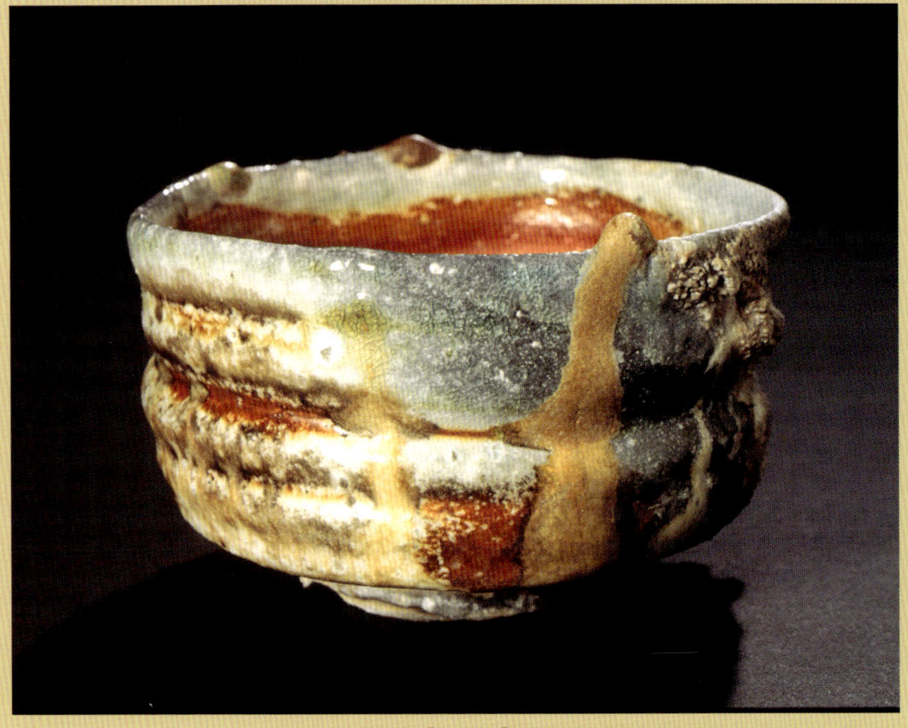

www.joebruhin.com

My kiln is an Anagama, which translates to cave kiln, it is half buried underground and measures 40 feet long. It requires ten days of constant attending and ten cords of split pine to achieve the results I seek and to complete one firing. The works from this kiln have a natural glaze, I do not apply glaze to the pots. The color and texture is caused by the climate, age and type of wood being used, atmospheric conditions inside the kiln caused by my intuition and experience, placement of the works, wood ash from the burning fuel melting into the clay, fire flashing the work and coals being maintained on the pots themselves. The blending of these variables results in endless variety of effects. **For more information on Joe's work, visit http://joebruhin.com or e-mail Joe at JoeBruhin@gmail.com.**

JOE BRUHIN

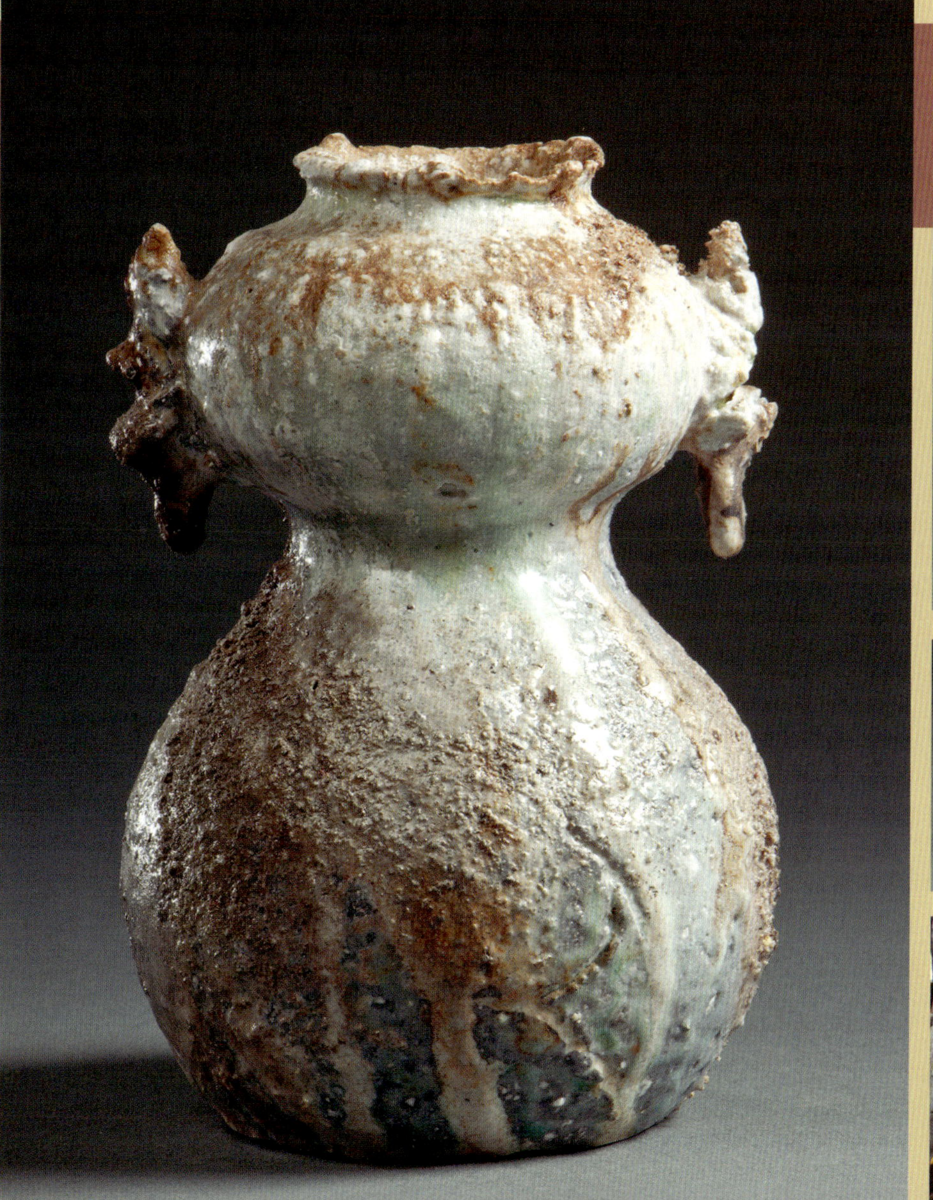

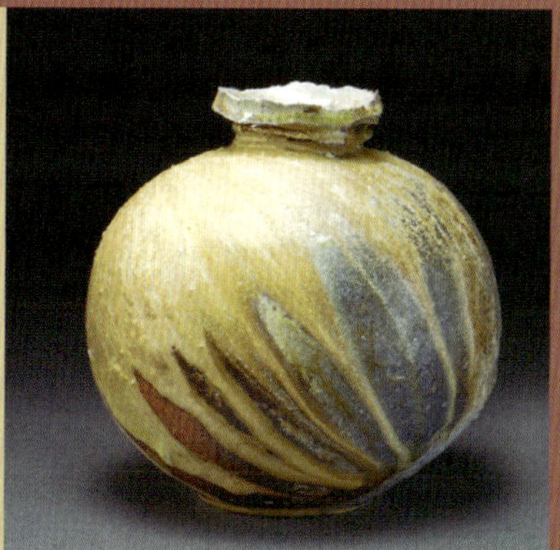

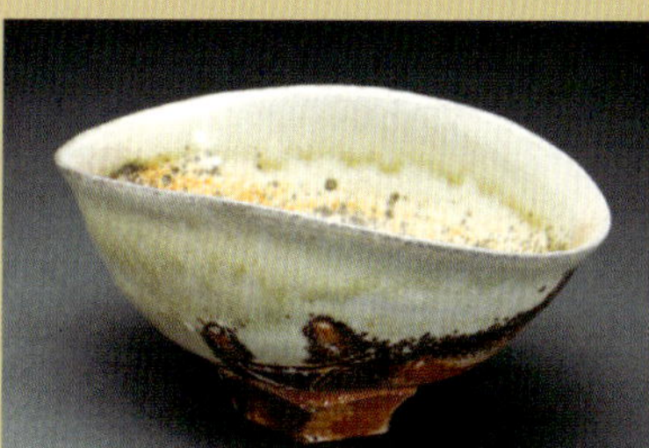

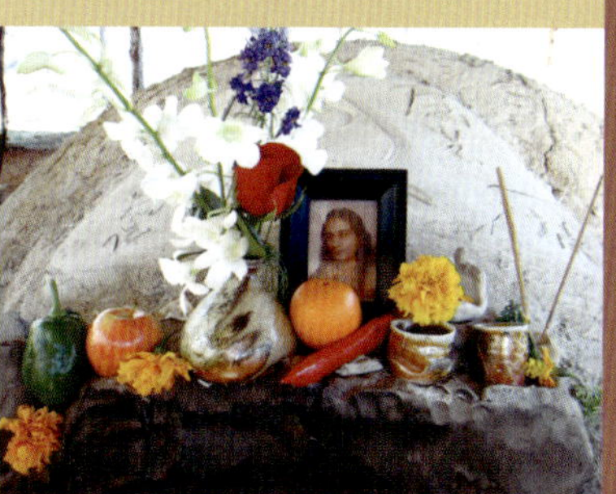

PHIL MUNDT

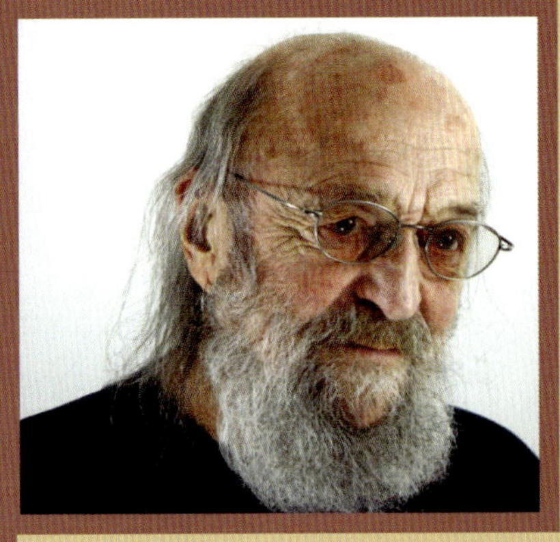

After receiving my B.S. and M.S. degrees in Art Education from the University of Wisconsin, I studied with such legendary glass and clay artisans as Harvey Littleton, Robert Turner, Don Reitz, Dale Chihuly and Kent Ipsen.

I taught ceramics for 18 years at Rich East high school in Park Forest, Illinois. My work has appeared at many of the top national art shows throughout the country and in galleries from Chicago to Santa Fe and Sedona.

I specialize in the process of Raku, an ancient Japanese form of pottery known for its spontaneity and random results. My forms are created with a combination of wheel throwing and slab building techniques. My inspiration comes from my respect for primitive art from many cultures.

In 2004, I moved to Yellville Arkansas and continue to show my work at art shows around the country. **For more information on Phil's work, visit: http://thorncreekstudio.com or e-mail: rakuphil@yahoo.com.**

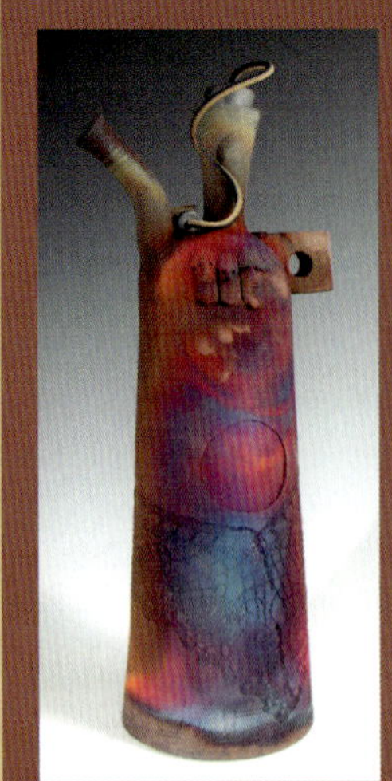

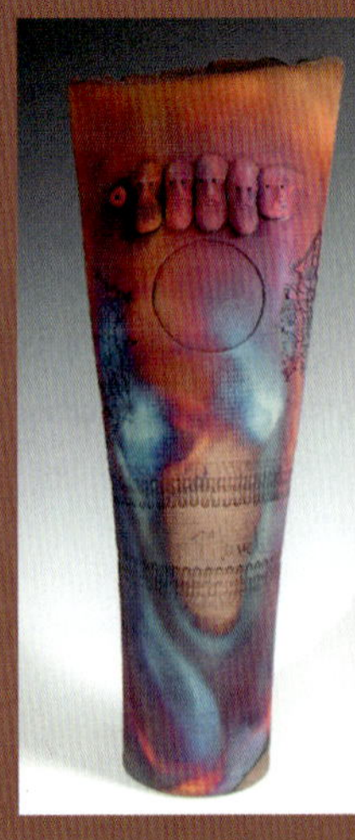

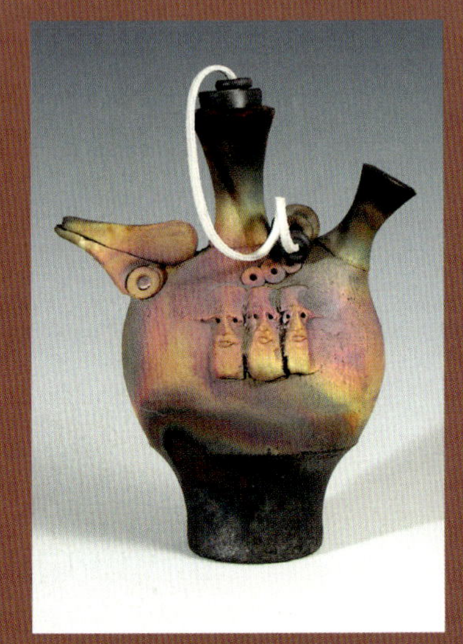

RAMONA JANE BUSS

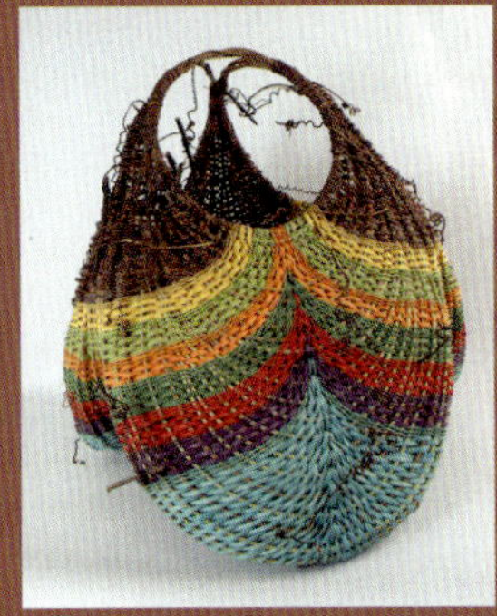

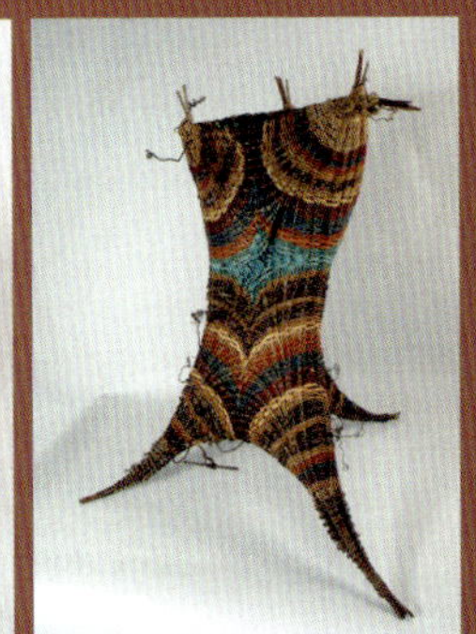

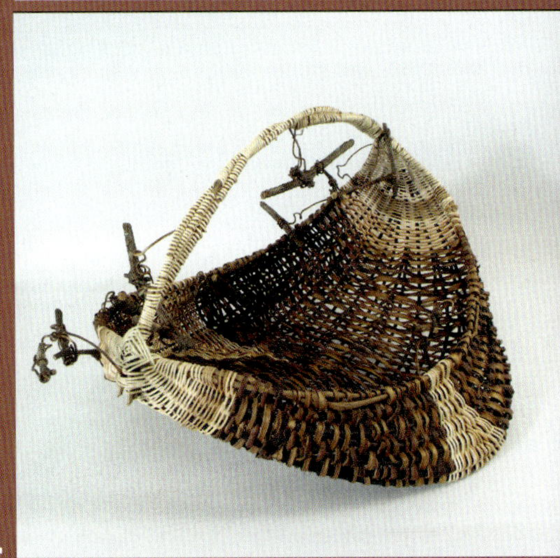

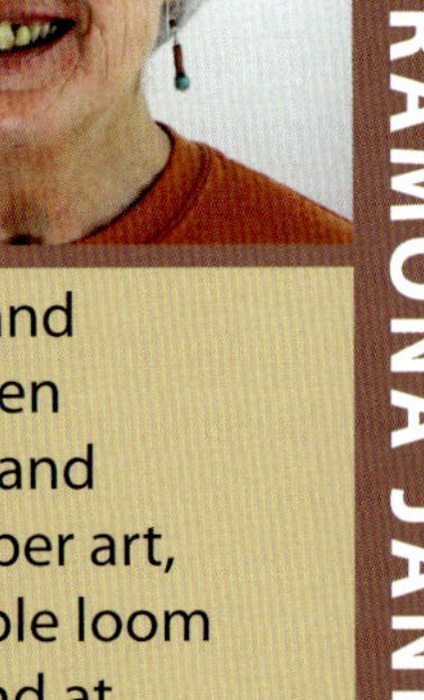

As a child, I spent my time playing in the woods near our farm house learning to appreciate nature and the wild flowe4rs in the spring and summer.

In 1975 I moved to Yellville, Arkansas where I found the woods to be more beautiful and pristine than any I had ever been in. I then began my study in the natural sciences and incorporated my long held interest in fiber art, including weaving, crocheting and simple loom weaving. All of this led me to try my hand at basket weaving, which allowed me to spend my time in nature gathering vine, bark and branches to use in my weaving.

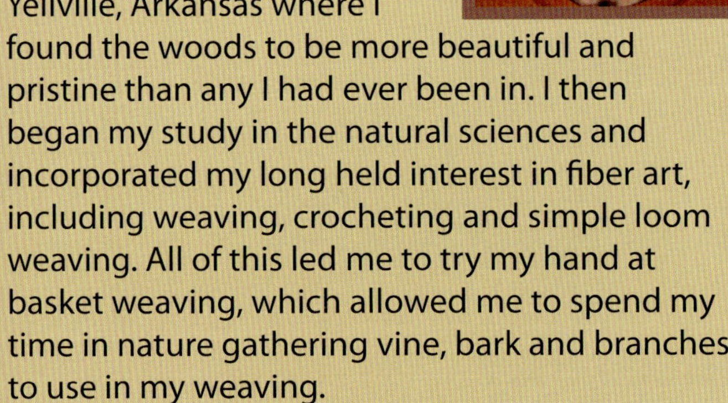

I have been showing my work as a professional fiber artist at top national shows throughout the country for many years. **For more information about Ramona's work, visit her at: http://www.thorncreekstudio.com.**

Susan Edgmon, an award winning artist, began painting in 1996. By her second painting, she knew art was going to be her destiny. She considers her style to be "realistic, with a flair." Subjects include all things in nature such as flowers, animals, landscapes and people.

Her originals and prints are in collections in the USA, as well as seven foreign countries. She is a signature member of the Artists of Northwest Arkansas and the Ozark Pastel Society. Her paintings have been published in two books, "The Best of American Pastel, Vol II" and "The Best of American Watermedia, Vol II." Susan teaches workshops and classes at her studio and gallery, Edgmon Art, in Gravette, Arkansas.
http://www.susanedgmon.com

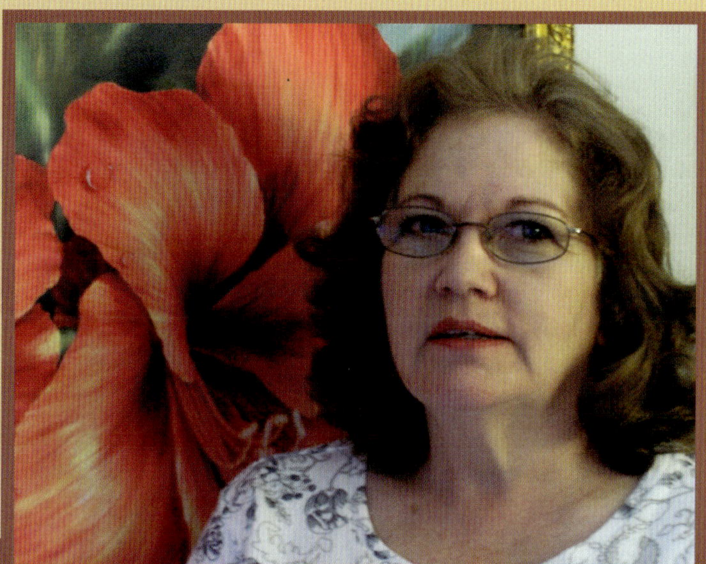

SUSAN EDGMON

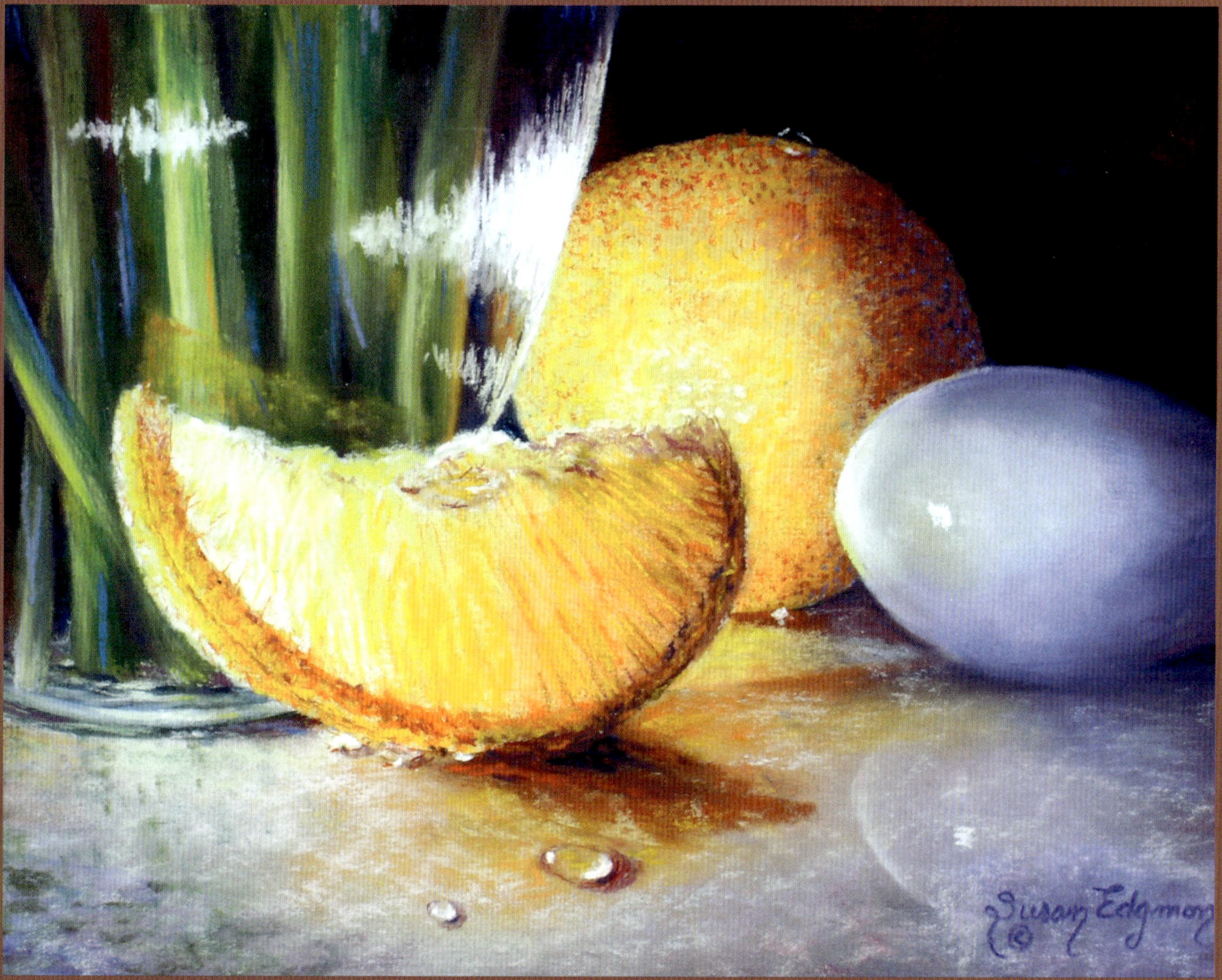

"Painting has brought an acute awareness of the joy and wonderful beauty that is all around us every day, no matter the weather or the season. You don't need a large landscape to appreciate the beauty in the world; you can find it in an area as small as a single flower."

For more information on Susan's work, visit her website at: http://www.susanedgmon.com or check out her shopping area at: http://www.shop.edgmonart.com.

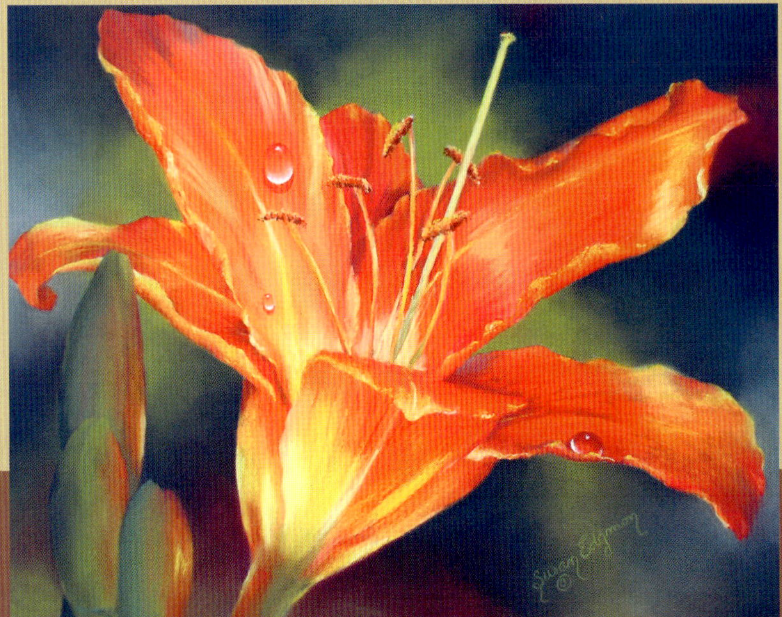

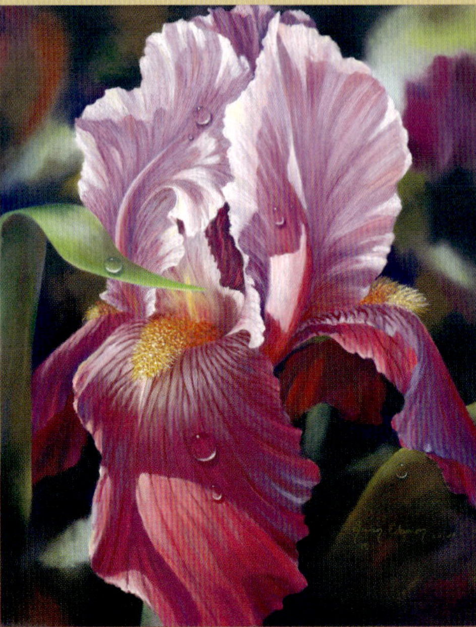

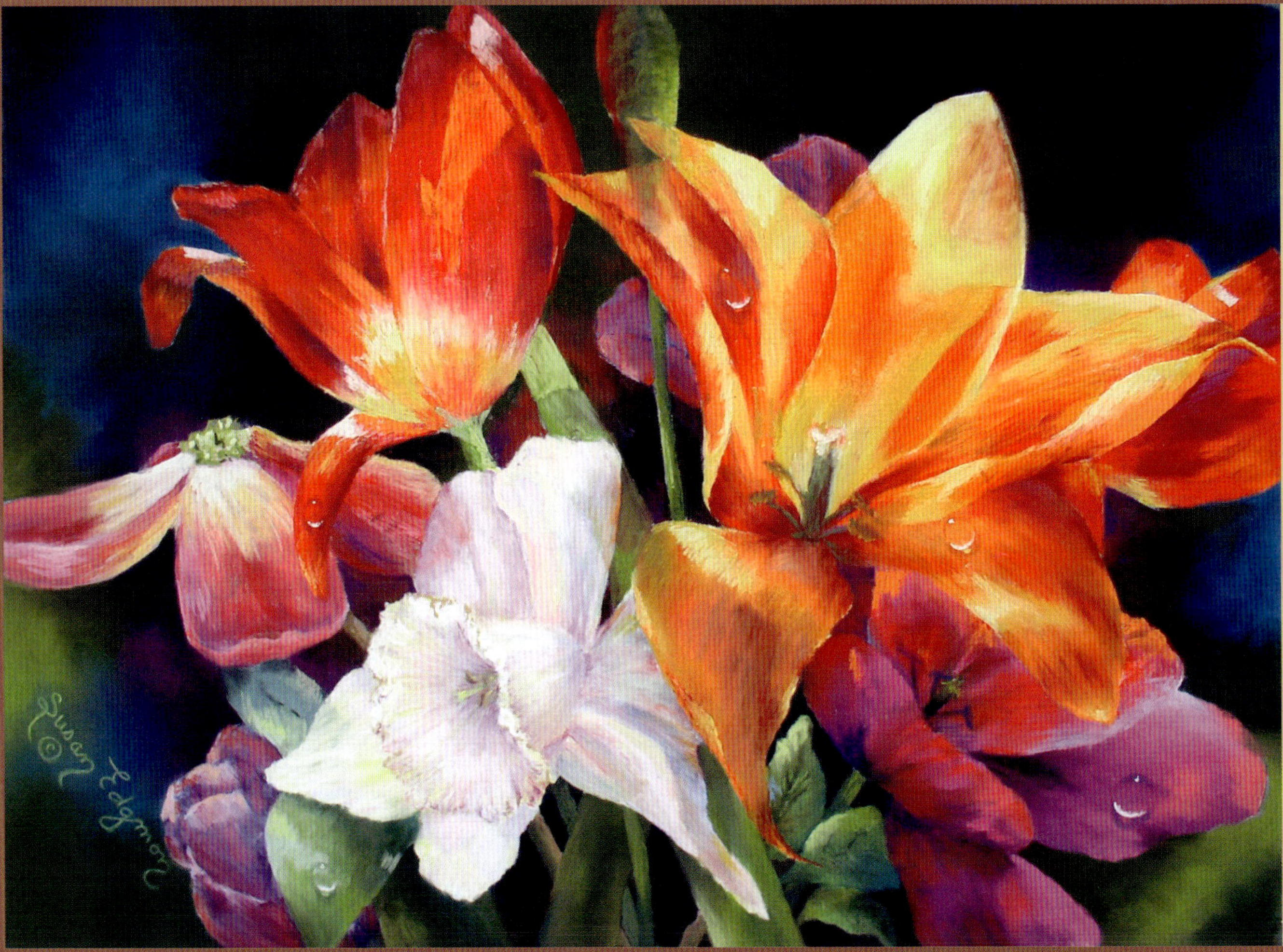

In addition to painting, Susan has taken her experience as an artist to create, design and patent a unique Plein Aire and travel box. The Edgmon Easel Box is a combination easel and storage box that mounts on a camera tripod. Each box is custom made out of Alder at the family woodshop in beautiful northwest Arkansas. Each is a piece of art. They are made by Artists for Artists. She has traveled with groups of artists to France and Italy to paint on location using the Edgmon Easel Box. **For more information, visit http://www.edgmonart.com or e-mail Susan directly at: susan@susanedgmon.com.**

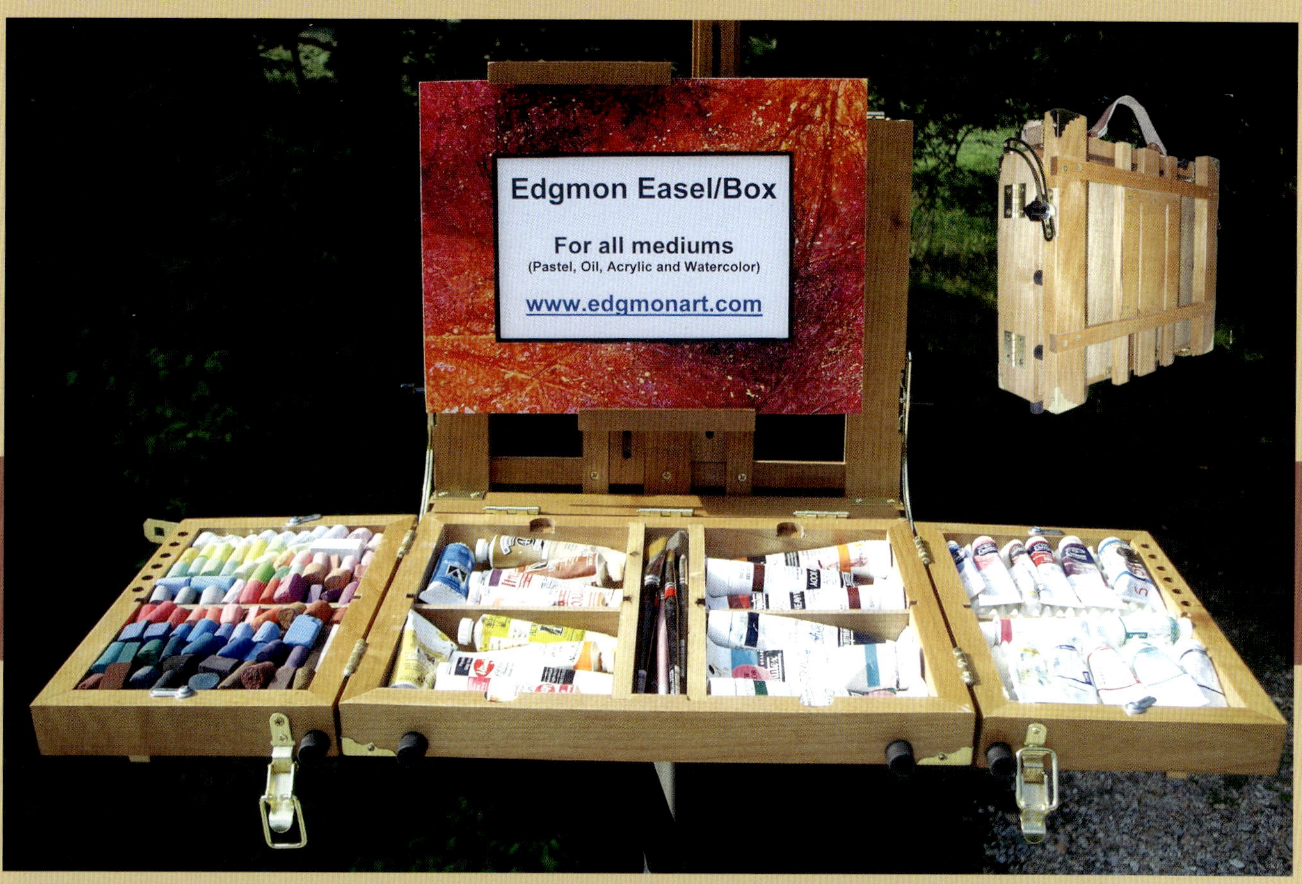

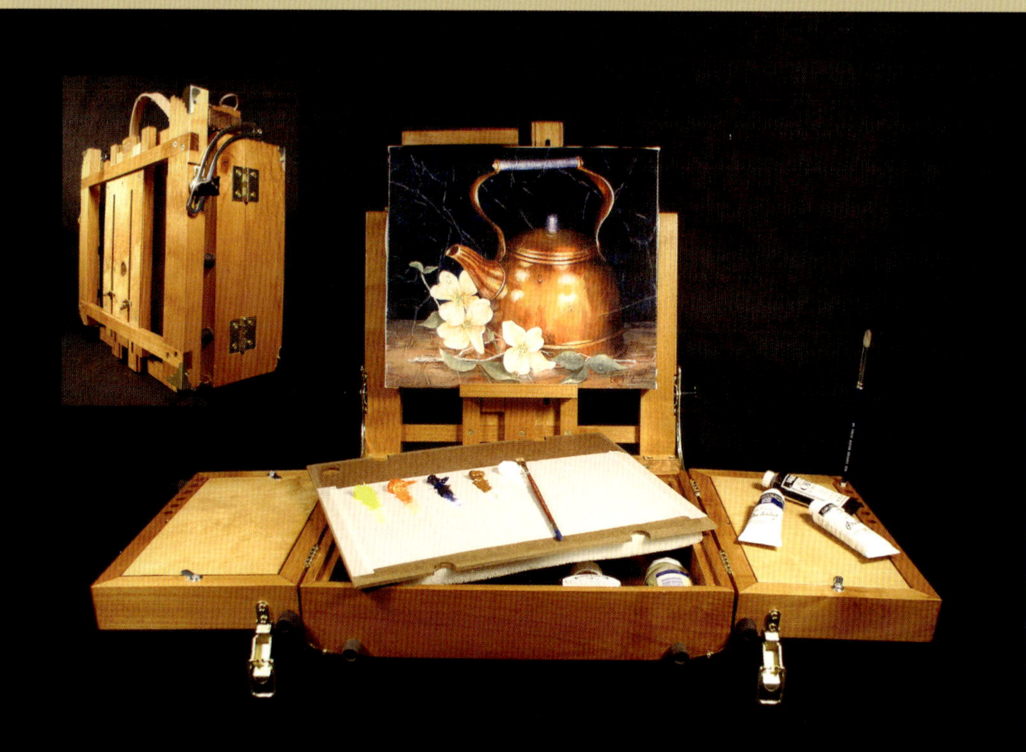

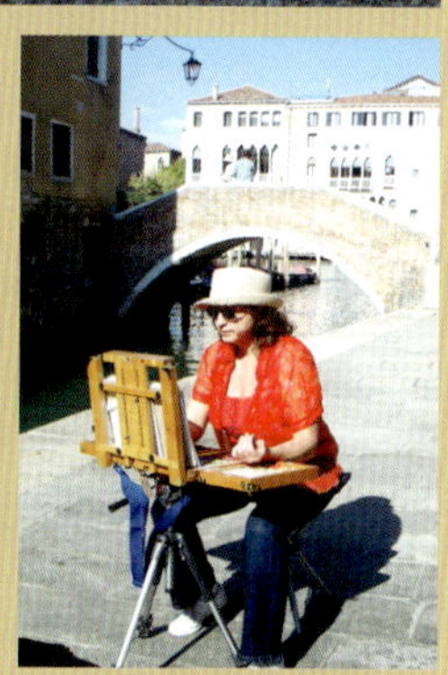

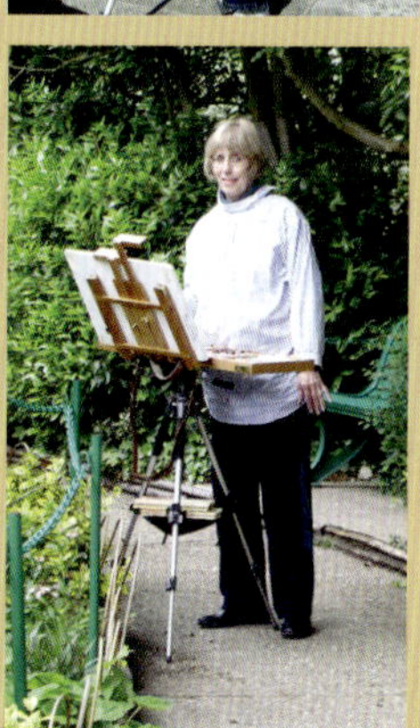

BARBARA CHAPPELL

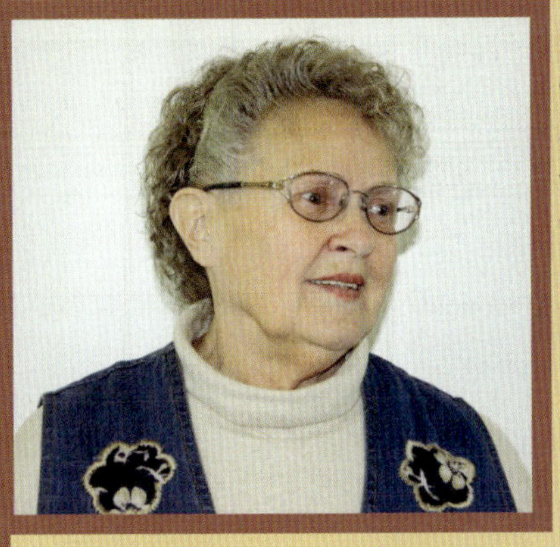

Barbara Chappell was born and raised in West Texas. As an adult she has lived and vacationed in several states. When she visited the Ozarks, she knew this was where she wanted to retire.

Barbara has always loved "Wood Art." In her travels to the Caribbean Islands and down the Amazon, she collected "found wood," native wood carvings and other wood souvenirs.

After retiring to Peel, Arkansas in 2005, she focused her efforts in wood carving and working with unusually shaped "found wood."

Her carving talent has earned her a "Best of Show" and numerous blue ribbons in the county, district and State fairs. She has also displayed her art at various art festivals in the Ozarks.
For more information about Barbara's work, visit: http://paletteartleague.org/BarbaraChappell.html.

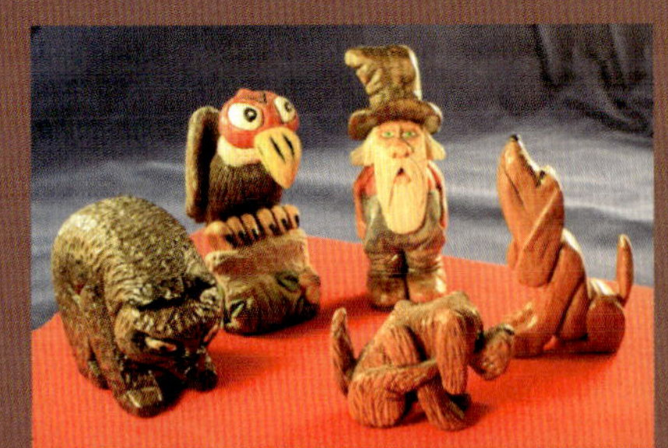

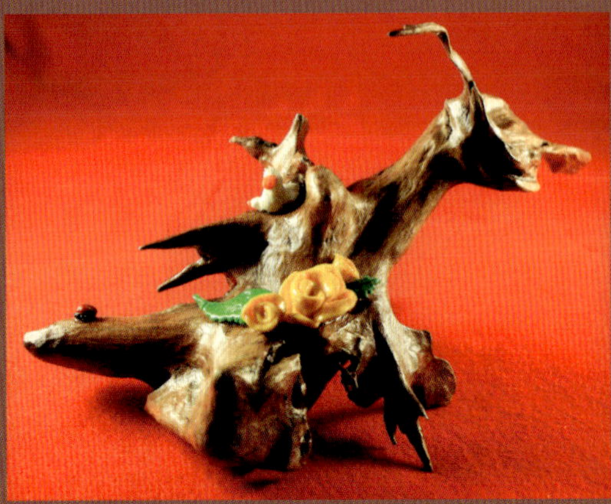

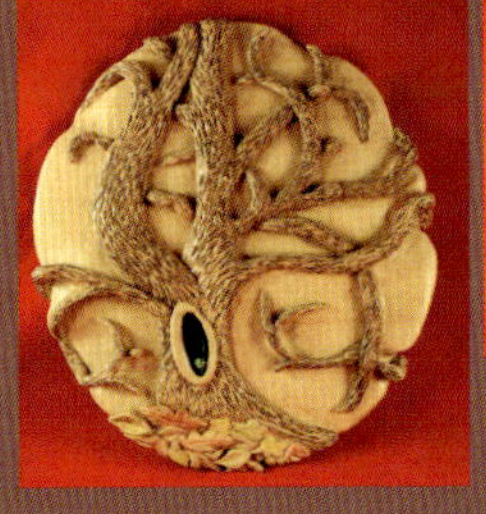

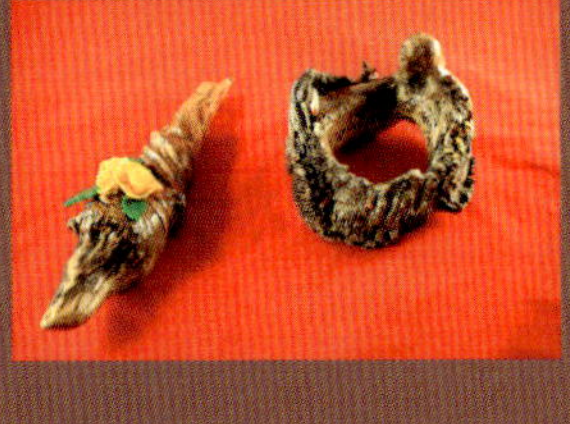

STEVE AND SUSIE HOSKINSON

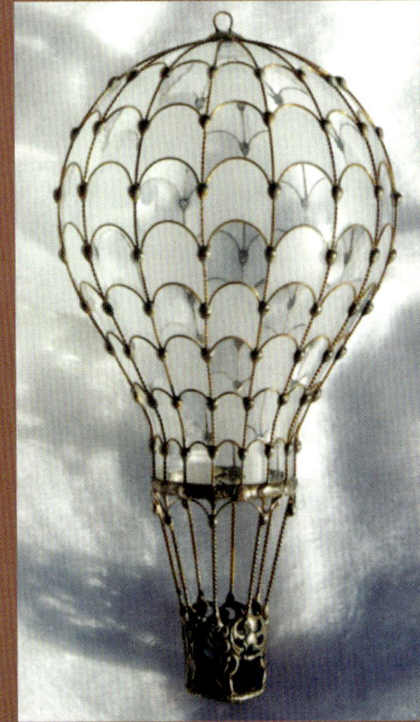

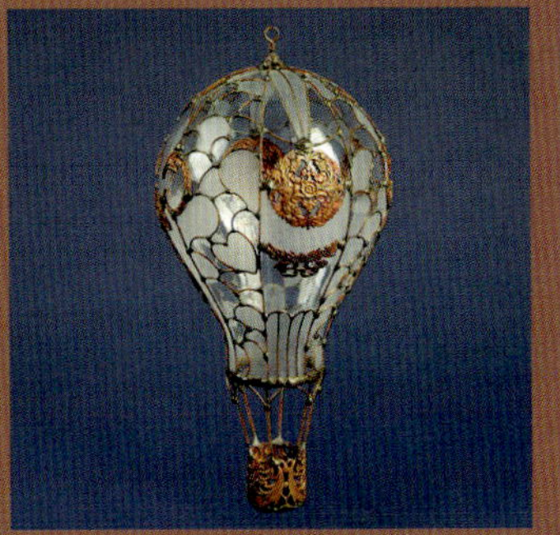

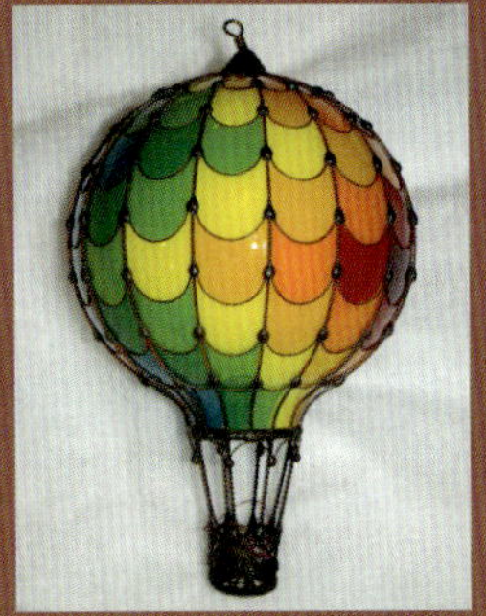

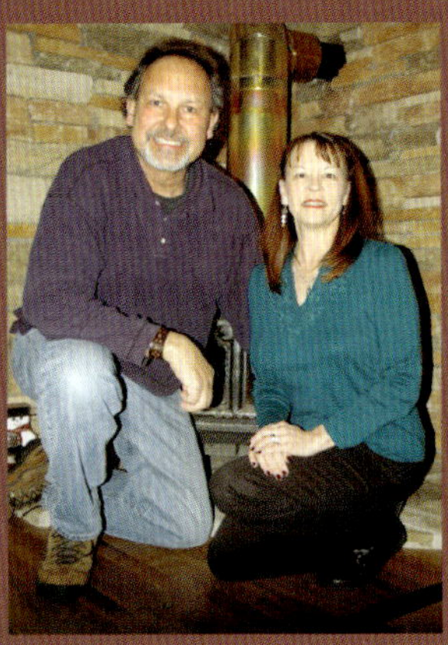

Steve & Susie Hoskinson are artists in the most traditional sense of the word. When they learned that the creator and only artisan who specialized in this art form was retiring and had no one to pass the tradition on to, Steve & Susie stepped in and have never looked back! Not only is their artwork beautiful and whimsical, but it is also Green". Their art is created by recycling light bulbs. So, the next time someone asks you what the old energy guzzling light bulbs are good for, you can tell them they are perfectly suited to become Glass Hot Air Balloon Collectibles. **For more information on Steve & Susie Hoskinson's work, visit their website at www.designsbysteveandsusie.com or call them at 417-725-9223.**

I have always loved the Ozarks, but my husband, my four children and I had to move to Texas to make a living. We first moved to Fayetteville Arkansas where I majored in all-level Art Education. We left there to take a job at Texas A&M Commerce where I finished my degree.

Over the years I have taught children's art in my own studio and Adult Continued Education at the University.

After retirement and thirty years later, we returned to our beloved Cotter, Arkansas where we renovated our family home, Hopkinswood, built in 1914 into a B&B.

I decided to pursue my interest in art more seriously since retiring. I joined three art associations and I've taken classes in four of our communities. Every day is an adventure in painting. Whether it is interpreting our surroundings or our emotions, it's a labor of love. **For more information on Marilyn's work, visit: http://paletteartleague.org/MarilynMorris.html.**

MARILYN MORRIS

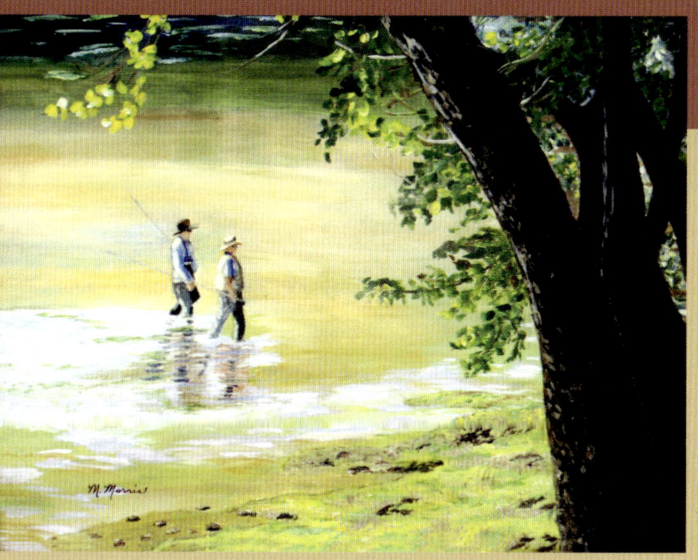

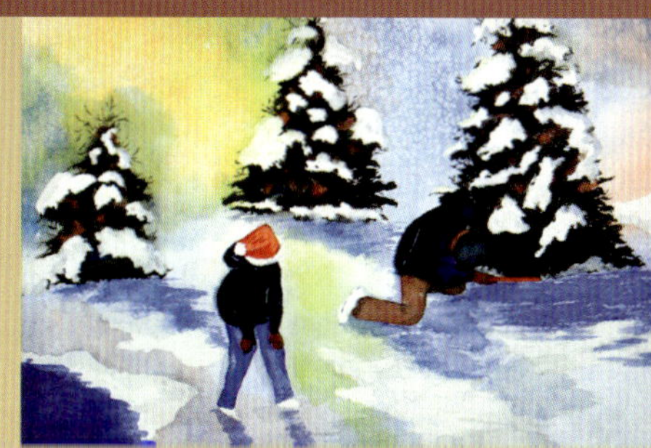

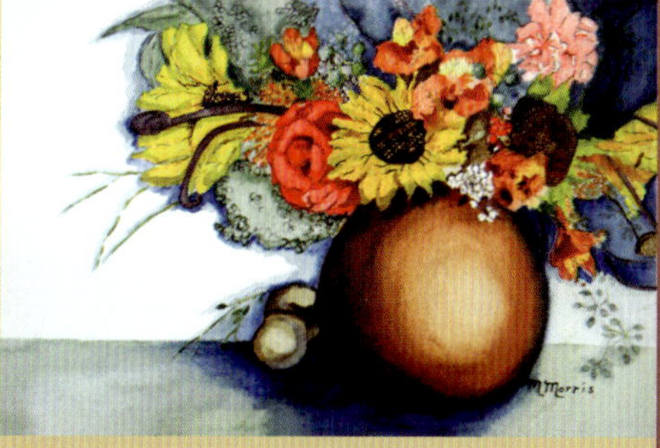

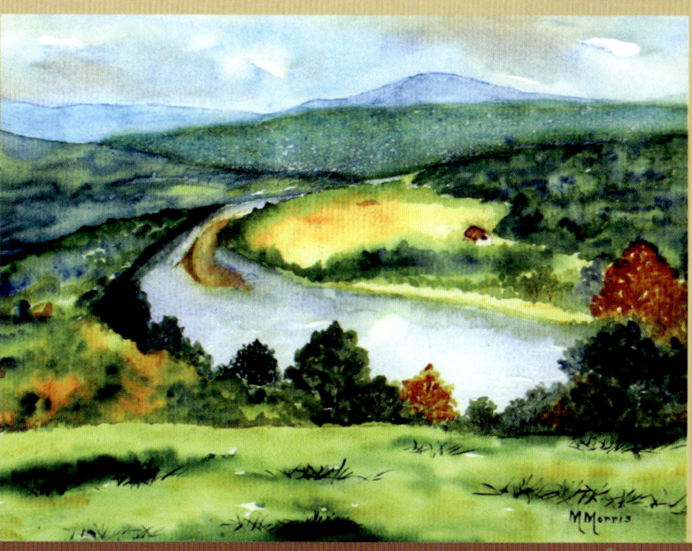

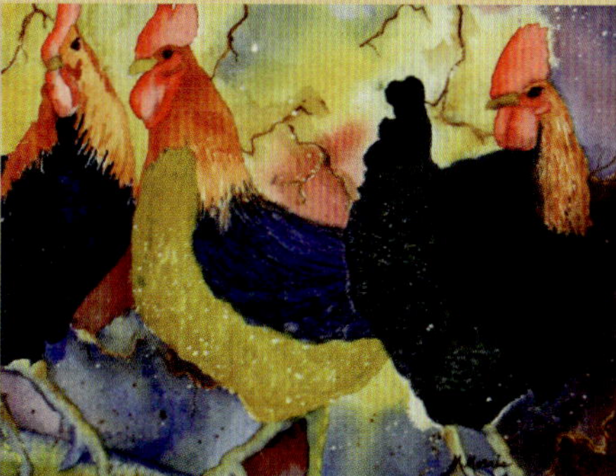

DONNA J. CRENSHAW

Donna J. Crenshaw, a Tennessee native, has lived and studied in Arkansas most of her adult life. She currently resides in Hot Spring, Arkansas. Striving to more fully express her inner visions and a mood or statement about her subject, she continues to study techniques. Primarily a portraitist, she interviews her client and the subject, followed by one to three photo sessions and a quick color study. After photographing her subjects she usually requests a brief sitting before completing the portrait in oil.

"I strive to make a statement about my subject's personality in each composition. A mood or feeling about the subject should be evoked, and sometimes one is able to achieve a composition appealing in its own right. This is always my goal." **For more information about Donna's work, visit: http://paletteartleague.org/DonnaCrenshaw.html.**

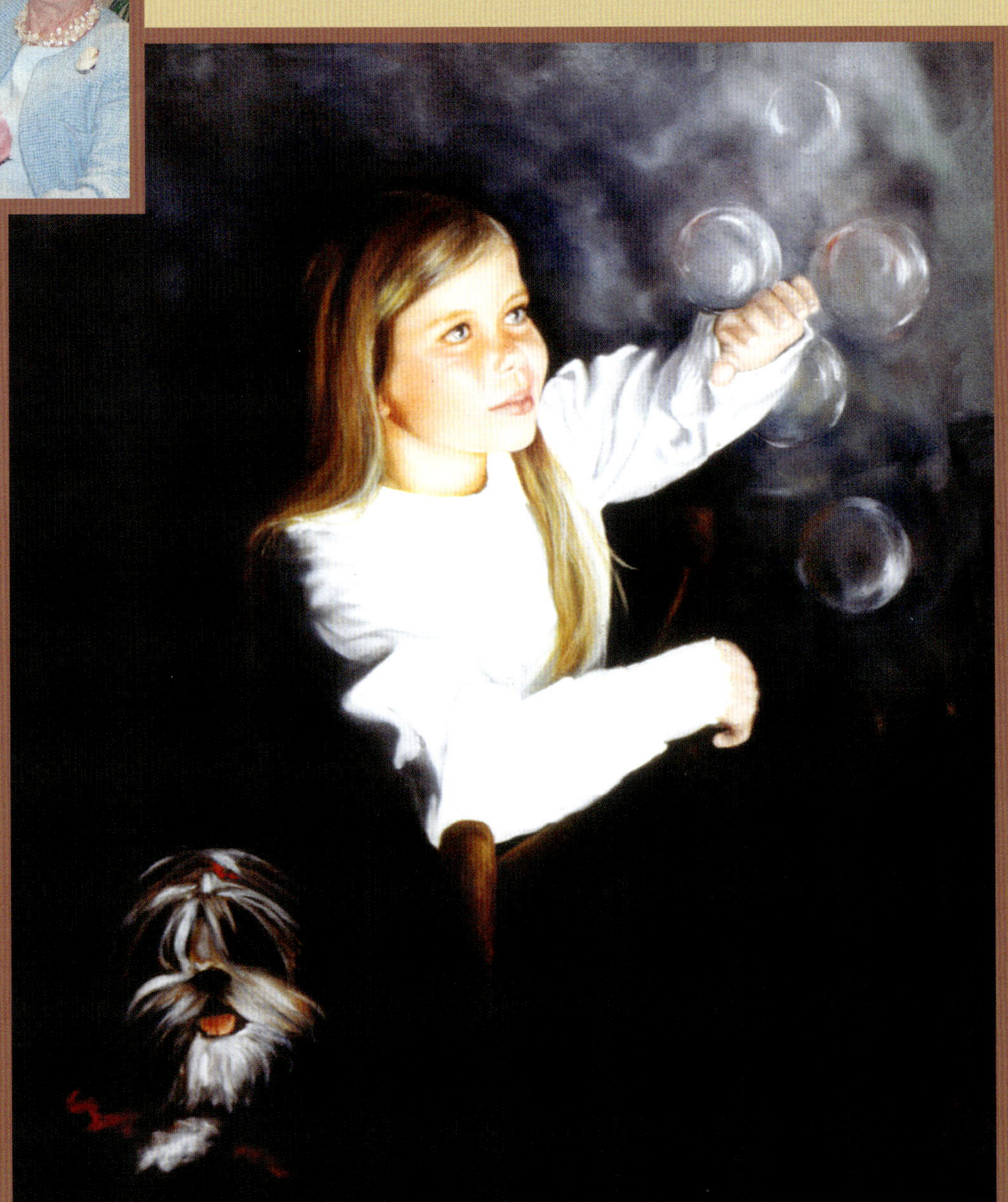

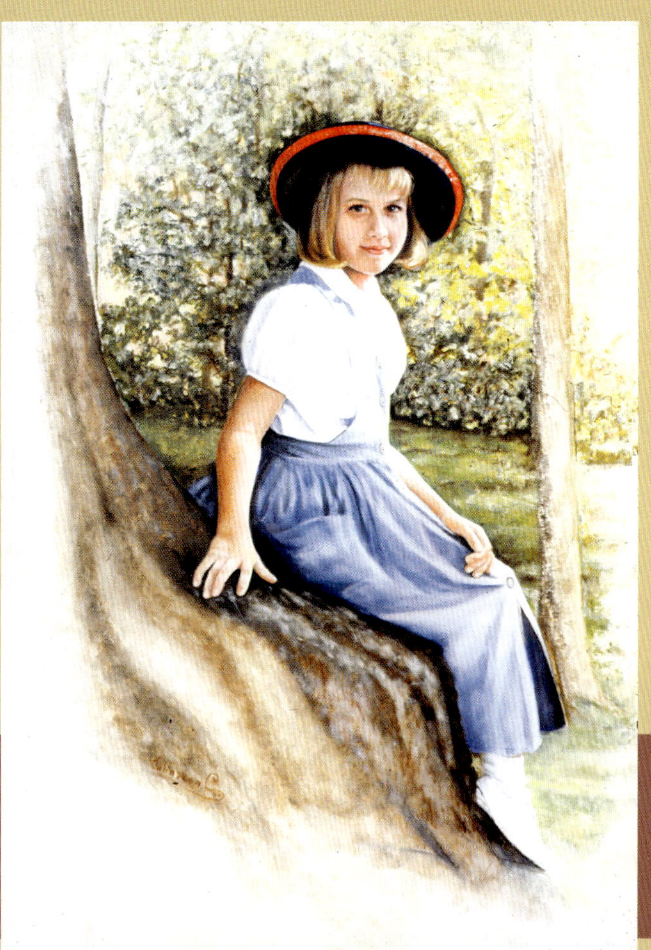
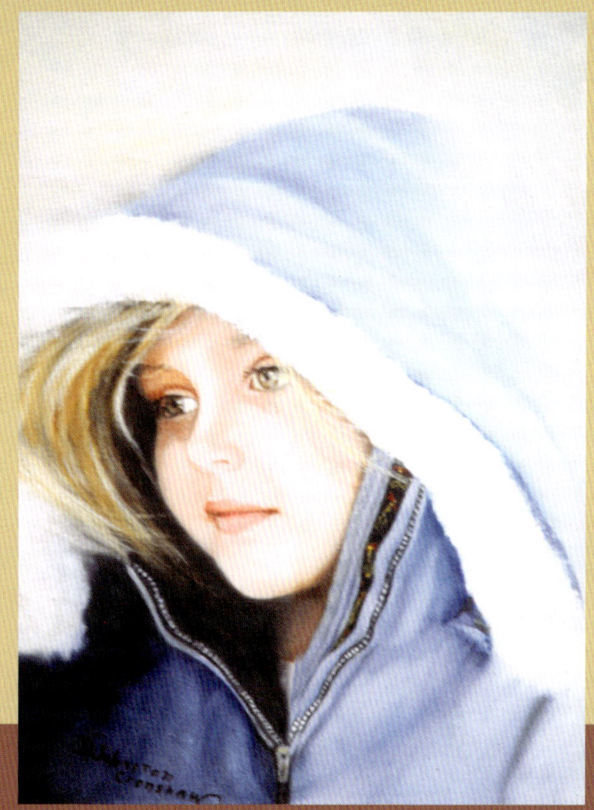
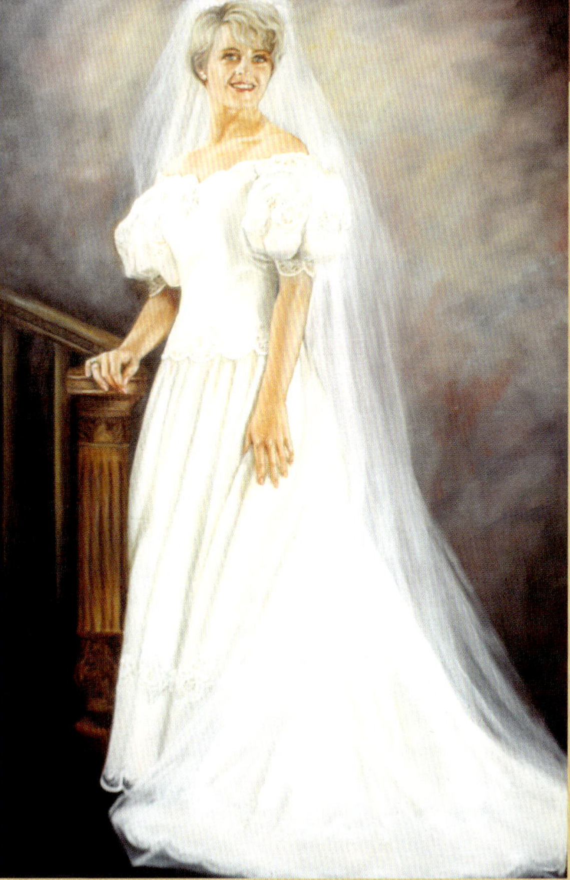
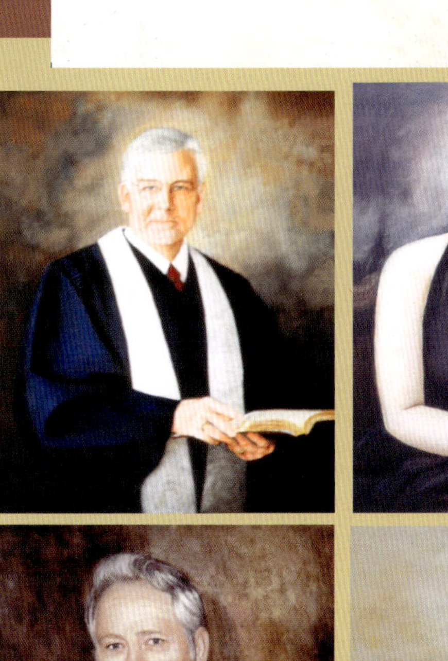
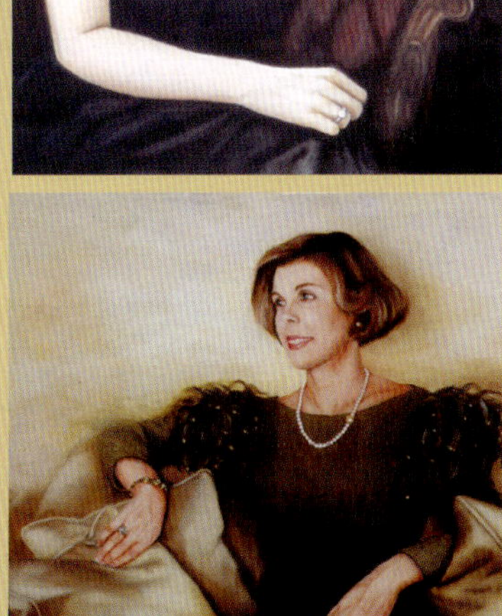
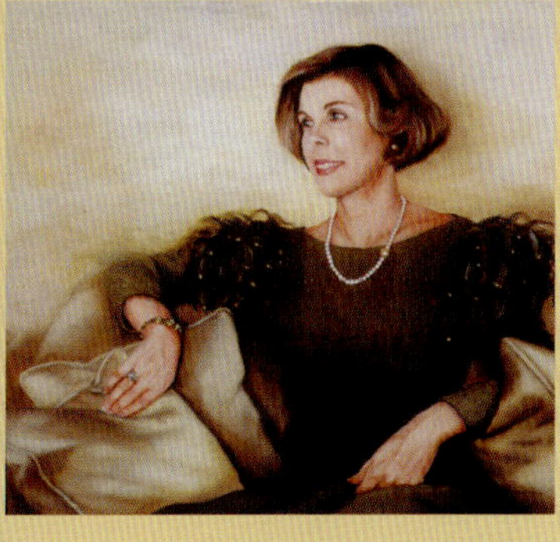

DONNA J. CRENSHAW

RICK COOK

Rick's love of art began at an early age and continued with UAFS art classes. His enjoyment of the outdoors is reflected in his art subjects. Furniture, wall art, and table art are hand-carved or lathe worked primarily using natural wood tones. In addition, he paints landscapes in oils. His art has shown in several galleries and art shows including The Arkansas Studies Institute Gallery in Little Rock, Arkansas. A wood sculpture, Autumn Trails in Arkansas, was in the Governor's 2009 Arkansas Artist Calendar and shown with Senator Mark Pryor's, A Celebration of Arkansas Artists, in 2009. A wood sculpture is on permanent display at Mt. Magazine Lodge.

Rick and his wife Pam have one son, Ryan who is happily married to Shalee. Rick and Pam are also the proud grandparents of Natalee 3 and Drake 1-month. **For more information on Rick's work, visit: http://paletteartleague.org/RickCook.html or e-mail Rick at pcook356@gmail.com.**

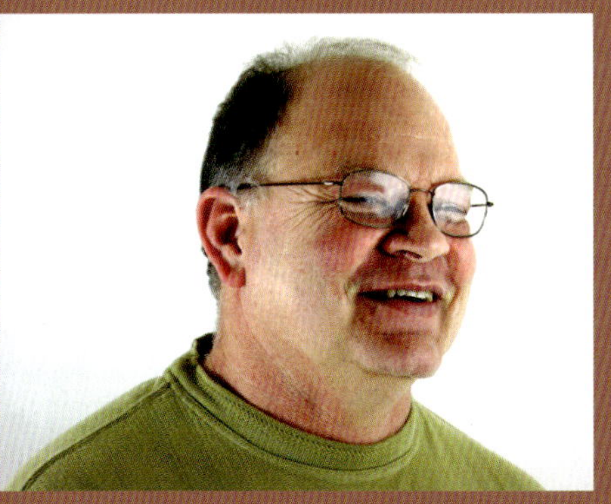

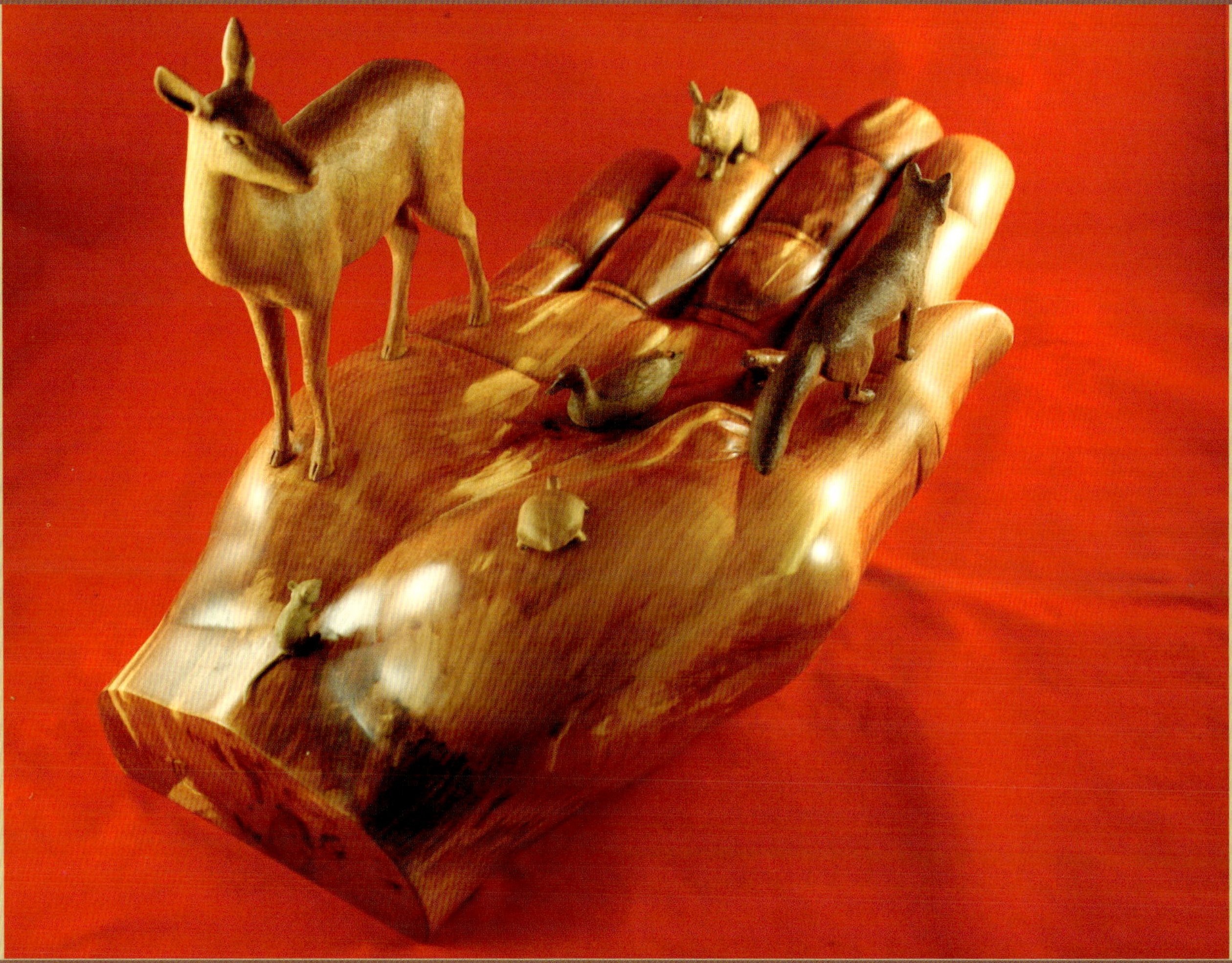

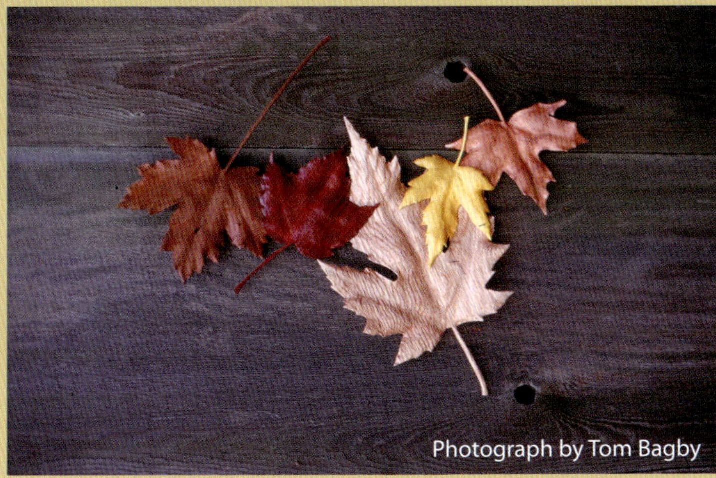
Photograph by Tom Bagby

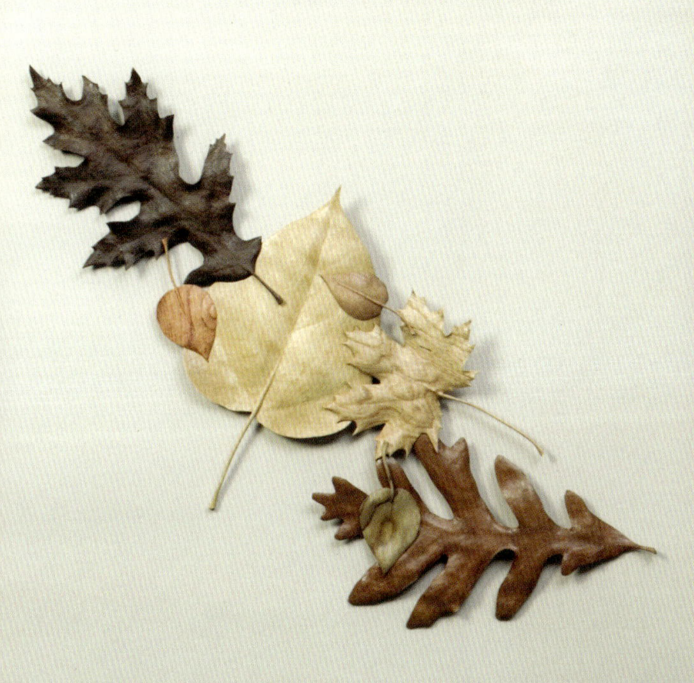
Photograph by Cindy Momchilou

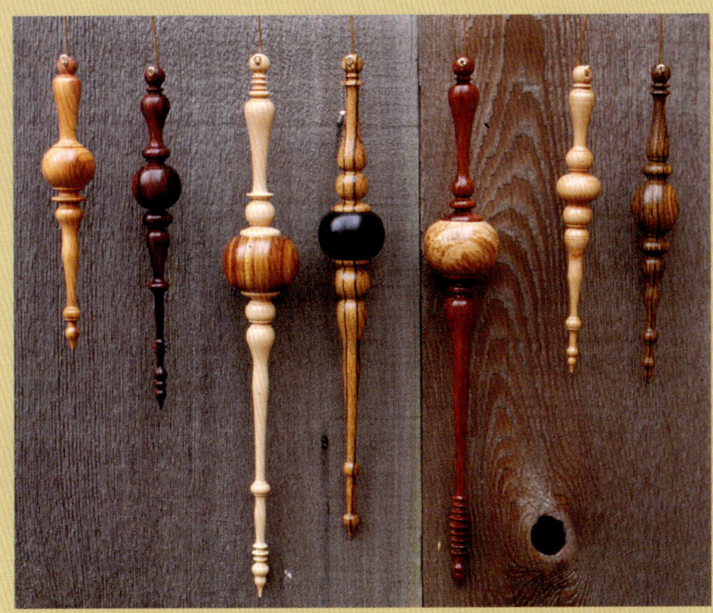
Photograph by Tom Bagby

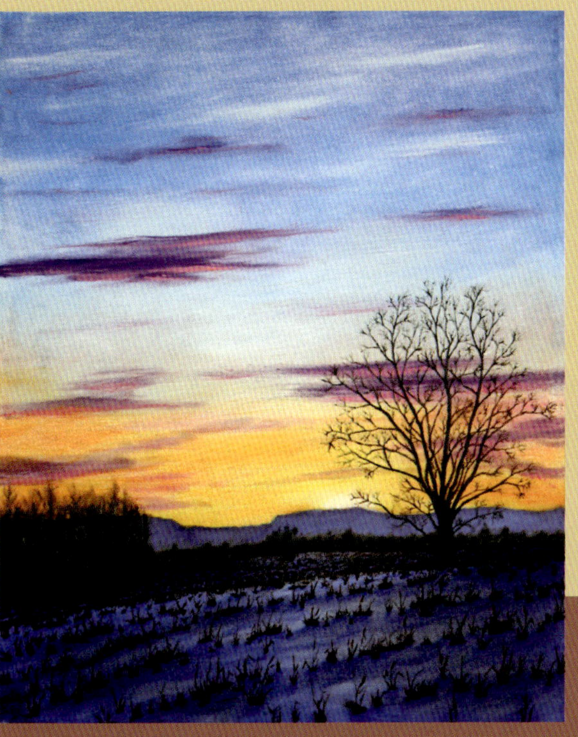

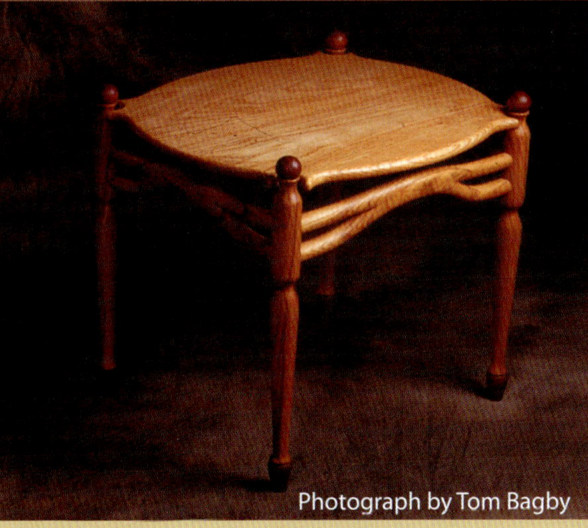
Photograph by Tom Bagby

DANA JOHNSON

Moving from west Texas as a teenager, to the beautiful Ozarks, I discovered that I had found my true home, "the green Ozark Mountains". After graduating from High School, I worked at a variety of jobs while pursing my art. I studied Art at the local college and was fortunate enough to attend many workshops with top Ozark artists.

My artistic experiences have primarily developed from the continuous absorption and observations of my ever-changing surroundings. I attribute much of my success and inherited talent to Jo Rowell who is not only a distinguished and successful instructor here in the Ozarks, but she is also my mother and mentor.

I enjoy painting commissioned portraits, florals, Ozarks landscapes and area wildlife. I work in many mediums, including oils, pastel, watercolor, pen and ink, and fine china painting.

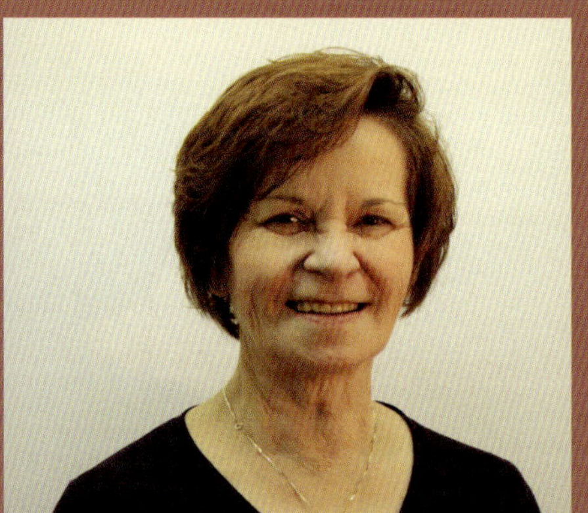

I have shown in many galleries in Arkansas and Texas. I currently have work being shown in The Palette Art League's Fine Art Gallery in Yellville, Arkansas. My artwork may be found in private collections in Arkansas, Oklahoma, Texas, Missouri, Mississippi, Wyoming and several countries in Europe.

For more information on Dana's work, visit her website at: http://paletteartleague.org/DanaJohnson.html.

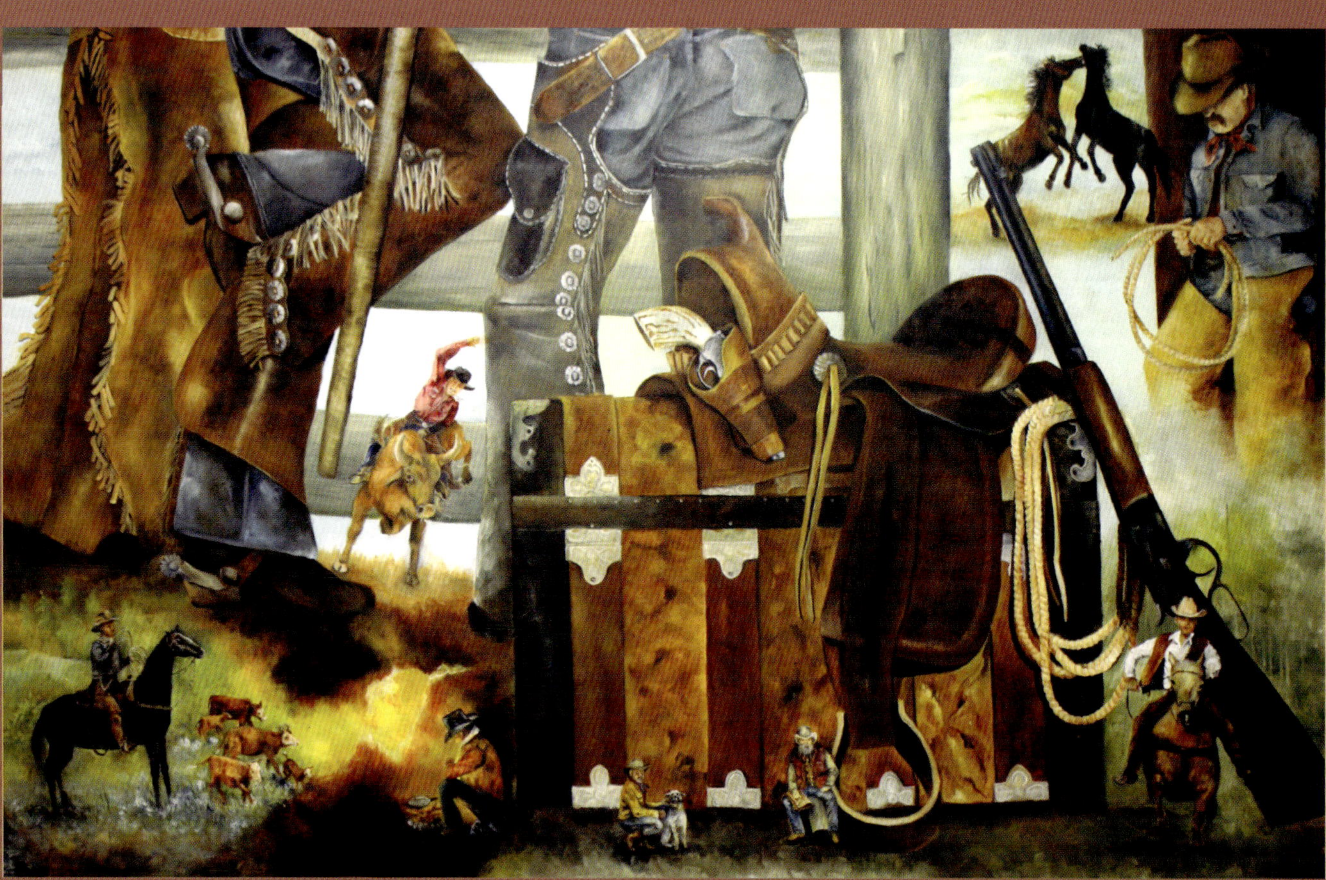

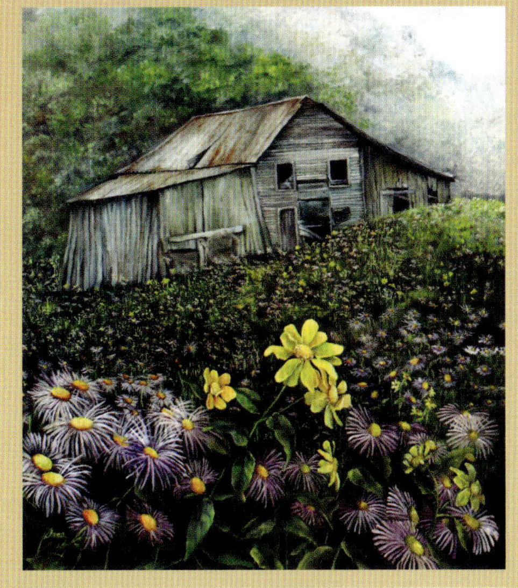
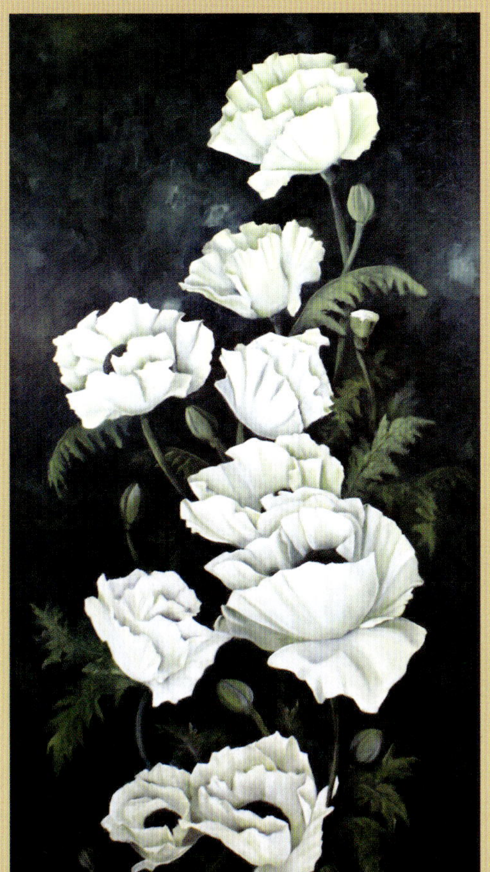
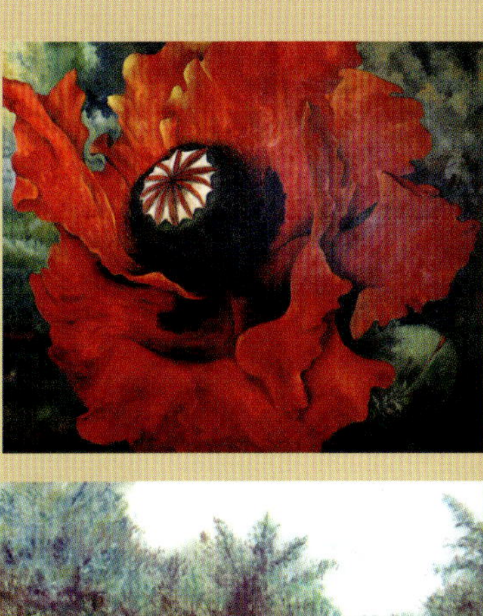
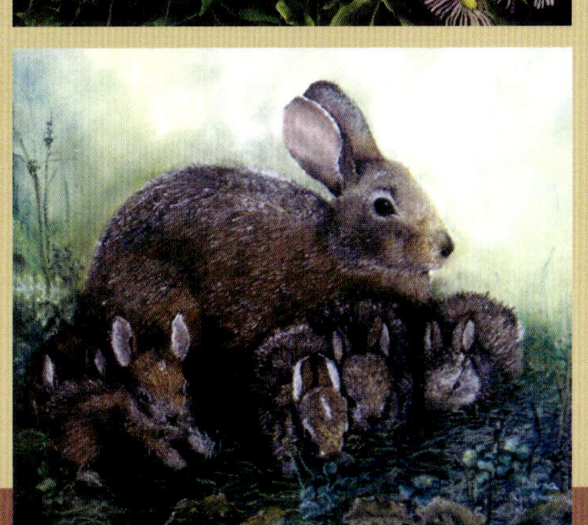
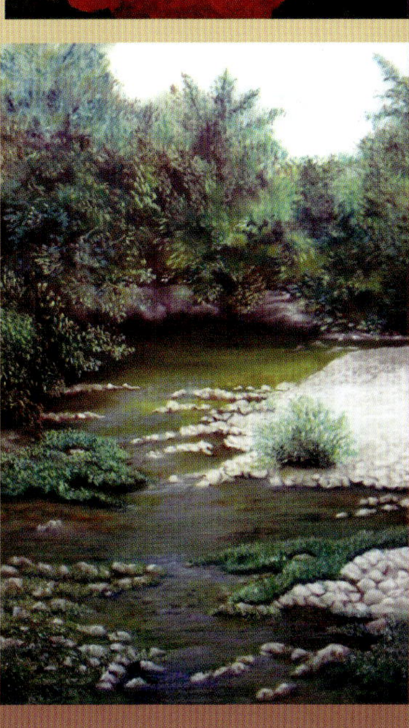

DANA JOHNSON

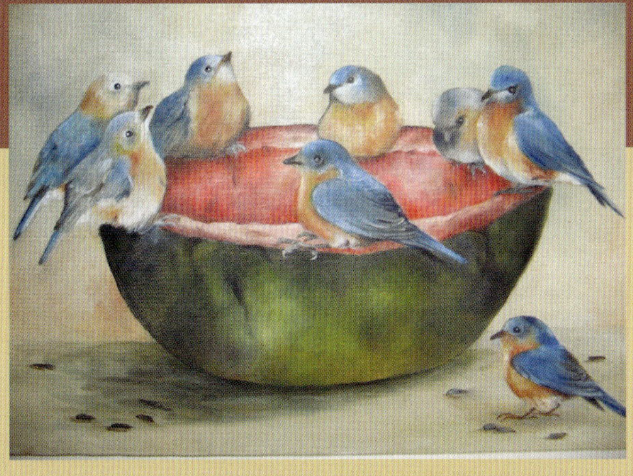
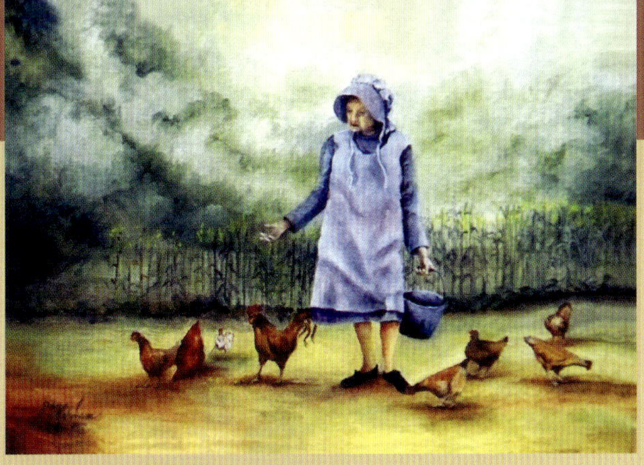
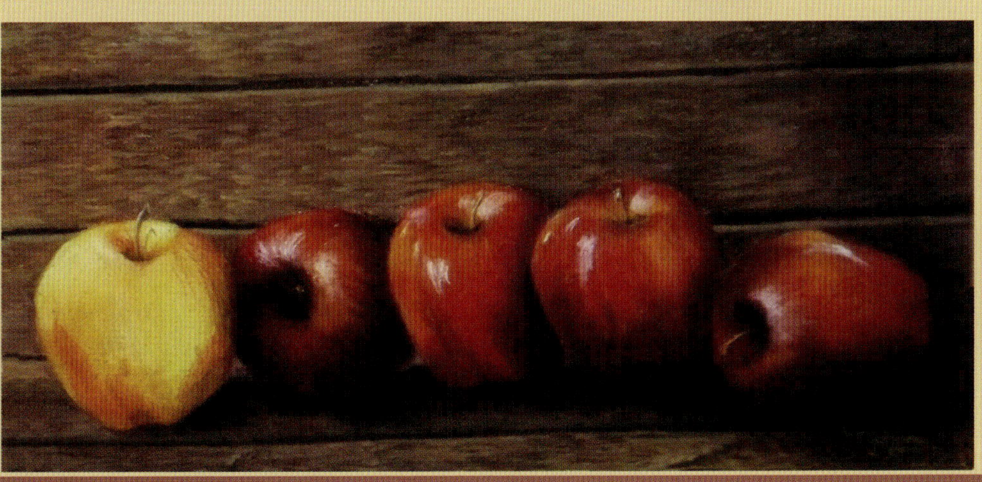
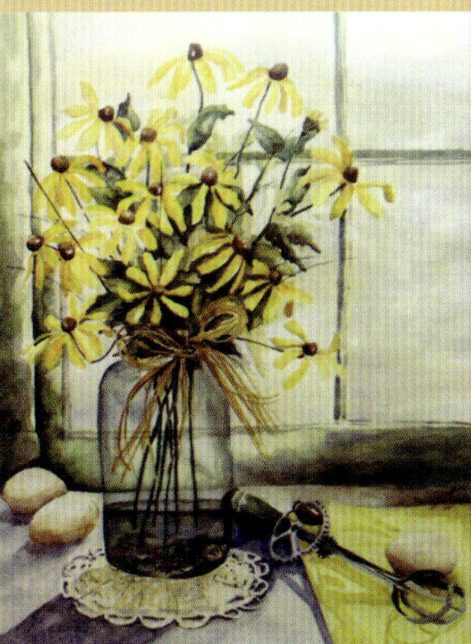

MISTY BAKER

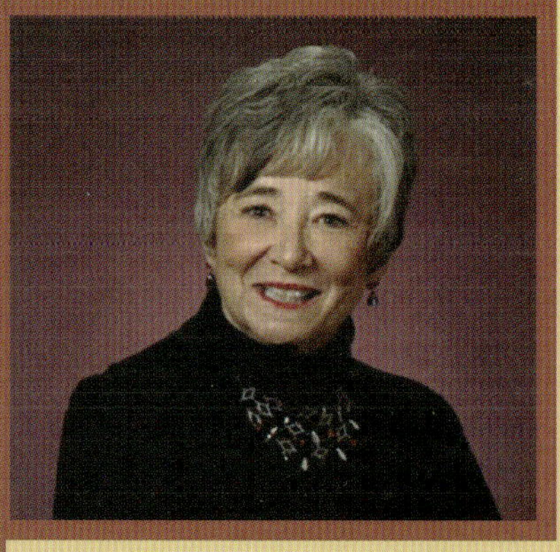

A great love of being busy and developing new ideas is what I thrive on. My father was an artist and did stained glass for 30+ years until lead poisoning stopped him. He passed away, but the idea for my Elegant DeLites actually came to me in the middle of a night. Could I develop a process to appear as stained glass on the bottles, and light them besides? It took me over 18 months to prefect the process – ordering supplies from other countries and mixing my own paints.

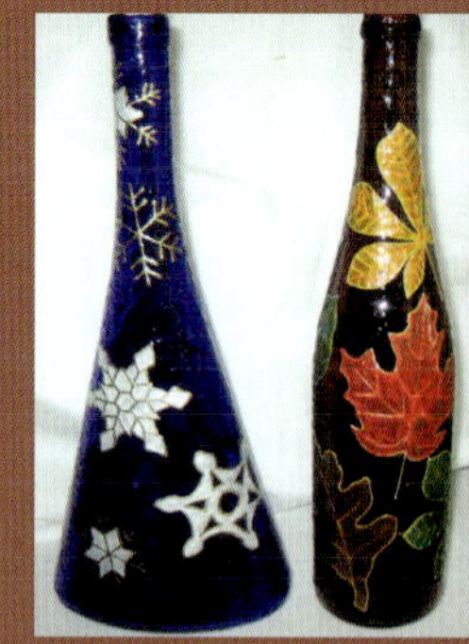

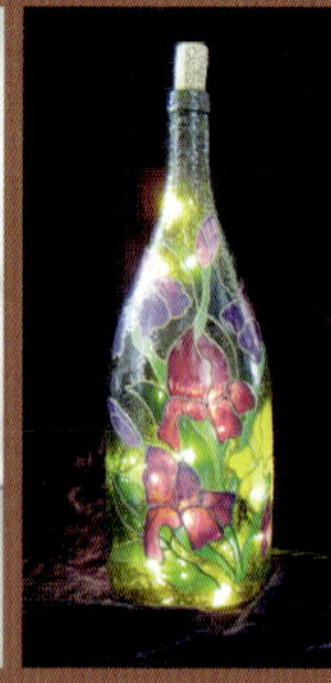

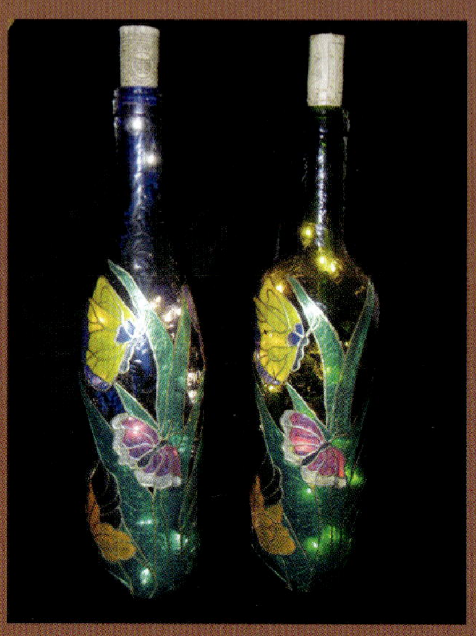

I love what I am doing! Even if others copy this unique art, I will never lose the wonderful feeling of sharing my Elegant DeLites with my dad! I share every "WOW!" with him. **For more information on Misty's work, visit her at http://www.elegantdelites.com or e-mail her at misty@elegantdelites.com.**

BECCA MARIE

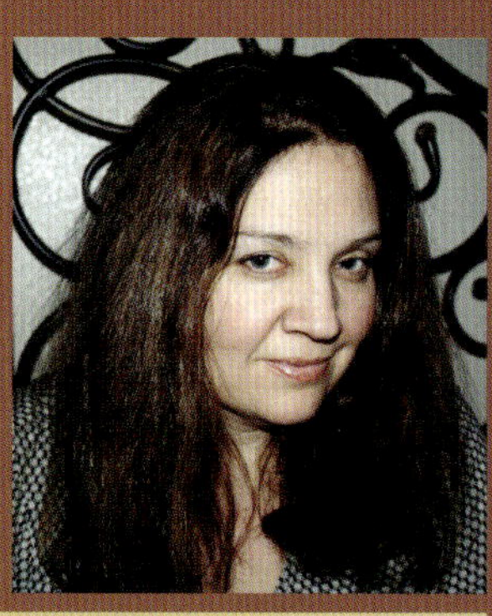

Born 1972 in Arkansas, I began showing interest in art as soon as I was old enough to crawl up on the bathroom counter and smudge lipstick and toothpaste all over the mirror. I quickly advanced to crayons and pencils, since mothers and older sisters become very angry with lipstick artists!

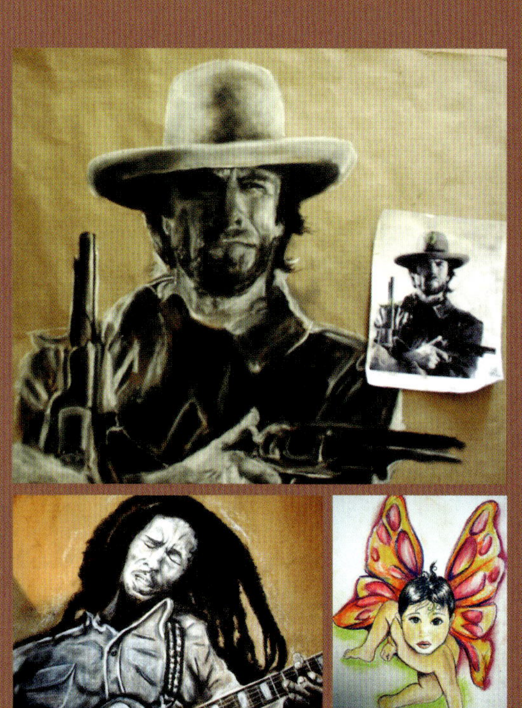

I now work with different types of media, specializing on commission portrait work. I have done family portraits from photographs for clients who are thousands of miles away. My art has been published in books, sold on the internet, and in various shops in N.W Arkansas. As you can see from my work, portraits are my first love, whether of a Hollywood celebrity or of the celebrities who are near and dear to your heart in your own family.

For more information you can email me at: becmarierw@yahoo.com or visit my facebook page at: http://www.Facebook.com/BeccaMarieEscobar.

Meg Simons began painting at the age of ten years old. She is a founding member of the Palette Art League, and currently serves as a director. Meg is always the first one to volunteer to face paint at various fund raising events. Her favorite medium is oil paints on canvas with a palette knife. She prefers to paint people (especially children) and animals, but will paint anything, when the mood hits. She has even painted a study in feet, children's feet, of course.

Meg sold her first painting at age 13. She was selected to exhibit her art in the Barrett Hamilton Young Artist Exhibit at the Arkansas Art Center in little Rock, while still in high school. Meg grew up in the Ozarks, and lives with her husband, Doc Roger and son in Bull Shoals, Arkansas. Meg feels that painting is a natural way of relieving the stress of the day to day grind of life and makes life far more enjoyable, interesting and enriching.

She and her husband collect art of all kinds from local, American Indian; to the unusual pieces they pick up on their travels.

For more information on Meg's work, visit: http://paletteartleague.org/MegSimons.html.

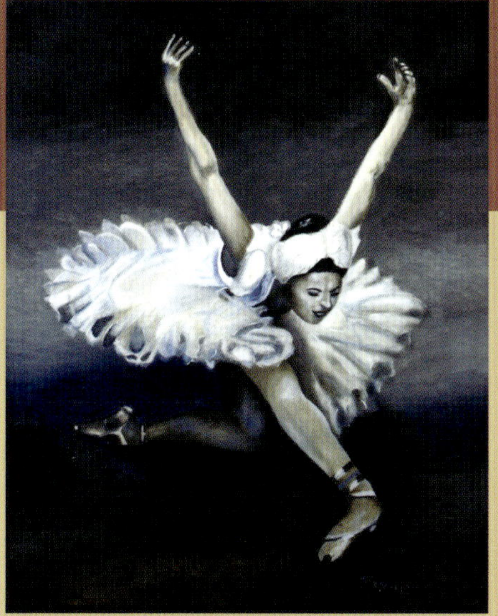

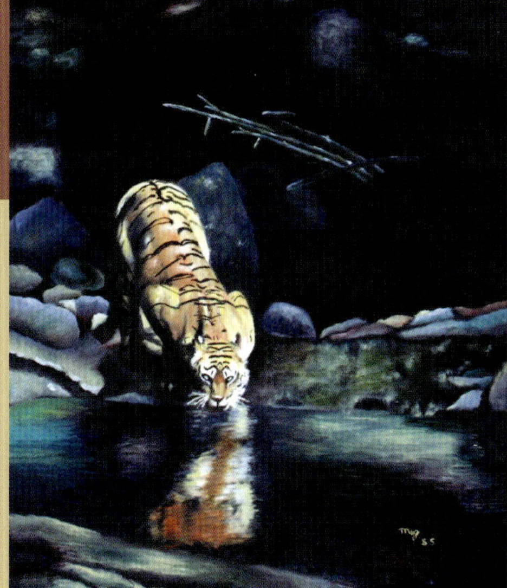

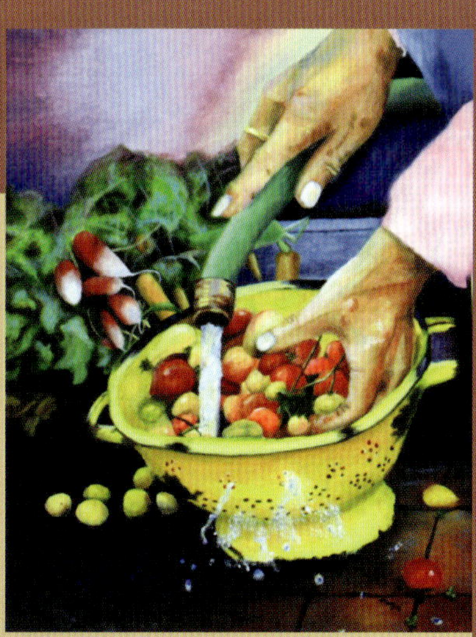

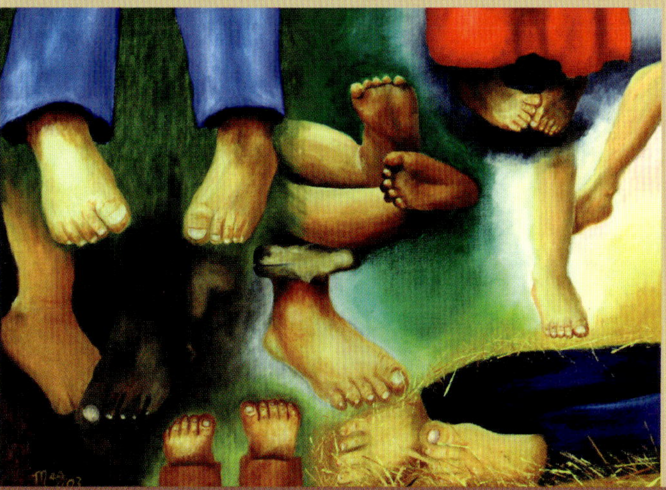

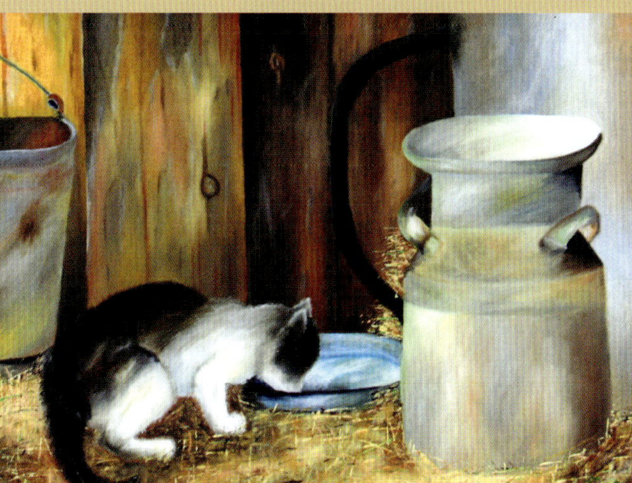

Keith R. Probert was born in England in 1951 and moved to the USA in 1988. His career as a "clay modeler" for the auto industry allowed him to travel the world before coming to the States.

Always an avid photographer, Keith was able to take his work to the next level after marrying a woman who wrote magazine articles and books. This allowed Keith to travel and to showcase his work in publications around North America.

Now that he is officially retired from the auto design world, Keith and his wife have found their home here in the heart of the Ozarks where Keith now has the time to serve on the Board of Directors of several community-based organizations in NW Arkansas and to pursue his photography.

For more information on Keith's work, visit http://paletteartleague.org/KeithProbert.html.

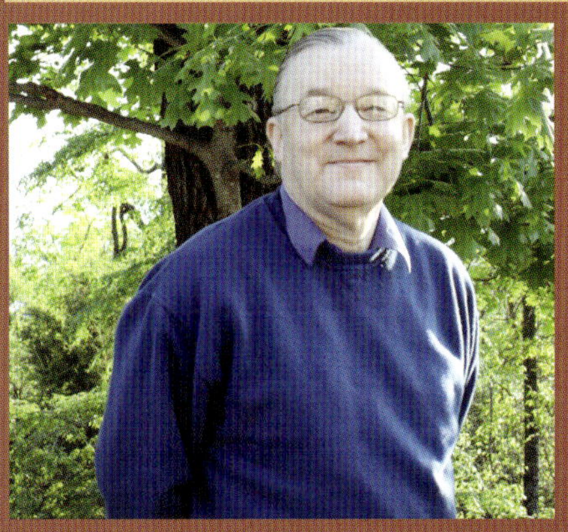

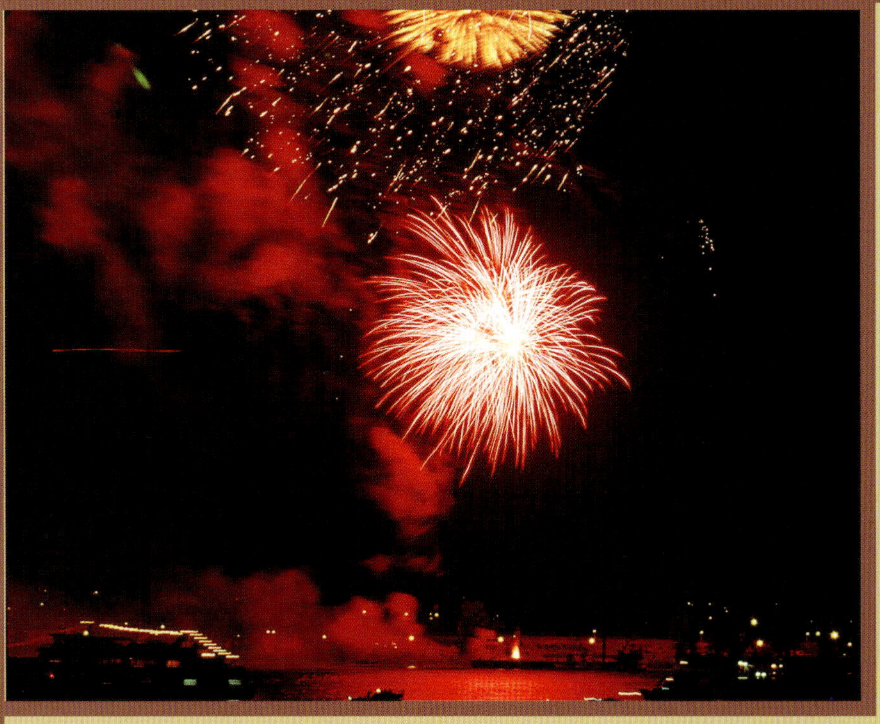

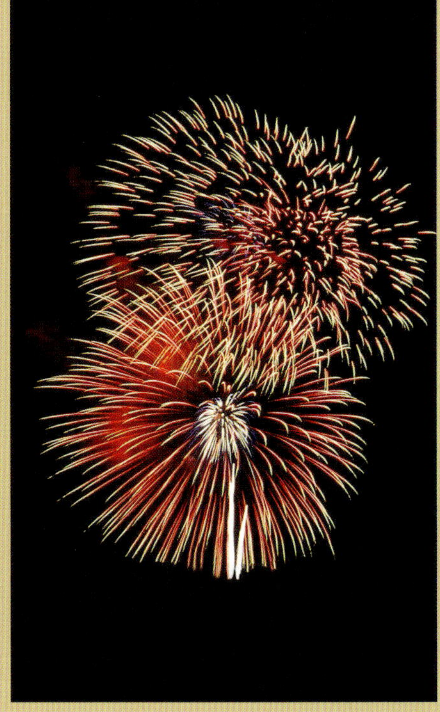

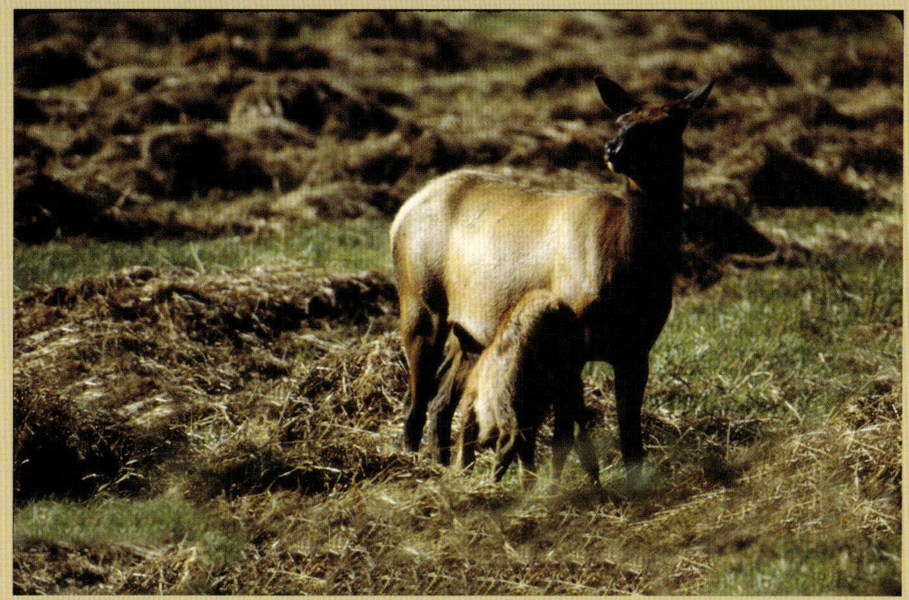

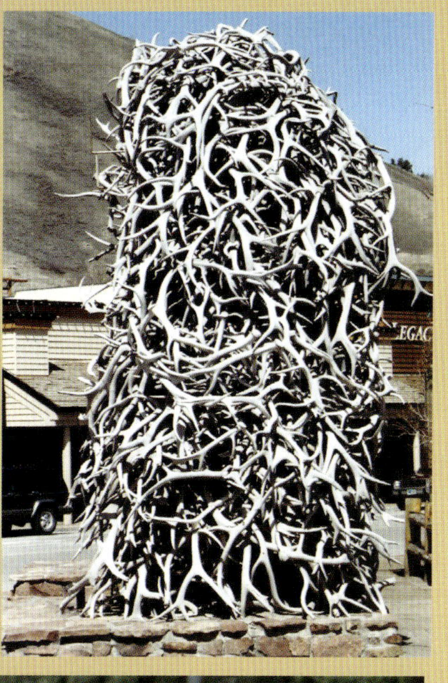

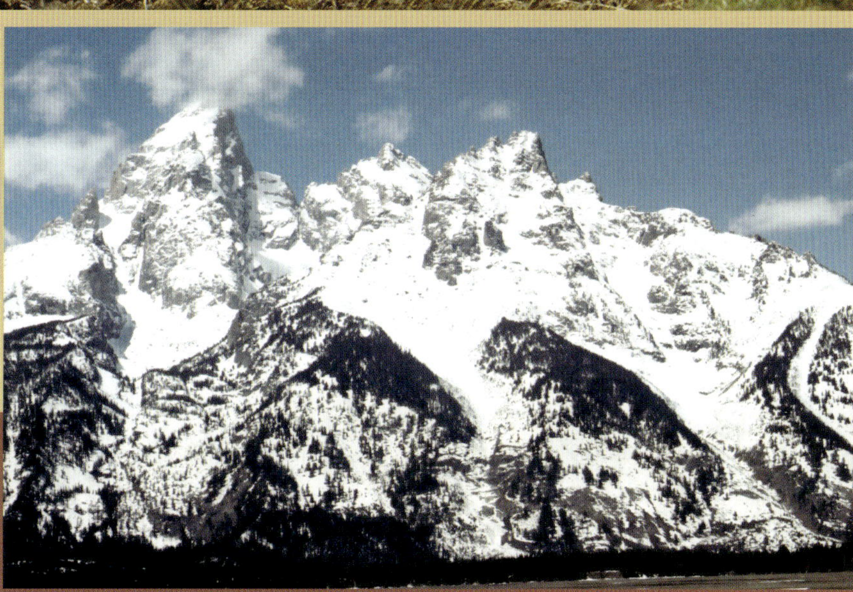

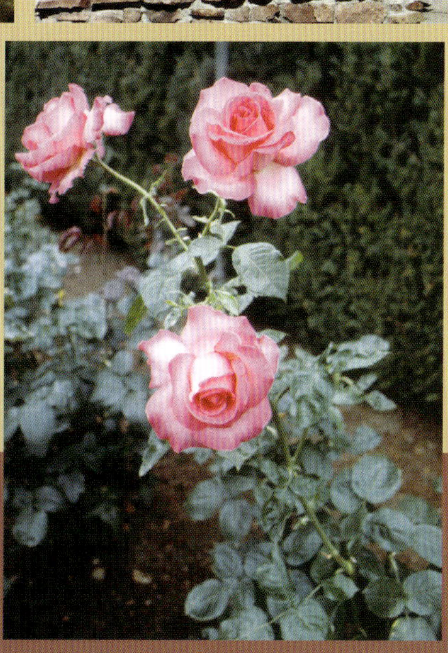

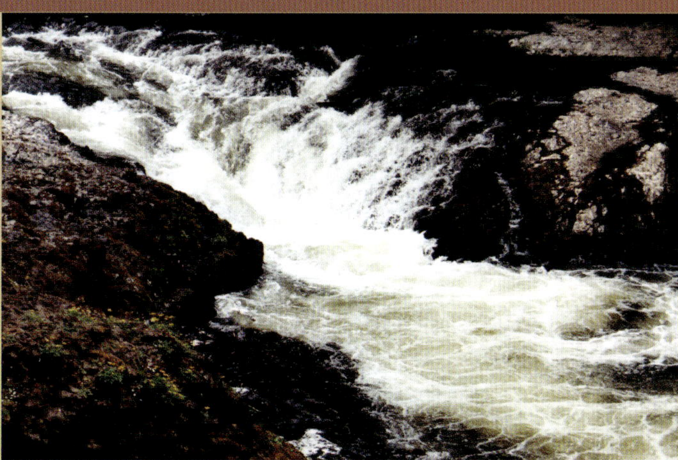

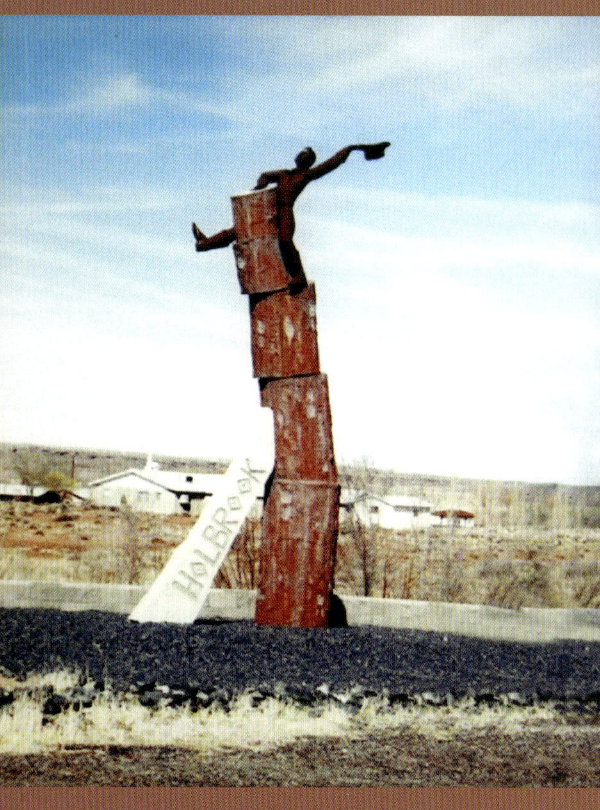
HOLBROOK

JO ROWELL

Jo Rowell is a rare artist indeed. Not only is she an amazingly talented painter but she is also driven and filled with the tenacity it takes to create (with the help of a handful of other tenacious artists), an organization to promote the Arts in the Ozarks and to help nurture that same organization for more than 15 years.

In addition to being one of the founding members of the Palette Art League, Jo is responsible for sparking a love of the Arts in countless numbers of children (and adults) across the Ozarks over the decades. Her young students often come back to visit her as adults now and share their appreciation for her and for the gift of Art that she gave to them.

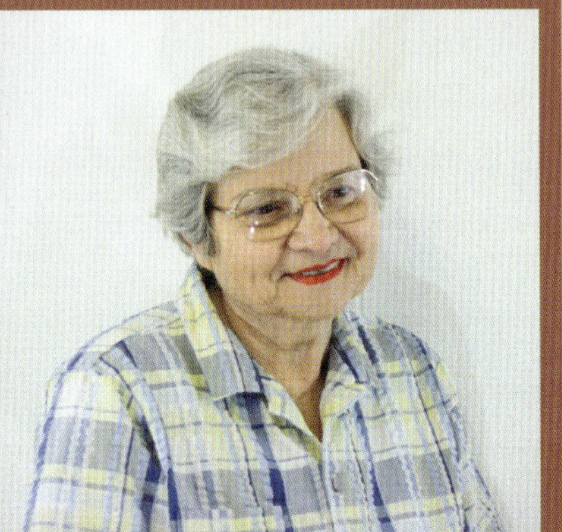

For more information on Jo's work, visit: http://paletteartleague.org/JoRowell.html.

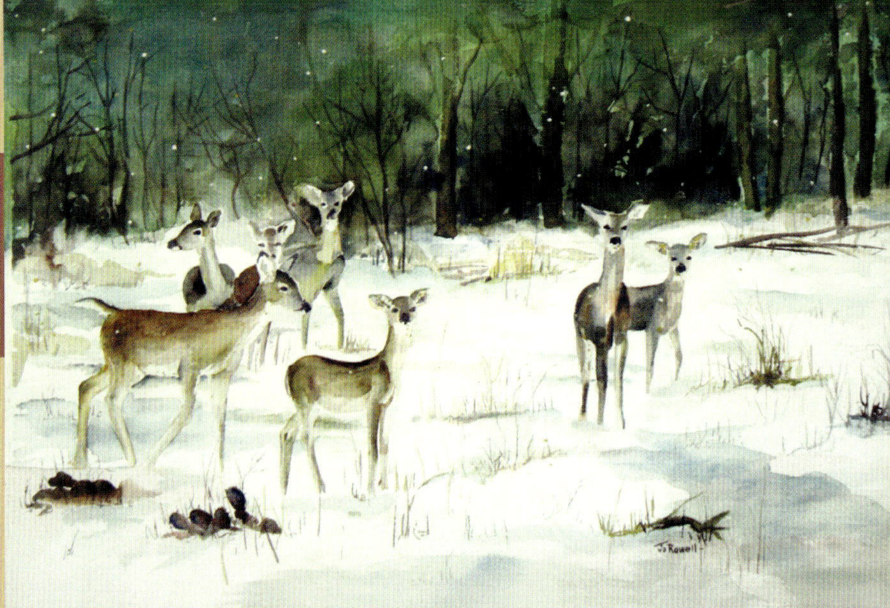

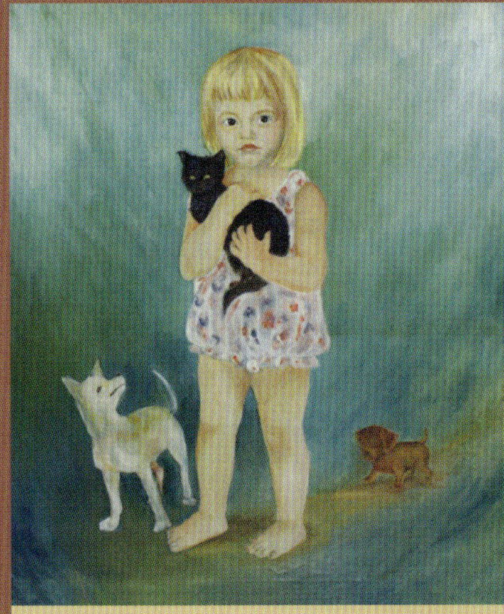

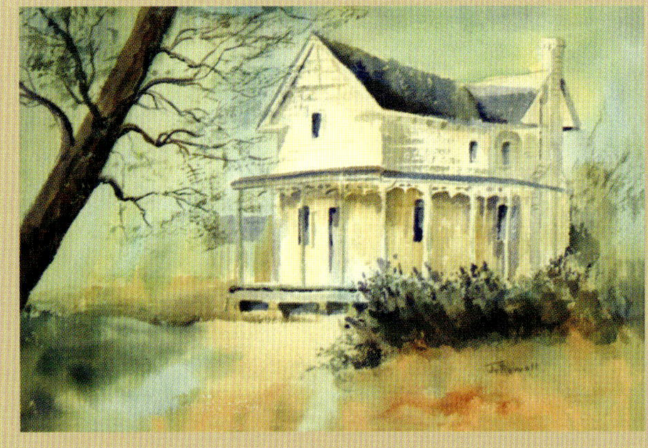

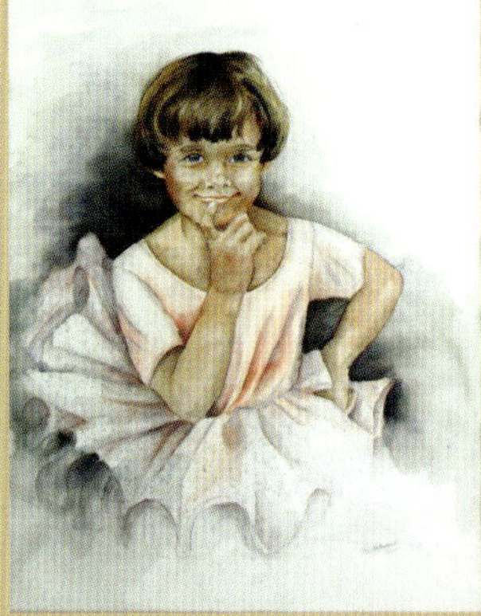

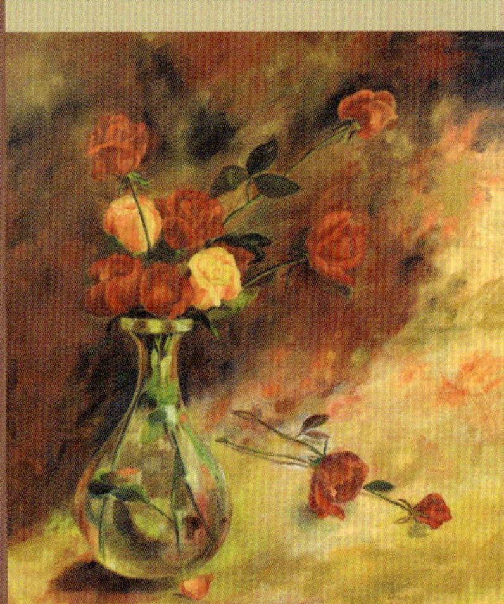

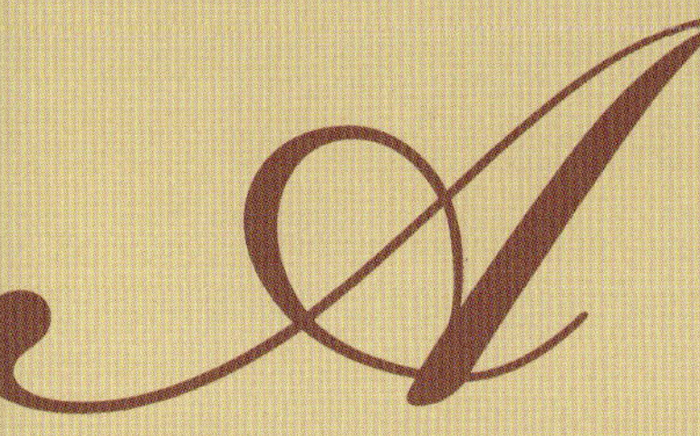

rtisan, Laurel Dyer (logo OZARKADU), was raised on the east coast and in New England. Later, she spent several years in California before coming to Arkansas. Laurel has studied with two top artists in the Ozarks, studying pastels and tight watercolor.

In the last few years, Laurel has also branched out to other media including lost wax jewelry making. She enjoys other areas of crafting including sewing, leather work, spinning, knitting and crochet. Her hobbies include gardening and raising French Alpine dairy goats. **For more information on Laurel's work, visit: http://paletteartleague.org/LaurelDyer.html.**

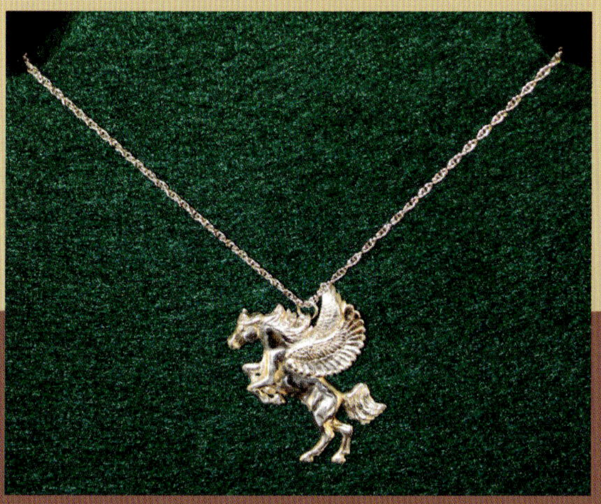

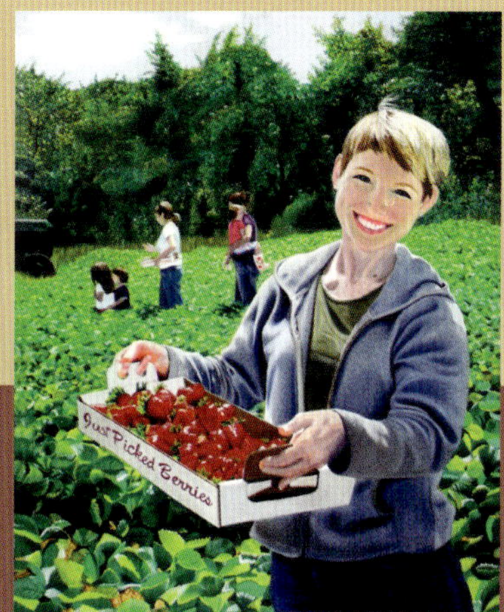

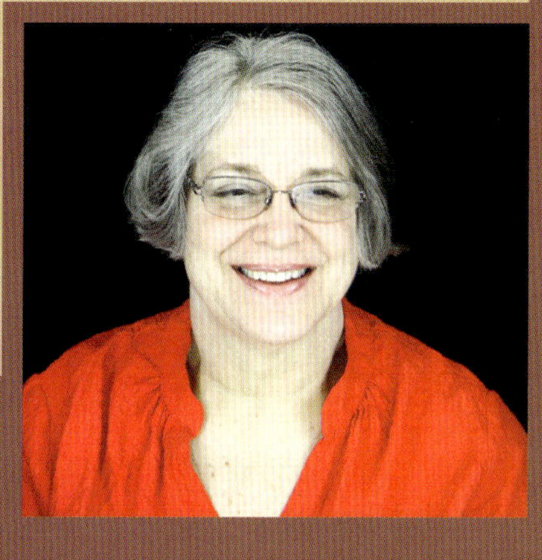

LAUREL DYER

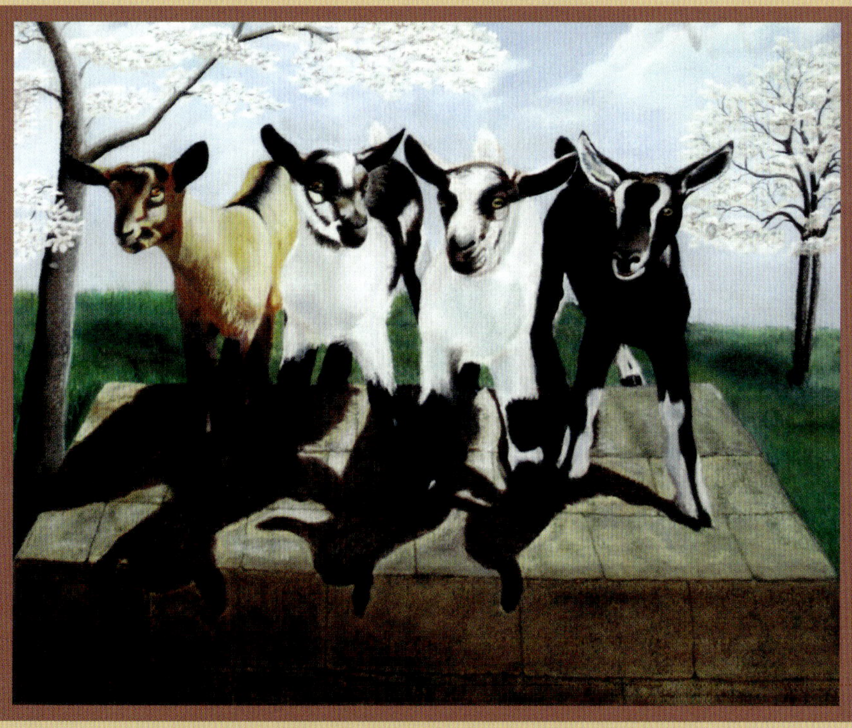

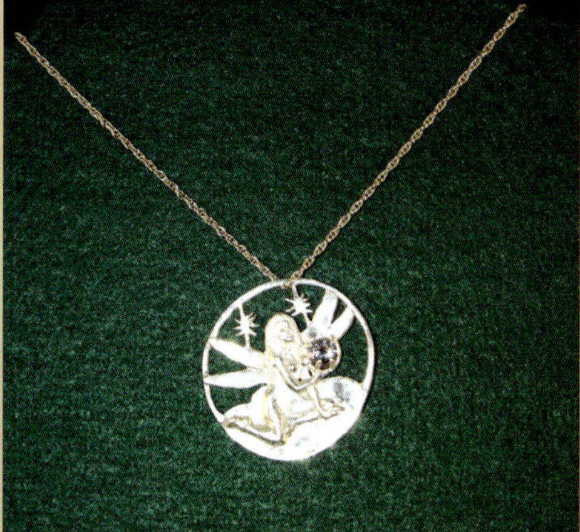

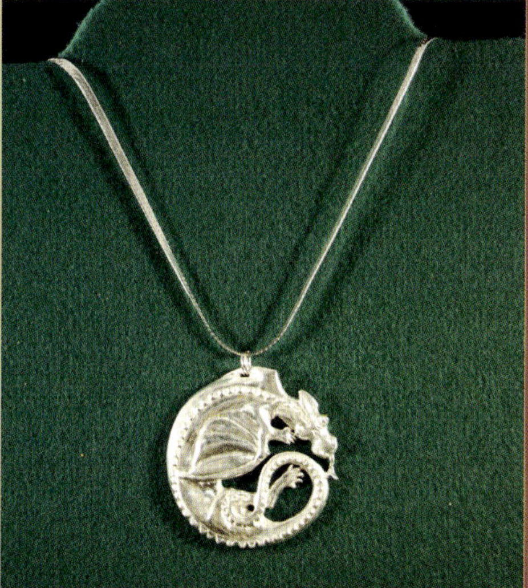

APRIL WILLIAMS

April Williams is a wonderfully talented, award winning Ozark artist who works in multiple mediums. Her work is always evolving and maturing. April is currently attending school full time, while pursuing her art part-time. She has a promising future in the art world. Watch for April in the years to come!

For more information on April's work, visit: http://paletteartleague.org/AprilWilliams.html.

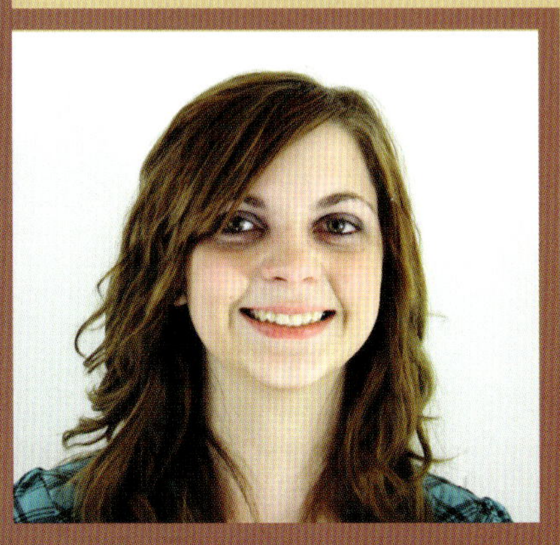

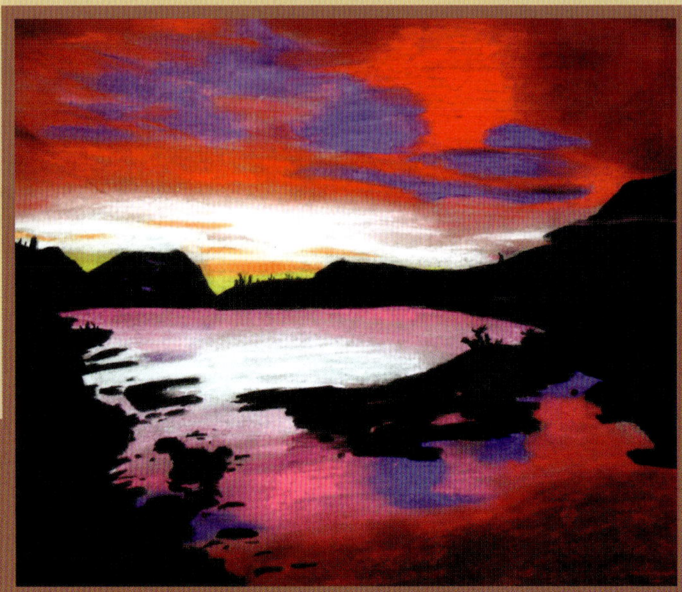

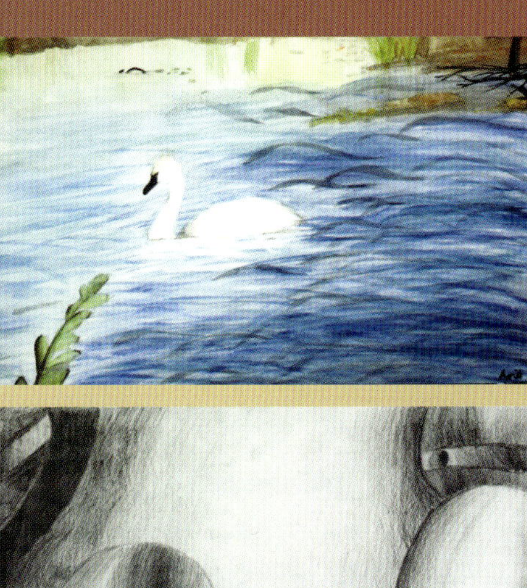

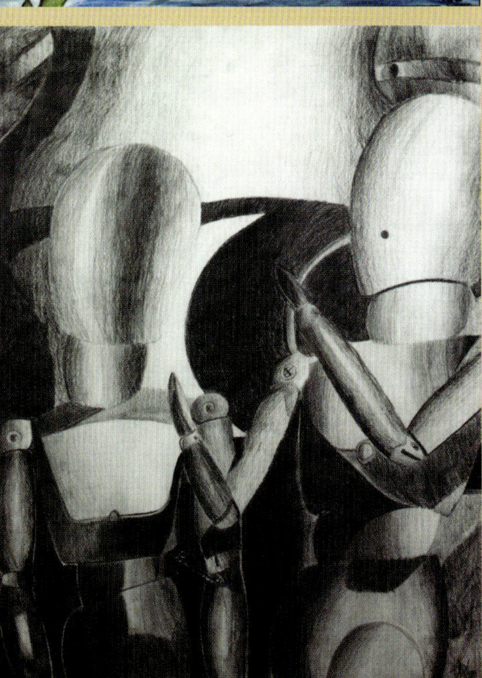

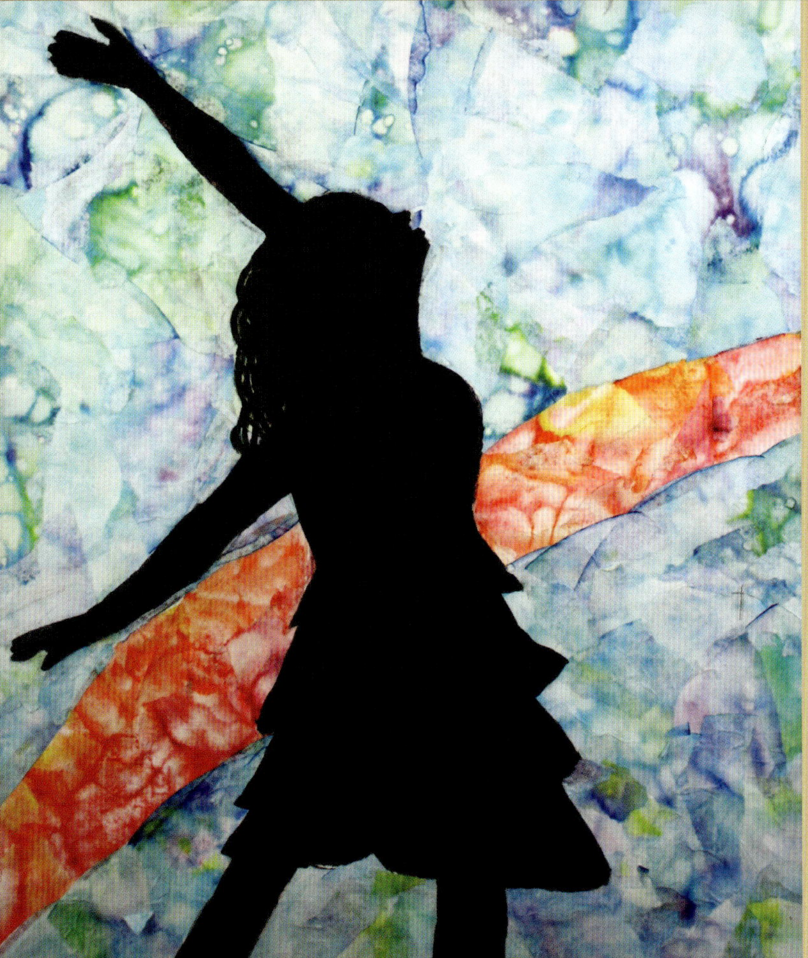

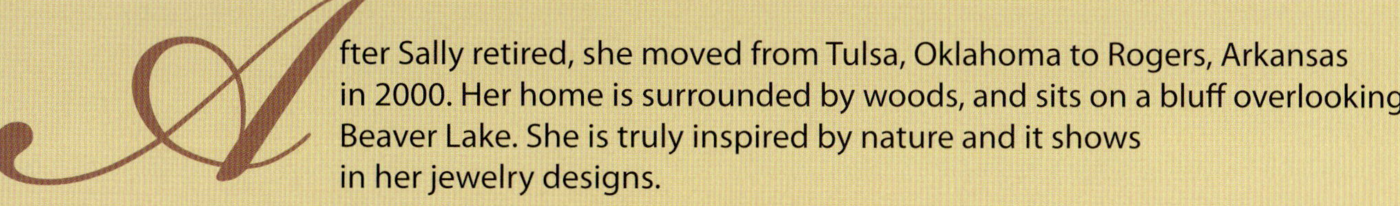

After Sally retired, she moved from Tulsa, Oklahoma to Rogers, Arkansas in 2000. Her home is surrounded by woods, and sits on a bluff overlooking Beaver Lake. She is truly inspired by nature and it shows in her jewelry designs.

Looking for something new to do after retirement, she began to make pottery, which led her to making jewelry. Sally makes hand built pendants and beads of clay and uses Raku glazes and various firing techniques using a Raku kiln. Each necklace is enhanced with stones, fossils and various beads.

Sally was once told that her jewelry looked like an actual archeological find. Her jewelry definitely has a look of antiquity about it. Each piece is one of a kind, striking and truly a conversation piece. **For more information on Sally's work, visit: http://paletteartleague.org/SallyBowen.html.**

SALLY BOWEN

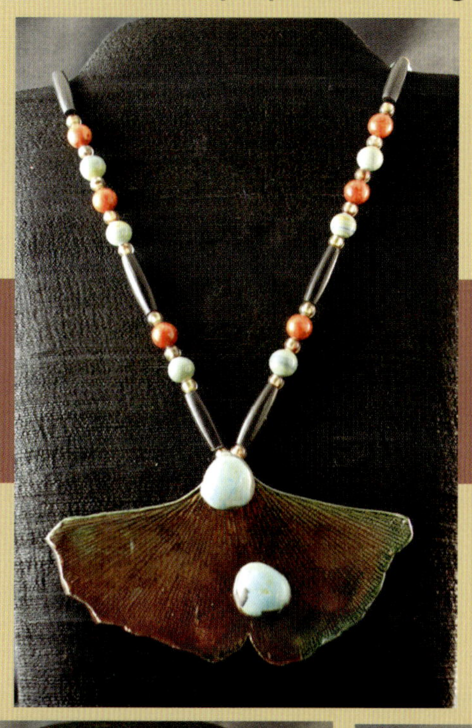

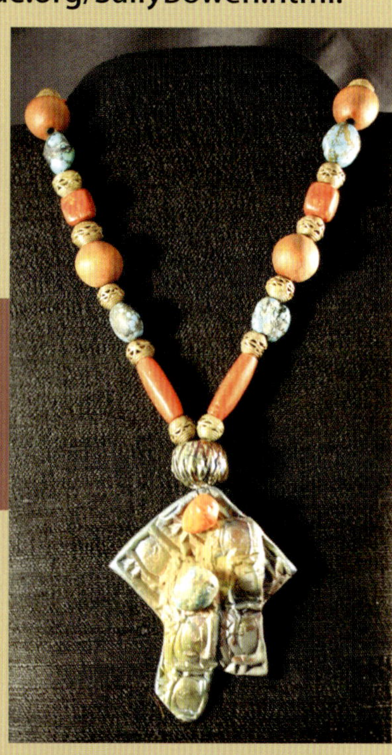

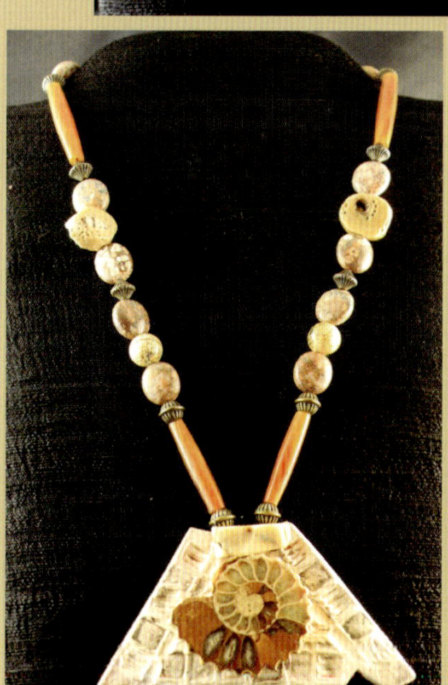

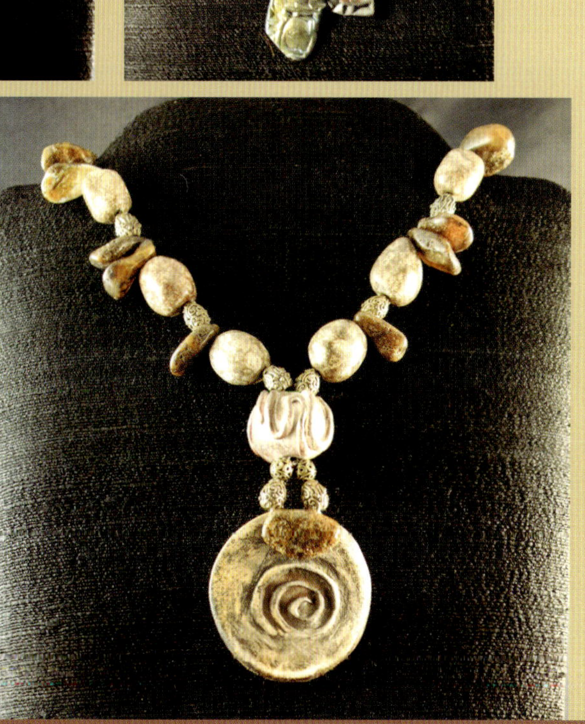

JACK DIVINE

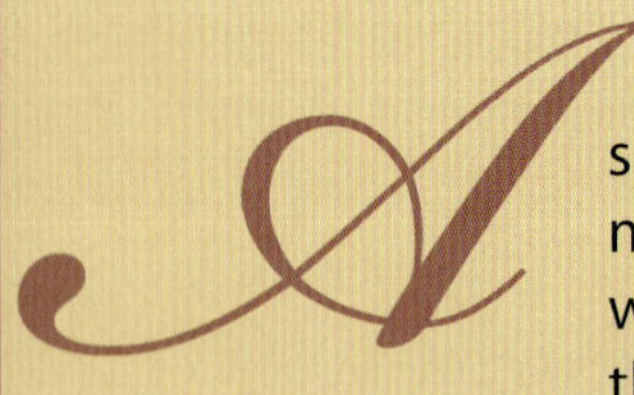

As a child, my dad worked in the timber in the western states and made much of our furniture. Working from plans and copying other's designs is where I began. In recent years, less time in the real world and more time in the Ozark woods has led me to a different philosophy.

My original work of gluing, carving, sanding and cutting wood into shapes has given way to working with the natural wood I find in the woods. Instead of forcing the wood into the design of my choosing, I now work with what I find in nature and let that determine my design path.

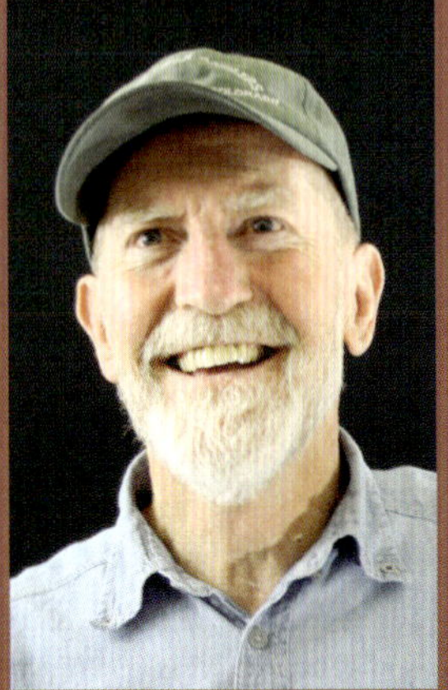

Most of my wood comes to me from storm damage, recycled and reclaimed materials. I hope my artwork calls you to touch it, to use it, to be a part of its natural origins and above all, to enjoy it!

For more information about Jack's work, visit: http://paletteartleague.org/JackDivine.html or e-mail jwdivine@hughes.net.

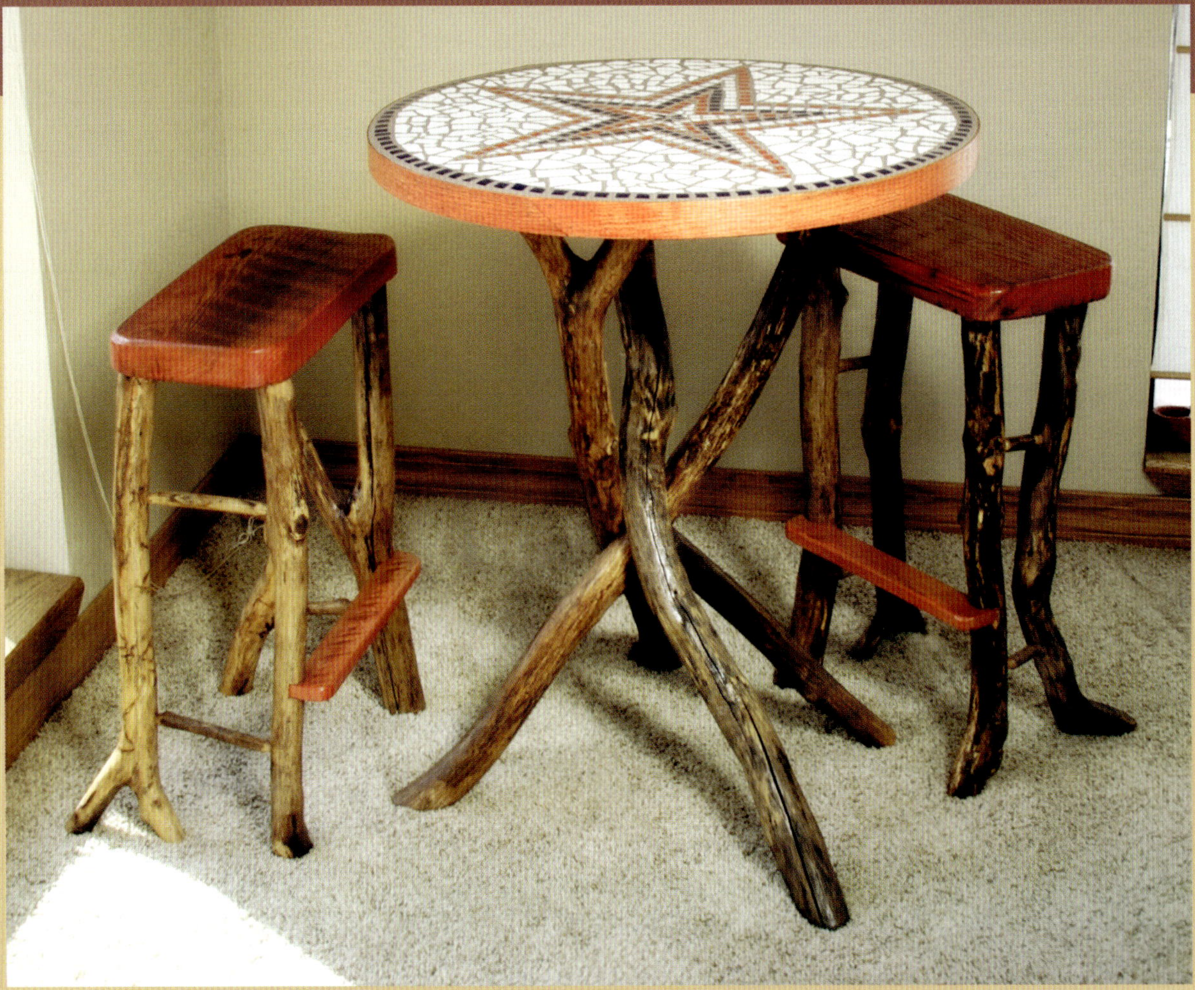

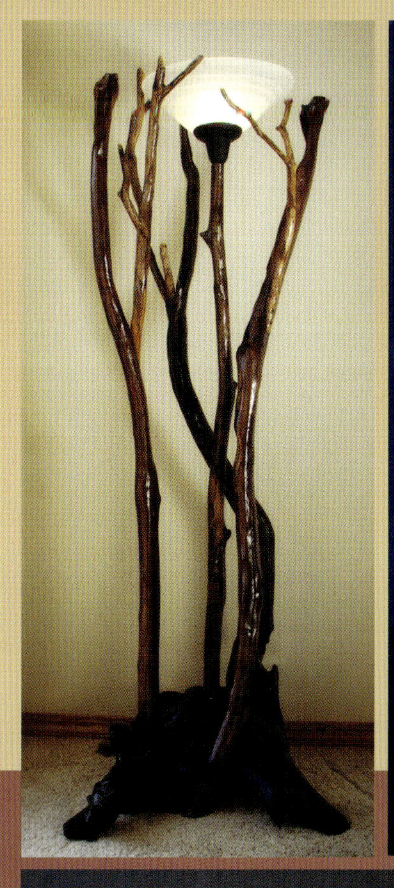
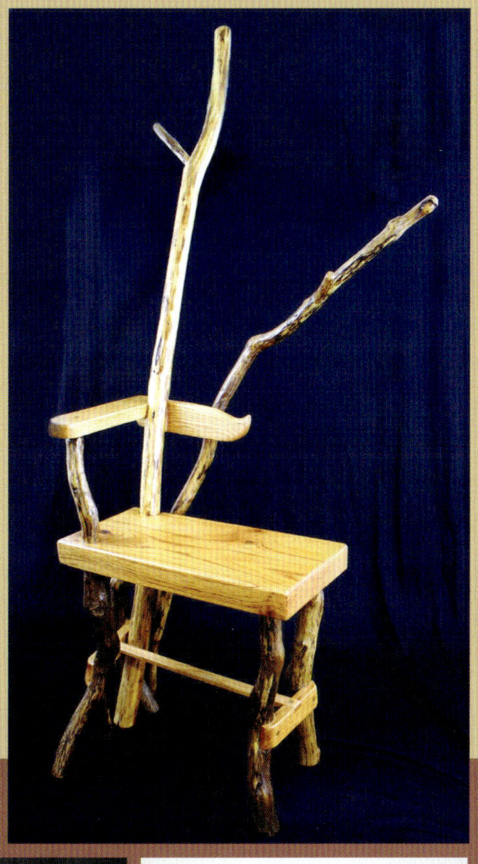
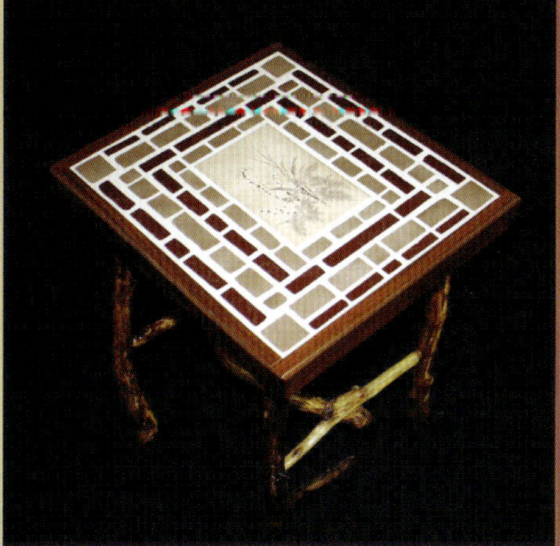
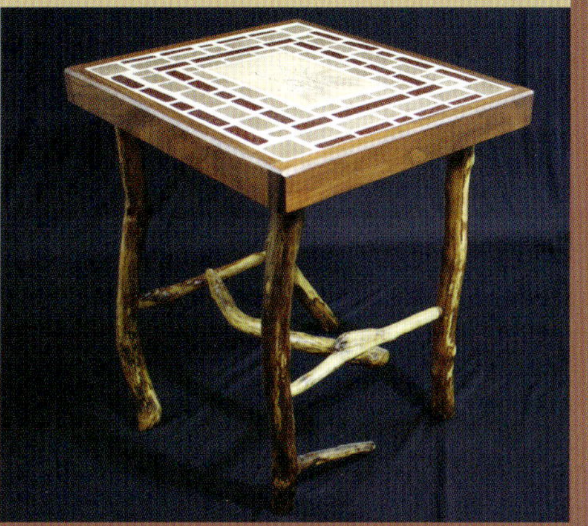

JACK DIVINE

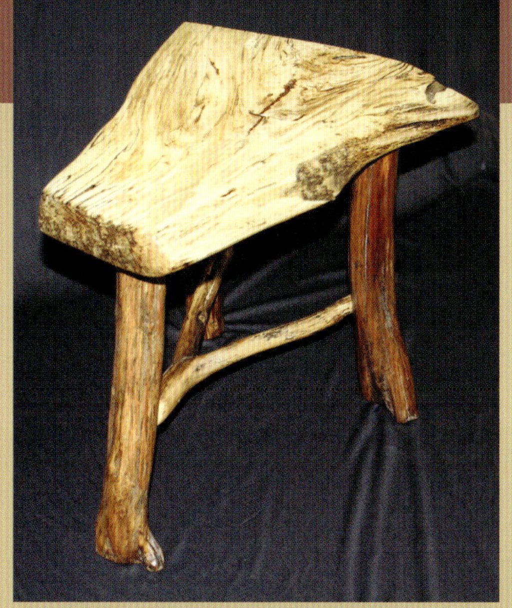
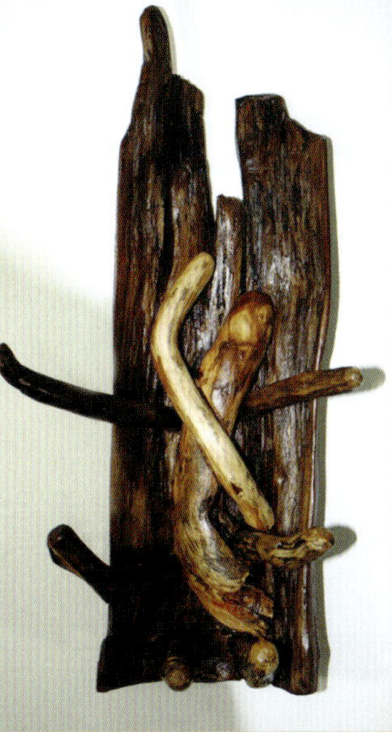
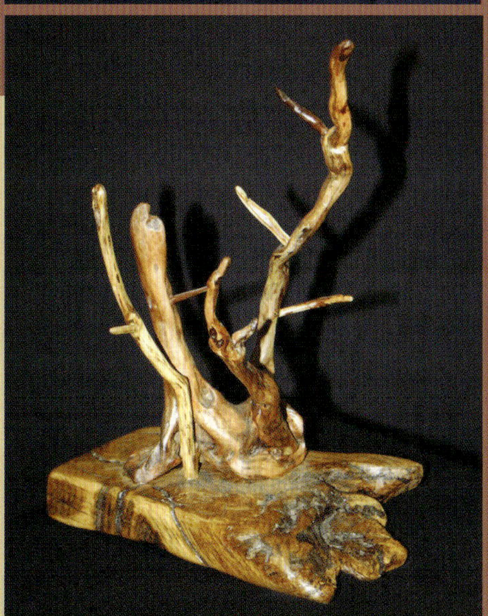
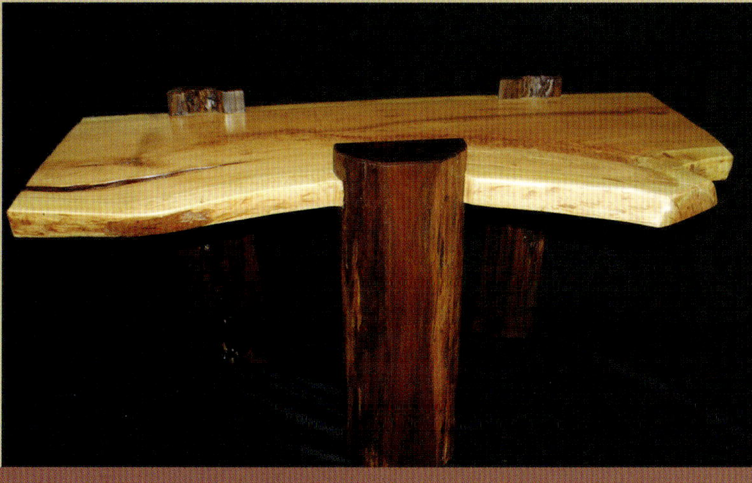
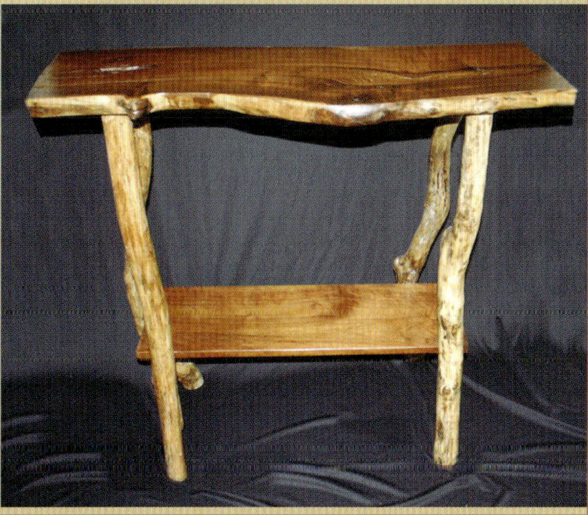

PAUL O'NEILL

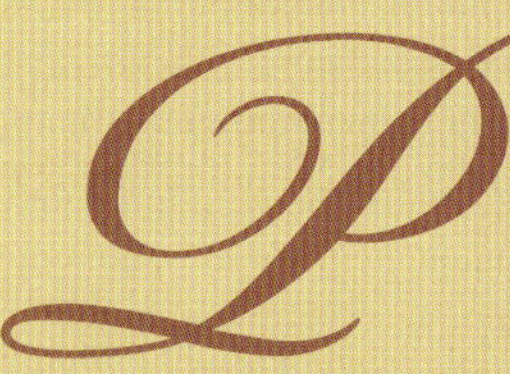aul O'Neill, a graduate of Paier College of Art, has spent his entire life as a working artist. O'Neill's work is noticeably influenced by the American Plein Air Impressionists. While much of Paul's work is impressionistic, he is an accomplished realist painter as well. In his still life, residence and marine paintings, his keen exactitude in draftsmanship and perspective is clearly shown.

His ability to capture those qualities that endear us to our treasured memories of home and hearth has put him in high demand for his architectural and marine portraits. O'Neill works from reference (photographs) as well as on site.

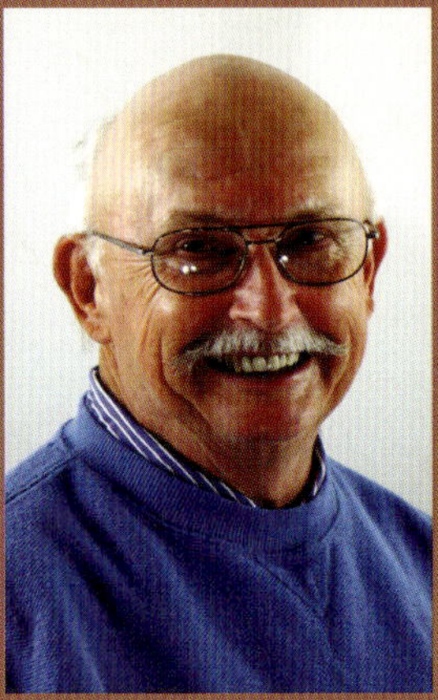

Paul can create a painting of your cherished family home from photographs, that you will cherish for generations. **For more information, please contact Paul at www.kingsriverfinearts.com or via e-mail at mail@KingsRiverFineArts.com.**

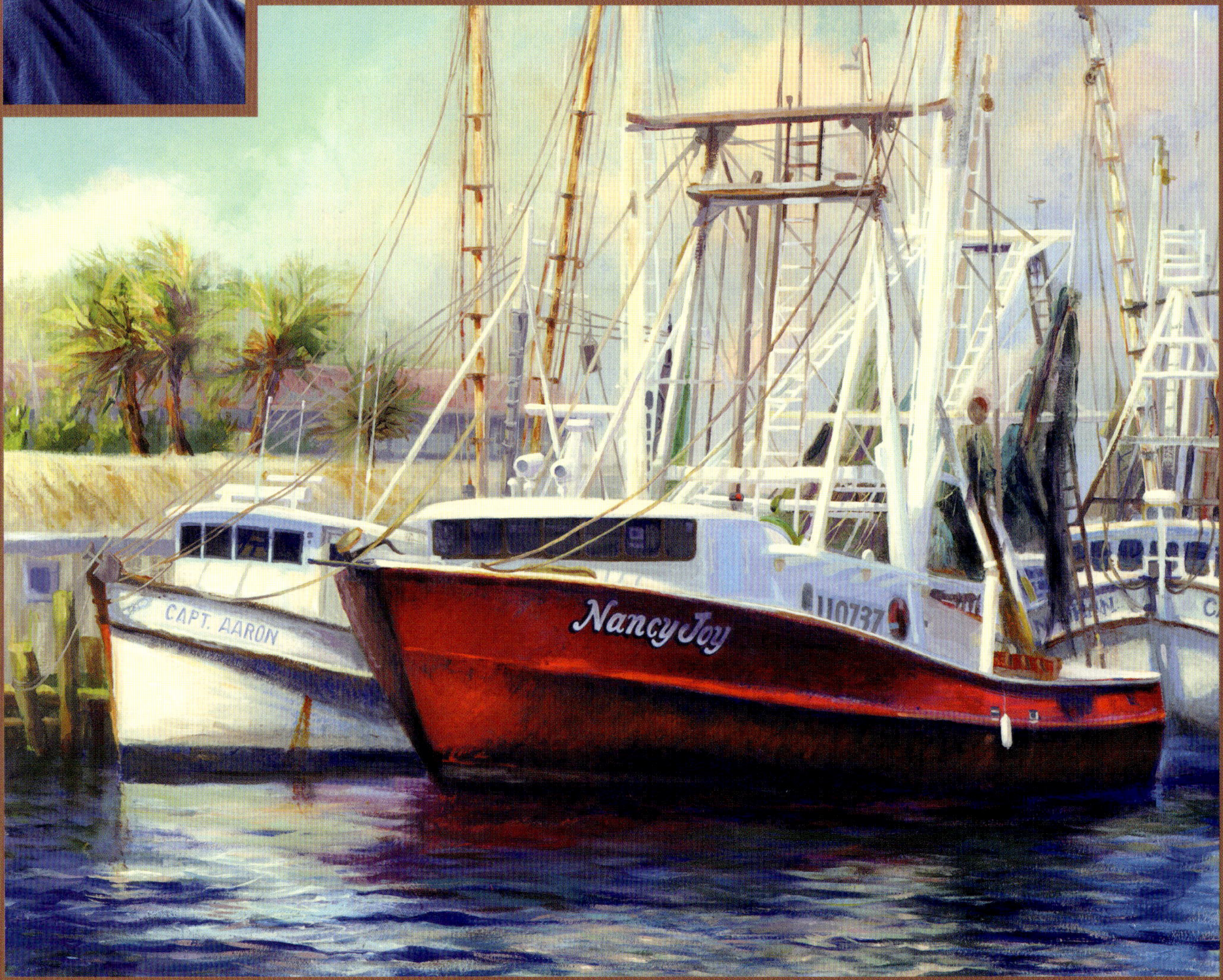

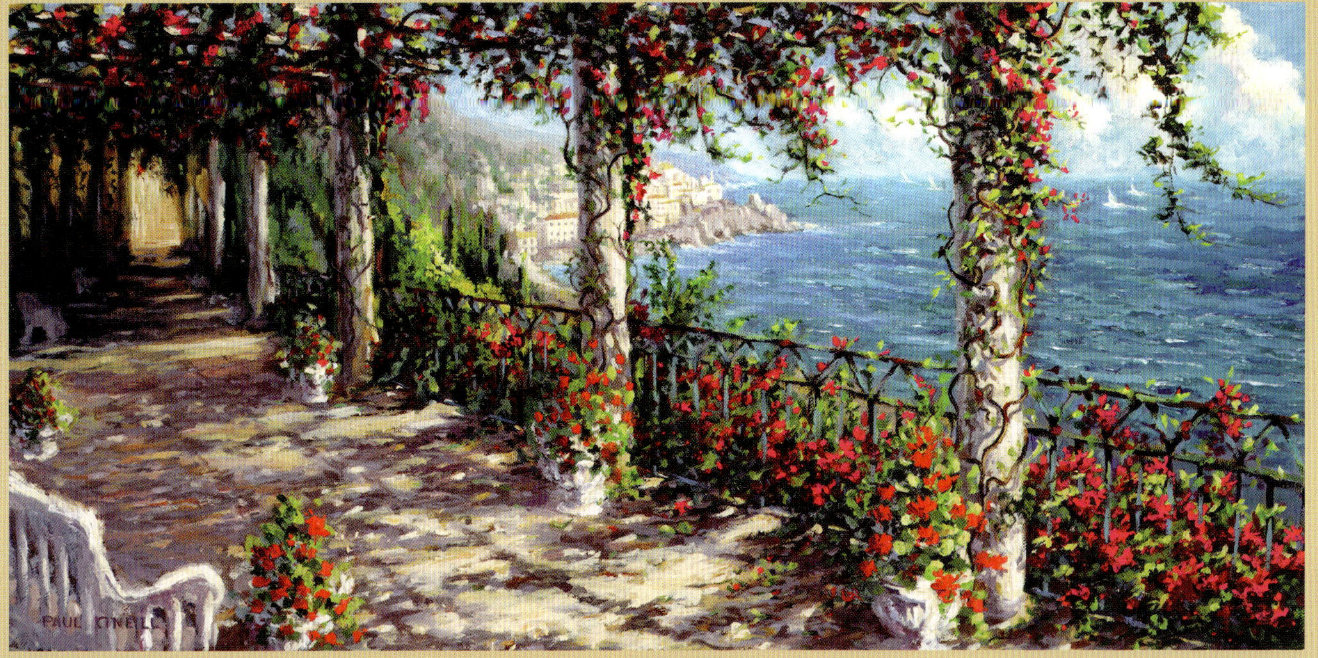

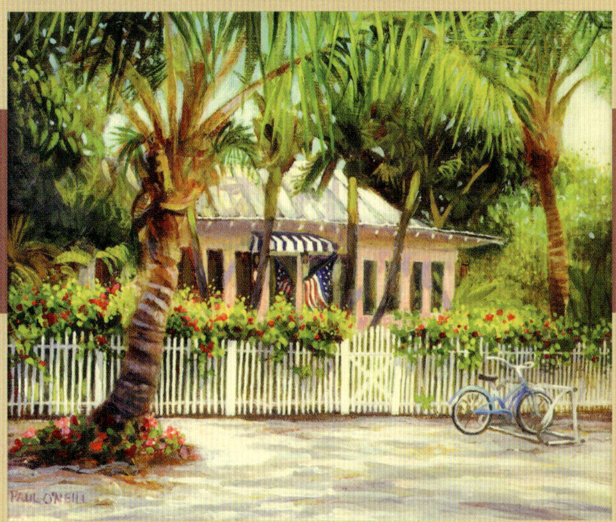

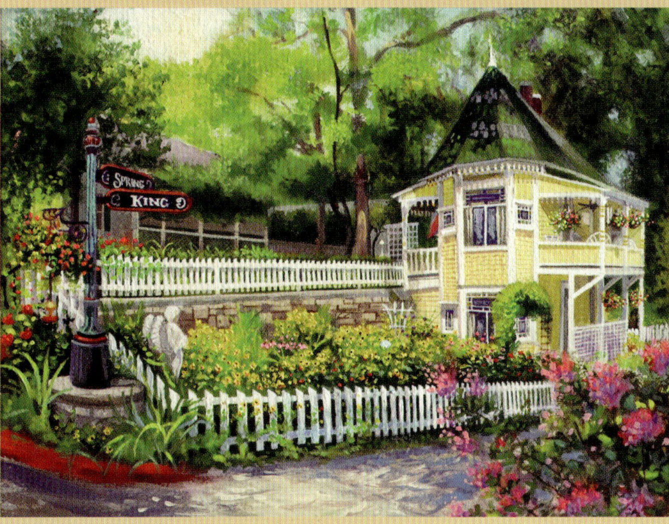

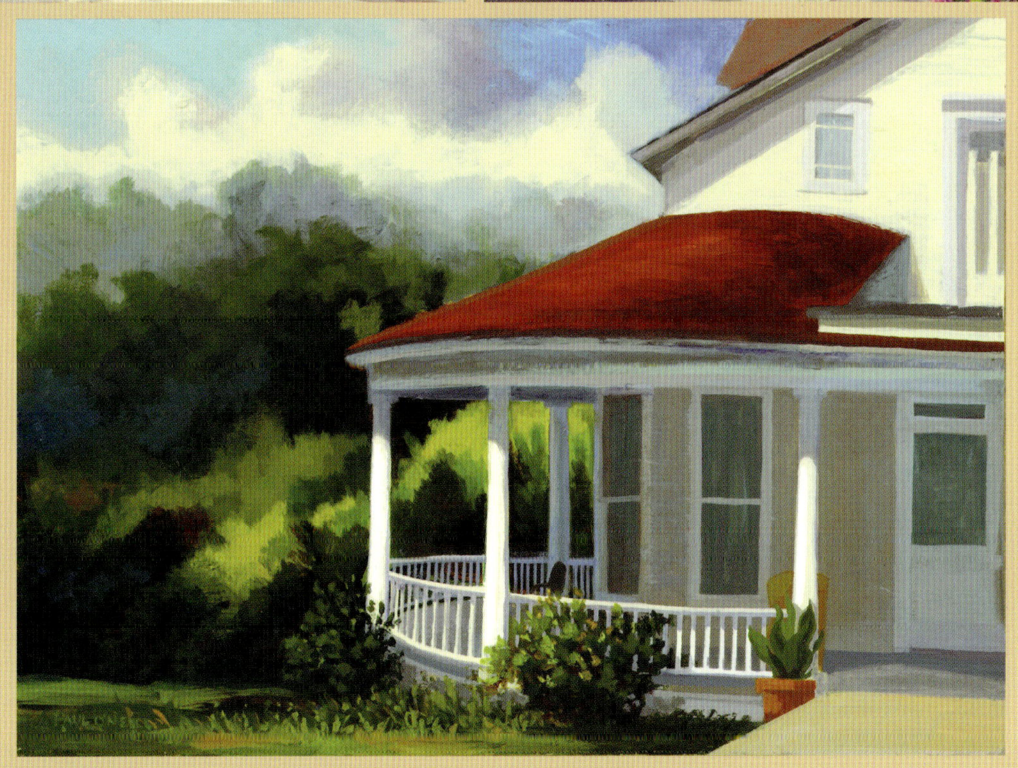

PAUL O'NEILL

SUE SNELL

I was much inspired to paint as a young child, when visiting an older, married sister's home and seeing her art work, paints, brushes etc. I knew that I wanted to do that some day!

In 1984 my husband retired from his job with the FAA and we moved to a farm near Yellville, Arkansas.

God, having blessed us with a wonderful family of five children, sixteen grandchildren and sixteen great-grandchildren and allowing us to live on a beautiful farm provides me with my two most favorite subject-matters. I love to paint the wildlife I see here and my latest and greatest challenge is doing portraits. My favorite mediums are pastels and oils.
For more information on Sue's work, visit: http://paletteartleague.org/SueSnell.html.

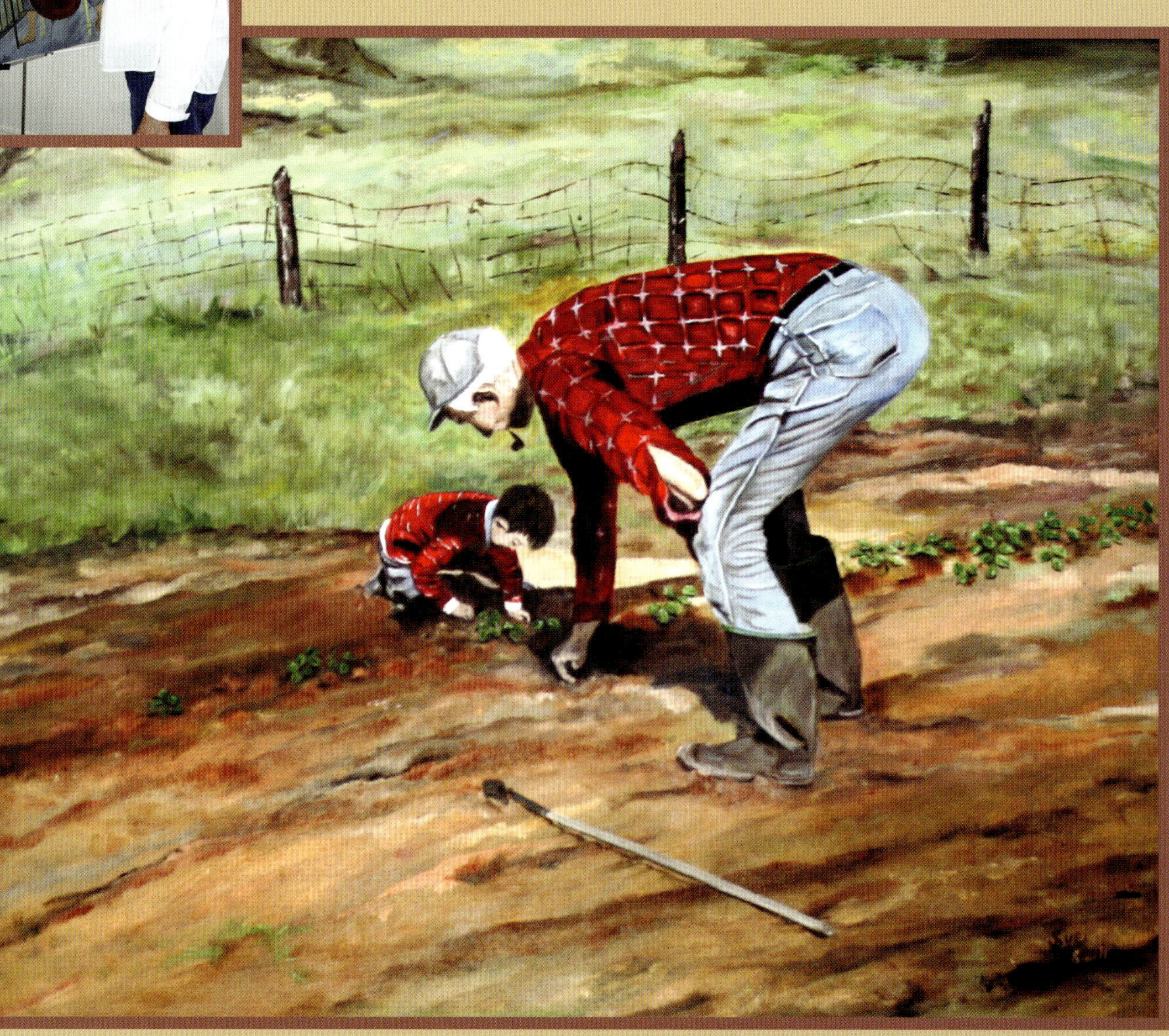

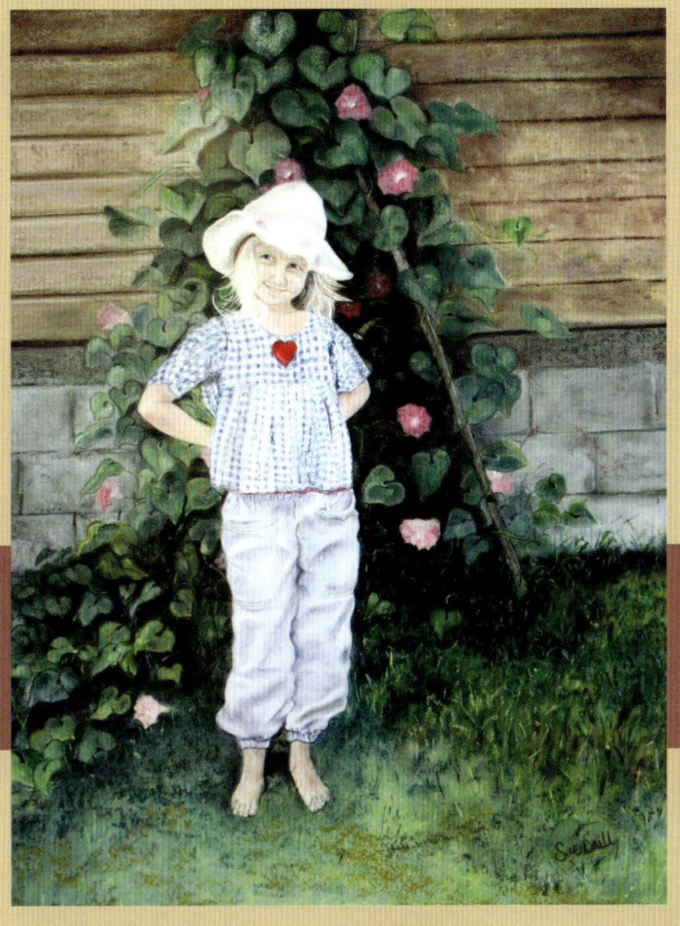

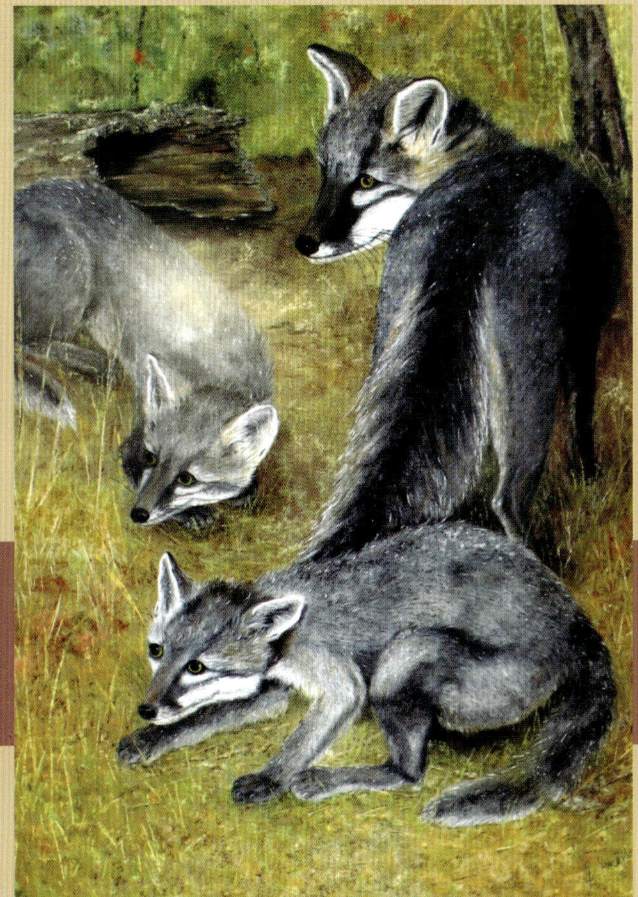

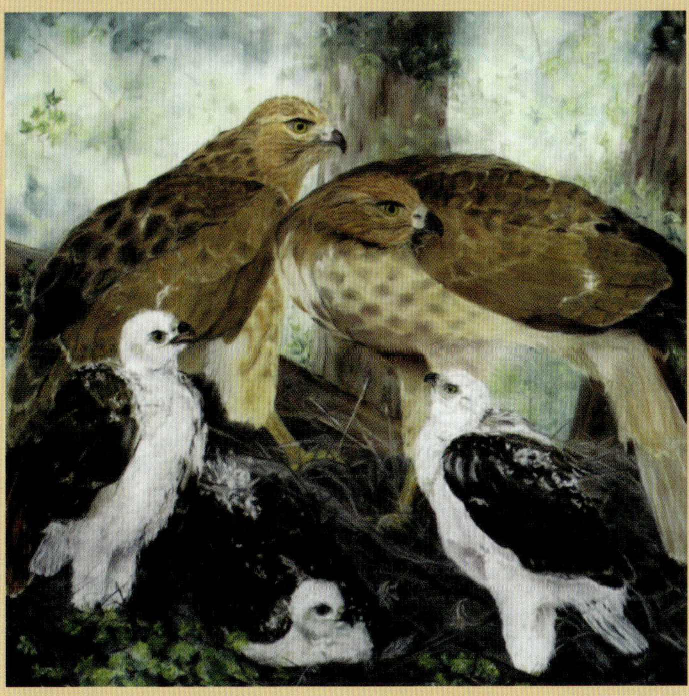

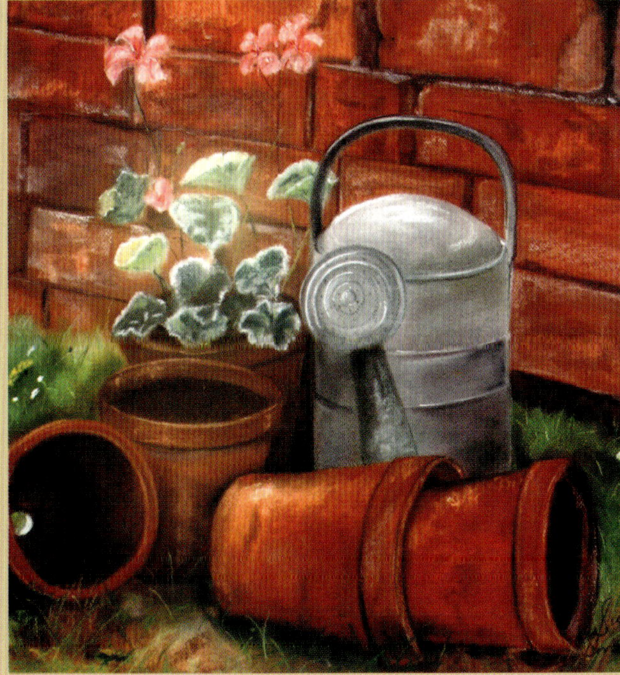

SUE SNELL

RON UFKES

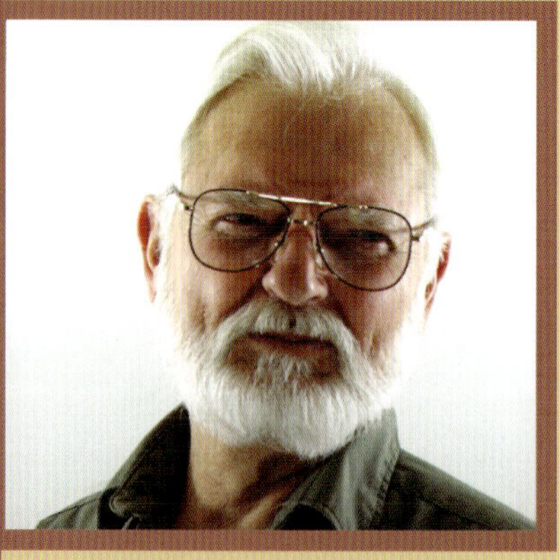

After a stint in the U. S. Army and earning a BS degree from the University of Illinois, I worked as a park ranger with the National Park Service. From there, I worked for 20-years with the San Bernardino County Sheriff's Department in California. My wife Janice and I retired to the small town of Lakeview, a few miles west of Mountain Home, Arkansas.

I can usually be found now in my shop (which is a real mess), working on the lathe. I enjoy the sound of the tools cutting into the wood blank and watching the ever-changing patterns in the wood as the waste is cut away.

For more information on Ron's work, visit: http://paletteartleague.org/RonUfkes.html or e-mail him at ronjan1@suddenlink.net.

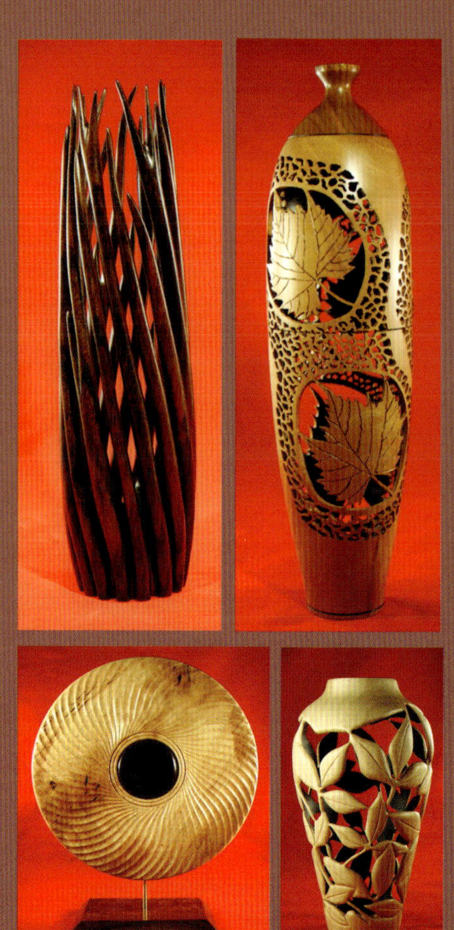

MATTHEW BUTLER

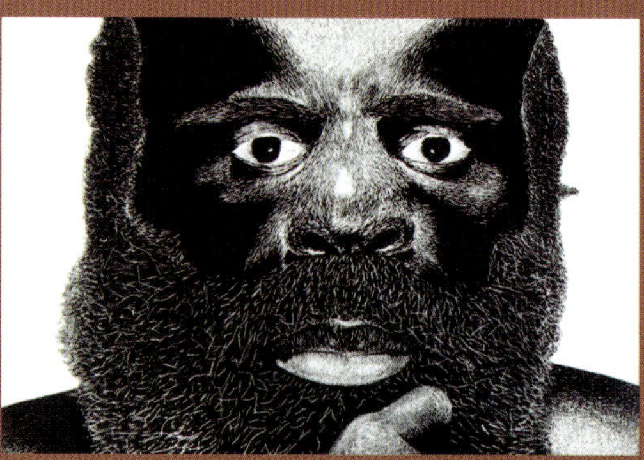

Kimbo Slice famous MMA fighter

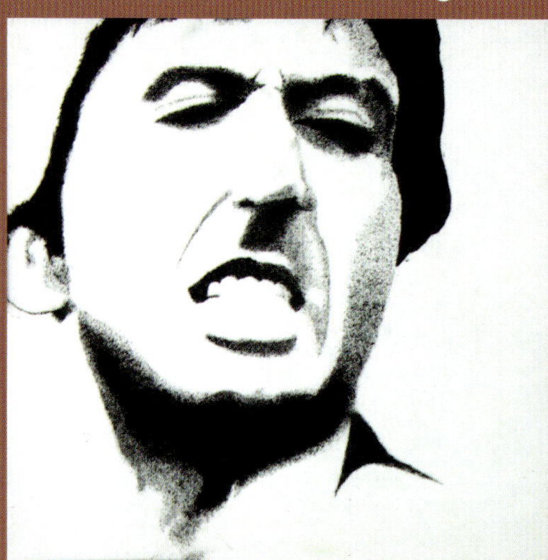

Al Pacino as Tony Montana

Matthew Butler was born in Orlando, Florida. He relocated to Arkansas in 1999 with his mother Dauna Tyson and family. He is a sophomore and has studied art for several years. Matthew also loves bowling and just recently went to state finals with his school team. He won second in the North Region State Art contest with his ink drawing of the character, Tony Montana from the very famous movie, Scarface. Matthew's talent for drawing started at a very young age. He is able to draw both with his left and right hands.

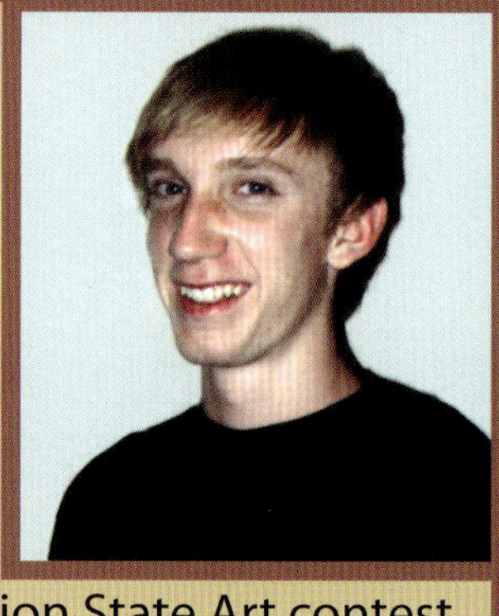

For more information on Matthew's work, e-mail daunatyson@yahoo.com.

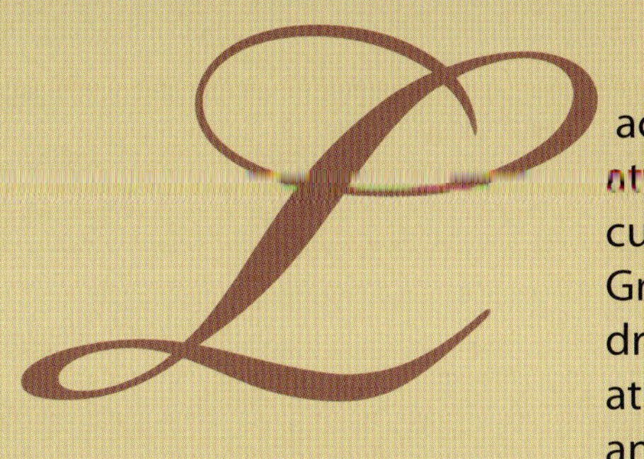

Lacey Rhoads was born in Mountain Home, Arkansas and attended Cotter High School. She graduated in 2007, and is currently a junior at Arkansas Tech University. She is majoring in Graphic Design, but is also passionate about painting and drawing. Her artwork has been displayed in group exhibitions at the River Valley Arts Center, Lake Point Conference Center, and the Arkansas Tech Juried Student Show. **For more information on Lacey's work, you can contact her by calling 870-405-3845.**

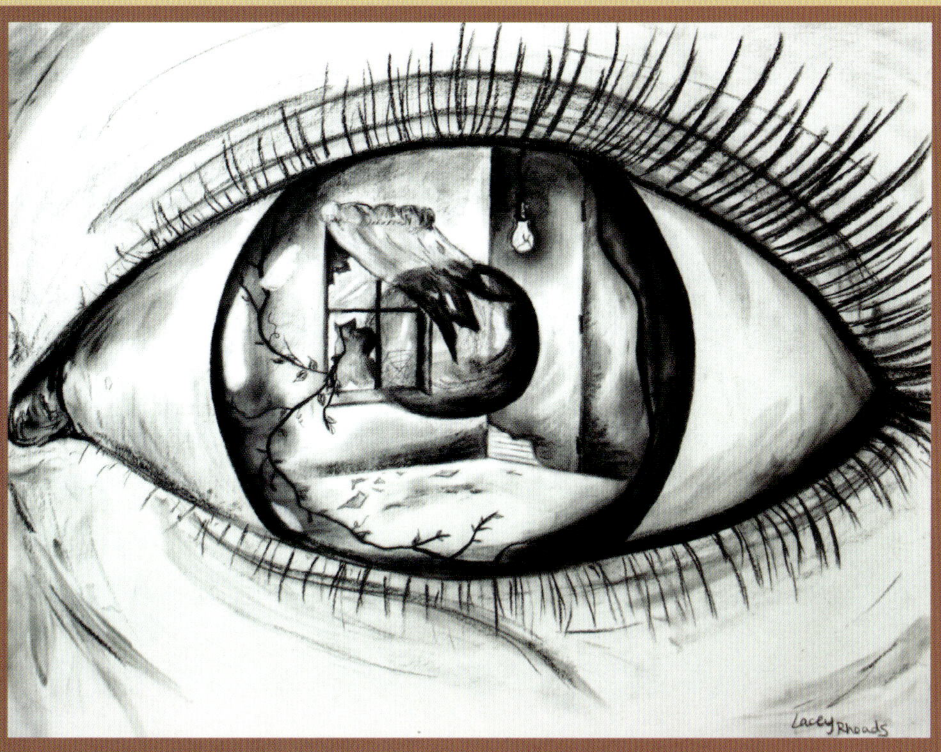

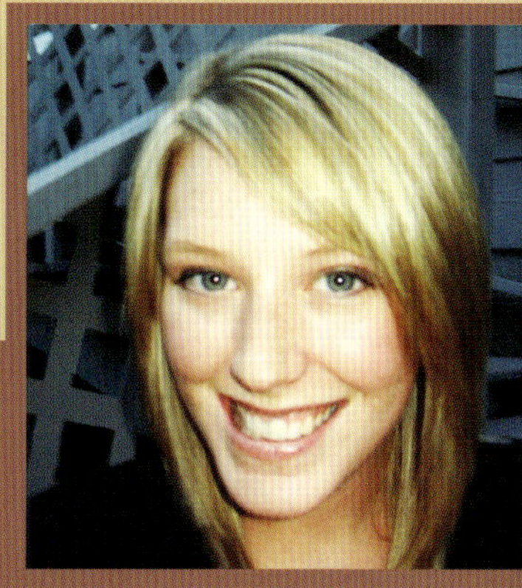

LACEY RHOADS

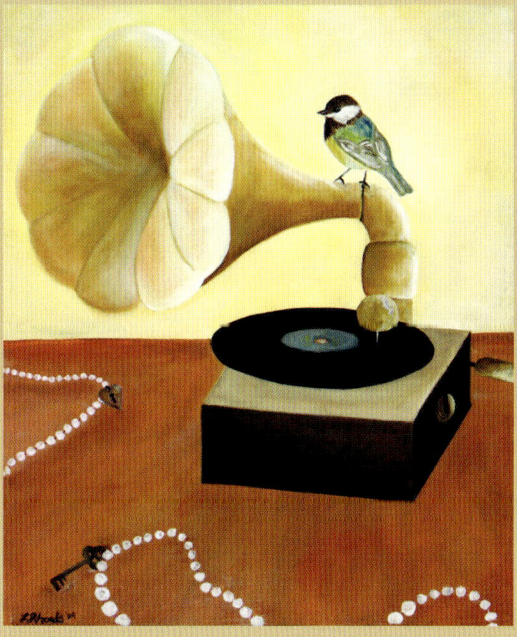

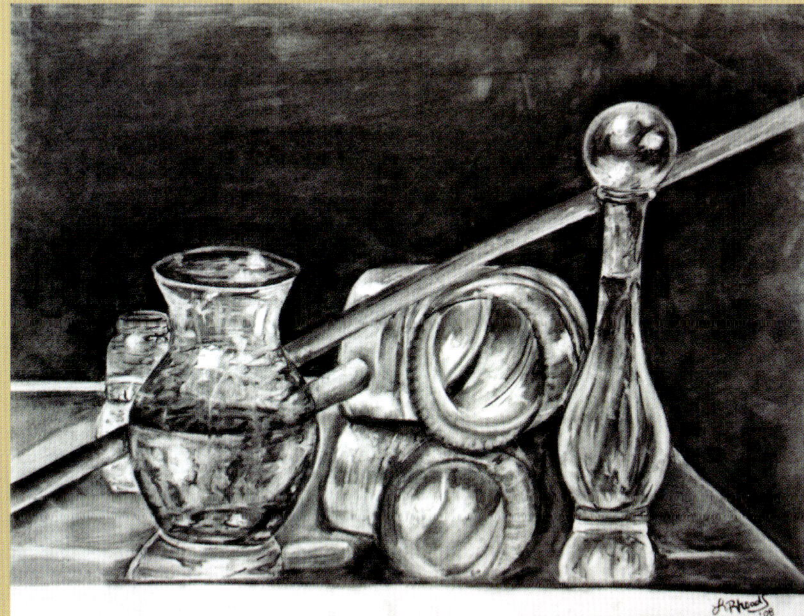

LIDA CRINER

Lida Adkins Criner comes from a long line of artists but was self-taught from girlhood. Lida lives in Limestone, Arkansas near the Buffalo National Forest. She develops and teaches internet courses in reading and writing and in the humanities for two universities. Painting portraits and landscapes from old photographs of people and places is a hobby that she shares with those who wish to renew the past, when they commission her to paint their ancestors and old home places. "Beholding beauty with the eye of the mind he will be enabled to bring forth not images of beauty, but realities because he has hold not of an image but of a reality" (Plato). **For more information on Lida's work or to inquire about prints or commission work, visit her website at: http://paletteartleague.org/LidaCriner.html or e-mail: earl1844@gmail.com.**

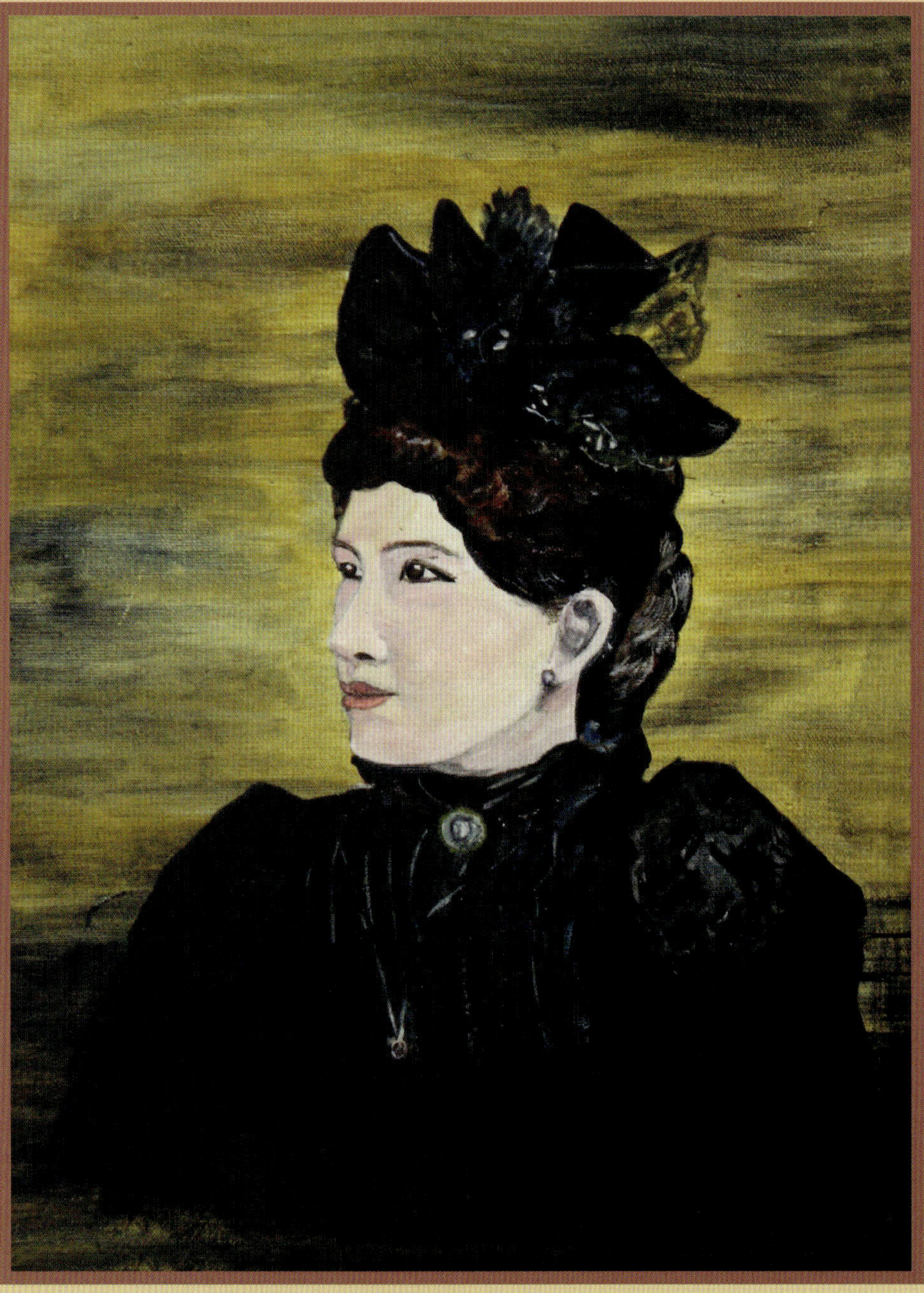

Great Grandmother Maria Luisa Earle
boarding ship in Port Cortez Central America 1898

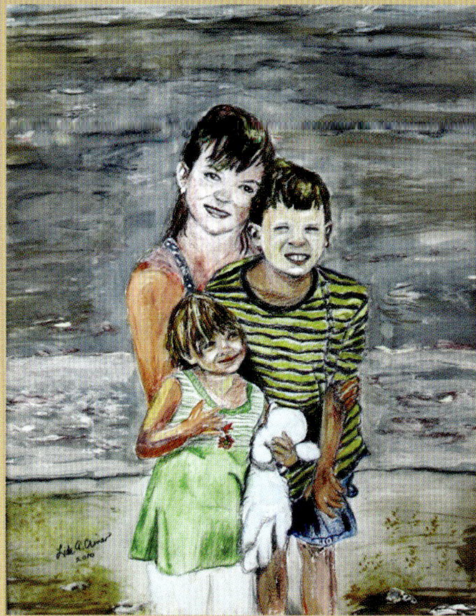
Grandkids on the Pensacola Beach
Elizabeth Hassig Berry,
Dustin & Suzannah Baker

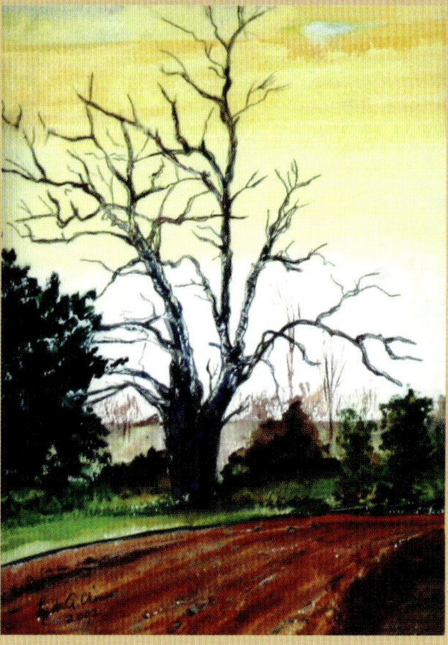
Norma Ogden's tree at limestone

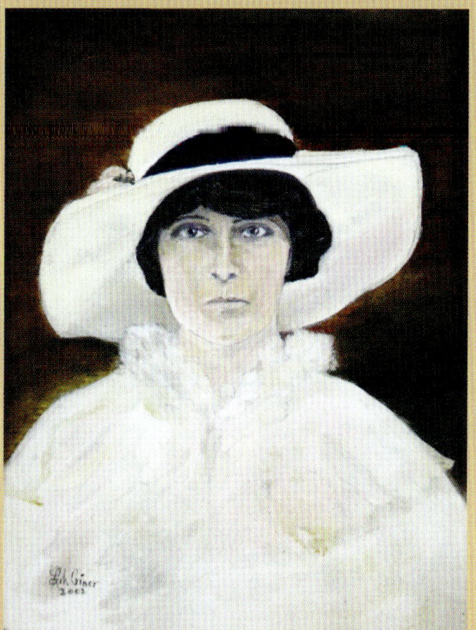
Miss Ethel Jones Criner
wedding day 1918

LIDA CRINER

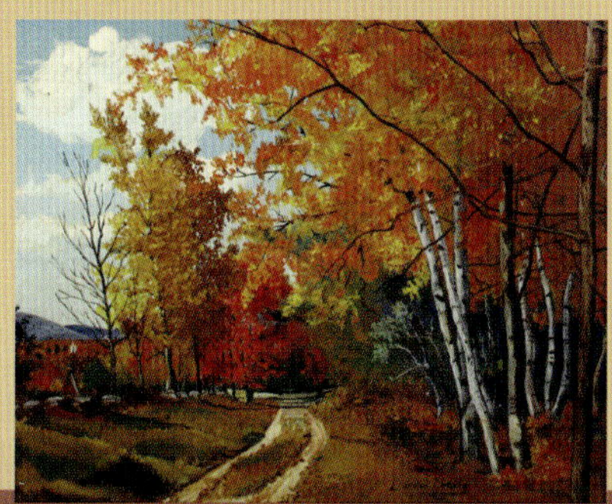
Aspen Colorado

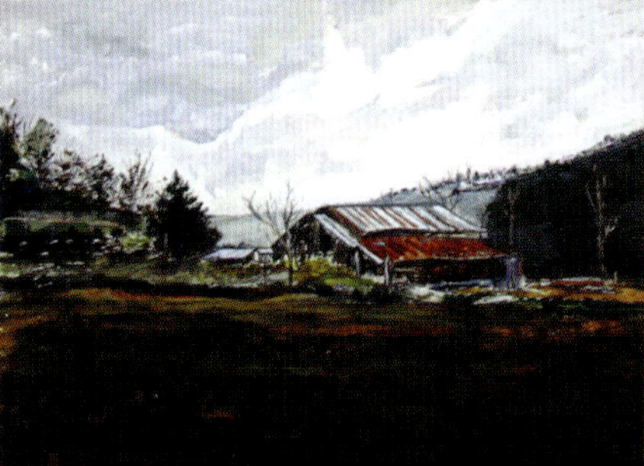
Glen Sams' old barn at
Limestone Arkansas

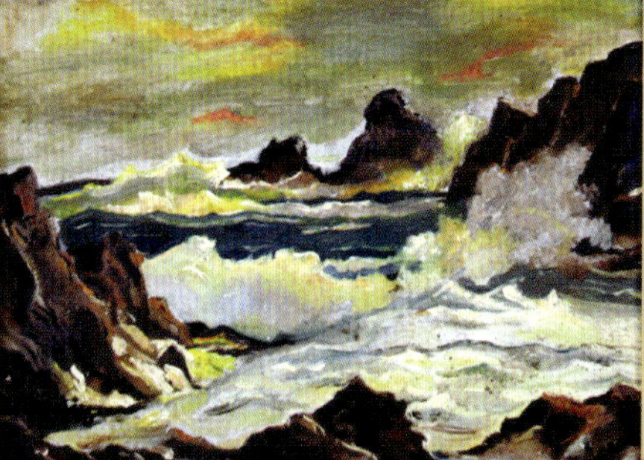
Maine Seascape

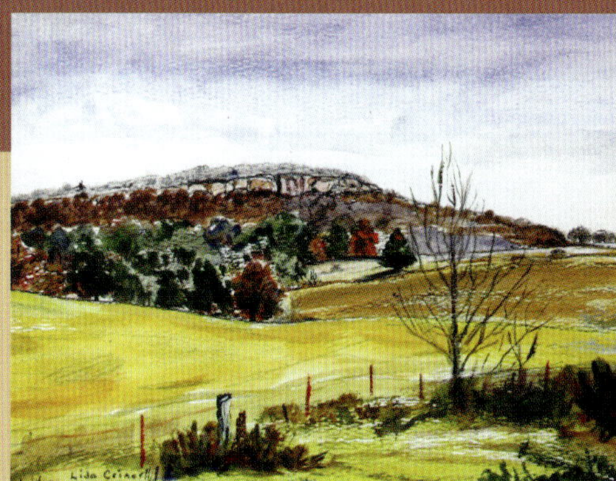
Red Rock
Newton County Arkansas

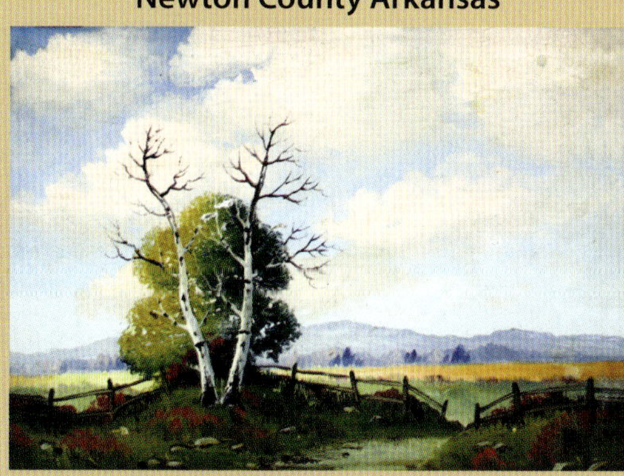
scene as taught by master painter
Glen Swedlun

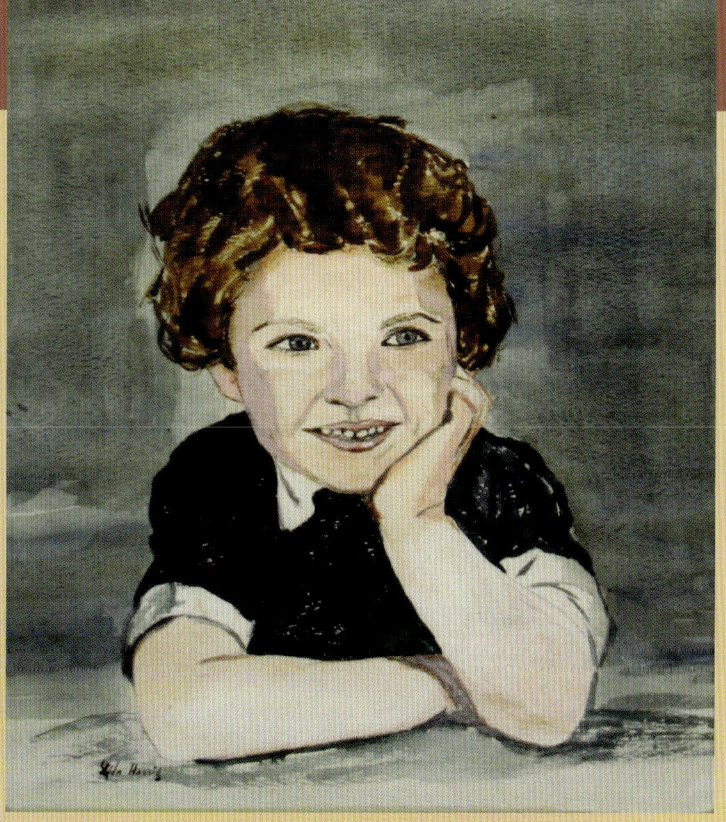
Renee Ragland in Bruno-Pyatt age 4

PAULINE BEATRICE "MACA" BANES (1921 – 2007)

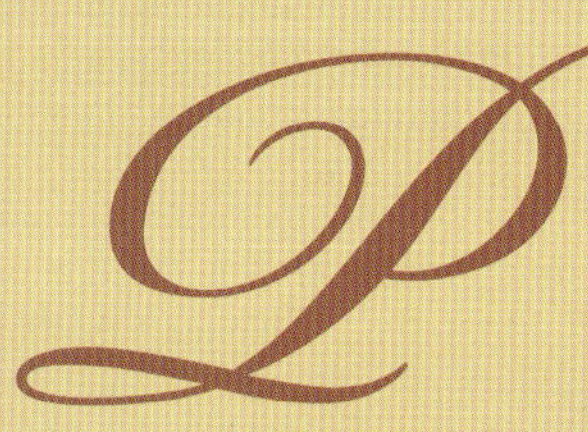

Pauline Beatrice "Maca" Banes (1921 – 2007), grew up in Bisbee, Arizona, married and came to Arkansas where she lived with her four children, Lida, Sue, Bill and Theresa. All of her children as well as her sister, the late Agnes Armstrong were artistically inclined. Pauline, whose grandfather was George Frederick Earle, of Maine (1844 – 1898), was happy to learn that she had come from a long line of well-known American artists. She said, "It means so much to know from where we came, and who we are." Ms. Banes painted landscapes of scenes near her home in the Ozarks at Western Grove, Arkansas. She began studying with Joanne Steiler, of Deer, Arkansas late in life and discovered that she had more talent than she imagined. Ms. Banes loved trees, clouds and streams and focused her talent on those ideas. **For more nformation on Ms. Banes's life and work, visit: http://paletteartleague.org/PaulineBanes.html.**

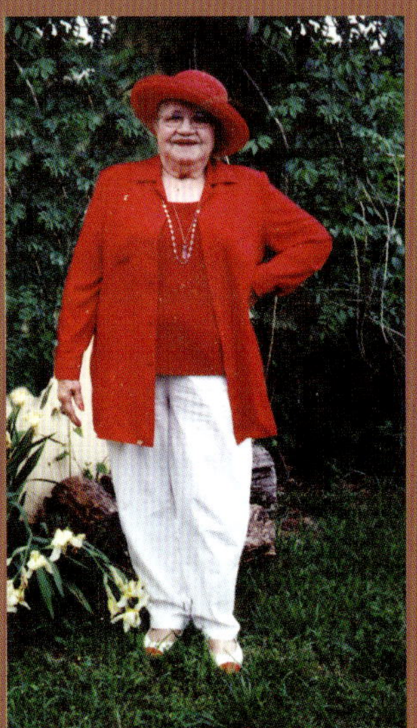

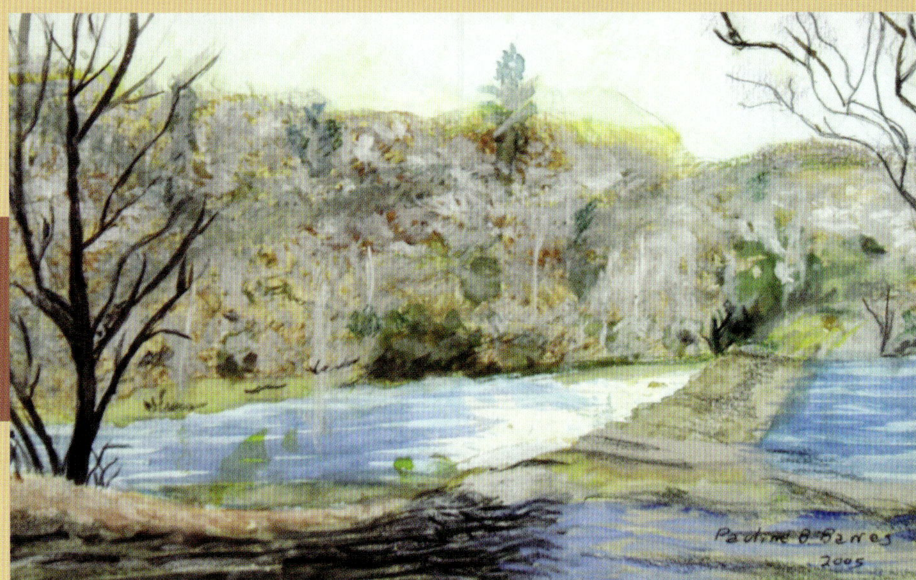

low water bridge at Hasty Arkansas

Mom's Dolls

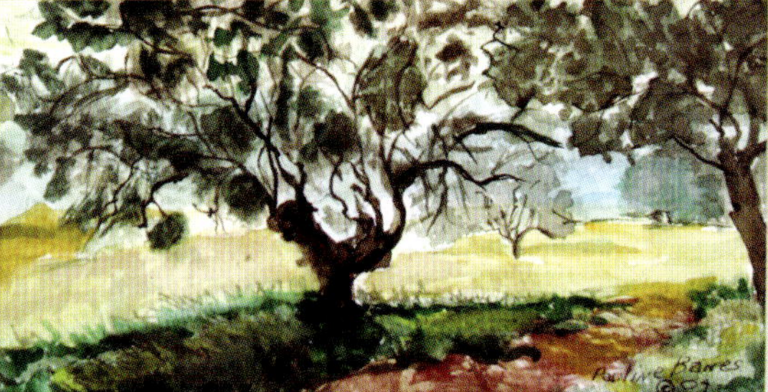

Joanne Steiler's watercolor lesson

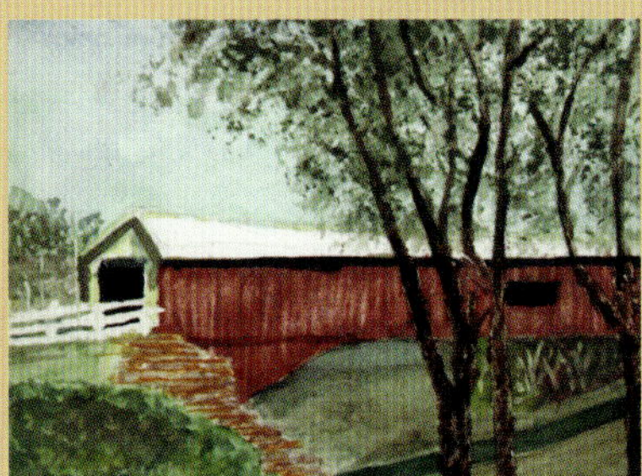

old covered bridge

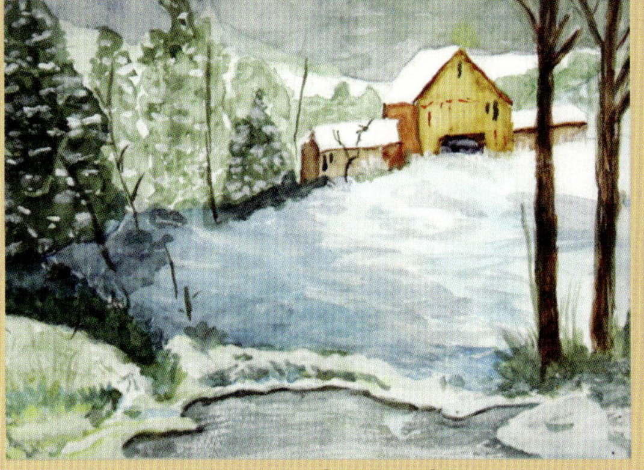

winter in the Ozarks

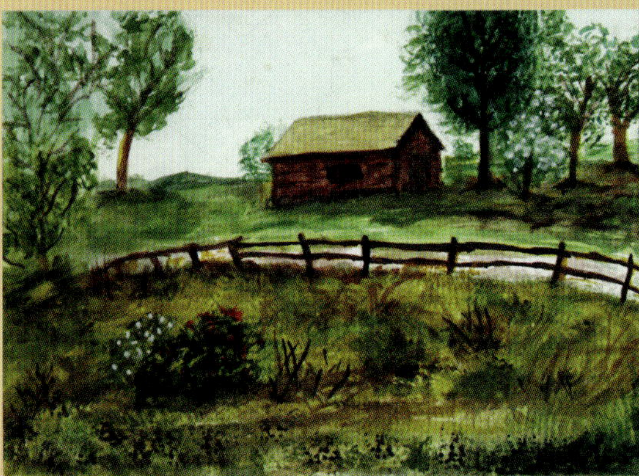

wild roses at the old cabin

LORETTA BABAK

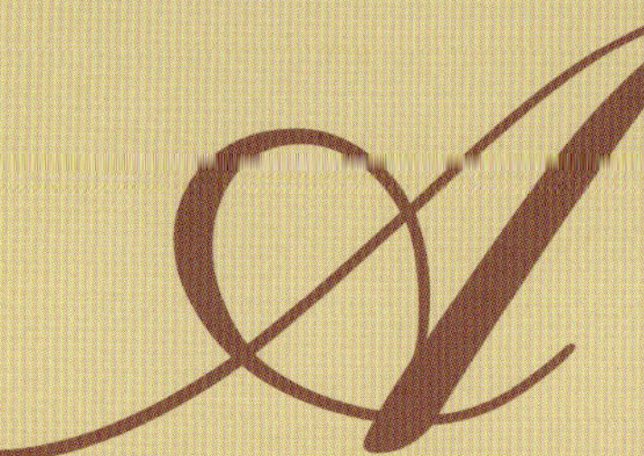

A passion for painting, combined with love of nature, paves the way for Loretta's creations. Many of her paintings of wildlife are on wood that has nature's flaws (knots, etc.) Incorporated into scenery, that is not only lovely, but fanciful.

Retirement brought about the move from Michigan to Mountain View, Arkansas. Building where there are bluffs, a creek, woodlands with rock landscapes, and wildlife, all help to feed her imagination.

Art doesn't have boundaries for Loretta. Her art ranges from wildlife, scenery, seascapes, western, to portraits. Paintings also range from oil, acrylic, to watercolor.

Membership in Off the Beaten Path Studio Tour, Mountain View Art Guild, Mid-Southern Watercolorists, and the Palette Art League, gives the opportunity to participate in functions with like minded people.

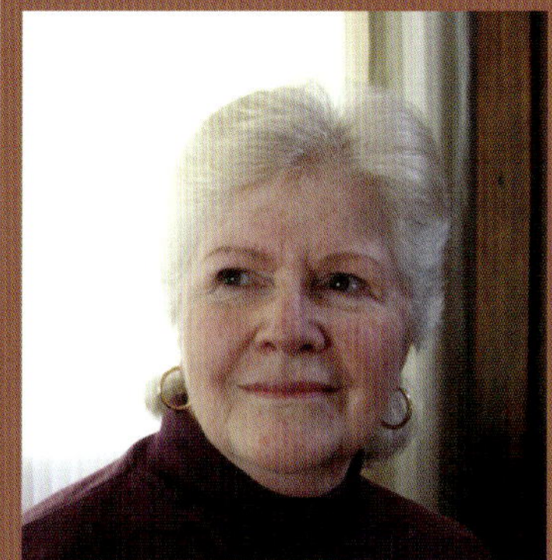

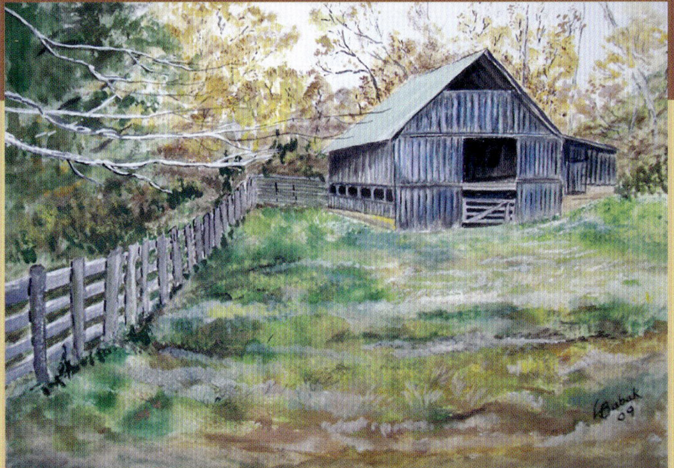

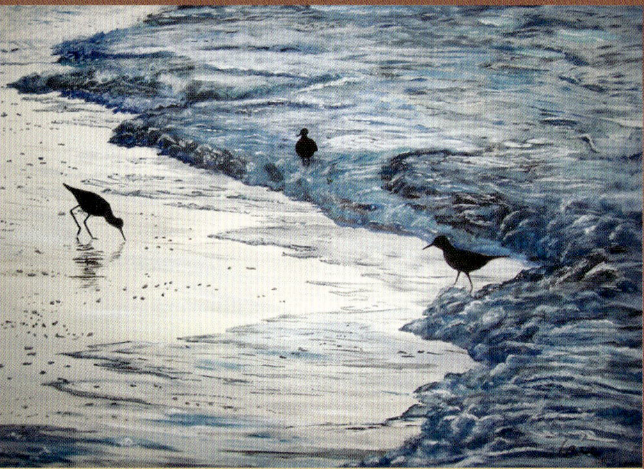

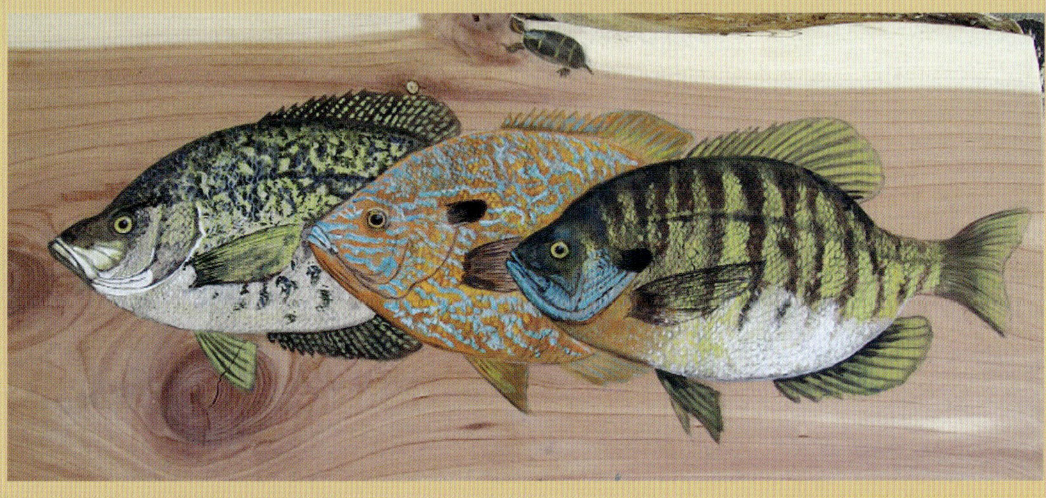

VICTORIA RAUB

I had never picked up a paintbrush before taking Phyllis Bailey's Painting I class at Arkansas State University, Mountain Home in 2007 and I haven't put the brush down since. After 25 years in the corporate world, I have found what I was meant to do. I work in oil, acrylic and watercolor. My paintings are full of color and texture and usually show some evidence of my other passion – flowers – by which I am continually inspired.

I am fortunate to have a wonderful studio in my home where my current focus is in oils. As a member of the Area Art Club, Palette Art League and Artists of the Ozarks, I participate in various local art competitions and exhibit my work at several local galleries.

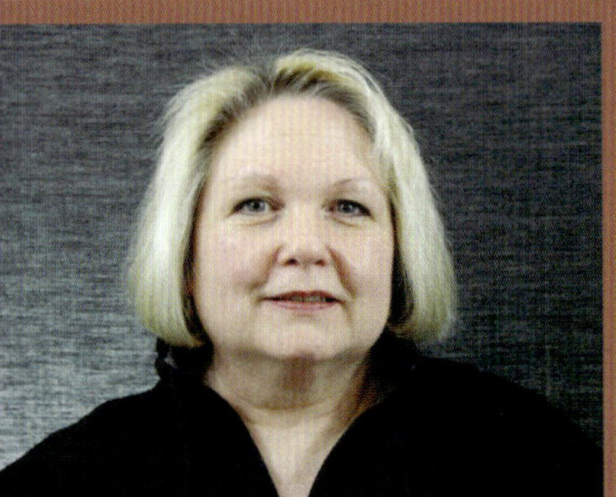

You may view more of my work at http://paletteartleague.org/VictoriaRaub.html or e-mail me at victoriaraub@bellsouth.net.

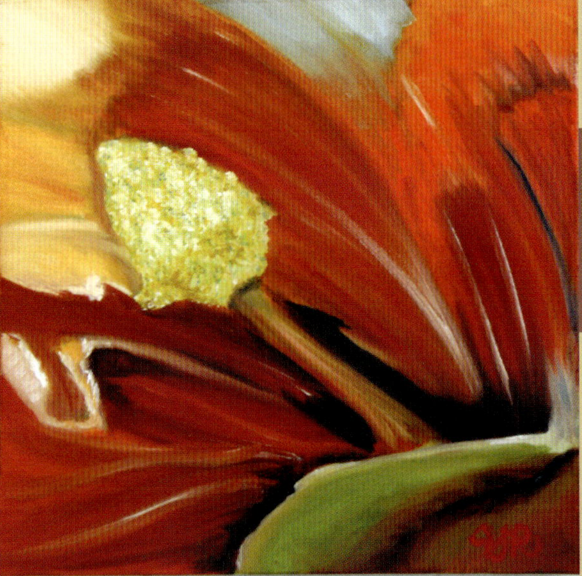

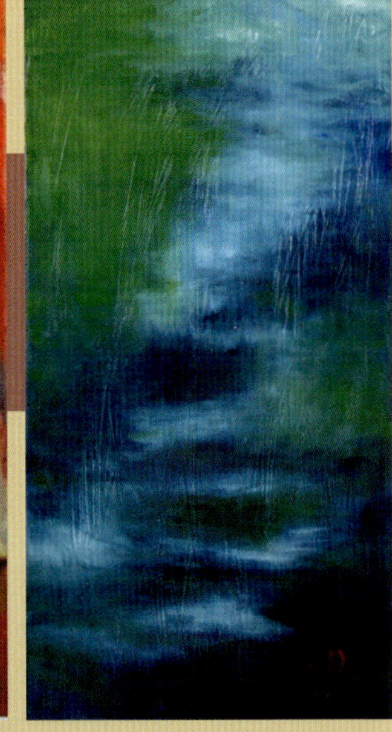

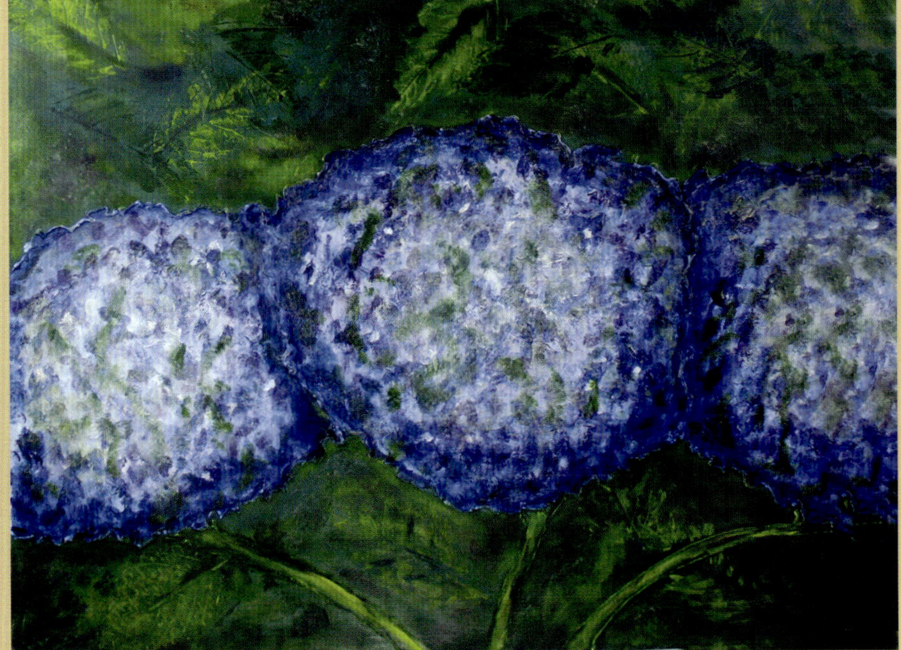

Brandon Smith, 23, of Yellville Arkansas, has been expressing his artistic talents since the age of three. He has a natural gift of transferring ideas from imagination to paper. As Brandon's talent grew, so did the attention he received. He's won numerous local and regional awards. Brandon has designed team mascots, automotive paint and styling ideas, tattoos and murals both commercially and for friends and family. Brandon enjoys working with pastels, pencil, charcoal and oils. Combining an interest in literature with his art, Brandon is currently working on creating graphic novels. His future interests are automotive design and art education, but where ever Brandon's road leads, his passion for art will no doubt be part of it. **For more information on Brandon's work, visit: http://paletteartleague.org/BrandonSmith.html.**

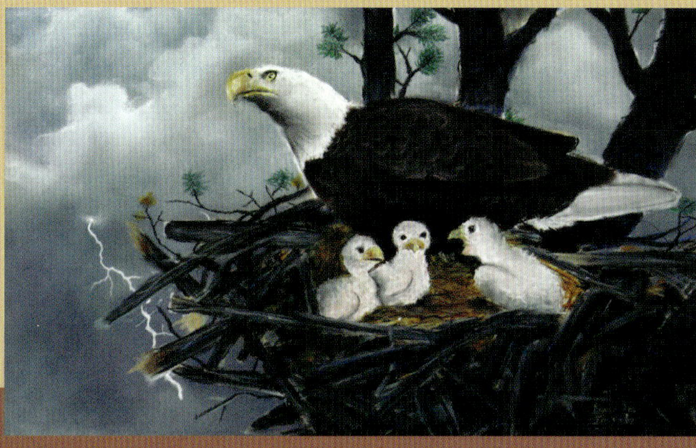

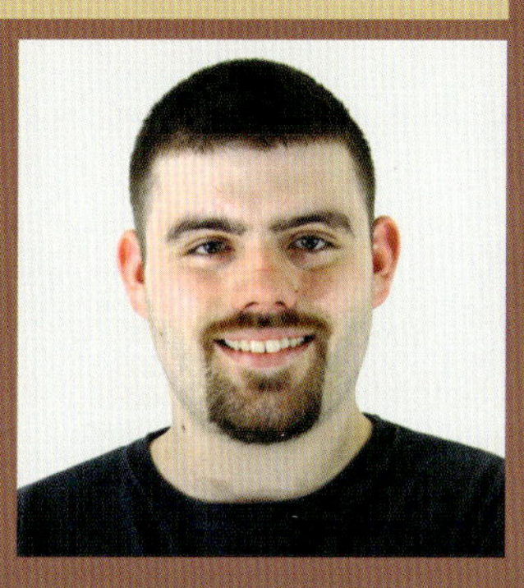

BRANDON SMITH

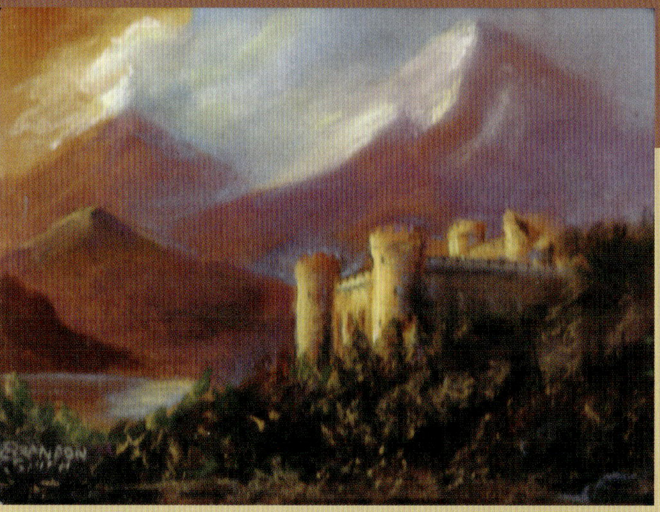

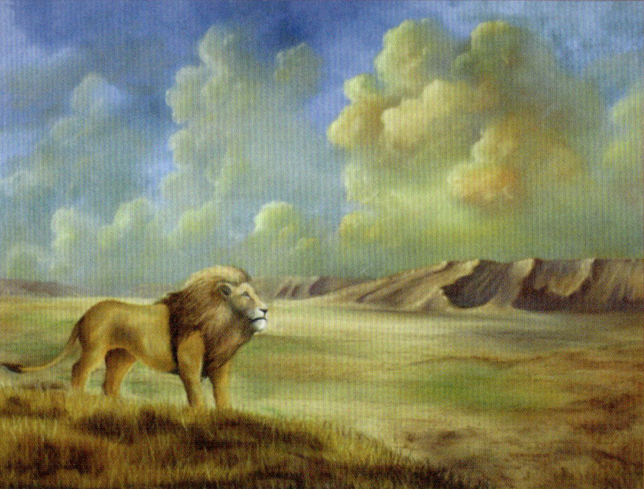

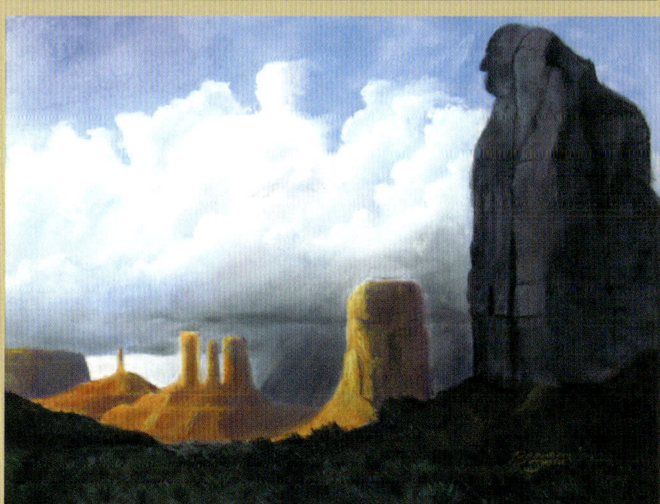

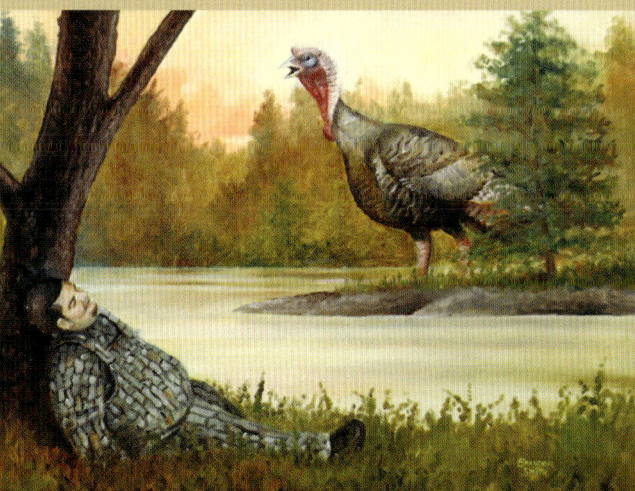

DAUNA TYSON

Dauna Tyson was born in Memphis, Tennessee but moved to the Ozarks in 1977. She lived in Arkansas until the tender age of 13 when her family moved to Tampa, Florida where she lived for the next 15 years. While in Florida, Dauna missed the mountains, creeks, lakes and rivers of the Ozarks. More than that, she really missed the solitude and the friendly people that the Ozarks are famous for. Her late father loved this area. He called it, "God's Country". He wanted Dauna and her children to move back to Arkansas in the late 90's, and they did.

Her passion for photography began in her teens. She loves capturing the beauty of nature and this is one of the most scenic places in the United States. Dauna also loves photographing children, "they are only young once", she says. She has three beautiful children. Lindsey Butler who is the model in some of Dauna's photos and wants to pursue modeling as she is very photogenic. Matthew Butler, an aspiring young artist who is also in this book. And her youngest son Taylor who is the next generation of talented artist in their home.

Dauna is a licensed real estate agent in the Ozarks and now has a photography business. **She can be contacted at: 870-656-3500 or email her at: daunatyson@yahoo.com. The name of her photography business is, "Ozarks Impressions, by Dauna Tyson". Dauna is the Creative Director for The Art and Artisans of the Ozarks.**

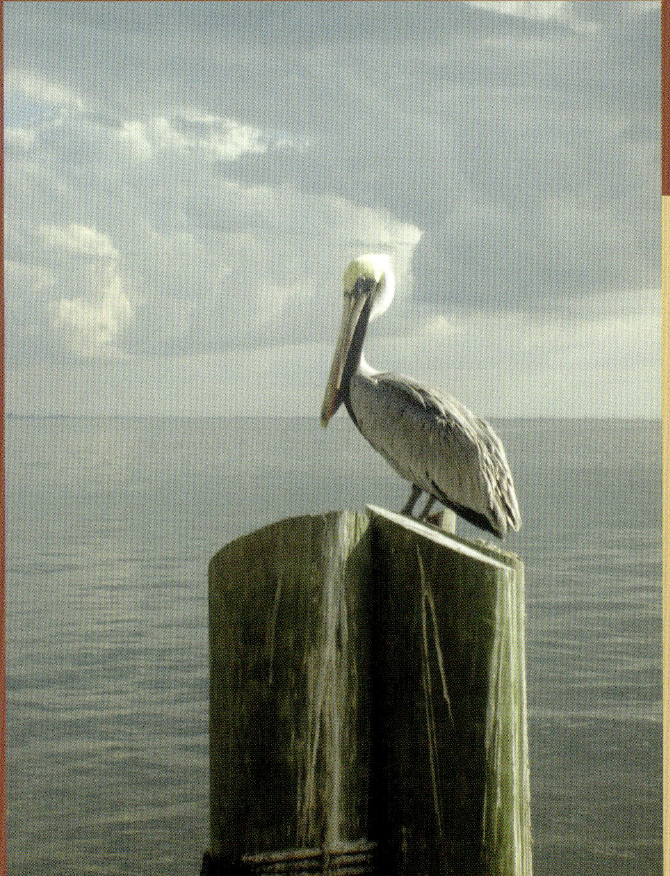

Pelican, St. Petersburg, Florida

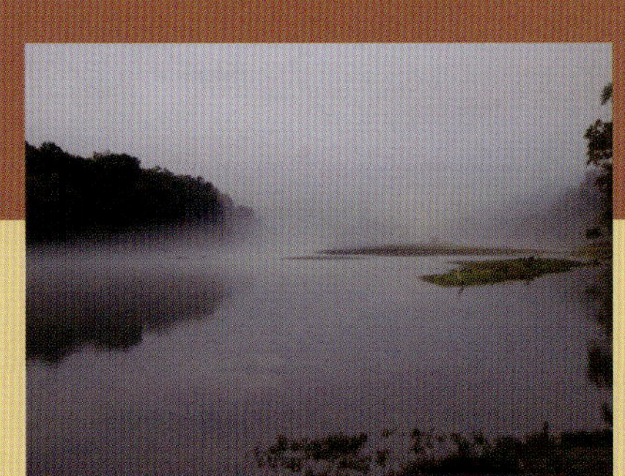

White River Mist

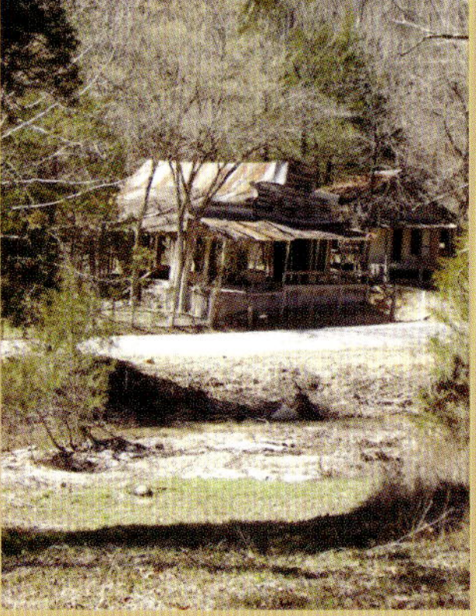

Old Mining Town, Rush, Arkansas

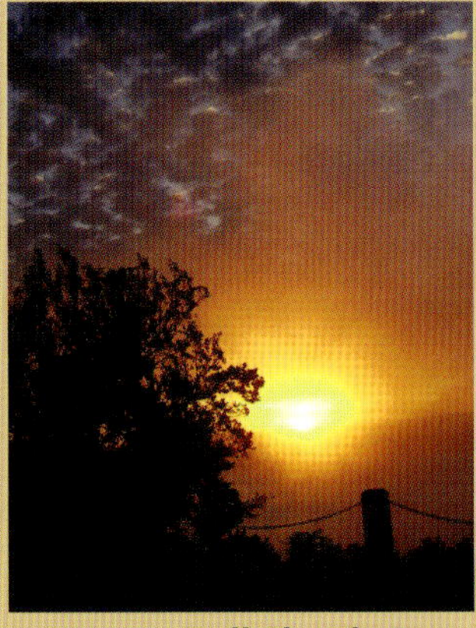

Sunset at Bull Shoals Dam, Bull Shoals, Arkansas

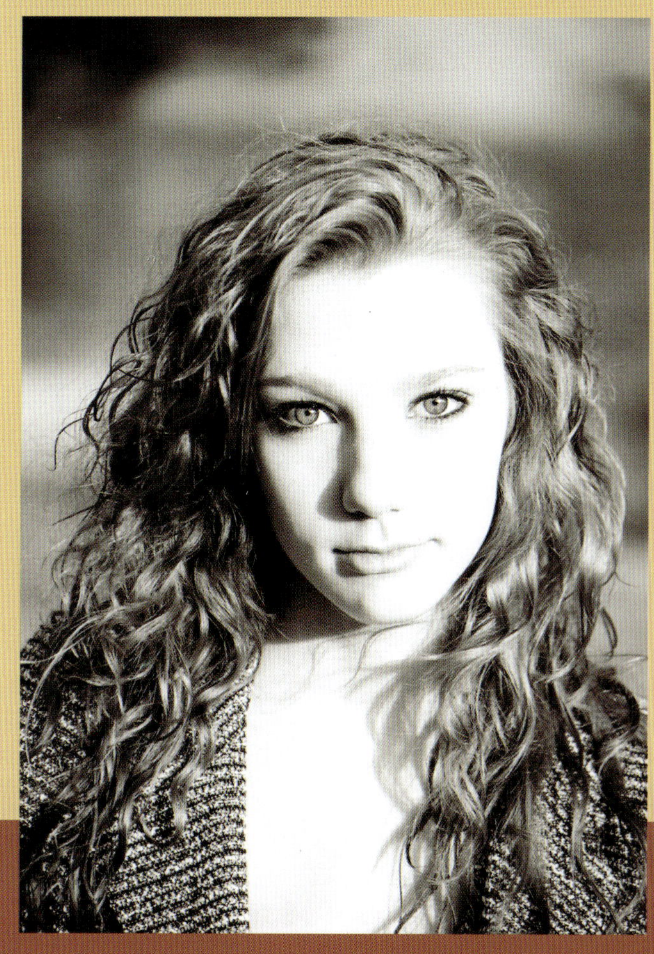
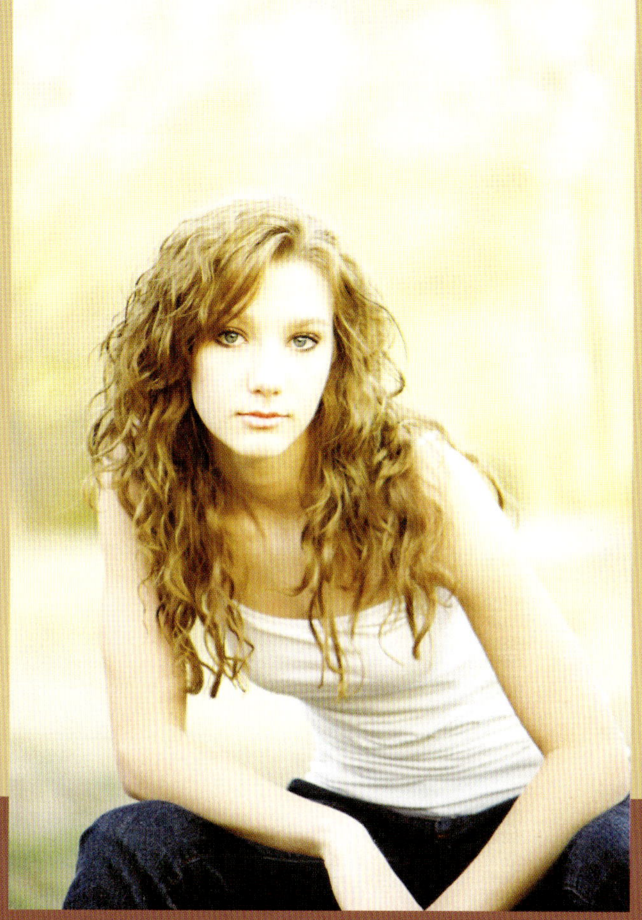

DAUNA TYSON

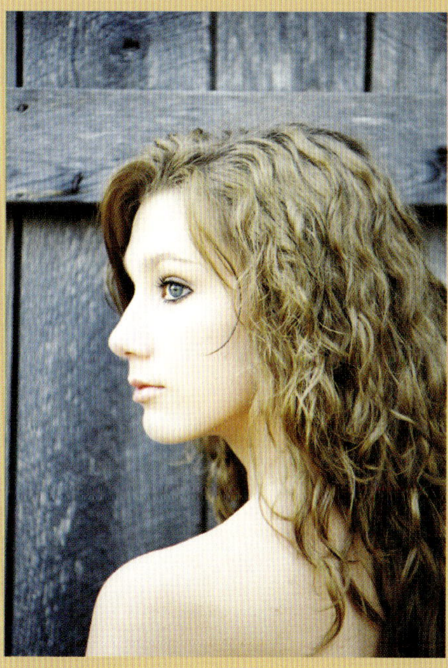
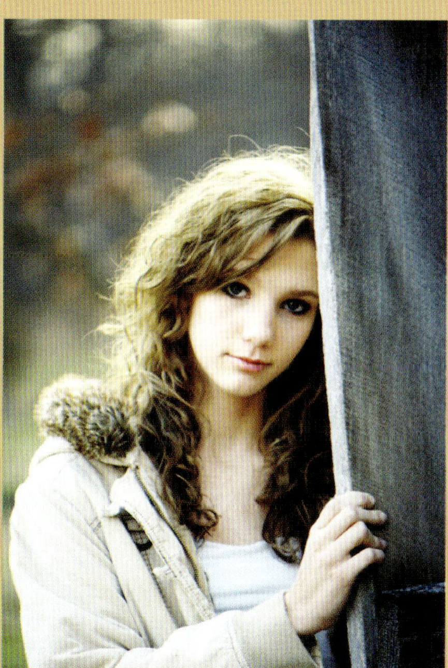
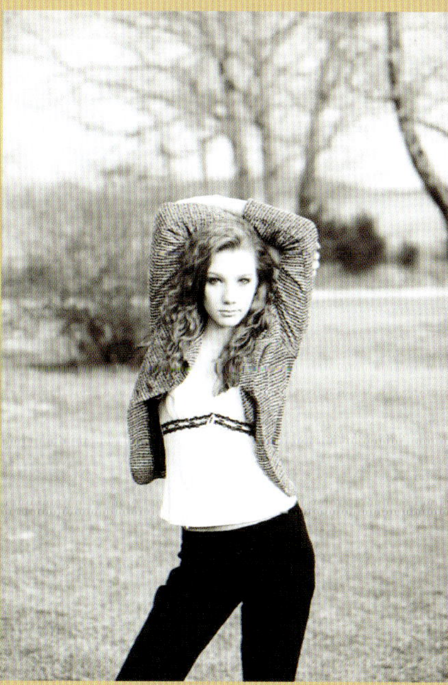

SARAH ELIZABETH MILLER

Miss Sarah Elizabeth Miller was born in Pocahontas, Arkansas. She completed her Masters of Art Degree from Arkansas State University in Jonesboro, AR where she worked for the Fowler Center and Bradbury Gallery since their opening in 2003. She has held positions as both gallery docent and graduate assistant for the gallery through out her education. Miller has also been employed as the House Manager for the Fowler Center and has served as the curatorial assistant for the Hardwired Café at ASU. She is currently a teaching candidate, pursuing her Masters in Secondary Education with the University of Arkansas in Little Rock. She is employed as an Art Specialist with the Jacksonville Lighthouse Charter School.

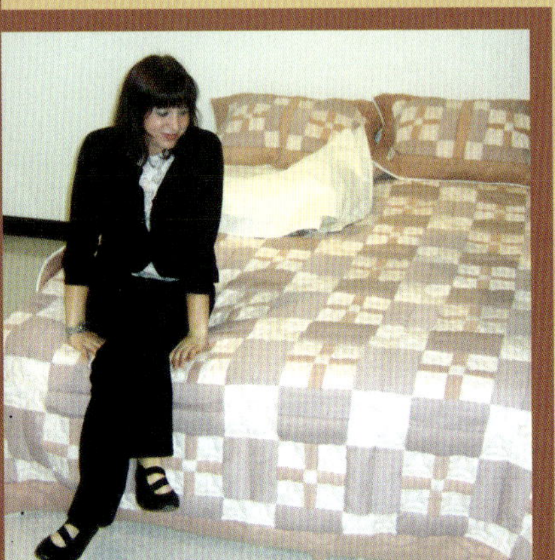

She is a practicing contemporary artist, and is currently in an exhibition with L.A.C.D.A. in Los Angeles, CA. Her mixed media objects and paintings have been presented in solo as well as group exhibitions through out the state. Other exhibition locations include; Memphis, Tennessee, St. Louis, Missouri, Los Angeles, California, Wakefield, Rhode Island, Atlanta, Georgia, Washington, DC, Philadelphia, Pennsylvania, Boston, Massachusetts, Chicago, Illinois, and Brooklyn, New York.

Her work has been recognized with scholarships, assistantships and grants from Arkansas State University where she received her BFA in December of 2003. Miller was awarded the Durst Award for her study with the U of A and served as the Vice-President for both the Art Graduate Student Association and the Contemporary Sculpture Society. She has also studied at Scuola Lorenzo De'Medici and the Florence University for the Arts in Florence, Italy and Teiko University in Maastricht, Netherlands.

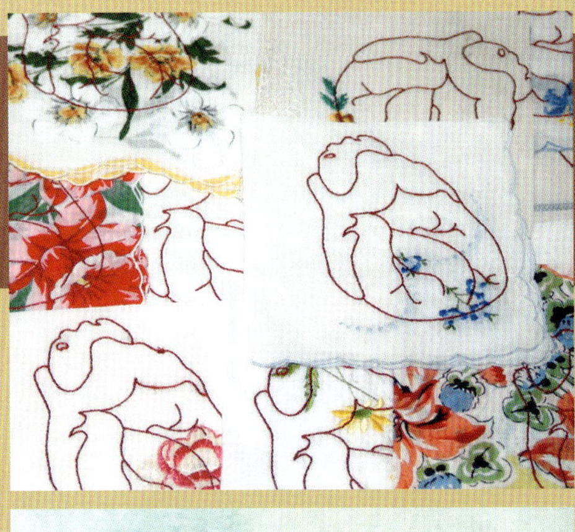

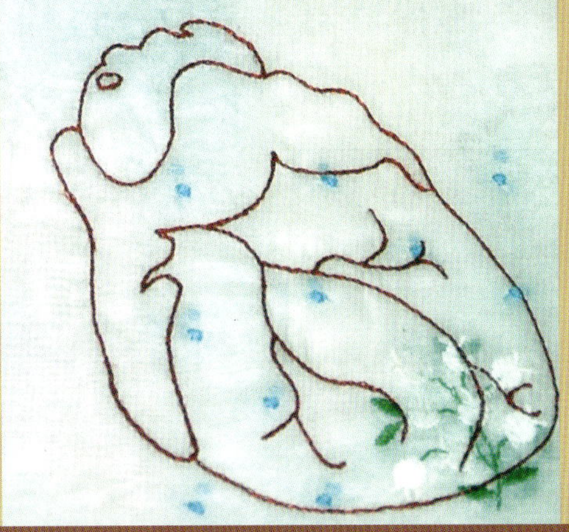

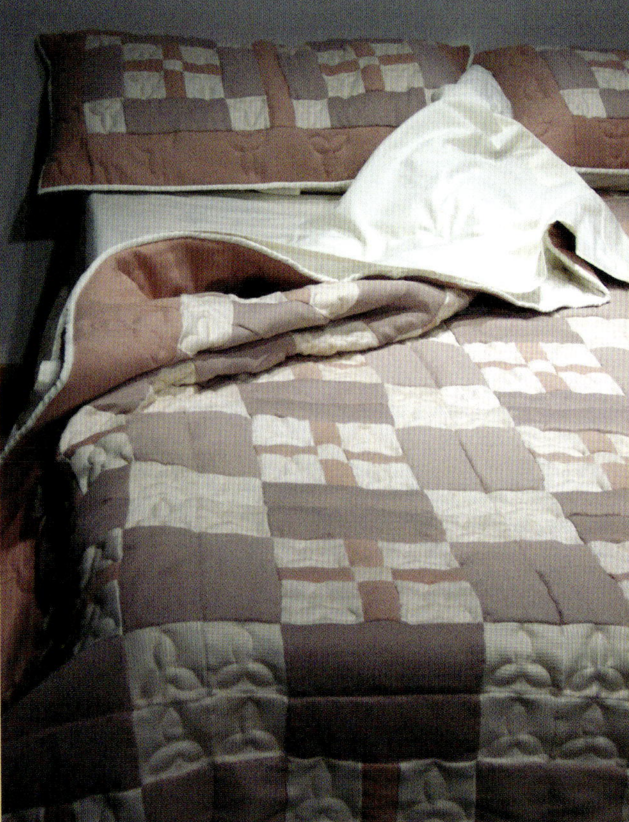

RHODA DOERR

Born and raised in Alaska, Rhoda Doerr has lived in the Pacific Northwest and Wisconsin before moving to Arkansas.

Rhoda's oil painting is part of the permanent collection at the Waukesha County Courthouse. Juried shows include Carroll University and the Cedarburg Wisconsin Art Fair and a one-woman show at Brookfield Academy. She was featured artist/storyteller at Fine Arts Day in local schools.

In Arkansas, Rhoda's awards at the area Art Club Show include Best in Oil and the Josie Schliemann Award. Her work was featured at the Olive Tree gallery in Mountain View Arkansas as well as the Ozark Folk Center. She is a member of the Mountain Home Area Art Club, the Mountain View Art Guild and the Arkansas Pastel Society. **For more information on Rhoda's work, visit http://paletteartleague.org/RhodaDoerr.html.**

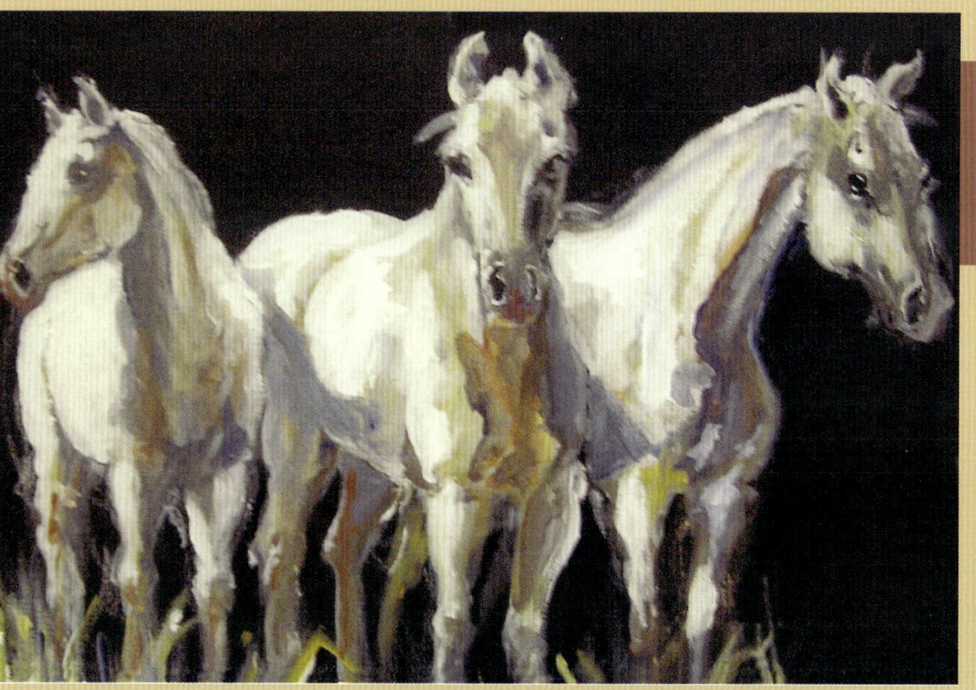

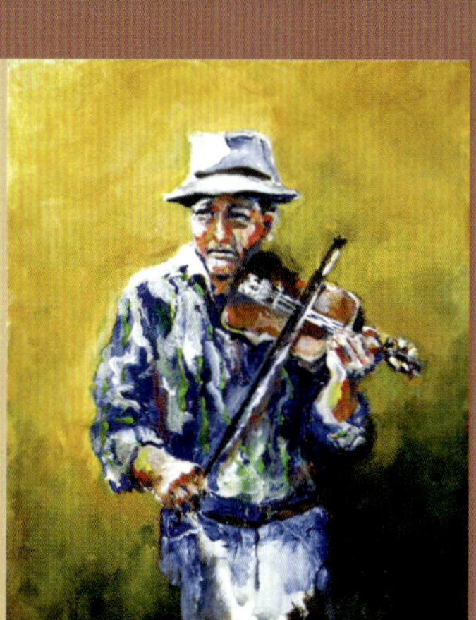

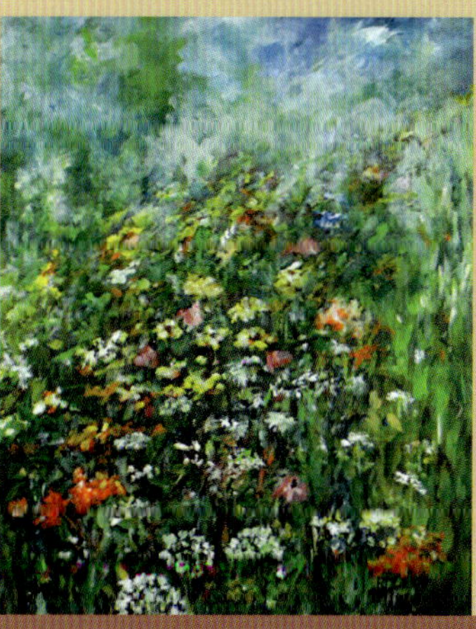

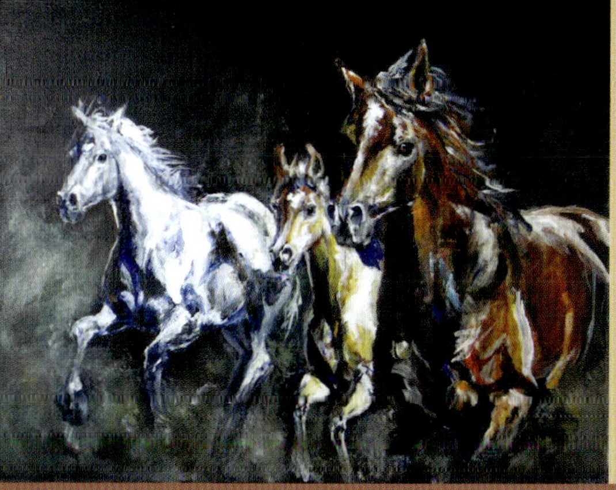

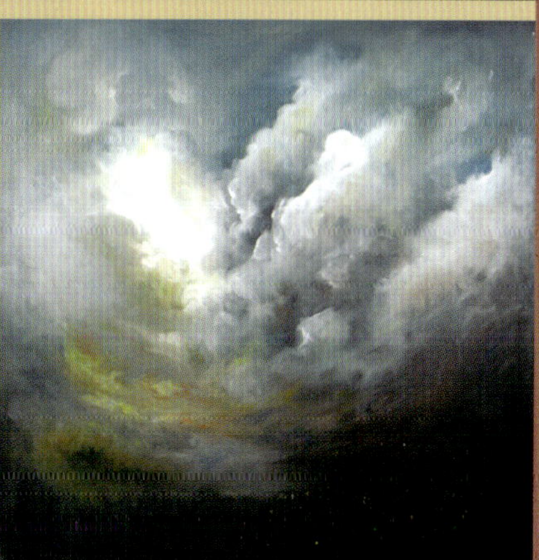

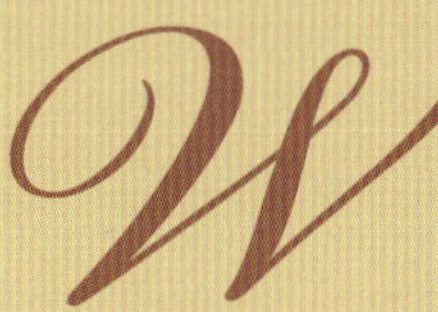

When I was six years old, my uncle asked what I wanted to be when I grew up. I answered, "an artist."

My interest in art followed me all through my life in various forms, from working with papier-mâché, painting custom aircraft on shirts, quilting, etc. It wasn't until 2002, however, that I discovered the joy of working with clay. It all began with a sculpture class – I knew I had found my niche! From that point, I went on to experience the art of creating functional pottery under the guidance of a Master Potter.

Currently, I enjoy my own studio where I continue to create hand-built pottery and experiment with a variety of glaze combinations.

This is a journey. This is my passion! **For more information on Phyllis's work, visit: http://paletteartleague.org/PhyllisAnderson.html.**

PHYLLIS ANDERSON

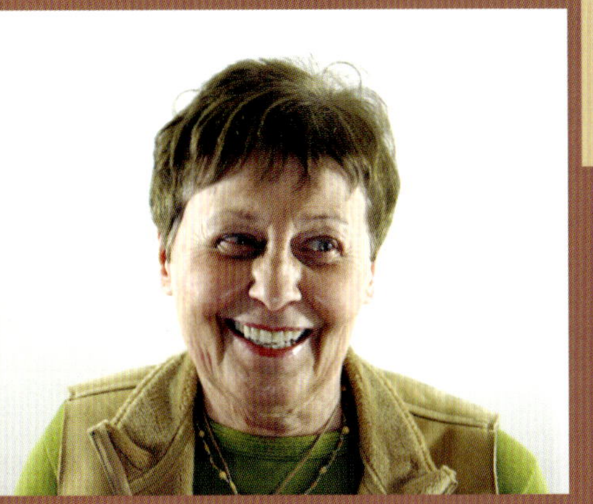

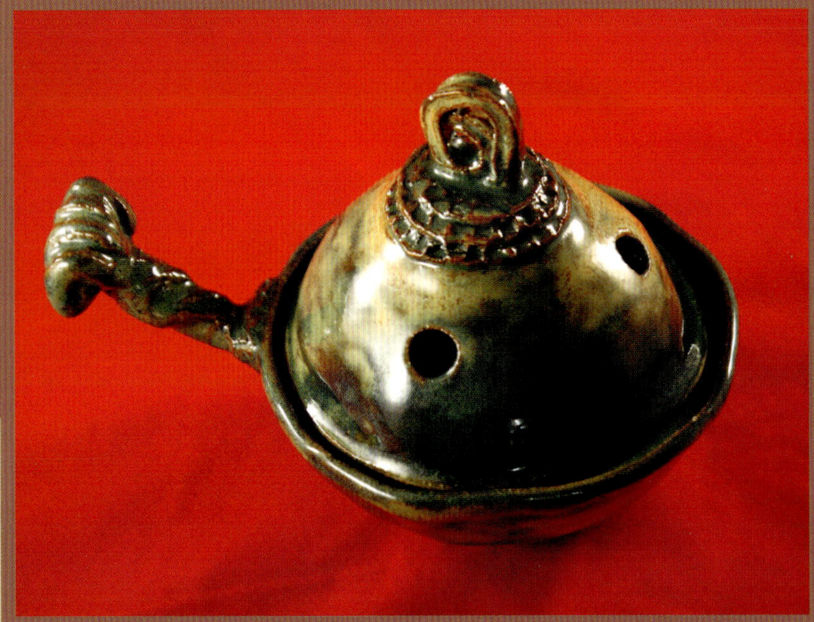

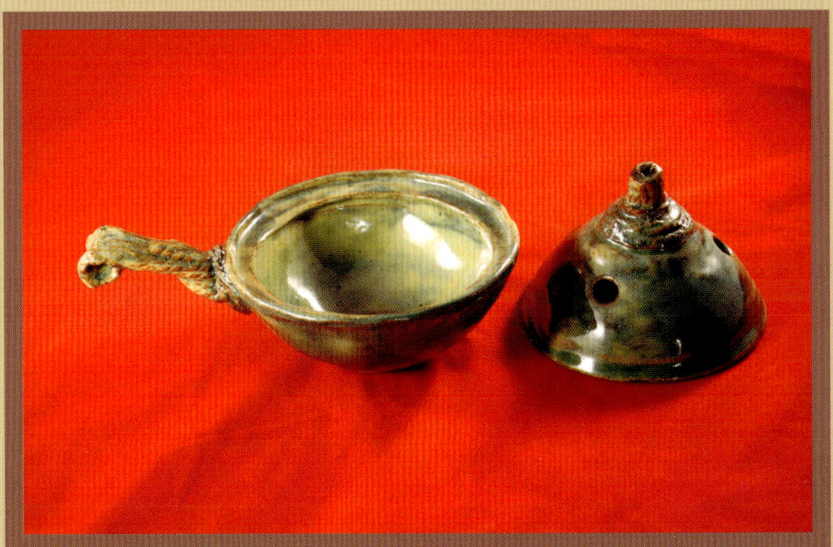

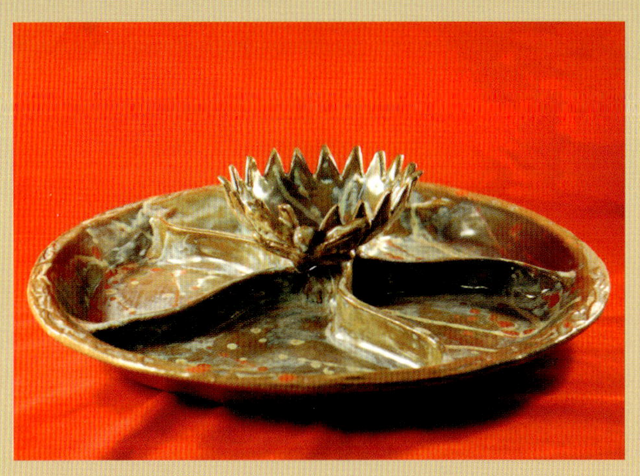

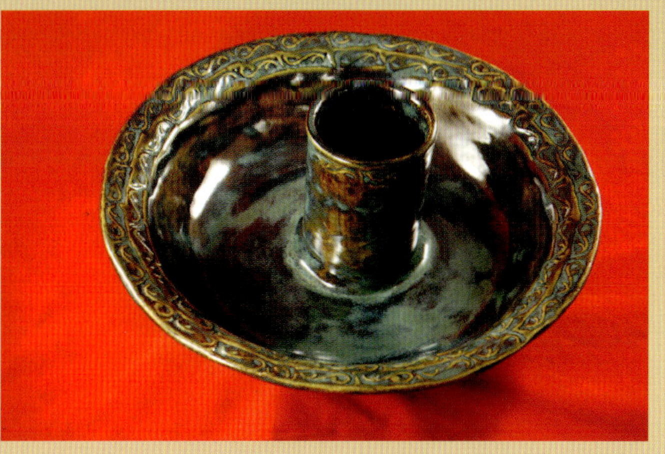

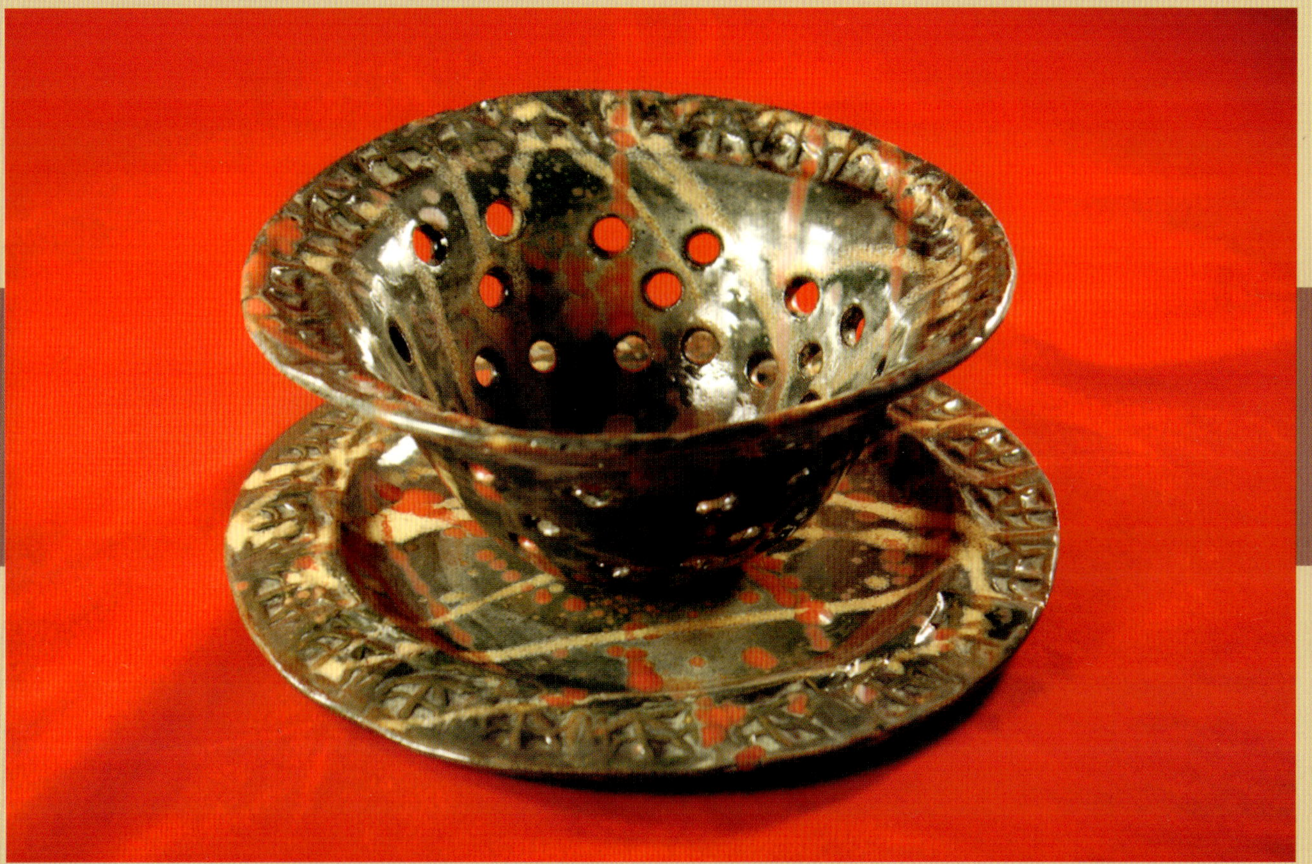

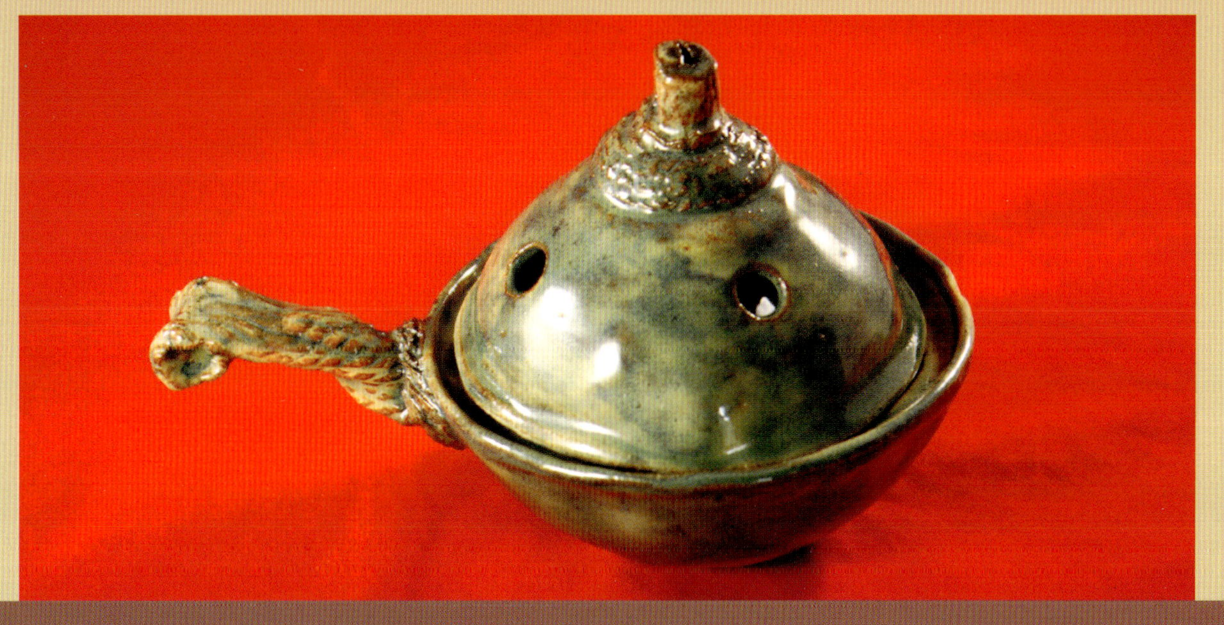

Alphabetic Index

Index

Index (continued)

New Members Are Always Welcome!

If you would like to become a member of the Palette Art League, visit our website at: http://paletteartleague.org/shop to sign-up today!

The Palette Art League is all inclusive in its membership. If you would like to help support the Arts and be a part of art education and art appreciation, we welcome you to become a member. We offer several different levels of membership and one is sure to fit your needs.

Business sponsors are always welcome and we are always happy to find volunteers who enjoy helping at the Gallery, at events and at workshops hosted at the Gallery.

As is the case with all volunteer organizations, we can't exist without our volunteers!

Our goal throughout the book was to provide you with information about each artist, about their work and to provide you with their contact information so you can conveniently learn more about them.

We hope that you have enjoyed volume 1 of The Art & Artisans of the Ozarks and watch for future volumes in the years to come!

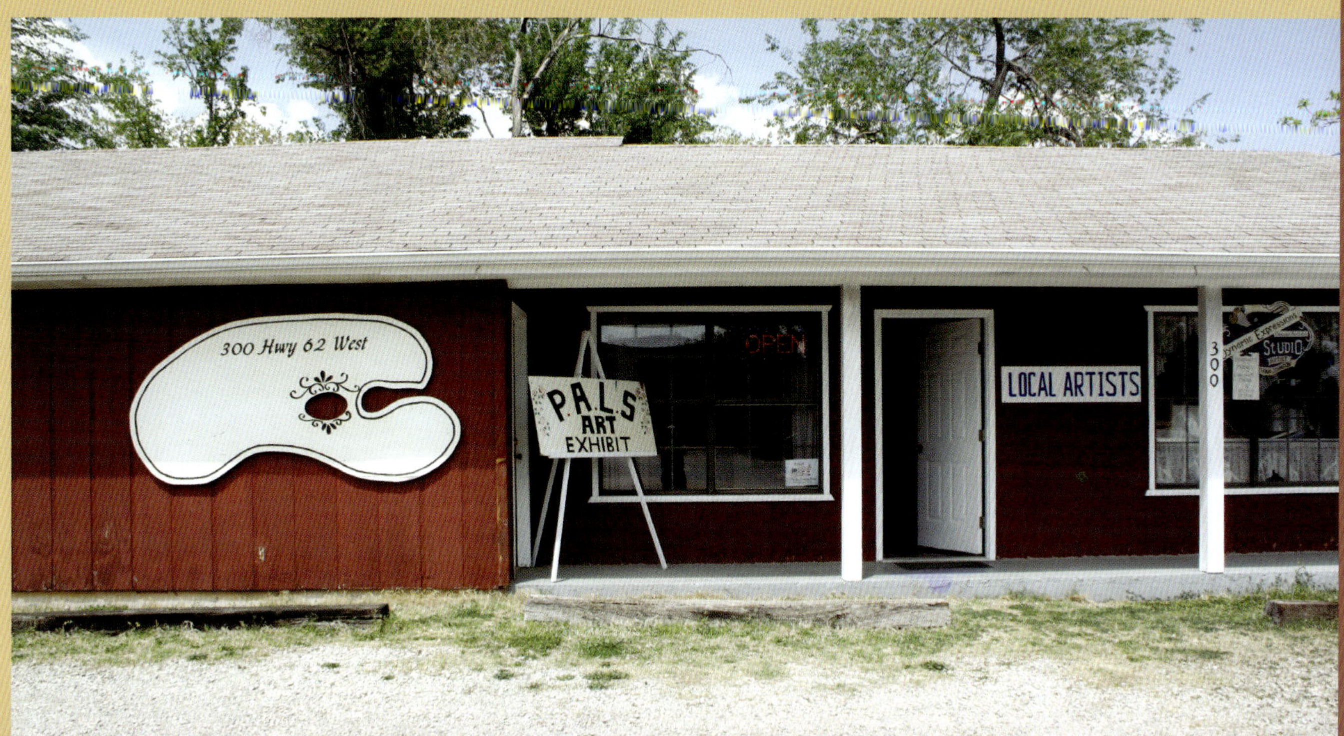

PALETTE ART LEAGUEGALLERY

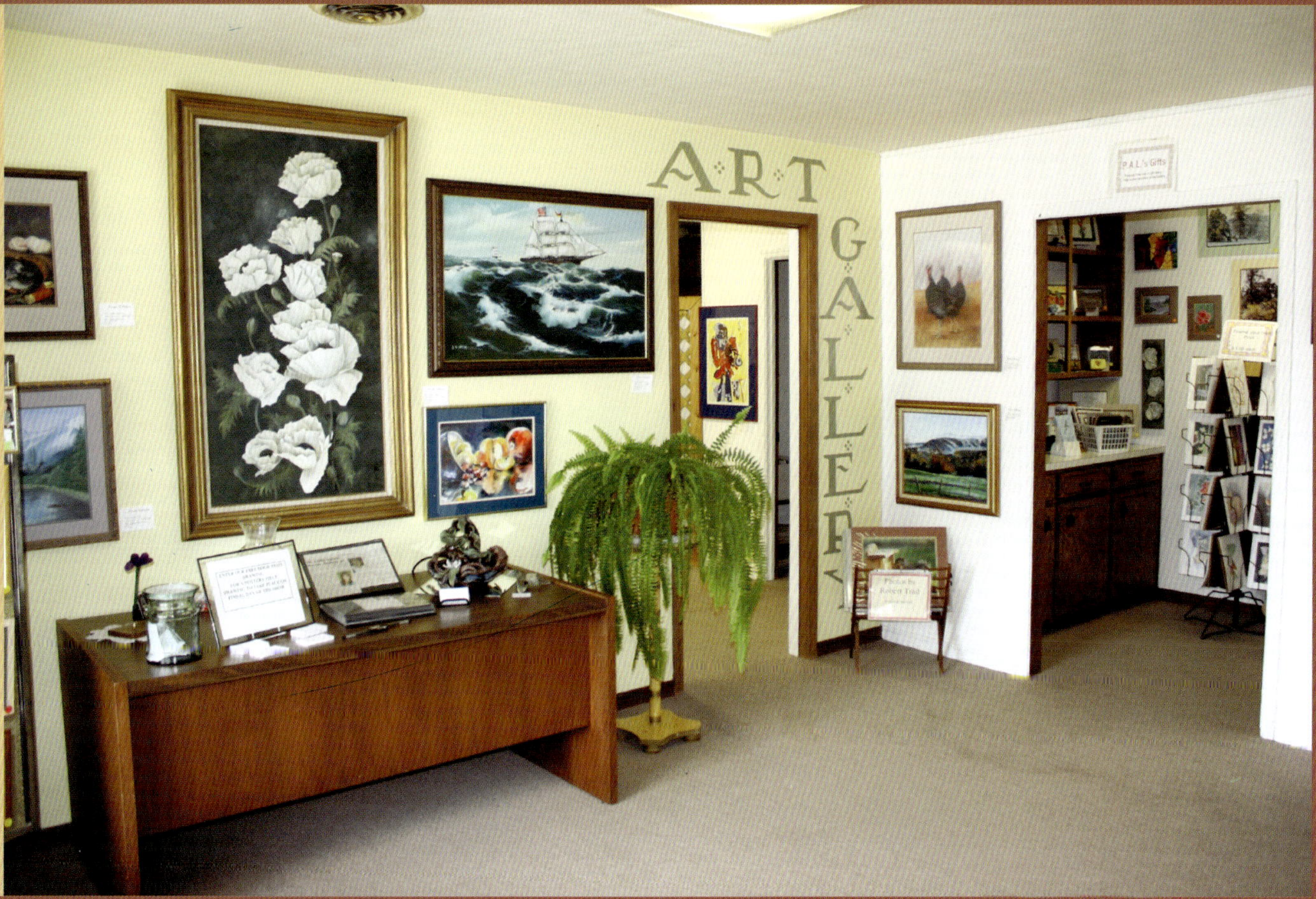

THE PALETTE ART LEAGUE

THE PALETTE ART LEAGUE

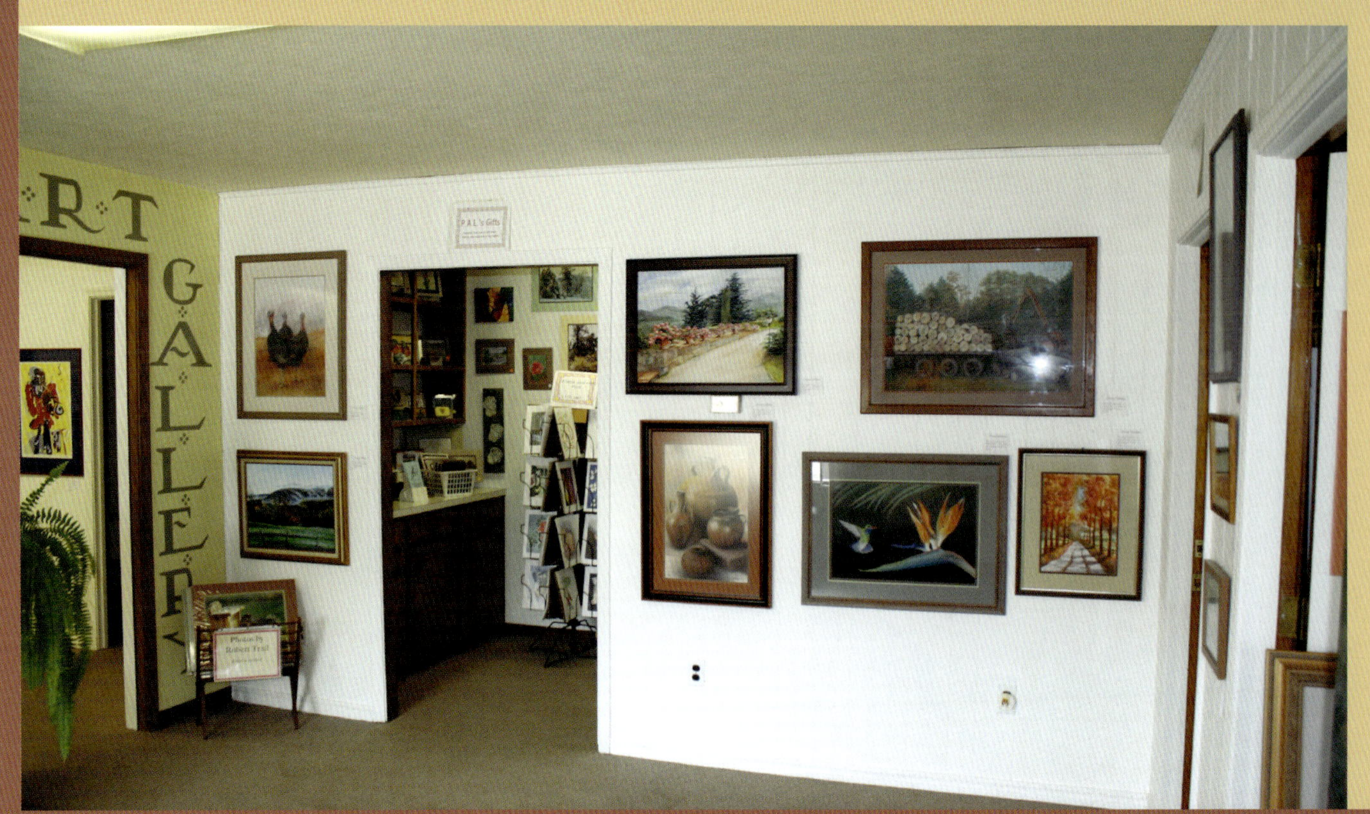

PALETTEARTLEAGUE.ORG

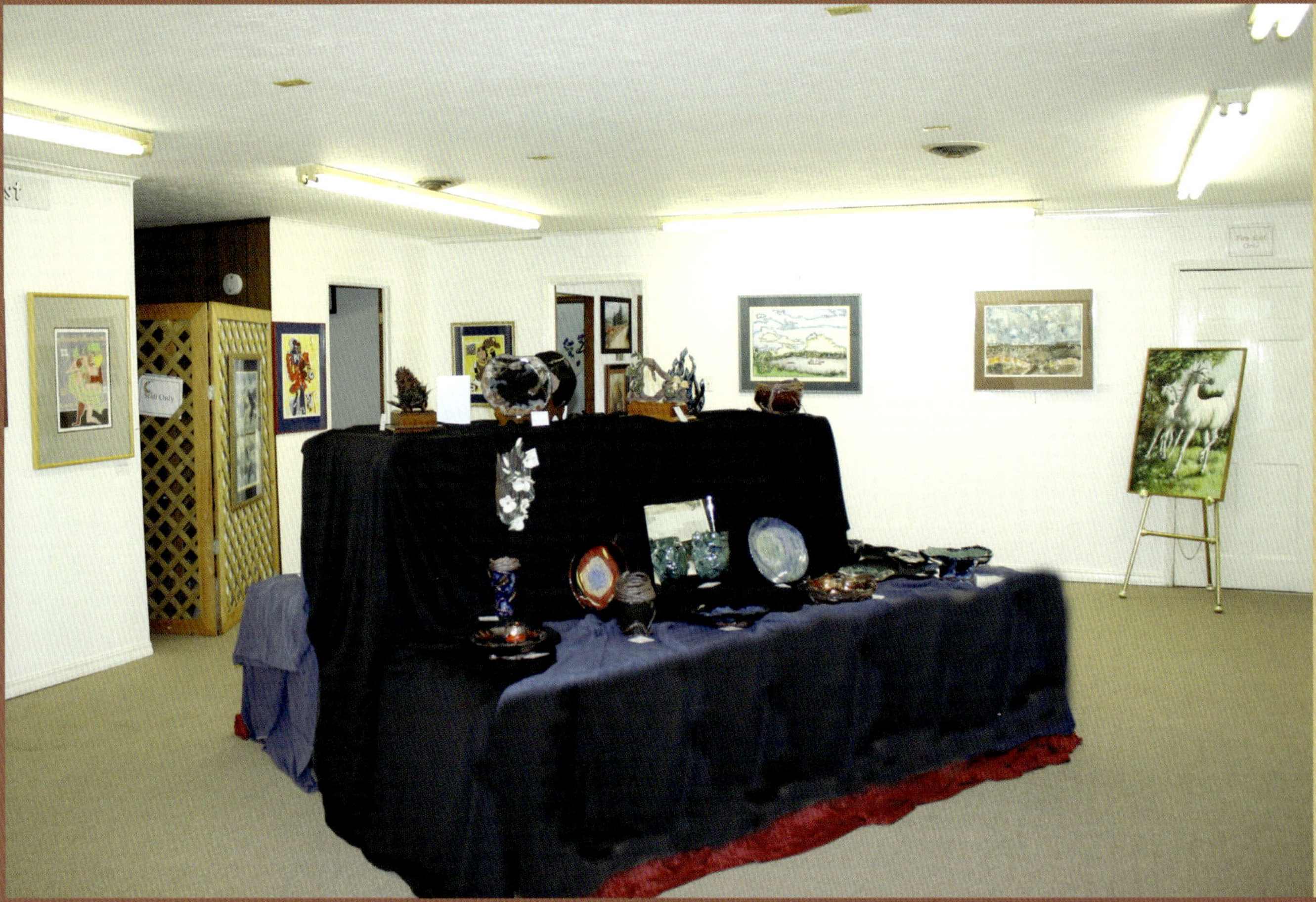

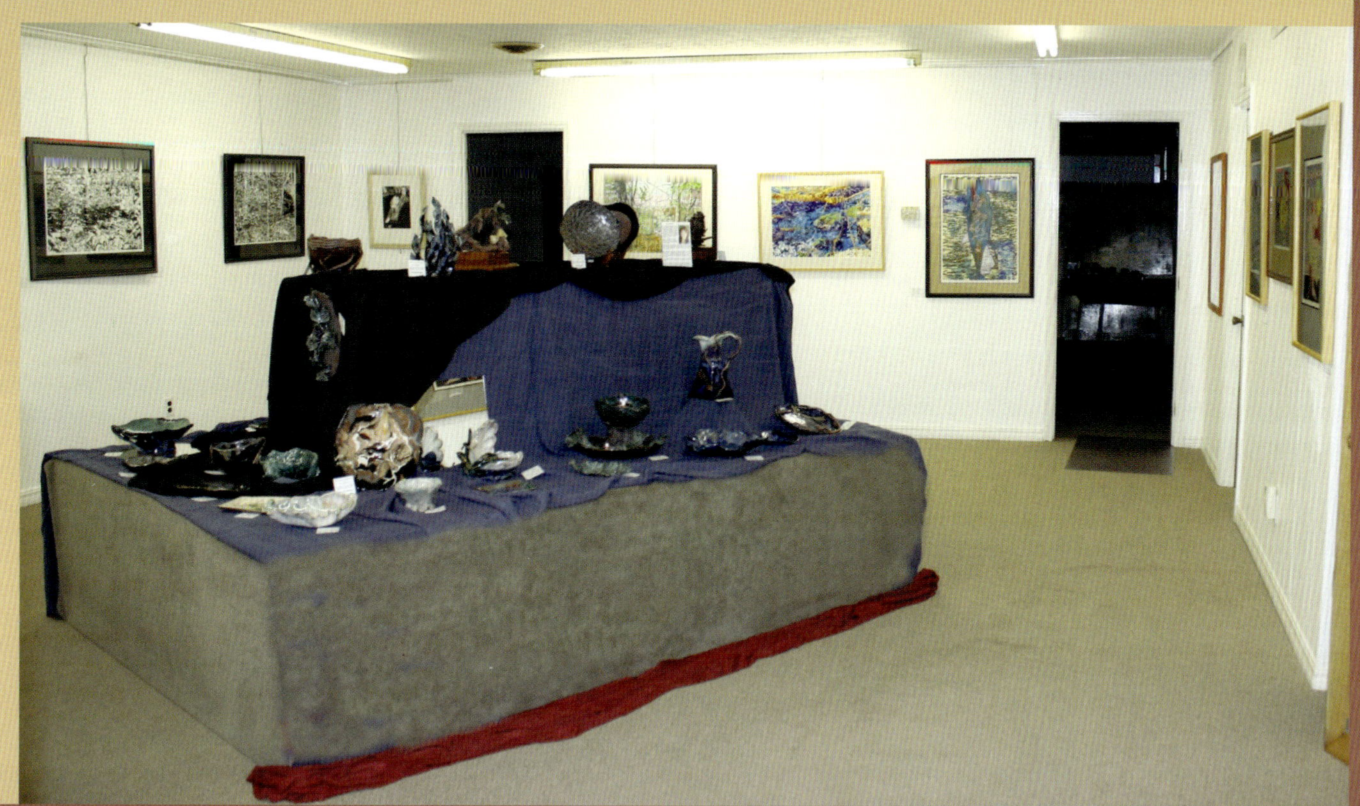

PALETTEARTLEAGUE.ORG

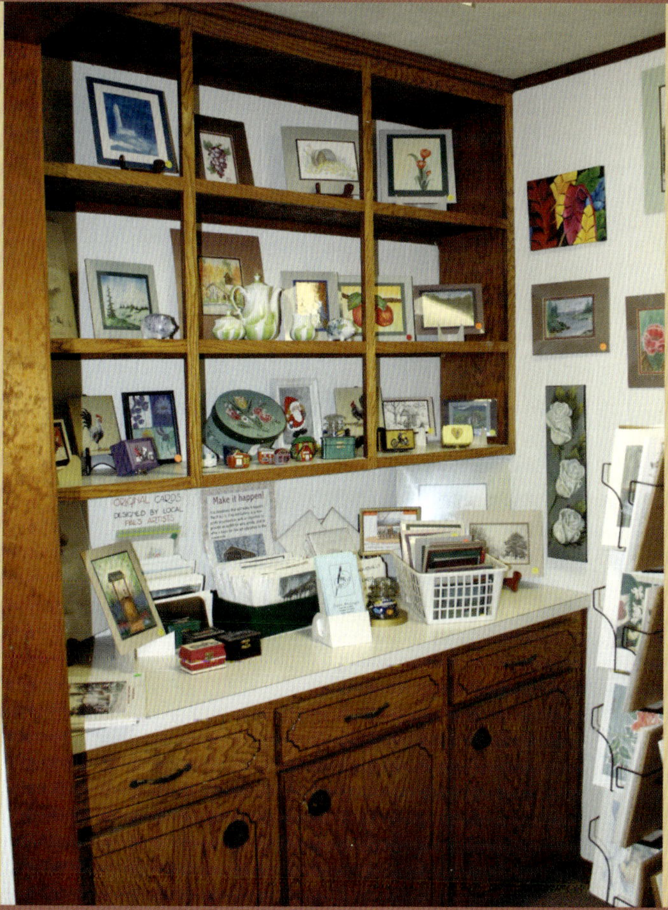

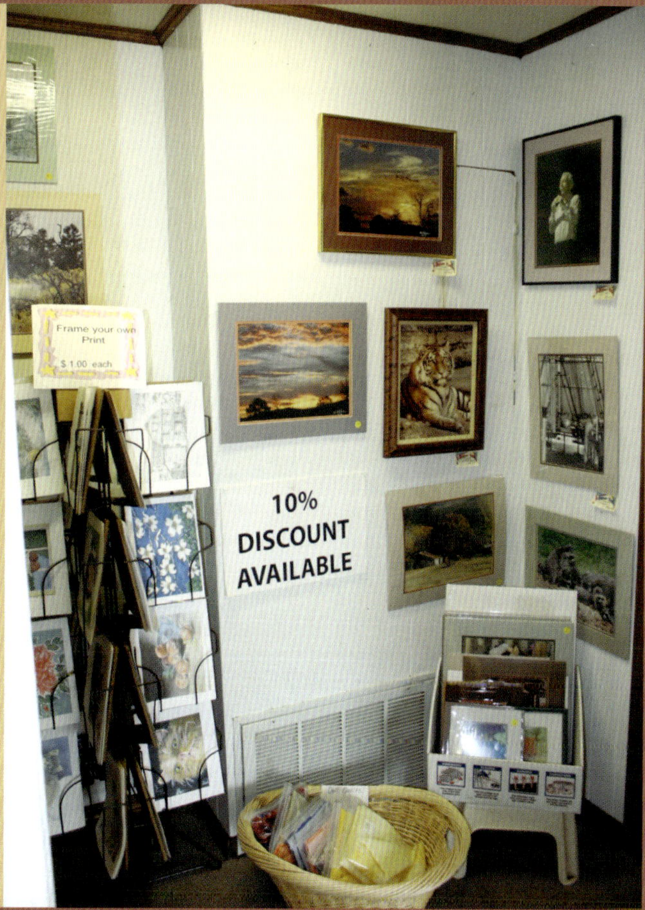

THE PALETTE ART LEAGUE

THE PALETTE ART LEAGUE

Order Page for The Art & Artisans of the Ozarks

For your convenience, you can place your order on-line at
http://paletteartleague.org/shop
or by using the order form below

Quantity Ordered	Book Title	Price	Total
____	The Art & Artisans of the Ozarks, Volume 1	$24.95 (each)	$__________
Shipping & Handling		$4.00 (per book)	$__________
Total Amount Enclosed			$__________

_____ Personal Check
_____ Credit Card – ___Amex, ____MC, ____Visa
Card Number: ____
Expiration Date: ____
CVV Code: (3 digit code on the reverse side of your card) ________
Name on the Card: ____
Phone Number: ____
Billing Address: ____
City/State: ____
Zip: ____

Shipping Information:

Please ship my books to:

Full Name: ___________________________
Street: ___________________________
City: ___________________________
State: ___________________________
Zip Code: ___________________________
E-mail: ___________________________

Please mail your order and payment to:
The Palette Art League
300 Hwy 62 West
Yellville, Arkansas 72687